IRISH AND SCOTCH-IRISH ANCESTRAL RESEARCH

A Guide to the Genealogical Records, Methods and Sources in Ireland

VOLUME II
BIBLIOGRAPHY AND FAMILY INDEX

BY

MARGARET DICKSON FALLEY, B.S.

Fellow of the American Society of Genealogists

GENEALOGICAL PUBLISHING CO., INC.

Baltimore 1984

Originally published: Strasburg, Virginia, 1962
Reprinted: Genealogical Publishing Co., Inc.
First printing: Baltimore, 1981
Second printing: Baltimore, 1984

Library of Congress Catalogue Card Number 80-83867
International Standard Book Number: Volume II: 0-8063-0917-2
Set Number: 0-8063-0916-4
Made in the United States of America

Contents of Volume II

PART ONE

PUBLISHED RECORDS

A Selected Bibliography of Publications Containing Genealogy and Family History, Pedigrees, Family Notes, Biography, and Materials for Compiling Genealogy

PART TWO

UNPUBLISHED FAMILY RECORDS

A Selected Bibliography and Family Index of Genealogy, Family History, Pedigrees, Notes and Collections of Family Documents

PART THREE

PUBLISHED SOURCES

A BIBLIOGRAPHY OF REFERENCE MATERIALS FOR GENEALOGICAL RESEARCH

PART FOUR

MICROFILMS

Collections of Microfilms for Reference, With a Key to Location of Records

PART FIVE

A BIBLIOGRAPHY FOR PRELIMINARY RESEARCH IN THE UNITED STATES

For the Purpose of Obtaining Basic Information Regarding the Immigrant Ancestor

PART ONE

PUBLISHED RECORDS

A SELECTED BIBLIOGRAPHY OF PUBLICATIONS CONTAINING GENEALOGY AND FAMILY HISTORY, PEDIGREES, FAMILY NOTES, BIOGRAPHY, AND MATERIALS FOR COMPILING GENEALOGY

CHAPTER I

BOOKS OF COMPILED FAMILY HISTORY AND GENEALOGY

(With a locating key)

The following bibliography has been compiled from many sources in Ireland. The accession lists of published genealogy and family history in the larger libraries have been copied and the collections examined in the smaller repositories. In the course of the work, this compiler has visited, repeatedly, the National Library of Ireland and the Genealogical Office in Dublin; the County Library, the City Library and the University Library in Cork; the Public Library in Waterford; the Public Record Office of Northern Ireland; the Linen Hall Library, and the Presbyterian Historical Society in Belfast; the Magee University College Library in Londonderry; and other County and Public Libraries. This compiler has also repeatedly searched many book shops in Ireland and, since 1951, has received the current sales catalogues from the Hodges Figgis Book Shop in Dublin and from the Cathedral Book Shop in Belfast. Thus, many books recorded in this bibliography have been listed for sale since 1951.

A family history or genealogy is most often found in a library located in the general area where the subject family or the compiler lived. Accordingly, the three libraries in Cork have the more complete collection of published works regarding the families which have resided in the south of Ireland, while the libraries in Belfast, Armagh, Londonderry, etc., have the larger Ulster collections. The Dublin libraries have the oldest, most complete and extensive deposits.

Anyone interested in purchasing books listed in this bibliography should write to the Hodges Figgis Book Shop, 6 Dawson Street, Dublin, or to the Cathedral Book Shop (Mr. Hugh Greer), 18 Gresham Street, Belfast, and request a catalogue, or make inquiry about the book desired. If a desired book is not available, one may ask to be put on a waiting list and notified when the requested book comes in to the shop. If one wishes a book of an early publication date, it is probably best to send a fee to have the book shop advertise for it. This compiler has resorted to advertising in some cases and, after requesting a particular book, has often been on a waiting list for more than a year.

Probably the largest collections in America of published Irish family histories and genealogies are in the American Irish Historical Society, New York City; the New York Public Library; the Library of Congress, Washington, D. C.; and in the Genealogical Society of Utah, Salt Lake City.

To aid in locating the books listed in this chapter, a key letter has been assigned to each of the four principal places where the volumes may be located. This key letter, in parenthesis, will be shown opposite the title of the book, where applicable.

(A) The National Library of Ireland, Kildare Street, Dublin.

(B) The Linen Hall Library, Donegall Square North, Belfast.

(C) Hodges Figgis & Company, Ltd. (Book Shop), 6 Dawson Street, Dublin.

(D) The Cathedral Book Shop (Mr. Hugh Greer), 18 Gresham Street, Belfast.

* * * *

ADAMS. A Genealogical History of Adams of Cavan, etc. By the late Rev. Benjamin William Adams, D.D. Edited and revised by Maxwell R. W. P. Adams. London, 1903.

ADARE. Memorials of Adare Manor—with Historical Notices of Adare, by her son, the Earl of Dunraven. By Caroline, Countess of Dunraven. Oxford, 1865. (C)

ADARE. Notes on the History of Adare. By the Hon. V. Wyndham-Quin. 1930. (C)

ALEXANDER. Memorials of the Earl of Sterling and the House of Alexander. By the Rev. Charles Rogers, LL.D. 2 vols. Edinburgh, 1877. (C)

AMORY. The Descendants of Hugh Amory, 1605-1805. By G. E. Meredith. London, 1901.

ANCKETILL. A Short History with Notes and References of the Ancient and Honorable Family of Ancketill or Ancketell. Compiled by one of its members. Belfast, 1901. (A)

ANKETILL. See Corry.

ARCHDALE. Memoirs of the Archdales, with the descents of some allied families. By Henry B. Archdale. 1925. (A)

ARMAR. See Corry.

ASH. The Ash Mss., written in the year 1735, by Lieut. Col. Thomas Ash, and other family records. By Henry Tyler, J. P., Limavady. Edited by the Rev. Edward T. Martin. Belfast, 1890. (C)

AUCHINLECK. See Corry.

AYLMER. The Aylmers of Ireland. By Sir Fenton J. Aylmer. London, 1931. (A)

BAGENAL. Vicissitudes of an Anglo-Irish Family, 1530-1800. By Philip H. Bagenal. London, 1925. (A)

BAGGE. Genealogical Account of the Bagge Family of County Waterford. Dublin, 1860.

BAILIE. History and Genealogy of the Family of Bailie of the North of Ireland. By George A. Bailie. Augusta, 1902.

BAIRDS, WAUCHOPES, COCHRANS, GIBSONS, WASSONS: British and American Origins. Pedigrees from Ulster. Edited by R. M. Sibbett. Belfast, 1931. (A)

BALL. Records of Anglo-Irish Families of Ball. By the Rev. W. B. Wright. Dublin, 1887. (B)

BALL. Ball Family Records. By the Rev. William Ball Wright, M. A. York, 1908.

BALLIQUIN. O'Ruark; or Chronicles of the Balliquin Family. By Henry J. Monahan. Dublin: J. Duffy, 1852. (C)

BANTRY, BEREHAVEN AND THE O'SULLIVAN SEPT. By T. D. Sullivan. Dublin, 1908. (C)

BARNARD. The Barnards. Londonderry, 1897.

BARRINGTON. The Barringtons. A Family History. By Amy Barrington. Dublin, 1917. (A)

BARRY. Barrymore: Records of the Barrys of County Cork, from the Earliest to the Present Time; with Pedigrees. By E. Barry. Cork, 1902. (C)

BARRY. The Last Earls of Barrymore. By G. J. Robinson. London, 1894.

BARTON. Some Account of the Family of Barton. Drawn from manuscripts and records, together with pedigrees of the various branches of the house. By Bertram F. Barton. Dublin, 1902. (A)

BEAMISH. A Genealogical Study of a Family in County Cork and Elsewhere. By C. T. M. Beamish. 1950. (A)

BEAMISH. Pedigrees of the Families of Beamish. By R. P. Beamish. Cork, 1892.

BECK. A Brief History of the Family of Beck. By John W. Beck. (Pamphlet.)

BERNARD. A Memoir of James Bernard, M. P., His Son, the First Earl of Bandon, and their Descendants. 1875.

BERNARD. The Bernards of Kerry. By John H. Bernard, Provost of Trinity College, Dublin. 1922. (A) (C)

BERRY. See Fleetwood.

BESSBOROUGH. Bessborough (Henrietta Frances, Countess of) : Lady Bessborough and her family circle. Edited by the Earl of Bessborough, in collaboration with A. Aspinall. 1940. (A)

BEWLEY. The Bewleys of Cumberland and Their Irish Descendants. By Sir E. T. Bewley. Dublin, 1902.

BINGHAM. Memoirs of the Binghams. By R. E. McCalmont. London, 1913.

BIRMINGHAM. Connaught to Chicago. By G. A. Birmingham. 1914. (D)

BLACKER. History of the Family of Blacker of Carrickblacker in Ireland. By L. C. M. Blacker. Dublin, 1901.

BLACKWOOD. Helen's Tower. By the Hon. Harold Nicolson. London, 1937. (C)

BLAKE. Castle Bourke formerly Kelboynell Castle in Carra Barony, Co. Mayo. With notes on the history of the ancient owners, the Clan MacEvilly (Stauntons) ; and on the history of the family of Bourke, Viscounts Mayo. By Martin J. Blake. 1929. (A)

BLAKE. Blake Family Records. By Martin J. Blake. 2 vols. London, 1902-5.

BLAYNEY. The Family of Blayney. Notes relating to the Blayney Family of Montgomeryshire and Ireland and to the estates of Arthur Blayney of Gregynog. By E. Rowley-Morris. 1890. (A)

BOLTON. Bolton Families in Ireland, with their English and American kindred, based in part upon original records which no longer exist. By Charles Knowles Bolton. Boston, 1937. (A)

BOYLE. The Orrery Papers (History of the Boyle Family). Edited by the Countess of Cork and Orrery. 2 vols. London, 1903. (C)

BOYLE. Memoirs of the Illustrious Family of the Boyles. By J. Esdale. 1754. (D)

BOYLE. Memoirs of the Lives and Characters of the Illustrious Family of Boyles. By Eustace Budgell. 1737. Also Dublin, 1755. (D)

BOYLE. Genealogical Memoranda Relating to the Family of Boyle of Limavady. By Edward M. F. G. Boyle. Londonderry, 1903. (A)

BRABAZON. Genealogical History of the Family of Brabazon, from its origin to 1825. By Sir William John Brabazon. Paris, 1825. (D)

BROWNE. The Kenmare Manuscripts. (The Browne Family of County Kerry.) Edited by Edward MacLysaght. Dublin, 1942. (C)

BUCHANAN. The Buchanan Book. By A. W. P. Buchanan, K. C. Montreal, 1911.

BULLOCK. Bullock or Bullick of Northern Ireland. Compiled by J. W. Beck. London, 1931.

BUTLER. Some Account of the Family of Butler, but more particularly of the late Duke of Ormonde, etc. London, 1716. (D)

BUTLER. Genealogical Memoranda of the Butler Family. By W. Butler. Sibsagor, Assam, 1845.

BUTLER. A Genealogical History of the Noble . . . House of Butler in England and Ireland, etc. London, 1771.

BUTLER. Testamentary Records of the Butler Family in Ireland (Genealogical Abstracts). Edited by the Rev. Wallace Clare. Peterborough, 1932. (A)

CAIRNS. History of the Family of Cairns or Cairnes and its Connections and Family Pedigrees (contains also the Elliot family; the Montgomeries of Lisduff and Ballymagowan; the Moores of Moore Hall; the Lawlor family). By H. C. Lawlor. London, 1906. (B) (D)

CALDWELL. "The Caldwell Family of Castle Caldwell, County Fermanagh." In the genealogy, *Bagshawes of Ford Hall, Darby*. By W. H. Greaves-Bagshawe.

CALLWELL. See Magee.

CAMAC. Memoirs of the Camacs, County Down, with some account of their predecessors. By Frank O. Fisher. Norwich, 1897. (A)

CAMPBELL. Campbell of Skeldon and New Grange, County Meath.

CAMPBELL. The Genealogy of Robert Campbell, a Record of the Descendants of Robert Campbell of County Tyrone. By the Rev. F. Campbell. Brooklyn, New York, 1909.

CARDEN. Some Particulars about the Family and Descendants of the First John Carden of Templemore, County Tipperary, and Priscilla, his wife. By John Carden. 1912. (A)

CARSON. Carsons of Shanroe, County Monaghan. By the Rev. W. T. Carson. Dublin, 1879.

CARSON. The Carsons of Monanton, Ballybay, County Monaghan. By J. Carson. 1907. (In the Public Record Office of Northern Ireland, Belfast.)

CAULFIELD. A Short Biographical Notice of Clan Cathmaoil or the Caulfield Family. By Bernard Connor. Dublin, 1808.

CHAMPION. Leitrim Castle, County Cork. A Genealogy of the Champion Family. By Col. James Grove White. (Reprint from the *Journal of the Cork Historical and Archaeological Society*, 1917.) (C)

CHICHESTER. The History of the Family of Chichester. By Sir Alexander P. B. Chichester. 1871.

CLARK. The History and Genealogy of the Clark Family and its Connections. By Charles Lamartine Clark. (The Clarks of Ulster and America.) Detroit, 1898. (C)

CLAYTON. Some Account of the Clayton Family of Thelwall, County Chester; afterwards of St. Dominick's Abbey, Doneraile and Mallow, County Cork. By J. P. Rylands. Liverpool, 1880.

COCHRANS. See Bairds.

CODDINGTON. See Croslegh. (A)

COFFEY. Genealogy and Historical Records of the Sept Cobhthaigh, now Coffey. By H. Coffey. Dublin, 1863.

COLE. Genealogy of the Family of Cole, County Devon, with Branches in Ireland. By James E. Cole. 1867.

COLE. The Cole Family of West Carbery. By the Rev. R. L. Cole. Belfast, 1943.

COLLES. A Record of the Colles Family. By R. W. Colles. Dublin, 1892.

CONOLLY. Speaker Conolly and His Connections. 1907. (C)

CONWAY. See O'Mahony.

CONYNGHAM. An Old Ulster House and the People who lived in it. By Mina Lenox - Conyngham. (A History of the Conyngham Family.) Dundalk, 1946. (D)

COOPER. See O'Haras.

COOTE. History and Genealogical Records of the Coote Family. Lausanne, 1900. (C)

COPINGER. History of the Copingers or Coppingers of County Cork. By W. A. Copinger.

CORCA LAIDHE. Genealogy of Corca Laidhe. Edited by J. O'Donovan. 1849. (B)

CORRY. The History of the Corry Family of Castlecoole. (With genealogies of the allied families of Crawford, Johnston, Anketill, Mervyn, Leslie, Armar, Lowry, Auchinleck, etc.) By the Earl of Belmore. London, Dublin, 1891. (A) (D)

CORRY. The Corry and Lowry Families, 1655-1802. In *The History of Two Ulster Manors of Finagh, in the County of Tyrone, and Coole, Otherwise Manor Atkinson, in the County of Fermanagh, and their Owners*. By the Earl of Belmore. London, 1881. (C)

COX. Claim of J. H. R. Cox to the Baronetcy of Cox of Dunmanway, County Cork. With Ancestry Evidence. By John H. R. Cox. London, 1912-1914. (A)

CRAWFORD. The Crawfords of Donegal and How They Came There. By Robert Crawford. Dublin, 1886. (A)

CRAWFORD. See Corry.

CRICHTON. The Genealogy of the Earls of Erne. By J. H. Steele. Edinburgh, 1910.

CRISPIN. The Crispins of Kingston-on-Hull. By M. Jackson Crispin. 1928. (A)

CROFTON. Crofton Memoirs: Account of John Crofton of Ballymurray, County Roscommon . . . His Ancestors and Descendants and others bearing the name. By the Rev. William Ball Wright, M. A., and Helen Crofton. York, 1911.

CROSLEGH. Descent and Alliances of Croslegh of Scaitliffe; and Coddington of Oldbridge; and Evans of Eyton Hall. By Charles Croslegh. 1904. (A)

CROSSLE. Descent and Alliances of Croslegh, or Crossle, or Crossley, of Scaitliffe. By the Rev. Charles Croslegh, D.D., London, 1904. (A)

D'ARCY. An Historical Sketch of the Family of D'Arcy from the Norman Conquest to the year 1853. First published in 1882. Reprint, Leeds, 1901.

D'ARCY. Complete Pedigree of the English and Irish Branches of the D'Arcy Family. London, 1901.

DAUNT. Account of the Family of Daunt. By John Daunt. Newcastle-on-Tyne, 1881.

DAVIES. Journal of the Very Rev. Rowland Davies, LL.D., from March 8, 1688-9, to September 29, 1690. With notes and an appendix, and some account of the author and his family. Edited by Richard Caulfield. 1857. (C)

DAVYS. The Davys Family Records. Records kept by members of the Davys family, formerly of Cloonbonny, near Lanesborough and of Martinstown near Roscommon. By S. F. O'Clanain. Longford, 1931. (A)

DECOURCY. A Genealogical History of the Milesian Families of Ireland, with the monument to Brian Boroimhe. The Chart of the Armorial Bearings of the same families. Compiled and edited by B. W. DeCourcy. 1880. (A)

DENHAM. Denham of Dublin. By Charles Holmes Denham, M.D. Dublin, 1936. (A)

DENNY. Denny Genealogy; Second Book. The Descendants of William Denny of Chester County, Pa., and the allied families of Culbertson, Gaston . . . and descendants of George Denny of Lincoln County, North Carolina. 1947. (A)

DESMONDE. The Olde Countess of Desmonde; Her Identitie; Her Portraiture; Her Descente, with . . . and genealogical table. By A. B. Rowan. Dublin, 1860. (C)

DEVENISH. Records of the Devenish Families. By Robert T. Devenish and Charles H. MacLaughlin. Chicago, 1948. (C)

DEVEREUX. Account of the Anglo-Norman Family of Devereux of Balmagir, County Wexford. By Gabriel O'C. Redmond, M. D. Dublin, 1891.

DICKSON. Dickson Genealogy. By C. T. M'Cready. Dublin, 1868.

DILL. The Dill Worthies. By the Rev. James R. Dill. Belfast, 1888. 2nd edition, Belfast, 1892. (A)

DILLON. Lineage of Gerald D. F. Dillon, Gent. By Gerald D. F. Dillon. (A)

DOBBS. Arthur Dobbs, Esquire, 1689-1765. Surveyor-General of Ireland, Prospector, and Governor of North Carolina. By Desmond Clarke. London, 1957. (C)

DODD. The Dodd Family Abroad. By Charles Lever. (C)

DOWNEY. A History of the Protestant Downeys of the counties of Sligo, Leitrim, Fermanagh and Donegal, and their Descendants. Also of the Hawksby Family of the counties of Leitrim and Sligo. Compiled by Cairncross C. Downey. New York, 1931. (D)

DOWSE. History of the Dowse Family. 1926. (In the Public Record Office of Northern Ireland, Belfast.)

DRENNAN. The Drennan Letters. Being a selection from the correspondence which passed between William Drennan, M. D., and his brother-in-law and sister, Samuel and Martha McTier, during the years 1776-1819. Edited by D. A. Chart. Belfast, 1931. (C)

DUFFERIN. See Blackwood *(Helen's Tower)*. The Dufferin Family is included.

DUNLEVY. A Genealogical History of the Dunlevy Family. Don Leve, Donlevy, Dunleavy, Dunlavey, Dunlevey. By Gwendolyn Dunlevy Kelley. Columbus, Ohio. 1901. (A)

EAGAR. The Eagar Family in the County of Kerry. By E. F. Eagar. London, 1958. (C)

EAGAR. The Eagar Family in the County of Kerry, with an Appendix containing Brief Notices of Other Families of the Name. And an Account of the Lineage of these Families. By Frederick John Eagar. Dublin, 1860-61.

EAGAR. Genealogical History of the Eagar Family. By F. J. Eagar. Dublin, 1861.

ECHLIN. Genealogical Memoirs of the Echlin Family . . . By the Rev. J. R. Echlin. Edinburgh.

EDGEWORTH. The Black Book of Edgeworthstown and other Edgeworth Memories, 1585-1816. Edited by Harriet Jessie Butler and Harold Edgeworth Butler. London, 1917. (A)

ELLIOT. See Cairns. (B)

ELLIS. Fourth and Last Supplement to Notices of the Ellises of England, Scotland, and Ireland, from the Conquest to the present time, including the families of Alis, Fitz-Elys, Helles, etc. By William Smith Ellis. London, 1857, 1881. (A)

EMISON. The Emison Families, with partial genealogies of collateral families. By James Wade Emison, Jr. Indiana, 1947. (C)

EMMET. The Emmet Family, with some Incidents relating to Irish History, and a Biographical Sketch of Prof. John P. Emmet, M. D., and other members. By Thomas A. Emmet, M. D. New York, 1898.

ERNE. Genealogy of the Earls of Erne. By John H. Steele. 1910. (A)

EVANS. The Last Six Generations of the Evans Family, now represented by Nicholas Evans of Lough Park, Castlepollard, Westmeath. By W. Sloane Evans. 1864.

EVANS. See Croslegh. (A)

EYRE. A Short Account of the Eyre Family of Eyre Court, and Eyre of Eyreville, in County Galway. By the Rev. Allen S. Hartigan, M. A. Reading, n.d. (A)

FALKINER. A Pedigree with Personal Sketches of the Falkiners of Mount Falcon. By Frederick B. Falkiner. Dublin, 1894.

FALKINER. The Falkiners of Abbotstown, County Dublin. By George H. Falkiner. Nuttall, Dublin, 1917. (Reprint from *Journal of the County Kildare Archaeological Society*. Vol. VIII, pt. 5, pp. 331-363.) (A)

FARNHAM. Seize Quartiers, connected with Royal Descents of Henry Maxwell, K. P., Seventh Lord Farnham. Cavan, 1850.

FARNHAM. Farnham Descents. Part I, Paternal Descent. Part II, Maternal Descent. Part III, Lady Farnham's Descent. By Henry Maxwell, Lord Farnham. Cavan, 1860.

FEATHERSTONE. The Featherstones and Halls. Gleanings from old family letters and manuscripts. By Margaret Irwine. 1890. (A)

FERGUSON. Records of the Clan and Name of Fergusson or Ferguson and Fergus. Edited by James Ferguson and Robert Menzies Fergusson. Edinburgh, 1895. (C)

FITZGERALD. Descents of the Earls of Kildare and their Wives. By the Marquis of Kildare. Dublin, 1869. (C)

FITZGERALD. The Earls of Kildare and their Ancestors, from 1057-1773. By the Marquis of Kildare. (The Fitzgerald Family.) Dublin, 1858, 1862.

FITZGERALD. Geraldines, Earls of Desmond. By the Rev. C. P. Meehan. Dublin, 1852.

FITZGERALD. Initium, Incrementum et Exitus Familiae Geraldinorum Desmoniae Comitum, Palatinorum Kyerriae in Hybernia, etc. By Dominic O'Daly. 1655.

FITZGERALD. The Life of Lord Edward Fitzgerald, 1763-1798. By Ida A. Taylor. (C)

FITZGERALD. Memoirs of an Irish Family, Fitzgerald of Decies, etc. By Mrs. M. MacKenzie. Dublin, 1905.

FITZGERALD. The Memoirs of Lord Edward Fitzgerald. By Thomas Moore. London, 1897. (C)

FITZGERALD. Pedigree of Fitzgerald, Knight of Kerry; Fitzgerald Seneschal of Imokilly; and of Fitzgerald of Cloyne. See Geraldine Documents, vol. 2, n. d. (B)

FITZGERALD. Sketch of the History and Descent of the Geraldines of Queen's County, Mountmellick. 1913.

FITZGIBBON. Pedigrees of the White Knight (and) the Sept of the Old Knight. See Geraldine Documents, vols. 4 and 7. 1881. (B)

FLEETWOOD. An Irish Branch of the Fleetwood Family. By Sir Edmund T. Bewley. Exeter, 1908.

FLEETWOOD. Some Royal Descents of the Families of Fleetwood, Berry and Homan-Mulock. Edited by Sir Ed. T. Bewley. 1908. (D)

FLEMING. Historical and Genealogical Memoir of the Family of Fleming of Slane. By Sir William Betham. 1829.

FOLLIN. Follin Family. By G. Edmonston. Washington, 1911.

FOLLIOTT. The Folliotts of Londonderry and Chester. By Sir E. T. Bewley. 1902.

FORBES. Memoirs of the Earls of Granard. By Admiral, the Hon. John Forbes. London, 1868.

FOX. Some Notes on the Fox Family of Kilcoursey in King's County. By M. E. Stone. Chicago, 1890.

FRAZER. Notes and Papers connected with Persifor Frazer in Glasslough, Ireland, and his son, John Frazer, of Philadelphia, 1735-1763. By P. Frazer, 1906.

FREKE. Mrs. Elizabeth Freke, Her Diary, 1671-1714. Edited by Mary Carbery, Cork, 1913. (C)

FRENCH. The Families of French of Belturbet, and Nixon of Fermanagh, and their Descendants. By the Rev. Henry Biddall Swanzy. Dublin, 1908. (D)

FRENCH. Memoir of the French Family (De la Freyne, De Freyne, Frenshe, ffrench), . . . By John D'Alton. Dublin, 1847.

FULLER. Some Royal, Noble and Gentle Descents of the Kerry Branch of the Fuller Family. Compiled for his Descendants. By J. F. Fuller. Dublin, 1880.

FULLER. Pedigree of the Family of Fuller of Cork, Kerry and Halstead. By J. F. Fuller. 1909.

FULTON. Memoirs of the Fultons of Lisburn. By Sir Theodore Hope. 1903. (A)

GAEDHAL. Irish Family History; being an historical and genealogical account of the Gaedhals. By Richard F. Cronnelly. Vol. I, 1865. (A)

GALWAY, GALWEY. The Galweys of Lota. By C. J. Bennett. Dublin, 1909. (D)

GAYER. Memoirs of the Gayer Family in Ireland. By Arthur Edward Gayer. Westminster, 1870.

GERALDINES. Dromona: the Memoirs of an Irish Family. An Account of the Geraldines and the Villiers Family. By Theresa Muir Mackenzie. Dublin, 1906. (C)

GERALDINES. The Rise, Increase, and Exit of the Geraldines, Earls of Desmond — Translated from the Latin — with Memoir and Notes. By C. P. Meehan. Dublin, 1878. (C)

GIBBON. Recollections from 1796 to 1829. By Skeffington Gibbon. (A)

GIBSON. See Baird.

GILLMAN. Searches Into the History of the Gillman or Gilman Family . . . in Ireland . . . by A. W. Gillman. London, 1895.

GORGES. The Story of a Family Through Eleven Centuries. By Raymond Gorges. Boston, 1944.

GOUGH. The Story of an Irish Property. A History of the Family of Gough. By Robert S. Rait. Oxford, 1908. (C)

GRACE. Memoirs of the Family of Grace. By Sheffield Grace. 2 vols. London, 1823. (A) (D)

GRACE. A Survey of Tullaroan, etc., being a genealogical history of the family of Grace. Dublin, 1819.

GRANDISON. Speeches delivered by the Council upon the Claim to the Barony of Grandison. With the Attorney General's Reply before the Lords' Committee for Privileges. London, 1855. (C)

GREATRAKES. Notes on the Family of Greatrakes. By the Rev. Samuel Hayman. 1863. (C)

GREEN. The Family of Green of Youghal, County Cork. The Descendants of Simon Green. By the Rev. Henry Biddall Swanzy and Thomas George Hennis Green. Dublin, 1902. (C)

GREENE. Pedigree of the Family of Greene. By Lt. Col. J. Greene. Dublin, 1899.

GREGORY. The House of Gregory. By Vere R. T. Gregory. Dublin, 1943. (D)

GROVE. Caherduggan Castle and Parish. (The Grove Family.) By Col. James Grove White. 1911. (C)

GUINNESS. See Magennis.

HAMILTON. The Hamilton Manuscripts. Printed from the Original Mss., by Sir James Hamilton, Knight. Edited by T. K. Lowry, Esq., LL.D. Belfast, 1867. (A) (C)

HAMILTON. Pedigree of the Hamilton Family of Fermegan, County Tyrone. By James F. Fuller. London, 1889.

HAMILTON. Hamilton Memoirs; being historical and genealogical notices of a branch of that family which settled in Ireland in the Reign of James I. By Everard Hamilton. Dundalk, 1920. (A)

HAMILTON. Genealogical Tables of the Descendants of John Hamilton of Locust Hill, Lexington, Virginia; born 1789 . . died 1825. Privately printed. 1933. (A)

HAMILTON. Hamilton Family, *ca.* 1600-1860; the descendants of James Hamilton, Viscount Clandeboye, d. 1643. (Genealogical chart included in *Helen's Tower.*) By Harold Nicolson. London, 1937.

HART. Family History of Hart of Donegal. By H. T. Hart. 1907.

HARVEY. The Harvey Families of Inishowen, County Donegal, and Maen, County Cornwall (with supplemental index). By Lt. Col. Gardiner H. Harvey. Folkstone, 1927. (A)

HASSARD. Some Account of the Family of Hassard; with a list of descendants in England and Ireland. By the Rev. Henry Biddall Swanzy, M. A. Dublin, 1903. (D)

HAUGHTON. Memoirs of the Family of Haughton in Ireland. By T. W. Haughton. Cullybackey, 1929. (In Public Record Office, Northern Ireland, Belfast.)

HAWKSBY. See Downey.

HEFFERNAN. The Heffernans and Their Times; A Study in Irish History. By Patrick Heffernan. London, 1940. (A)

HEWETSON. Memoirs of the House of Hewetson or Hewson in Ireland. By John Hewetson. London, 1901.

HEWSON. The Hewsons of Finuge, Kerry, of Royal Descent. By John Hewson. 1907.

HILL. The House of Downshire from 1600-1868. By H. McCall. 1880.

HOARE. Account of the Early History and Genealogy, with Pedigrees from 1330 unbroken to the Present Time, of the Families of Hore and Hoare, with all their Branches. By Capt. Edward Hoare of Cork. London, 1883. (A)

HOMAN-MULOCK. See Fleetwood.

HOVENDEN. The Lineage of the Family of Hovenden (Irish Branch). By a Member of the Family. London, 1892.

HOVENDEN. See O'Neill. By John J. Marshall.

JACOB. Historical and Genealogical Narration of the Families of Jacob. By Archibald Hamilton Jacob of Dublin, and J. H. Glascott. Dublin, 1875.

JACOB. History of the Families of Jacob of Bridgewater, Tiverton and Southern Ireland. By H. W. Jacob, M. A. Taunton, 1929.

JOHNSTON. See Corry.

JONES. The Jones in Ireland: Chapter of Hitherto Unwritten Genealogy, with a Slight Sketch of their Time. By Robert Leach. Yonkers, New York, 1866.

KEATING. Records of the Keating Family. By Thomas Matthews.

KENMARE. The Kenmare Manuscripts. A Calendar of the Correspondence, Rentals, Estate Accounts, Legal Documents, etc., of the Earls of Kenmare during the 18th Century. Edited by Edward MacLysaght. Dublin, 1942. (C)

KENNEY. Pedigree of the Kenney Family of Kelclogher, County Galway. By J. C. F. Kenney. Dublin, 1868.

KERR. Joseph Kerr of Ballygoney and His Descendants. Compiled by Mary Alice Kerr Arbuckle. New York, 1904.

KILDARE. The Earls of Kildare and their Ancestors, 1057-1773. By Charles W. Fitzgerald, 4th Duke of Leinster. 1857. 2nd edition, 3 vols. 1858-66. (A)

KINGSTON. The Kingston Family in West Cork. By Delmege Trimble. 1929. (In Public Record Office, Northern Ireland, Belfast.)

KIRWAN. Pedigree of the Kirwan Family, Compiled from the Originals. By Denis Agar Richard Kirwan and John Waters Kirwan. (A)

LACY. The Roll of the House of Lacy; pedigrees, military memoirs . . . and a memoir of the Browns (Camas). By Edward Delacy-Bellincari. Baltimore, 1928. (A)

LANDAFF. Genealogy of the Earls of Landaff of Thomastown, County Tipperary, Ireland. (A)

LANGTON. Memorials of the Family of Langton of Kilkenny. By J. G. A. Prim. Dublin, 1864.

LA TOUCHE. Genealogy of the "De La Touche" Family seated in . . . France, prior to and continued after a branch of it settled in Ireland, 1690-95. By Sir A. B. Stransham. London, 1882.

LAWLER, LAWLOR. The Lawlor Family. See Cairns. (B)

LE FANU. Memoir of the Le Fanu Family. By Thomas Le Fanu. Manchester, 1924. (A)

LEFROY. Notes and Documents relating to the Leffroy Family . . . now Represented by the Families of Lefroy of Carrickglass, County Longford, etc. By a Cadet (Sir John Henry Lefroy), 1868.

LEINSTER. Emily, Duchess of Leinster, 1731-1814. A Study of Her Life and Times. By Brian Fitzgerald. 1849. (A)

LENOX-CONYNGHAM. See Conyngham. (A)

LE POER TRENCH. Memoirs of the Le Poer Trench Family, written by Richard, 2nd Earl of Clancarty, about 1805, and now printed . . . by his grandson. Dublin, 1874. (A) (B) (C)

LESLIE. The Leslies of Tarbert, County Kerry and their Forebears. By Pierce Leslie Pielou. Dublin, 1935. (A)

LESLIE. Leslie of Glaslough in the Kingdom of Oriel, and of Noted Men that have dwelt there. By Seymour Leslie. Glaslough, 1913.

LESLIE. See Corry.

LEVINGE. Historical Notes on the Levinge Family, Baronets of Ireland. By J. C. Lyons. Ladestown, 1853.

LEVINGE. Jottings for Early History of the Levinge Family, Part I. By Sir Richard Levinge. Dublin, 1873. (C)

LINDESAY. The Lindesays of Loughry, County Tyrone; A Genealogical History. Compiled by Ernest H. Godfrey. London, 1949. (C)

LLOYD. Genealogical Notes on the Lloyd Family in County Waterford. By A. R. Lloyd. n. d.

LOWRY. The History of the Two Ulster Manors of Finagh in the County of Tyrone, and Coole, Otherwise Manor Atkinson, in the County of Fermanagh, and of their Owners. (Includes the families of Lowery, Atkinson, Champion, Corry, and Armar.) By the Earl of Belmore. London, Dublin, 1881. (A) (C)

LOWTHER. Lowthers in Ireland in the 17th Century. By Sir E. T. Bewley. 1902.

LUDLOW. Memoirs of Edmund Ludlow, Esq., Lieutenant General of the Horse, Commander-in-Chief of the Forces in Ireland. 3 vols. 2nd edition. London, 1721. (C)

LYNCH. Genealogical Memoranda Relating to the Family of Lynch. London, 1883.

LYNCH. Lynch Record, containing biographical sketches of the men of the name Lynch, 16th to 20th Century. By Elizabeth C. Lynch. New York, 1925. (A)

LYONS. Historical Notice of the Lyons Family and their Connections. By John C. Lyons. Ladestown, 1853.

LYSTER. Memorials of an Ancient House. By the Rev. H. Lyster Denny. 1913.

MACCARTHY. A Historical Pedigree of the Sliochd Feidhlimidh, the MacCarthys of Gleannacroim. By Daniel MacCarthy. Exeter, 1849. (D)

MacCarthy. A Historical Pedigree of the MacCarthys. By Daniel MacCarthy. Exeter, 1880.

Macdonald. A Romantic Chapter in Family History. By Alice B. Macdonald. 1911.

Macdonnell. An Historical Account of the Macdonnells of Antrim: including notices of some other Septs, Irish and Scottish. By Rev. George Hill. Belfast, 1873. (A) (B) (C)

MacEgan. The MacEgan Family. By Marie O. MacEgan. 1941. (C)

MacLaughlin. The MacLaughlins, or Clan Owen. By John P. Brown. Boston, 1879.

MacLysaght. Short Study of a Transplanted Family in the 17th Century. By E. MacLysaght. Dublin, 1935.

MacLysaght. Index to the Family Map in the Heraldic Museum. By Edward MacLysaght. 1945. (A)

MacManus. Genealogical Memoranda Relating to the Sotheron Family and the Sept MacManus. By C. Sotheron. 1871-1873.

Macnamara. The Story of an Irish Sept. By N. MacNamara. London, 1896.

Macnamara. The Pedigrees of MacConmara of . . . County Clare. By R. W. Twigge. 1908.

Macnamara. The Pedigree of John Macnamara, Esquire, with some family reminiscences. By R. W. Twigge. 1908. (A)

MacRory. The Past MacRorys of Duneane, Castle-dawson, Limavady, and Belfast. By R. A. MacRory. Belfast.

Madden, Madan. The Madan Family and Maddens in Ireland and England. By Falconer Madan. Oxford University Press. 1933. (A)

Magee. The Magees of Belfast and Dublin, . . . with some notes on the Willson, Callwell and other Belfast families. The M'Calmonts and their Relations. Collected by Francis Joseph Bigger. Belfast, 1916. (A) (D)

Magennis. Notes on the Family of Magennis, formerly Lords of Iveagh, Newry and Mourne. By Edmund F. Danne. Salt Lake City, 1878.

MAGENNIS. The Magennises of Clanconnell. By the Rev. E. D. Atkinson. 1895.

MAGENNIS. Pedigree of the Magennis (Guinness) Family of North Ireland and of Dublin. By Richard Linn. Christchurch, New Zealand, 1897.

MARTIN. The Martins of Cro Martin. 2 vols. By Charles Lever. (C)

MASSY. Genealogical Account of the Massy Family. Dublin, 1890.

MATHEW. Genealogy of the Earls of Landaff, of Thomastown, County Tipperary. 1904.

MAUNSELL. History of the Maunsell or Mansel Family. By Robert G. Maunsell. Cork, 1903.

MAXWELL. Farnham Descents. By Henry Maxwell, Lord Farnham. Cavan, 1860.

M'CALMONT. See Magee.

MCCARTHY. Three Kerry Families. By Samuel T. McCarthy. 1923. (A)

MCCARTHY. The McCarthys of Munster. By Samuel T. McCarthy. 1922. (A)

MCCORMICK. Genealogical Tables of the Descendants of Robert McCormick of Walnut Grove, Rockbridge County, Virginia; Born 1780-died 1846. Privately printed, 1934. (A)

MCCREADY. McCreery (McCready) Genealogy. By C. T. McCready. Dublin, 1868.

MCGOVERN. An Irish Sept; by two of its scions. By the Rev. J. B. and J. H. McGovern. Manchester, 1886.

MCGOVERN. Genealogy and Historical Notes of the MacGauran or McGovern Clan. By J. H. McGovern. Liverpool, 1890.

MCKEE. A History of the Descendants of David McKee, with a General Sketch of the Early McKees. By James McKee. Philadelphia, 1872.

MEADE. The Meades of Ineshannon. By J. A. Meade. Victoria, B. C., 1956.

MEADE. The Meades of Meaghstown Castle and Tissaxon. By J. A. Meade. n.d.

MERCER. The Mercer Chronicle; An Epitome of Family History. By E. S. Mercer. 1866.

MERVYN. See Corry.

MOLYNEUX. An Account of the Family and Descendants of Thomas Molyneux. By Capel Molyneux. Evesham, 1820.

MOLYNEUX. Pedigree of Molyneux, of Castle Dillon, County Armagh. By Sir T. Phillips. Evesham, 1819.

MONROE. Foulis Castle and the Monroes of Lower Iveagh. By Horace G. Monroe. 1929. (A)

MONTGOMERY. A Genealogical History of the Family of Montgomery, of Mount Alexander, etc. By Mrs. E. O'Reilly. 1842.

MONTGOMERY. The Montgomery Manuscripts. (Printed from Original Manuscripts and Transcripts of Manuscripts, composed by William Montgomery, 1698-1704.) Belfast, 1830.

MONTGOMERY. The Montgomery Manuscripts (1603-1706). Compiled from Family Papers by William Montgomery of Rosemont, Esq., and edited with notes, by the Rev. George Hill. Belfast, 1869. (A) (B) (C)

MONTGOMERY. A Family History of Montgomery of Ballyleck, County Monaghan. By G. S. M. Belfast, 1887 and 1891.

MONTGOMERY. Montgomeries of Lisduff and Ballymagowan. See Cairns. (B)

MONTGOMERY. Origin and History of the Montgomerys. By B. G. de Montgomery. 1948. (A)

MOORE. The Genealogy of John William Moore, B.A., M.D., Dublin, 1900.

MOORE. The Family of Moore. By Anne T. Moore, Countess of Drogheda. Dublin, 1906. (A)

MOORE. The Moores of Moore Hall. By Joseph Hone, London, 1939. (See Cairns.) (B)

MORRIS. Morris of Ballybeggan and Castle Morris, County Kerry. By the Marquis of Ruvigny and Raineval. 1904.

MORRIS. Memoirs of My Family; Together with some Researches into the Early History of the Morris Families of Tipperary, Galway and Mayo. By E. Naomi Chapman. Frome, 1928.

MULOCK. The Family of Mulock. By Sir Edmund Bewley. Dublin, 1905.

MUNRO. The Munro Family of Coleraine. *Story of St. Patrick's Coleraine.* By Sam Henry, pp. 42-46. (D)

NASH. The Genealogy of the Nash Family of Farrihy, etc., Ireland. 1910.

NESBITT. History of the Family of Nesbitt or Nisbitt, from Memoranda of Alexander Nesbitt, of Lismore. Completed by his Widow, Cecilia Nesbitt. Torquay, 1898.

NESBITT. A Genealogy of the Nesbit, Ross, Porter Families, of Pennsylvania. By Blanche T. Hartman. Pittsburgh, Pa., 1929.

NESBITT. History of the Nesbitt Family. By Dr. R. Nesbitt. 1930. (In the Public Record Office of Northern Ireland, Belfast.)

NIXON. The Family of Nixon of Nixon Hall, County Fermanagh—with a Short Account of the Families of Erskine of Cavan and Allin of Youghal. By Henry Biddall Swanzy. Dublin, 1899. (C)

NIXON. See French.

NUGENT. Historical Sketch of the Nugent Family. By J. C. Lyons. Ladestown, 1853.

O'BRIEN. Historical Memoir of the O'Briens, with Notes, Appendix, and a Genealogical Table of their Several Branches. Compiled from the Irish Annalists. By John O'Donoghue. Dublin, 1860. (C)

O'BRIEN. The O'Briens. By W. A. Lindsay. London, 1876. (C)

O'BRIEN. Genealogical Notes on the O'Briens of Kilcor, County Cork. 1887. (C)

O'BRIEN. History of the O'Briens from Brian Boroimhe, A. D. 1000 to 1945, plus Genealogical Table. By Hon. Donough O'Brien. London, Batsford, 1949. (A)

O'BYRNE. Historical Reminiscences of O'Byrnes, O'Tooles, O'Kavanaghs and Other Irish Chieftains. By O'Byrne. London, 1843. (A)

O'BYRNE. The O'Byrnes and their Descendants. Dublin, 1879. (C)

O'BRYNE. The History of the Clan O'Toole and other Leinster Septs. (See also O'Toole.) By the Rev. P. L. O'Toole. Dublin, 1890. (C)

O'CARROLL. History of the Ely O'Carroll Territory or Ancient Ormond. By the Rev. John Gleeson. 1915. (A)

O'CARROLL. Pedigree of the O'Carroll Family. 1883.

O'CLERY. The O'Cleirigh Family of Tir Conaill. By Father Paul Walsh. Dublin, 1938.

O'CONNELL. O'Connell Family Tracts: Nos. I-II. Edited by Basil Morgan O'Connell. Dublin, 1947, 1948. (A)

O'CONNELL. The Last Colonel of the Irish Brigade; Count O'Connell, and Old Irish Life at Home and Abroad, 1745-1833. By Mrs. Morgan John O'Connell. 2 vols. London, 1892. (C)

O'CONNOR. The O'Connors of Ballinahinch. By Mrs. Hungerford. London, 1893. (C)

O'CONNOR. Memoirs of Charles O'Conor, of Belenagare, with Historical Account of the Family of O'Conor. By the Rev. C. O'Conor. Dublin, 1796.

O'CONNOR. The O'Conors of Connaught. An History; Memoir, compiled from the Mss. of the late John O'Donovan, LL.D., with additions from the State Papers and Public Records. By the Rt. Hon. Charles Owen O'Conor. Dublin, 1891. (B)

O'CONNOR. Memoir of the O'Connors of Ballintubber, County Roscommon, showing . . . the true representatives of the family. By Roderic O'Connor. 1859. (A)

O'CONNOR. Lineal Descent of the O'Connors of County Roscommon. By R. O. O'Connor. Dublin, 1862.

O'CONNOR. Historical and Genealogical Memoir of the O'-Connors, Kings of Connaught and their Descendants. By Roderic O'Connor, Esq., B. L. Dublin, 1861. (A)

O'DALY. The O'Dalys of Muintuavara; Story of a Bardic Family. By Dominick Daly. Dublin, 1821.

O'DALY. Historical Account of the Family of O'Daly. By John O'Donovan. Dublin, 1852. (B)

O'DALY. History of the O'Dalys. The Story of the Ancient Irish Sept. The Race of Dalach of Corca Adaimh. By Edmund Emmet O'Daly. New York, New Haven, 1937. (A)

O'DELEVIN. The O'Delevins of Tyrone: The Story of an Irish Sept, now represented by the Families of Devlin, Develin, Develyn, Develon and Devellen. By Joseph Chubb Develin. Rutland, Vermont, 1938. (A)

O'DEMPSEY. An Account of the O'Dempseys, Chiefs of Clan Maliere. By Thomas Mathews. Dublin, 1903. (C)

O'DONNELL. John O'Donnell of Baltimore; His Forbears and Descendants. Compiled by E. Thornton Cook. London, 1934. (A)

O'DONOVAN. The Tribes and Territories of Ancient Ossory. By John O'Donovan. 1851. (A)

O'DOWDA. Genealogies, Tribes, and Customs of Hy-Fiachrach, commonly called O'Dowda's Country. By J. O'Donovan. 1844.

O'DWYER. The O'Dwyers of Kilnamanagh; the History of an Irish Sept. By Sir Michael O'Dwyer. London, 1933. (Also see O'Kennedy.) (A)

O'GOWAN. A Memoir of the Name of O'Gowan, or Smith. By an O'Gowan. Co. Tyrone, 1837. (A)

O'HARAS. History and Antiquities and Present State of the Parishes of Ballysadare and Kilvarnet, in the County of Sligo; with Notices of the O'Haras, the Coopers, the Percevals and other local families. By Terence O'Rorke. Dublin, 1878. (A)

O'HART. The Last Princes of Tara, or a brief sketch of the O'Hart ancient royal family. By J. O'Hart. Dublin, 1873. (A)

O'HEGERTY. O'Hegerty Pedigree (French Descent of Denis O'Hegerty of Clunsullagh, Brookhiel, County Donegal) 1622-1926. By J. Hagerty, Esq., Cohasset, Mass., U. S. A.

O'HURLEY (O'HURLY). The Family of O'Hurley. By the Rev. P. Hurley. Cork, 1906.

O'KELLY. Tribes and Customs of Hy-Many—Commonly Called O'Kelly's Country. By J. O'Donovan. 1843. (B)

O'KELLY. Secret History of the War of the Revolution in Ireland, 1688-1691, —. By Charles O'Kelly—edited with notes, etc., and a memoir of the Author and his Descendants. By John Cornelius O'Callaghan. Dublin, 1850. (C)

O'KENNEDY. Records of Four Tipperary Septs; the O'Kennedys, O'Dwyers, O'Mulryans, O'Meaghers. By Martin Callahan. Galway, 1938. (A)

OLIVER. The Olivers of Cloghanodfoy and their Descendants. By Major General J. R. Oliver. 2nd edition. London, 1904. (A)

O'MADDEN. Records of the O'Maddens of Hy-Many. By Dr. John More Madden. Dublin, 1894.

O'MAHONY. Three Kerry Families; O'Mahony, Conway, and Spotswood. By Samuel Trant MacCarthy. Folkstone (1923). (C)

O'MALLEY. Genealogy of the O'Malleys of the Owals. Philadelphia, 1913.

O'MEAGHER. Historical Notices of the O'Meaghers of Ikerrin. By John C. O'Meagher. London, 1886. (A) (B) (C)

O'MEAGHER. See O'Kennedy.

O'MULLALLY. History of O'Mullally and Lally Clans. By D. P. O'Mullally. 1941.

O'MULRYAN. See O'Kennedy.

O'NEIL. The O'Neills of Ulster; Their History and Genealogy. By Thomas Matthews. 3 vols. Dublin, 1907. (B)

O'NEILL. The Fate and Fortunes of Hugh O'Neill, Earl of Tyrone, and Rory O'Donel, Earl of Tyrconnell; their Flight from Ireland and Death in Exile. By C. P. Meehan. 2nd edition. Dublin, 1870. (C)

O'NEILL. The Will and Family of Hugh O'Neill, 2nd Earl of Tyrone (with appendix of genealogies). Edited by the Rev. Paul Walsh. Dublin, 1930. (A)

O'NEILL. History of the Parish of Tynan, in the County of Armagh. With notices of the O'Neill, Hovenden, Stronge, and other families connected with the district. By John J. Marshall. Dungannon, Co. Tyrone, 1932. (A)

O'REILLY. The O'Reillys of Templemills, Celbridge, and a pedigree from the old Irish manuscripts brought up to date, with a note on the history of the Clan Ui-Raighilligh in general. By M. W. O'Reilly, Esq. (From the O'Hanluain (Enri Ms.).) Dublin, 1940. (A)

ORMSBY. Pedigree of the Ormsby Family, formerly of Lincolnshire, now Ireland. By J. F. Fuller. 1886.

ORPEN. The Orpen Family: Being an Account of the Life and Writings of Richard Orpen of Killowen, County Kerry, together with some Researches into the Early History of his Forbears in England. By Goddard H. Orpen. Frome, 1930. (A)

O'SULLIVAN. Bantry, Berehaven, and the O'Sullivan Sept. By T. D. Sullivan. Dublin, 1908. (C)

O'TOOLE. The O'Tooles, Anciently Lords of Powerscourt Feracualan, Fertire and Imale; with some notices of Feagh Machugh O'Byrne, Chief of Clan Ranelagh. By John O'Toole. Dublin. (A) (C)

O'TOOLE. See O'Byrne.

PALMER. Genealogical and Historical Account of the Palmer Family of Kenmare, County Kerry. By the Rev. A. H. Palmer. 1872.

PALMER. Account of the Palmer Family of Rahan, County Kildare. By T. Prince. New York, 1903.

PARNELL. A Historical Sketch of Parnell and Parnells. By R. Johnston. Dublin, 1888. (A)

PARSONS. Notes on Families and Individuals of the Name of Parsons. London, 1903.

PATTERSON. Some Family Notes. By William Hugh Patterson. Belfast, 1911.

PENTHENY. Memoir of the Ancient Family of Pentheny, or De Pentheny, of County Meath. Dublin, 1821.

PERCEVAL. See O'Haras.

PILKINGTON. Harland's History and Pedigrees of the Pilkingtons. Edited by R. G. Pilkington. 4th edition. Dublin, 1906. (C)

PILKINGTON. Harland's History of the Pilkingtons, from the Saxon times . . . to the present time. 2nd edition. Dublin, 1886.

PLUNKET. The Family of Plunket. By W. Lynch (in his *View of the Legal Institutions*), 1830. (B)

POE. Origin and Early History of the Family of Poë or Poe, with Full Pedigrees of the Irish Branch of the Family, and a Discussion on the True Ancestry of Edgar Allen Poe, the American Poet. By Sir E. T. Bewley. Dublin, 1906.

POLLOCK. The Family of Pollock. By the Rev. Allen S. Hartigan. Folkstone, n. d.

POOL. The Pools of Mayfield and Other Irish Families. By Rosemary ffolliott. Dublin, 1958. (C)

PORTER. See Nesbitt.

POWER. An Historical Account of the Pohers, Poers and Powers. By G. O'C. Redmond, M.D. Dublin, 1897.

POWER. Notes and Pedigrees Relating to the Family of Poher, Poer or Power. By Edmund, 17th Lord Power. Clonmel, n. d.

PRATT. Pratt Family Records; an Account of the Pratts of Youghal and Castlemartyr, County Cork, and their Descendants. By John Pratt. Millom, 1931. (D)

PRATT. The Family of Pratt of Gawsworth, Carrigrohane, County Cork. By John Pratt. 1925. (A)

RAM. The Ram Family. By Willett Ram and Francis Robert Ram. Halesworth, Suffolk, 1940. (C)

REA. Memoirs of the Rea Family, 1798-1857. By A. H. Thornton. (B)

REA. The Rea Genealogy. By J. Harris Rea. Banbridge, 1927. (In the Public Record Office of Northern Ireland, Belfast.)

RENTOUL. A Record of the Family and Lineage of Alexander Rentoul, LL.D., M.P. By E. Rentoul. Belfast, 1890.

RICHARDSON. Six Generations of Friends (Quakers) in Ireland. By J. M. R. London, 1890.

ROBERTS. A Roberts Family quondam Quakers of Queen's County. By E. J. Adeir Impey. London, 1939.

ROSBOROUGH. Later History of the Family of Rosborough of Mullinagoan, County Fermanagh. By H. B. Swanzy. 1897.

ROSS. See Nesbitt.

RUDKIN. The Rudkins of the County Carlow. By Sir E. T. Bewley. Exeter, 1905.

SANDYS. Some Notes for a History of the Sandys Family of Great Britain and Ireland. By C. Vivian and Col. T. M. Sandys. 1907.

SANKEY. Pedigree of the Sankeys of England and Ireland. 1881.

SAUNDERSON. The Saundersons of Castle Saunderson. By Henry Saunderson. Frome, 1936. (A)

SAVAGE. The Ancient and Noble Family of Savages of Ards, with sketches of English and American Branches of the House of Savage. By George F. Savage-Armstrong. London, 1888. (B) (D)

SAVAGE. A Genealogical History of the Savage Family of Ulster, being a Revision and Enlargement of Certain Chapters of "The Savages of the Ards". Edited by George F. Savage-Armstrong. London, 1906. (A) (B)

SEAVER. History of the Seaver Family. By the Rev. George Seaver. Dundalk, 1950.

SEGRAVE. The Segrave Family, 1066 to 1935. By Charles W. Segrave, assisted by Thomas U. Sadleir, Deputy Ulster King of Arms. London, 1936. (A)

SHERIDAN. The Lives of the Sheridans. 2 vols. By Percy Fitzgerald. 1886. (A)

SHERIDAN. The Sheridan Family, 1687-1867; the descendants of Thomas Sheridan of Quilca. (Included in *Helen's Tower*. By Harold Nicolson. London, 1937. Genealogical chart.) (C)

SHIRLEY. Stemmata Shirleiana, or Annals of the Shirley Family. By E. P. Shirley. 1873.

SINCLAIR. The Sinclair Genealogy. By C. T. McCready. 1868.

SINCLAIR. Genealogy of the Sinclairs of Ulster. By Sir John Sinclair. 1810.

SINNETT, SENNOTT, SYNNOTT. The Sinnett Genealogy . . . with records of Sennetts, Sinnotts, etc., in Ireland and America. By the Rev. C. N. Sinnett. Concord, New Hampshire, 1910.

SIRR. A Genealogical History of the Family of Sirr of Dublin. London, 1903.

SLACKE. Records of the Slacke Family in Ireland. By Helen A. Crofton. 1900-1902. (A) (D)

SMITH. The Chronicles of a Puritan Family in Ireland. (Smith (formerly) of Glasshouse.) By G. N. Nuttall-Smith, M. A. London, 1923. (C)

SMITH. The Smith Family, being a popular account of most branches of the name . . . from the 14th Century. By Compton Reade. 1904. (A)

SMYTH. Généalogie de I'Ancienne et Noble Famille de Smyth de Ballyntary, Comte de Waterford en Irelande.

SOMERVILLE. Records of the Somerville Family of Castlehaven and Drishane from 1174 to 1904. Compiled by E. Somerville and Boyle Townshend Somerville. Cork, 1940.

SPEDDING. The Spedding Family, with Short Accounts of a Few Families Allied by Marriage. By Captain John C. D. Spedding. Dublin, 1909.

SPOTSWOOD. See O'Mahony.

STEWART. The Stewarts of Ballintoy, with Notes on Families of the District. By the Rev. George Hill. Coleraine, 1865. (B)

STONEY. Some Old Annals of the Stoney Family. By Maj. F. S. Stoney, R. A. London, 1879. (A)

STRONGE. See O'Neill. By John J. Marshall.

STUART. Genealogical and Historical Sketch of the Stuarts of the House of Castle Stuart in Ireland. By the Hon. and Rev. Andrew Godfrey Stuart. Edinburgh, 1854. (A)

SULLIVAN. Materials for a history of the family of John Sullivan of Berwick, New England, and of the O'Sullivans of Ardea, Ireland. Chiefly collected by . . . T. C. Amory. (Edited by Miss G. E. Meredith.) With a pedigree of O'Sullivan Beare, by Sir J. Bernard Burke. Cambridge, Mass., 1893. (A)

SULLIVAN. A Family Chronicle derived from the Notes and Letters selected by Lady Grey and edited by Gertrude Lyster. London, 1908.

SULLIVAN. Bantry, Berehaven and the O'Sullivan Sept. By T. D. Sullivan. Dublin, 1908.

SYNGE. The Family of Synge or Sing: Pedigree tables of families bearing the above name and notes . . . dealing chiefly with the family of Synge or Sing, of Bridgnorth in Shropshire, and its branches in Ireland, America, etc. By Katherine C. Synge. Southampton, 1940. (C)

TAAFFE. Memoirs of the Family of Taafe. Compiled by Count E. F. J. Taaffe. Vienna, 1856.

TALBOT. Genealogical Memoir of the Ancient and Noble Family of Talbot of Malahide, County Dublin. 1829.

TERRY. The Pedigrees and Papers of James Terry, Athlone Herald, at the Court of James II, in France, 1690-1725; together with other pedigrees and naturalizations from the Manuscripts d'Hozier and other sources in France. By Charles E. Lart. Exeter, 1938. (A)

TIERNAN. The Tiernan and Other Families. By Charles B. Tiernan. Baltimore, 1901. (A)

TOWNSHEND. An Officer of the Long Parliament and his Descendants, being an Account of the Life and Times of Colonel Richard Townshend of Castletown (Castle Townshend), and a Chronicle of his Family. By Richard and Dorothea Townshend. London, 1892.

TRACY. Tracy Peerage Case. Case of Benjamin Wheatley Tracy, Esq., . . . Claiming the Titles, Honors and Dignities of Viscount and Baron Tracy. Folio, 1853. (D)

TRANT. The Trant Family. By Samuel T. McCarthy. 1924. (A)

TRENCH. A Memoir of the Trench Family. By Thomas R. F. Cooke-Trench. 1897. (A)

TUTHILL. Pedigree of Tuthill of Peamore, County Devon, and of Kilmore and Fhaa, County Limerick. By Lt. Col. P. B. Tuthill.

TWEEDY. The Dublin Tweedys. The Story of a Dublin Family. By Owen Tweedy. London, 1956. (C)

TYRCONNEL. Illustrated Handbook of the Scenery and Antiquities of S. W. Donegal. With historical notes on the Clan of Tir-Connel, MacSwine of the Battle Axe, etc. 1872. (B)

TYRRELL. Genealogical History of the Tyrrells of Castleknock, in County Westmeath, and now of Grange Castle, County Meath. By J. H. Tyrrell. 1904.

USSHER. The Ussher Memoirs, or Genealogical Memoirs of the Ussher Families in Ireland. By the Rev. William Ball Wright. London, 1899.

VANCE. An Account Historical and Genealogical of the Family of Vance in Ireland. By W. Balbirnie. Cork, 1860.

VILLIERS. Pedigree of the Family of Villiers of Hanbury, County Stafford, and of Kilpeacon, County Limerick. By Lt. Col. P. B. Tuthill. London, 1907.

VILLIERS. See Geraldines.

WALSH. The Family of Walsh. A Royalist Family. Irish and French (1689-1789) and Prince Charles Edward. 1904. (A) (C)

WALSH. The Lament for John MacWalter Walsh. With notes on the history of the family of Walsh from 1170-1690. With a foreword by James J. Walsh. New York, 1925. (A)

WANDESFORDE. The Story of the Family of Wandesforde of Kirklington and Castlecomer. By Harry Bertram M'Call. London, 1904.

WARBURTON. Memoir of the Warburton Family of Garryhinch, King's County. Dublin, 1848. 2nd edition, Dublin, 1881.

WARREN. The Warren Saga, plus Pedigree. By Edward O'Boyle. Londonderry, 1946.

WARREN. History of the Warren Family. By the Rev. Thomas Warren. 1902.

WASSONS. See Baird.

WATERS or WALTER. The Waters or Walter Family of Cork. By Eaton W. Waters. Cork, 1939. (With Genealogical Chart, 13th Century to 20th Century.) (C)

WAUCHOPE. The Ulster Branch of the Family of Wauchope, Wauhope, Wahab, Waughop, etc., with notes on the main Scottish family and on branches in America and Australia. Edited by Gladys M. Wauchope. London, 1928. (A)

WAUCHOPE. See Baird.

WHITE. The History of the Family of White of Limerick, Knockcentry, etc. By John D. White. Cashel, 1887.

WILDE. The Wildes of Merrion Square: the family of Oscar Wilde. By Patrick Byrne. London, 1954. (C)

WILKINSON. Fragments of Family History. By S. P. Flory. London, 1896.

WILLIAMS. The Groves and Lappan; County Monaghan, Ireland. An Account of . . . in search of the genealogy of the Williams Family. By J. F. Williams. St. Paul, U. S. A., 1889.

WILLSON. See Magee.

WILSON. Ancestors of Woodrow Wilson. By H. W. Walker. 1915. (B)

WILSON. A Brief Journal of the Life—of Thomas Wilson (Quaker). Who departed this Life at his own Habitation near Edenderry, in the Kingdom of Ireland. By John Stoddart. Dublin, 1728. (C)

WINGFIELD. Muniments of the Family of Wingfield. By Viscount Powerscourt. London, 1894.

WINTHROP. Some Account of the Early Generations of the Winthrop Family in Ireland. Cambridge, Mass., 1883.

WOLFE. Wolfes of Forenaghts, Blackhall, Baronrath, County Kildare and County Tipperary. By Lt. Col. R. T. Wolfe. Guildford, 1893.

YARNER. A Collection Concerning the Family of Yarner of Wicklow. By J. C. H. 1870.

YOUNG. Three Hundred Years in Inishowen, being more particularly an account of the family of Young, of Cudaff, with short accounts of many other families connected with them during that period. By Amy J. Young. Belfast, 1929. (B)

CHAPTER II

PUBLISHED COLLECTIONS OF PEDIGREES, GENEALOGY AND FAMILY HISTORY

BURKE, SIR BERNARD. A Genealogical and Heraldic History of the Landed Gentry of Ireland. Revised and edited by A. C. Fox-Davies. London, 1912.

BURKE, SIR BERNARD. Genealogical and Heraldic History of the Peerages of England, Ireland and Scotland, Extinct, Dormant and in Abeyance. London, 1883.

BURKE, SIR BERNARD. General Armory of England, Scotland and Ireland. London, 1878.

BURKE, SIR BERNARD. Landed Gentry of Great Britain and Ireland. 2 vols. London, 1871.

BURKE, SIR BERNARD. Reminiscences Ancestral, Anecdotal and Historic (a remodeled and revised edition of *The Rise of Great Families*—). London.

BURKE, SIR BERNARD. A Visitation of Seats and Arms of the Noblemen and Gentlemen of Great Britain and Ireland. London, 1855.

BURKE, SIR JOHN BERNARD. Anecdotes of the Aristocracy and Episodes in Ancestral Story. 2 vols. London, 1849.

BURKE, JOHN. A Genealogical and Heraldic History of the Landed Gentry or Commoners of Great Britain and Ireland. 4 vols. London, 1837, 1838.

BURKE, JOHN and JOHN BERNARD. A Genealogical and Heraldic Dictionary of the Landed Gentry of Great Britain and Ireland. 3 vols. London, 1849.

BURKE, JOHN and JOHN BERNARD. Genealogical and Heraldic History of the Extinct and Dormant Baronetcies of England, Ireland and Scotland. London, 1844.

BURKE, SIR JOHN BERNARD. Romantic Records of Distinguished Families. 2 vols. London, 1851.

BURKE, SIR JOHN BERNARD. Family Romance; or, Episodes in the Domestic Annals of the Aristocracy. 2 vols. London, 1853.

BURKE, SIR JOHN BERNARD. General Armoury of England, Scotland, Ireland and Wales. London, 1878.

BURKE, O. J. History of the Lord Chancellors of Ireland, 1186-1874. London, 1879.

BURKE. Burke's Genealogical and Heraldic History of the Landed Gentry of Ireland. Edited by L. G. Pine. 4th edition. London, 1958.

COKAYNE, G. E. Complete Peerage of England, Scotland, Ireland, Great Britain and the United Kingdom, extant, extinct or dormant, new edition, revised and much enlarged by Hon. Vicary Gibbs and others, vols. 1-12, Pt. 1, and 13 (all published). 13 vols.

COKAYNE, G. E. The Complete Peerage of England, Scotland and Ireland, or a History of the House of Lords and all of its Members from the Earliest Times. Revised and enlarged: Edited by H. A. Doubleday and Lord Howard de Walden. 9 vols. London, 1936.

COKAYNE, G. E. State of the Peerage of Ireland, 1801-1889. With list of Knights of St. Patrick, 1783-1888. London, 1889.

CRISP, F. A. Visitation of Ireland. 6 vols. Edited by J. J. Howard and F. A. Crisp. London, 1897-1918.

CRONNELLY, RICHARD F. Cronnelly's Irish Genealogies. Dublin, 1864.

CRONNELLY, RICHARD F. Irish Family History. Dublin, 1864-1865.

CROSSLY, AARON. The Peerage of Ireland: or, An Exact Catalogue of the present Nobility both Spiritual and Temporal, with a Genealogical Account of them . . . Dublin. T. Hume. 1725.

DALTON, JOHN. Illustrations, Historical and Genealogical of King James's Irish Army List, 1689. Dublin, 1855. 2nd edition, 2 vols. 1860-1861.

FOSTER, J. Stemmata Britannica: A genealogical account of the untitled nobility and gentry of Great Britain and Ireland. 1877.

HOWARD, J. J. See Crisp, F. A.

KEATING, G. History of Ireland: Genealogies and Synchronisms. Edited by P. S. Denneen. 1914.

KIMBER. Kimber's Peerage of Ireland. 1788.

LART, CHARLES E. The Pedigrees and Papers of James Terry, Athlone Herald at the Court of James II, in France (1690-1725)—. Exeter, 1938.

LODGE, JOHN. The Peerage of Ireland or a Genealogical History of the Present Nobility of that Kingdom. 2nd edition, revised, enlarged and continued to the present time, by Mervyn Archdall. 7 vols. Dublin, 1789.

LYNCH. Feudal Dignities.

MACLYSAGHT, EDWARD. Irish Families, their Names, Arms and Origins. Dublin, 1957.

MAGEE, JAMES. Irish Genealogies, by James Magee of Magherlin.

O'CLERY. O'Clery's Book of Pedigrees—Ireland.

O'HART, JOHN. The Irish and Anglo-Irish Landed Gentry when Cromwell Came to Ireland. Dublin, 1884.

O'HART, JOHN. Irish Pedigrees or the Origin and Stem of the Irish Nation. 2 vols. 2nd edition, Dublin, 1878; 5th edition, Dublin, New York, 1887-1892.

PATERSON, JAMES. History of County Ayr, with a Genealogical Account of Families of Ayrshire (Scotland). 2 vols. 1853. (Vol. 3 published later.) (Listed for origins of Scotch-Irish families.)

PHILLIPS, T. Knights of Ireland.

ROBSON, T. The British Herald; or Cabinet of Armorial Bearings of the Nobility and Gentry of Great Britain and Ireland. Sunderland, 1830.

ROONEY, JOHN. A Genealogical History of Irish Families, with their Crests and Armorial Bearings. New York. (1896 ?.)

SALMON. A Short View of the Families of the Present Nobility—. London, 1759.

WHITE, COLONEL JAMES GROVE. Historical and Topographical Notes, Etc., on Buttevant, Castletownroche, Doneraile, Mallow, and Places in their Vicinity. Collected by Colonel James Grove White. 4 vols. Cork, Vol. I, 1905; Vol. II, 1911; Vol. III, 1913; Vol. IV, 1916.

CHAPTER III

BIOGRAPHICAL DICTIONARIES AND BIOGRAPHICAL SUCCESSION LISTS

BIOGRAPHICAL DICTIONARIES

AGNEW, D. C. Protestant Exiles from France in the Reign of Louis XIV, or the Huguenot Refugees. 2nd edition. London, 1871-1874.

BALL, F. ELRINGTON. The Judges in Ireland, 1221-1921. 2 vols. London, 1926. New York, 1927.

BROWN, REV. S. J. M. Ireland in Fiction. 2nd edition. Dublin, 1919.

BURTCHAELL, GEORGE DAMES. Genealogical Memoirs of the Members of Parliament for the County and City of Kilkenny, etc. Dublin, 1888.

CRONE, JOHN SMYTH. A Concise Dictionary of Irish Biography. Dublin, 1928. Revised and enlarged edition, Dublin, 1937.

DENNY, H. L. L. Handbook of County Kerry Family History, Biography, etc. 1923. (References.)

DICTIONARY OF NATIONAL BIOGRAPHY. London, 1908-1949.

DICTIONARY OF NATIONAL BIOGRAPHY. With index and epitome, and supplementary volumes. Edited by Sir L. Stephen and Sir S. Lee. 70 vols. 1885-1912.

GILBERT, J. T. History of the Viceroys of Ireland. 1865.

HAMILTON, THOMAS. Irish Worthies: A series of biographical sketches of eminent ministers and members of the Presbyterian Church of Ireland. Belfast, 1875.

HAYES, RICHARD. Biographical Dictionary of Irishmen in France. Dublin, 1949.

HERBERT, ROBERT. The Worthies of Thomond: A compendium of short lives of the most famous men and women of counties Limerick and Clare to the present day. 1st, 2nd and 3rd series. Limerick, 1946.

HORE, H. J., and JAMES GRAVES. The Social State of the Southern and Eastern Counties of Ireland in the 16th Century: being the Presentments of the Gentlemen, Commonalty and Citizens of Carlow, Cork, Kilkenny, Tipperary, and Wexford, made in the Reigns of Henry VIII and Elizabeth. Dublin, 1870.

KILLEN, REV. W. D. History of Congregations of the Presbyterian Church in Ireland and Biographical Notices of Eminent Presbyterian Ministers and Laymen. Belfast, 1886.

KING, JEREMIAH. County Kerry, Past and Present: A Handbook to the Local and Family History of the County. Dublin, 1931.

O'CALLAGHAN, J. C. History of the Irish Brigades in the Service of France. Dublin, 1854.

O'DONOGHUE, DAVID J. The Geographical Distribution of Irish Ability. Dublin, 1906.

O'DONOGHUE, DAVID J. The Poets of Ireland: A Biographical Dictionary with Bibliographical Particulars. London, 1892-3; Dublin, 1912.

O'MAHONY, C. The Viceroys of Ireland. London, 1912.

O'RAGHAELAIGH, DEASMUMHAN. Three Centuries of Irish Chemists. Cork, 1941.

O'RAHILLY, T. F. Irish Poets, Historians and Judges in English Documents, 1538-1615. In *Proceedings of the Royal Irish Academy*, vol. 36.

O'REILLY, EDWARD. A Chronological Account of nearly Four Hundred Irish Writers—to 1750. (*Transactions of the Iberno-Celtic Society*. Vol. 1, pt. 1. Dublin, 1820.)

PARLIAMENT, MEMBERS OF, 1213-1874: A Return of the name, year, etc., of each member of the Lower House of the Parliaments of England, Scotland and Ireland. 3 vols. London, 1878.

RONAN, REV. MYLES V. The Irish Martyrs of the Penal Laws. London, 1935.

RYAN, R. Biographical Dictionary of the Worthies of Ireland. 2 vols. 1821.

SADLEIR, T. U. Kildare Members of Parliament, 1559—. In the *Journal of the County Kildare Archaeological Society*, 1911-1924.

SMYTH, C. J. Chronicle of the Law Officers of Ireland. London, 1839.

STRICKLAND, W. C. Dictionary of Irish Artists. 2 vols. Dublin, 1913.

SWIFT, JOHN. History of the Dublin Bakers and Others. Dublin, 1949.

ULSTER BIOGRAPHICAL SKETCHES. 1884. (In Public Record Office of Northern Ireland, Belfast.)

WARE, SIR JAMES. History of the Bishops of Ireland; enlarged by Walter Harris. 1739.

WEAVER, J. R. H., *Ed.* Dictionary of National Biography. 1922-1930. Index, 1901-1930.

WEBB, ALFRED. A Compendium of Irish Biography. Dublin, 1878.

WILLS, JAMES. Lives of Illustrious and Distinguished Irishmen; from the earliest times to the present period. 12 vols. Dublin, 1842. Dublin, Edinburgh and London, 1847.

YOUNG, WILLIAM R. The Fighters of Derry; Biographical and Genealogical notes on those who were present at the Siege of Derry, 1689. London, 1932.

BIOGRAPHICAL SUCCESSION LISTS (OF THE IRISH CLERGY)

Early Catholic And Established Church Of Ireland

Cotton, Henry. Fasti Ecclesiae Hibernicae; The Succession of the Prelates and Members of the Cathedral Bodies in Ireland. 5 vols. and supplement. Dublin, 1847-1878.

Church of Ireland

Brady, W. Maziere. Clerical and Parochial Records of Cork, Cloyne and Ross; taken from Diocesan and Parish Registers, Manuscripts in the Principal Libraries and Public Record Offices of Oxford, Dublin and London and from private family papers. 3 vols. London, 1864.

Carmody, The Very Rev. W. P. Lisburn Cathedral and its Past Rectors. 1926.

Carroll, W. G. The Succession of Clergy in the Parishes of S. Bride, S. Michael le Pole and S. Stephen. Dublin, 1884.

Cole, Rev. J. H. Church and Parish Records of the United Diocese of Cork, Cloyne and Ross. 1903. (A continuation or supplement to Brady.)

Lawlor, Hugh Jackson. The Fasti of St. Patrick's, Dublin. Dublin, 1930.

Leslie, Rev. James B. Ardfert and Aghadoe Clergy and Parishes. 1940.

Leslie, Rev. James B. Armagh Clergy and Parishes. 1911.

Leslie, Rev. James B. Supplement to Armagh Clergy and Parishes. Dundalk, 1948.

Leslie, Rev. James B. Clogher Clergy and Parishes. 1908, 1929.

Leslie, Rev. James B. Derry Clergy and Parishes. 1937.

Leslie, Rev. James B., and Swanzy, Very Rev. H. B. Biographical Lists of the Clergy of the Diocese of Down. 1936.

LESLIE, REV. JAMES B., and Swanzy, Very Rev. H. B. Biographical Succession Lists of the Diocese of Dromore. Belfast, 1933.

LESLIE, REV. JAMES B. Ferns Clergy and Parishes. 1936.

LESLIE, REV. JAMES B. Ossory Clergy and Parishes. 1933.

LESLIE, REV. JAMES B. Raphoe Clergy and Parishes. 1940.

RENNISON, WILLIAM H. Succession List of the Bishops and Clergy of the Dioceses of Waterford and Lismore. Waterford, 1922.

PRESBYTERIAN

MCCONNELL, REV. JAMES. Fasti of the Irish Presbyterian Church, 1613-1840. Revised by Rev. S. G. McConnell. Edited by F. J. Paul and Rev. David Stewart. Belfast, *ca.* 1943.

CHAPTER IV

RECOMMENDED HISTORICAL AND GENEALOGICAL PERIODICALS

There are several important historical societies of county, regional, and national scope which publish journals or periodicals, usually semi-annually. The primary purpose of these societies is to encourage research of a historical, archaeological or genealogical nature, for the common benefit of the members. The results of this research have been compiled in historical accounts of antiquities and in collections of records of a character to preserve the history of families and persons belonging therein. These have been richly documented from primary sources. The genealogical work ranges in scope from full pedigrees of several generations, genealogical charts, family notes or biographies, to miscellaneous records such as transcripts or abstracts of wills, marriage bonds, entries of baptism, marriage and burial from parish registers, tombstone inscriptions, descriptions and records of armorial sculptured tombstones, abstracts of deeds, lists of local inhabitants at a given date, lists of taxpayers, public office holders, freemen's rolls, and much other material of use in compiling genealogy.

Before listing these periodicals, attention should be called to one recommended to this compiler by Dr. Richard J. Hayes, Director of the National Library of Ireland, entitled *Irish Historical Studies.* This is a joint journal of the Irish Historical Society and the Ulster Society for Irish Historical Studies. Publication was begun in March, 1938, and issues have appeared in March and September of each following year. It presents the well-documented work of scholars on many subjects of importance to historians and genealogists. Approximately fifty pages of each issue are devoted to reviews of all Irish historical and genealogical publications of the previous year which are thought to be worthy of note. Highly qualified persons contribute the critical and analytical book reviews, and note the articles of importance. Thus, the reviews constitute a selected bibliography and critical description of the newly published historical and genealogical works of Irish interest. Some American libraries have complete files of this periodical.

Special attention should also be given to the *Journal of the Royal Society of Antiquaries of Ireland.* Publication of this *Journal* began in 1849, and has continued in an uninterrupted series to date, representing the oldest historical society in Ireland. While the Society has undergone various changes of name, the *Journal* has been preserved as a continuous publication. The great historians, antiquarians and genealogists of Ireland have, for over a century, been among the elected fellows and members of this Society. They, with their interests and contributions to this *Journal,* have maintained its excellence. The reviews of current publications of Irish interest which appear in each issue have long set the standard of critical analysis in the field of Irish history, archaeology and genealogy. They provide a running annotated bibliography of great value to the student.

Each publication listed below has its specialized value according to the area and interests represented. Complete files of all are preserved in the National Library of Ireland. Local historical societies, county and public libraries, have the publications which represent their own area. The best known and most widely distributed journals will be found in the large genealogical libraries of America.

The National Library of Ireland now maintains a card index, by name and subject, for all except the *Journal of the Cork Historical and Archaeological Society,* the *Journal of the Royal Society of Antiquaries of Ireland,* and the *Ulster Journal of Archaeology.* Indexes to these three periodicals have been published by the respective societies. The index cards for the other journals and periodicals have been microfilmed by the National Library, under the direction of Dr. Hayes.

* * * * *

ANALECTA HIBERNICA. A journal which, since 1930, has been published from time to time by the Irish Manuscripts

Commission. Various documents and indexes of a historical and genealogical nature have been printed, such as the INDEX OF WILL ABSTRACTS IN THE GENEALOGICAL OFFICE, Dublin (*Analecta Hibernica*, No. 17, 1949). This and other items which appear are judged by the Commission to be valuable, but too short in length for publication in a separate volume.

ARCHIVIUM HIBERNICUM or IRISH HISTORICAL RECORDS. The Catholic Record Society of Ireland was established in 1911 for the publication of Irish historical documents. Many important documents, mainly Catholic, have been printed. The first journal was issued in 1912; it was published annually thereafter until 1917. In 1922, vol. 7 was issued, and vol. 8 did not appear until 1941. Vol. 8 contains A RENT ROLL OF ALL HOUSES AND LANDS BELONGING TO THE SEE OF ARMAGH (*ca.* 1620), compiled by Lawrence P. Murray, from records in the Muniment Room of the Diocesan Registry Office in Armagh. This same volume presents THE COUNTY ARMAGH HEARTHMONEY ROLLS, 1664, copied in the Public Record Office, Dublin, before 1922. This, in effect, is a census of the householders in County Armagh.

ARDAGH AND CLONMACNOISE ANTIQUARIAN SOCIETY JOURNAL. Publication began with Vol. I, no. 1, in 1926, and had reached Vol. II, no. 12, in 1951. The area of interest covered by this magazine comprises the counties of Cavan, Leitrim, Roscommon, Sligo and Westmeath.

ARMAGH DIOCESAN HISTORICAL SOCIETY JOURNAL. This Society was founded in May, 1953, under the patronage of His Eminence, Cardinal D'Alton. Its primary purpose is the study of local history on the highest ecclesiastical level. Published articles are compiled from the manuscripts in Catholic diocesan libraries which represent the labor of many priests who have spent their lives gathering materials for histories of their parishes. For local history of County Armagh, they contain a treasure-trove of miscellaneous information concerning individuals, families and communities during the times of political changes, Catholic persecution under Penal Laws, Protestant settlements, revolution and confiscation, as revealed in seventeenth century documents. Some of these comprise extracts from the Rent Rolls of the Archbishopric, 1615; Chancery Inquisitions (rich in family records); Hearthmoney Rolls, 1664; Ashe's Survey; Rental of the Manor of Armagh, 1714 (with names and location of the tenants); Tithe-payer's lists, 1835; and various spellings of townland names in the seventeenth century documents. It presents, largely, material for the compiling of local history and genealogy.

BELFAST MONTHLY MAGAZINE. Publications began with Vol. I, in 1808, and continued through Vol. XIII, in 1814. So far as is known, it was not published subsequent to that date.

BIOGRAPHICAL SOCIETY OF IRELAND (PUBLICATIONS). Beginning in 1918, when Vol. I appeared, the Society has published those papers of a biographical and genealogical nature, which were read before the members in Dublin.

CARLOVIANA: The Journal of the Old Carlow Society. This Society, which began publication with Vol. I, no. 1, in January, 1947, has made an important contribution to the printing of local and family history of County Carlow; little having appeared since John Ryan's *History of Carlow,* in 1834. The first number included three letters from emigrants to America, after the famine, *ca.* 1844. A list is also printed of the inhabitants of Carlow in 1824, as extracted from Pigott's *Directory.* A bibliography of County Carlow publications is presented (pp. 33-36). An account of "Killeshin Parish in the Nineteenth Century", with some genealogical material, is included.

CLOGHER RECORD. Publication of the *Journal* of the Clogher Historical Society began with Vol. I, no. 1, in 1953. This Catholic Society has for its area of interest the diocese of Clogher, which includes parts of counties Donegal, Fermanagh, Louth, Tyrone, and all of County Monaghan.

CLONMEL HISTORICAL AND ARCHAEOLOGICAL SOCIETY JOURNAL. The first issue of this publication appeared in 1952. Its interests include the city of Clonmel, County Tipperary, and the surrounding area.

CORK HISTORICAL AND ARCHAEOLOGICAL SOCIETY JOURNAL.

This Society was founded in 1891 and, the following year, began publication of a journal which has appeared in an uninterrupted series, reaching vol. 58, no. 187 (Jan.-June, 1953), and continuing to this date. An index to all numbers, 1892-1940, was compiled by Denis J. O. Donoghue (p. 104). The area of interest includes County Cork and the adjacent counties, owing to the fact that many County Cork families had interests in nearby counties through marriage and inheritance. The *Journal* is especially rich in genealogy, both as to quality and quantity. It, fortunately, has been strengthened by the membership and contributions of several of Ireland's most competent genealogists.

DONEGAL (COUNTY) HISTORICAL SOCIETY JOURNAL. Founded in 1947, it has for its purpose an emphasis on local and family history. Each number includes brief family histories, some genealogy, and a section entitled *Notes and Queries,* mostly of a genealogical nature. The County Donegal Catholic Qualification Rolls, 1778-1790, copied in the Public Record Office before 1922, was a contribution of Sean O Domhnaill, in Vol. I, no. 3 (December, 1949). This gives the names, residence and occupation of the Catholics who had taken and subscribed to the oath of allegiance. (See VOLUME I., PART THREE.)

DOWN AND CONNOR HISTORICAL SOCIETY'S JOURNAL. This Society was founded in 1926, to encourage the study of the local history, families and antiquities of the diocese, by the clergy and laity of Down and Connor. The diocese includes parts of the counties of Antrim, Down, and Londonderry.

DUBLIN HISTORICAL RECORD. The publication of the Old Dublin Society quarterly periodical has continued in an uninterrupted series since the founding of the Society in 1934.

DUBLIN MAGAZINE. An Irish monthly register. Vol. I, published in 1798, was continued for some time and contained genealogical information of this area.

DUBLIN SATURDAY MAGAZINE. Irish biography and antiquities included. Nos. 1-108, in one volume.

FRIENDS HISTORICAL SOCIETY JOURNAL. Publication began in 1903, and has continued to the present time. It is a rich source for Quaker genealogy.

GALWAY ARCHAEOLOGICAL SOCIETY JOURNAL. The Society was founded in 1900. The *Journal* has published excellent material on local history and genealogy of County Galway.

GENEALOGIST, THE. Published in London, 1877-1922, this contained some Irish as well as English genealogy.

GENEALOGISTS' MAGAZINE, THE. The official organ of the Society of Genealogists, London. Publication, beginning in 1925, has continued to the present date.

HERMATHENA. In vols. 58-61 (1946-1948), J. G. Smyly contributes installments of his calendar of "Old Deeds in Trinity College Library, 1348-1508".

IRISH BOOK LOVER. Founded in 1914, it has continued in an uninterrupted series to the present time. It devotes space to reviews of genealogical material and family subjects. Among these are "The Plunkett Genealogies."

IRISH ECCLESIASTICAL RECORD. A Catholic monthly journal under episcopal sanction, began publication in 1854, and has continued to the present time.

IRISH GENEALOGIST. This is the publication of the Irish Genealogical Society, under the editorship of the Rev. Wallace Clare. The Society was founded in London in September, 1936, and has collected a large library of books for genealogical reference and genealogical manuscripts. The published articles in the magazine are short, but valuable. They include brief transcripts of documents and lists of various classes of genealogical records.

IRISH HISTORICAL STUDIES. The joint journal of the Irish Historical Society and the Ulster Society for Irish Historical Studies. Published twice yearly from 1938 until the present time. Described at the beginning of this chapter.

IRISH REVIEW. Published in Dublin, 1911-1914, it contains material relating to family history.

IRISH SWORD. The Journal of the Military History of Ireland, it contains much military information, including lists and biographies of use to the genealogist.

KERRY: JOURNAL OF THE COUNTY KERRY ANTIQUARIAN SOCIETY. Publication began in 1908. The stated purpose of this *Journal* is to record matter pertaining to county history, antiquities, county genealogies, etc. Some Kerry records contain extracts from original documents and compiled family histories (1612-1800). The Rev. Sir Henry L. Denny, its editor in 1923, published a *Handbook of County Kerry Family History, Biography, etc.* This contains the references for compiling over two hundred County Kerry genealogies.

KILDARE: JOURNAL OF THE COUNTY KILDARE ARCHAEOLOGICAL SOCIETY. The Society was founded and the first issue of its journal appeared in 1891. Publication has continued in an uninterrupted series to the present time. Besides much family history, under the editorship of Thomas Ulick Sadleir it has run a continued series of "Kildare Diocesan Wills", and among miscellanea, a list of officers of the Kildare Militia, 1794-1817, contributed by the late Tenison Groves.

KILKENNY: OLD KILKENNY REVIEW. Founded in 1946, the first issue contained the history of the families connected with Foulksrath Castle.

KILKENNY: JOURNAL OF THE KILKENNY AND SOUTH EAST IRELAND ARCHAEOLOGICAL SOCIETY. See *Journal of the Royal Society of Antiquaries of Ireland.*

LIMERICK: THE JOURNAL OF THE LIMERICK FIELD CLUB. It first appeared in 1897, and ran until 1908. See *North Munster Antiquarian Society Journal.*

LIMERICK: JOURNAL OF THE OLD LIMERICK SOCIETY. Publication was started in December, 1946. Contains biographical notes on county families.

LOUTH: JOURNAL OF THE COUNTY LOUTH ARCHAEOLOGICAL SOCIETY. Founded in 1904, the Society has made its journal one of the finest in Ireland. It is a storehouse of information on the county and its people. Original documents have been the basis for many articles.

MUNSTER: NORTH MUNSTER ANTIQUARIAN SOCIETY JOURNAL. Vol. I, no. 1, October, 1936. *The Journal of the Limerick Field Club,* which first appeared in 1897 and ran until 1908, was continued in the following year by this journal which lapsed in 1919 at the termination of the Society. This Society was reorganized in 1929, as the Thomond Archaeological Society and the Field Club. In October, 1936, the Society again reorganized and began publication under the above name which has continued to the present time. Dr. Richard J. Hayes, in the first issue, contributed two articles: "The German Colony in County Limerick", which deals with the settlement, in 1709, of Protestant refugees from the Palatine, and "Some Limerick Doctors, from Dr. Thomas Arthur (1593-1674), to Sir Matthew Tierney (1776-1845)."

NOTES AND QUERIES. Publication began in London, in 1849. This magazine lays emphasis on genealogy. Besides many family records, a series was published in vols. 182-187; being 17th to 19th century wills of the people of the counties of Cavan, Donegal, Fermanagh, Galway, Kings, Longford, Mayo, Monaghan, Roscommon, Tipperary, Tyrone, and Westmeath. In vol. 187, the Walsh and Irwin pedigrees were printed.

ROYAL IRISH ACADEMY PROCEEDINGS. Published from time to time in Dublin, since 1836; material relating to family history is often presented.

ROYAL IRISH ACADEMY TRANSACTIONS. First published as a periodical in Dublin, 1785, it has appeared at intervals to the present day and contains information on records for compiling family history.

ROYAL SOCIETY OF ANTIQUARIES OF IRELAND. In 1849, the parent Society was founded as the Kilkenny Archaeological Society. In 1856, this was organized into the Kilkenny and South-East of Ireland Archaeological Society. In 1868, it became the Historical and Archaeological Association of Ireland. In 1870, it was formed into the Royal Historical and Archaeological Association of Ireland. In 1890, it was finally organized into the present Society. This Society is the oldest historical organization in Ireland, having published a periodical from its first year in 1849, and continued under the various changes of name in an uninterrupted series to the present time. No student of history or genealogy should complete his work without a search of this publication, as its interests extend throughout Ireland. In 1923, it had running through its numbers the "Ossory Marriage Licences", the "Ossory Intestate Administrations," and the "Kilkenny School Register (1685-1800)". In 1945, its numbers carried notes on "Eighteenth-Century Tombstones in County Wexford".

STUDIES. A periodical founded in 1912, it is among the most scholarly of Irish historical magazines. Dr. Richard J. Hayes has made numerous contributions to this magazine; among them being, "Irish Links with Bordeaux", an account of Irish families (and their origins) who settled there in the eighteenth century. His "Biographical Dictionary of Irishmen in France" (with their family connections) ran serially for years before it was published in book form in Dublin, in 1949. An Index to *Studies* (vols. 1-20), in typescript, is in the National Library and in the University College Library, Dublin. This is brought up to date with each issue.

TOPOGRAPHER AND GENEALOGIST. Published in three volumes, 1846-1858, only.

ULSTER JOURNAL OF ARCHAEOLOGY. First series, Belfast, 1853-1862. Second series, Belfast, 1895-1911. Third series, Belfast, 1938, to date. Not enough can be said for the genealogical importance of this publication, particularly with regard to Ulster. It is full of family records, compiled genealogies, and a great series of transcripts of primary records. Each volume is indexed. The larger American genealogical libraries have collections of this publication.

WATERFORD: JOURNAL OF THE WATERFORD AND SOUTH EAST OF IRELAND ARCHAEOLOGICAL SOCIETY. Founded in 1894, the Society published an uninterrupted series to 1920.

CHAPTER V

FAMILY INDEX TO ARTICLES IN IRISH PERIODICALS: RELATING TO FAMILY HISTORY, GENEALOGY, PEDIGREES, AND BIOGRAPHY

(With a key to the periodicals)

The principal Irish periodicals in which family history, genealogy, pedigrees, biography, transcripts of documents for compiling genealogy, etc., have appeared are listed below, followed by key numbers in parentheses. This key number in parenthesis, followed by volume and page numbers of the periodical, appears in each listing in the family index.

Complete files of these publications are deposited in the National Library of Ireland, Kildare Street, Dublin. The *Ulster Journal of Archaeology* will be found in Belfast, in the Public Record Office of Northern Ireland, and at the Presbyterian Historical Society.

Most of the important American genealogical libraries have full or partial files of the older and well-known Irish periodicals of this nature.

PERIODICALS

Ardagh And Clonmacnoise Antiquarian Society Journal. (1)

Belfast Witness. (2)

Breifny Antiquarian Society Journal. (3)

Carloviana. (4)

CORK: *Journal Of The Cork Historical And Archaeological Society.* (5)

DONEGAL: *Journal Of The County Donegal Historical Society.* (6)

Dublin Historical Record. (7)

GALWAY: *Journal Of The Galway Archaeological And Historical Society.* (8)

Huguenot Society of London, Proceedings. (London.) (9)

Irish Ecclesiastical Record. (10)

Irish Genealogist. (London.) (11)

Irish Sword. (12)

KERRY: *County Kerry Archaeological Society Journal.* (13)

KILDARE: *Journal Of The County Kildare Archaeological Society.* (14)

KILKENNY: *Journal Of The Kilkenny And South East Ireland Archaeological Society.* (See Royal Society of Antiquaries of Ireland, Chapter IV.) (15)

Londonderry Sentinel. (16)

LOUTH: *Journal Of The County Louth Archaeological Society.* (17)

MUNSTER: *North Munster Antiquarian Society Journal.* (18)

Notes and Queries. (London.) (19)

OSSORY: *Transactions Of The Ossary Archaeological Society.* (20)

Recorder (The). (21)

Royal Society of Antiquaries of Ireland (Journal Of). (22)

Ulster Journal Of Archaeology. (23)

WATERFORD: *Journal Of The Waterford And South East of Ireland Archaeological Society.* (24)

FAMILY INDEX

AGNEW. The Agnews in County Antrim (a brief account of family history previous to 1656). By John M. Dickson. (23) 2nd series, vol. 7, pp. 166-171. 1901.

ALEN. Alen of St. Wolstans. By J. B. Clements. (14) vol. 1, pp. 340-1. 1892-1895.

ALEN. An Account of the Family of Alen of St. Wolstans, County Kildare. By H. L. Lyster Denny. (14) vol. 4, no. 2, pp. 95-110, 1903-1905; vol. 5, pp. 344-347, 1906-1908.

ALLEN. Ladytown and the Allens. By Thomas U. Sadleir. (14) vol. 9, pp. 60-69. 1918-1921.

ARCHER. An Inquiry Into the Origin of the Family of Archer in Kilkenny, with notices of other families of the name in Ireland. By J. H. Lawrence-Archer. (22) vol. 9, pp. 220-232. 1867.

ARTHUR. The Arthur Manuscript. By Edward MacLysaght. (22) vol. 80, pt. 1, 1950.

ASTON. See Chamberlain.

AYLMER. The Aylmer Family. By Hans Hendrick Aylmer. (14) vol. 1, pp. 295-397. 1892-1895.

AYLMER. Donadea and the Aylmer Family. By the Rev. Canon Sherlock. (14) vol. 3, pp. 169-178. 1899-1902.

AYLMER. The Aylmers of Lyons, County Kildare. By Hans Hendrick Aylmer. (14) vol. 4, pp. 179-183. 1903-1905.

BAGOT. The Bagots of Nurney. By Charles M. Drury. (14) vol. 7, pp. 317-324. 1912-1914.

BARRON. Distinguished Waterford Families: Barron. By Father Stephen Barron. (24) vol. 17, pp. 47-65, 128-134, 137-152, 1914; vol. 18, pp. 69-87, 91-104, 1915.

BARRY; BARRYMORE. Records of the Barrys of County Cork, from the earliest to the present time, with pedigrees. By the Rev. E. Barry. (5) vol. 5, pp. 1-17, 77-92, 153-168, 209-224, 1899; vol. 6, pp. 1-11, 65-87, 129-146, 193-209, 1900; vol. 7, pp. 1-16, 65-80, 129-138, 193-204, 1901; vol. 8, pp. 1-17, 129-150, 1902.

BARRY-PLACE. Memoirs of the Barry-Place Family. Being a narrative of the family of the Rev. John Barry, of Bandon, Wesleyan minister, . . . Compiled by J. Barry Deane. 1911. (5) vol. 33, pp. 19-21. 1928.

BARTON. The Family of Barton. By the Rev. Canon Sherlock. (14) vol. 4, pp. 111-113. 1903-1905.

BELLEW. Some Notes on the Family of Bellew of Thomastown, County Louth. By the Hon. Mrs. Gerald Bellew. (17) vol. 5, pp. 193-197. 1923.

BERMINGHAM (Birmingham). Notes on the Bermingham Pedigree. By Goddard H. Orpen. (8) vol. 9, pp. 195-205. 1915-1916.

BERMINGHAM. The Bermingham Family of Athenry. By H. T. Knox. (8) vol. 10, pp. 139-154. 1917-1918.

BERMINGHAM. Carbury and the Berminghams' Country. By the Rev. Matthew Devitt. (14) vol. 2, pp. 85-110. 1896-1899.

BESNARD. Notes of the Besnard Family, from manuscripts written about 1870. By T. E. Evans. (5) vol. 39, pp. 92-99. 1934.

BLACK. The Black Family. Edited by Isaac W. Ward. (23) 2nd series, vol. 8, pp. 176-188. 1902.

BLENNERHASSETT. The Blennerhassetts of Kerry: Earlier English Stock. (13) vol. 5, pp. 34-39. 1919.

BOUCHIER. The Bouchier Tablet in the Cathedral Church of St. Canice, Kilkenny, with some account of that family. By Richard Langrishe. (22) vol. 34, pp. 365-369, 1904; vol. 35, pp. 21-33, 1905.

BOURKE. The Bourkes of Clanwilliam. By James G. Barry. (22) vol. 19, pp. 192-203. 1889.

BOURKE. The de Burgos or Bourkes of Illeagh. By M. Callanan. (18) vol. 1, pp. 67-77. 1936-1939.

BOWEN. Ballyadams in Queen's County, and the Bowen Family. By Lord Walter Fitzgerald. (14) vol. 7, pp. 3-32. 1912-1914.

BRADSHAW. The Bradshaws of Bangor, and Mile-Cross, in the County of Down. By Francis J. Bigger. (23) 2nd series, vol. 8, pp. 4-6, 55-57.

BROWNE. Pedigree of the Brownes of Castle MacGarrett. By Lord Oranmore and Brown. (8) vol. 5, pp. 48-59, 165-177, 227-238. 1907-1908.

BROWNLOW. See Chamberlain.

BURKE. The Rt. Hon. Edmund Burke (1729-1797); A Basis for a Pedigree. By Basil O'Connell. (5) vol. 60, pp. 69-74. 1955.

BURKE. Some Notes on the Burkes. By M. R. (8) vol. 1, pp. 196-197. 1900-1901.

BURKE. The De Burgo Clans of Galway. By H.T. Knox. (8) vol. 1, pp. 124-131, 1900-1901; vol. 3, pp. 46-58, 1903-1904; vol. 4, pp. 55-62, 1905-1906.

BURKE. Portumna and the Burkes. By H. T. Knox. (8) vol. 6, pp. 107-109. 1909-1910.

BURKE. The Burkes of Marble Hill. By Thomas U. Sadleir (8) vol. 8, pp. 1-11. 1913-1914.

BURKE. Seanchus na mBurcach and Historia et Genealogia Familiae De Burgo. By Thomas O'Reilly. (8) vol. 13, pp. 50-60, 101-137, 1926-1927; vol. 14, pp. 30-51, 142-166, 1928-1929.

BURKE. The de Burghs of Oldtown. By Lt. Col. Thomas J. de Burgh. (14) vol. 4, pp. 467-472. 1903-1905.

BURKE. The Family of Gall Burke, of Gallstown, in the County of Kilkenny. By John O'Donovan. (15) vol. 3, pp. 97-120. 1860.

BURNSIDE. Families of Burnside and Thomson, of County Tyrone: Genealogy from the time of James I, to *ca.* 1760. (2) December, 1876.

BURTON. The Burton Family. By Percy Poole. (4) vol. 1, pt. 2, pp. 10-12.

BUTLER. Original Documents Relating to the Butler Lordship of Achill, Burrishoole and Aughrim (1236-1640). By Prof. Edmund Curtis. (8) vol. 15, pp. 121-128. 1931-1933.

BUTLER. The Butlers of County Clare. By Sir Harry Blackhall. (18) vol. 6, pp. 108-129. 1952.

BUTLER. The Butlers of Duiske Abbey. By the Rev. James Hughes. (22) vol. 10, pp. 62-75. 1868-1869.

BUTLER. The Butlers of Dangan and Spidogue. By George D. Burtchaell. (22) vol. 30, pp. 330-333. 1900.

BUTLER. An Irish Legend of the Origins of the Barons of Cahir. By W. F. Butler. (22) vol. 55, pp. 6-14. 1925.

BUTLER. The Descendants of James, Ninth Earl of Ormond. By William F. Butler. (22) vol. 59, pp. 29-44. 1929.

BUTLER. The Butlers of Poulakerry and Kilcash. By P. J. Griffith. (24) vol. 15, pp. 24-29. 1912.

BYRNE. The Byrnes of County Louth. By Patrick Kirwan. (17) vol. 2, pp. 45-49. 1908-1911.

CAREW. County Cork Families; the Carew Pedigree. (5) vol. 24, facing p. 132. 1918.

CARROLL. True Version of the Pedigree of Carroll of Carrollton, Maryland, U.S.A. (22) vol. 16, pp. 187-194. 1883.

CHAMBERLAIN. The Chamberlains of Nizelrath. By T. G. F. Paterson. (17) vol. 10, pp. 324-326. 1944.

CHAMBERLAIN. The Chamberlains of Nizelrath; Genealogical Notes on the Allied Families of Clinton, Aston, O' Doherty, and Brownlow. By T. G. F. Paterson. (17) vol. 11, pp. 175-185. 1947.

CHETWOOD. The Chetwoods of Woodbrook, in Queen's County. By Walter G. Strickland. (14) vol. 9, pp. 205-226. 1918-1921.

CHINNERY. George Chinnery, 1774-1852, with some account of his Family and Genealogy. By W. H. Welply. (5) vol. 37, pp. 11-21, 1932; vol. 38, pp. 1-15, 1933.

CLAYTON. The Clayton Family, County Cork. By J. Buckley. (5) vol. 5, pp. 194-197. 1899.

CLINTON. Clinton Records. By T. G. F. Paterson. (17) vol. 12, pp. 109-116. 1950.

CLINTON. See Chamberlain.

CODD. Castletown Carne and Its Owners. By Lt. Col. W. O. Cavenagh. (22) vol. 41, pp. 246-258, 1911; vol. 42, pp. 34-45, 1912.

COGHILL. See Cramer.

COLVILLE. The Colville Family of Ulster. By John M. Dickson. (23) 2nd series, vol. 5, pp. 139-145, 202-210, 1899; vol. 6, pp. 12-16, 1900.

COMYN. Notes on the Comyn Pedigree. By David Comyn. (18) vol. 3, pp. 22-37. 1913.

CONWAY. The Conways of Kerry. By J. S. M. (13) vol. 5, pp. 71-91. 1920.

COTTER. The Cotter Family of Rockforest, County Cork. By J. C. (5) 2nd series, vol. 14, no. 77, pp. 1-12. 1908.

COTTER. The Cotter Family of Rockforest, County Cork. Edited by G. de P. Cotter. (5) 2nd series, vol. 43, pp. 21-31. 1938.

COWLEY. Some Notice of the Family of Cowley, in Kilkenny. By J. G. A. Prim. (15) and (22) vol. 2, pp. 102-114. 1852.

CRAMER. A Genealogical Note on the Family of Cramer or Coghill. (5) 2nd series; vol. 16. pp. 66-81. 1910.

CRAMER. Cramer Pedigree. By J. F. Fuller. (5) vol. 16, p. 143. 1910.

CURRAN. Curran and his Kinsfolk. (Family of John Philpot Curran.) By W. H. Welply. (19) CXCIV, pp. 266-8, 290-4, 338-41, 384-7. 1949.

DALY. Families of Daly of Galway, with Tabular Pedigrees. By Martin J. Blake. (8) vol. 13, p. 140. 1926-1927.

D'ARCY. Tabular Pedigrees of the D'Arcy Family. (8) vol. 10, facing p. 58. 1917-1918.

DAWSON. The Dawsons of Ardee. By the Rev. L. P. Murray. (17) vol. 8, pp. 22-33. 1933.

DE LACY. Notes on the Family of De Lacy in Ireland. By Nicholas J. Synnott. (22) vol. 49, pp. 113-131. 1919. (With Genealogical chart, 1600-1792-3.)

DENNY. Dennys of Cork. By the Rev. H. L. L. Denny. (5) 2nd series, vol. 18, pp. 45-46. 1922.

DE RIDELESFORD. The De Ridelesfords. By E. St. John Brooks. (22) vol. 82, pp. 45-61. 1952.

D'ESTERRE. Pedigree of Captain D'Esterre, who was fatally wounded . . . 1851. (5) vol. 34, p. 47. 1929.

DE VERDON. The De Verdons of Louth. By the Rev. Denis Murphy. (22) vol. 25, pp. 317-328. 1895.

DE VERDON. The De Verdons and the Draycots. By Charles MacNeill. (17) vol. 5, pp. 166-172. 1923.

DICKSON. The Right Rev. William Dickson, D. D., Lord Bishop of Down and Connor: Family Genealogical Notes. By Francis Joseph Bigger. (23) 2nd series, vol. 3, pp. 120-135. 1897.

DICKSON. William Steel Dickson, 1774-1824. In *Bulletin of the Irish Committee of Historical Sciences,* No. 50.

DIXON. Dixon of Kilkea Castle. By Henry B. Swanzy. (14) vol. 9, pp. 392-394. 1918-1921.

DOBBYN. Ancient and Illustrious Waterford Families. The Dobbyns and Waddings. By Patrick Higgins. (24) vol. 4, pp. 247-250. 1898.

DRAKE. The Drake Family. By Frederick W. Knight. (5) 2nd series, vol. 38, pp. 20-30. 1933.

DRAYCOT. See De Verdon.

DRAYCOTT. Some Early Documents Relating to English Uriel, and the Towns of Drogheda and Dundalk (in Ireland): *The Draycott Family.* By Charles McNeill. (17) vol. 5, pp. 270-275. 1924.

DRURY. Edmund, brother of Sir William Drury, Lord Justice of Ireland, and his Irish descendants. (19) vol. 171, pp. 279, 338, 374, 425. 1936.

EMMET. The Emmet Family Connections with Munster. By John T. Collins. (5) vol. 58, pp. 77-80. 1953.

ENGLEFIELD. Englefield, Roper and Wildman (Wileman) Families; 17th Century Family History. By Henry F. Reynolds. (19) vol. 181, pp. 12-13.

EUSTACE. Kilcullen New Abbey and the FitzEustaces. By James Fenton. (14) vol. 12, pp. 217-221. 1935-1945.

EYRE. Eyre Mss. (1720-1857) in University College, Galway. Part I presented by Dr. Marguerite Hayes-McCoy. (The Eyre family settled in Galway under Cromwell and were of some municipal importance for 80 years.) (8) vol. 20, pp. 57-74. 1942.

FITZEUSTACE. FitzEustace of Baltinglass. (24) vol. 5, pp. 190-195. 1899.

FITZGERALD. The Story of the Slught Edmund (1485-1819); An Episode in Kerry History. By S. M. (13) vol. 3, pp. 186-205. 1915.

FITZGERALD. The Fitzgeralds of Lackagh. By Lord Walter Fitzgerald. (14) vol. 1, pp. 245-264. 1892-1895.

FITZGERALD. The Fitzgeralds and the MacKenzies. By W. Fitzgerald. (14) vol. 2, p. 269. 1896-1899.

FITZGERALD. The Fitzgeralds of Ballyshannon, County Kildare, and their successors thereat. By Lord Walter Fitzgerald. (14) vol. 3, pp. 425-452. 1899-1902.

FITZGERALD. The History of Morett Castle and the Fitzgeralds. By Lord Walter Fitzgerald. (14) vol. 4, pp. 285-296. 1903-1905.

FITZGERALD. The Geraldines of Desmond. From Michael O'Clery's Book of Pedigrees. Edited by Canon Hayman. (22) vol. 15, pp. 215-235, 411-440, 1880-1881; vol. 17, pp. 66-92, 1885.

FITZGERALD. The Fitzgerald Family; Unpublished Geraldine Documents, edited by the Rev. Samuel Hayman. (22) vol. 10, pp. 356-416, 1869; vol. 11, pp. 591-616, 1871; vol. 14, pp. 14-52, 157-166, 246-264, 300-335, 1876-1877.

FITZGERALD. The Fitzgeralds of Rostellane, in County Cork. By R. G. Fitzgerald-Uniacke. (22) vol. 25, pp. 163-170. 1895.

FITZGERALD. The Geraldines of the County Kilkenny. By George Dames Burtchall. (22) vol. 22, pp. 358-376, 1892; vol. 23, pp. 179-186, 408-420, 1893; vol. 32, pp. 128-131, 1902.

FITZGERALD. The Desmonds' Castle at Newcastle Oconyll, County Limerick. By Thomas J. Westropp. (22) vol. 39, pp. 350-368. 1909.

FITZGERALD. The Fitzgeralds of Glenane, County Cork. By R. G. Fitzgerald-Uniacke. (22) vol. 42, pp. 164-169. 1912.

FITZGERALD. The Fitzgeralds, Barons of Offaly. By Goddard H. Orpen. (22) vol. 44, pp. 99-113. 1914.

FITZGERALD. The Descendants of the Last Earls of Desmond. By John O'Donovan. (23) vol. 6, pp. 91-97. 1858.

FITZGERALD. The Fitzgeralds of Farnane, County Waterford. By G. O.'C. Redmond. (24) vol. 14, pp. 27-39, 72-81, 1911; vol. 15, pp. 168-176, 1912.

FITZMAURICE. The Fitzmaurices, Lords of Kerry. By M. J. Bourke. (5) 2nd series, vol. 26, pp. 10-18. 1920.

FITZRERY. The FitzRerys, Welsh Lords of Cloghran, County Dublin. By E. Curtis. (17) pp. 13-17. 1921.

FLATESBURY. The Family of Flatesbury, of Ballynasculloge and Johnstown, County Kildare. By Sir Arthur Vicars. (14) vol. 4, pp. 87-94. 1903-1905.

FLEETWOOD. The Fleetwoods of the County Cork. By Sir Edmund T. Bewley. (22) vol. 38, pp. 103-125. 1908.

FLEMING. In Family History section of *Notes and Queries* (19), by Henry F. Reynolds:

1. Fleming of Ballenacara and Abbeyville, Co. Sligo. Vol. 180, pp. 40-43.
2. Fleming of Killmoney, Co. Kildare. Vol. 181, pp. 58-60.
3. Fleming of Kildare; Crowe. Vol. 181, pp. 201-203.
4. Fleming of Old Rock, County Sligo. Vol. 181, pp. 312-315.
5. Fleming of Roadstown, County Sligo. Vol. 181, pp. 329-330.
6. Fleming: 17th and 18th Century Wills and other Documents. Vol. 180, pp. 111-115, 167-169, 295-297, 369-370.

FRENCH. The Families of French of Dures, Cloghballymore, and Drumharsna, with tabular pedigree. By Martin J. Blake. (8) vol. 10, pp. 125-138. 1917-1918.

FRENCH. The Origin of the Families of French of Connaught, with tabular pedigree of John French of Grand-Terre in 1763. By Martin J. Blake. (8) vol. 11, pp. 142-149. 1920-1921.

FRENCH. Some Account of the Family of French of Belturbet. By the Rev. H. B. Swanzy. (23) vol. 8, pp. 155-160. 1902.

GALWEY. The Genealogy of Galwey of Lota. (5) vol. 30, pp. 59-74. 1925.

GARDE. The Garde Family. By R. Beckersteth. (5) vol. 5, pp. 200-202. 1899.

GERRARD. The Gerrards and Geraldines. By Capt. Henry Gerrard. (5) 2nd series, vol. 34, pp. 30-35, 71-75. 1929.

GRACE. The Origin of the Grace Family of Courtstown, Co. Kilkenny, and of their title to the Tullaroan estate. By Richard Langrishe. (22) vol. 30, pp. 319-324, 1900; vol. 32, pp. 64-67, 1902.

GRAHAM. See Colville.

GRANT. The Grants of Newry, A family group of teachers, 1740-1900. By J. Fitzsimmons. (10) vol. 69, pp. 405-414. 1947.

GRIERSON. Notes on the Family of Grierson of Dublin. By J. R. H. Greeves. (11) vol. 2, pp. 303-307.

HAMILTON. The Hamilton Family (Extracts of Family Genealogy and History from "The Hamilton Manuscripts"). (23) vol. 3, pp. 68-76, 236-249, 1855; vol. 5, pp. 21-32, 1857.

HAMILTON. Family History of Mona Castle, County Fermanagh and the Hamiltons. By the Rt. Hon. the Earl of Belmore. (23) 2nd series, vol. 1, pp. 195-208, 256-277, 259-270, 299-300. 1895. (Includes some notes on the Cathcart and Hume families and a pedigree of Hamilton of Mona Castle, *ca.* 1550-*ca.* 1800.) Vol. 4, pp. 139-151. 1898.

HANDY. Handy of Coolylough and Bracca Castle, County Westmeath. By Henry F. Reynolds. (19) vol. 182, pp. 160-162, 240.

HARTPOLE. Notes on the District of Ivory, Coolbanagher Castle, and the Hartpoles. By Lord Walter Fitzgerald. (14) vol. 4, pp. 297-311. 1903-1905.

HAUTENVILLE. The Huguenot Family of Hautenville in Ireland and some of its connections. By Major B. R. R. Rambaut. (9) vol. 17, pp. 262-266.

HEACOCK. Richard Heacock Pedigree. (5) 2nd series, vol. 11, p. 47. 1905.

HEALY. The Healys of Donoughmore. By John T. Collins. (5) 2nd series, vol. 48, pp. 124-132. 1943.

HENCHY. The O'Connor Henchys of Stonebrook. By V. Hussy-Walsh. (14) vol. 2, pp. 407-412. 1896-1899.

HENRY. The Henry Family of Kildare. By the Rev. Canon Sherlock. (14) vol. 3, pp. 386-388. 1899-1902.

HEWETSON. The Hewetsons of the County of Kildare. By John Hewetson. (22) vol. 39, pp. 146-163, 1909; vol. 39, pp. 369-392, 1909.

HEWETSON. The Hewetsons of Ballyshannon of Donegal. By John Hewetson. (22) vol. 40, p. 238-243. 1910.

HORT. The Horts of Hortland. By Sir Arthur F. Hort. (14) vol. 7, pp. 207-216. 1912-1914.

HUME. Hume, Family of; Pedigree and estate of; Castle of (County Fermanagh). By the Earl of Belmore. (23) 2nd series, vol. 1, pp. 257-259, 270-275. 1895.

IRWIN. The Irwins and Irvines of Sligo, Roscommon and Fermanagh. By R. W. Walsh. (19) vol. 187, pp. 141-143.

JACOB. The Dublin Family of Jacob (Quaker family, 17th Century). By W. J. Jacob. (7) vol. 2, pp. 134-140.

JEPHSON. The English Settlement in Ireland under the Jephson Family. By H. F. Berry. (5) 2nd series, vol. 12, pp. 1-26. 1906.

KAVANAGH. The Kavanaghs of Maine. (21) vol. 10, no. 6, pp. 22-25.

KAVANAGH. The Fall of the Clan of Kavanagh. By the Rev. James Hughes. (22) vol. 12, pp. 282-305. 1873.

KELLS. The Kells and Philpotts in Mallow, 1749. By H. J. Berry. (5) 2nd series, vol. 15, pp. 95-98. 1909.

KEMMIS. A Short Account of the Family of Kemmis in Ireland. By Lewis G. N. Kemmis. (14) vol. 12, pp. 144-169. 1935-1945.

LALLY. A Sept of O'Maolale (or Lally) of Hy-Maine. By Miss J. Martyn. (8) vol. 4, pp. 198-209. 1905-1906.

LANGTON. Memorials of the Family of Langton of Kilkenny. By John G. A. Prim. (22) vol. 8, pp. 59-108. 1864.

LATOUCHE. The LaTouche Family of Harristown, Co. Kildare. By Miss M. F. Young. (14) vol. 7, pp. 33-40. 1912-1914.

LATTIN. The Lattin and Mansfield Families, in the County Kildare. By the Rev. Canon Sherlock. (14) vol. 3, pp. 186-190. 1899-1902.

LATTIN. Notices of the Family of Lattin. By John M. Thunder. (22) vol. 18, pp. 183-188. 1887.

LAVALLIN. History of the Lavallins. By George Berkeley. (5) 2nd series, vol. 30, pp. 10-15, 75-83, 1925; vol. 31, pp. 36-43, 53-59. 1926.

LAWE. Lawe of Leixlip. By the Rev. H. L. L. Denny. (14) vol. 6, pp. 730-739. 1909-1911.

LENNON. Four Irish Pedigrees: Lennon of Cloncullen; Nicholson of Ballynegargen; Peyton of Carregard; Phibbs of Spotfield. By Edward Stewart Gray. (11) vol. 2, pp. 48-51. 1946.

LIMERICK. The Family of Limerick of Schull, County Cork. By the Rev. H. L. L. Denny. (5) 2nd series, vol. 13, pp. 120-127. 1907.

LLOYD. The Lloyds of Rockville and their Namesakes of Croghan. (11) vol. 1, p. 373.

LONG. The Longs of Muskerry and Kinalea. By John T. Collins. (5) vol. 51, pp. 1-9. 1946.

LOVETT. Mr. Lovett out of Ireland; 16th Century Buckinghamshire Family. By the Rt. Rev. E. Neville Lovett. (7) vol. 3, pp. 54-66.

LUTTREL. The Luttrels of Luttrelstown. By M. J. Bourke. (5) 2nd series, vol. 27, pp. 65-69. 1921.

LYNCH. Account of the Lynch Family and Memorable Events of the Town of Galway. By John Lynch. (8) pp. 76-93. 1913-1914.

LYNCH. Pedigree of Lynch of Lavally, County Galway. By Martin J. Blake. (8) vol. 10. pp. 66-69. 1917-1918.

MACARTNEY. See MacAulay.

MACAULAY. Gleanings in Family History from the Antrim Coast. The MacAulays and MacArtneys. By the Rev. George Hill. (23) vol. 8, pp. 196-210, 1860; vol. 9, pp. 1-15, 1861-1862.

MACCARTHY-MCCARTHY. Publications regarding the MacCarthy family in (5) 2nd series:

McCarthys, Branches of. Vol. 2, p. 501.

McCarthys, Castles of. Vol. 13, p. 159 n. Vol. 32, pp. 97-99.

McCarthys, Lands of. Vol. 22, pp. 25-32, 159-160, 162. Vol. 23, pp. 49-60. Vol. 33, pp. 3-7.

McCarthys in Iveragh. Vol. 34, pp. 16-18.

McCarthys, Lords of Muskerry, Historical Pedigree of, 1380-1641. Vol. 1 A. f. 192.

McCarthys of Carrignavar. Vol. 13, pp. 168-170, 173-174.
McCarthys, Genealogy of. Vol. 13, pp. 168-169.
McCarthys of Drishane. Vol. 23, pp. 114-115.
McCarthys of Sliocht Corky. Vol. 10, p. 74.
McCarthys of Tipperary. Vol. 2, A, pp. 100-101.
McCarthys, Senior Family in Ireland. Vol. 2, p. 213.

MACCARTHY. The MacFinnin MacCarthys of Ardtully. By Randal MacFinnin MacCarthy. (5) 2nd series, vol. 2, pp. 210-214. 1896.

MACCARTHY. The MacCarthys of Drishane. By S. T. MacCarthy. (5) 2nd series, vol. 23, pp. 114-115. 1917.

MACCARTHY. Some McCarthys of Blarney and Ballea. By John T. Collins. (5) 2nd series, vol. 59, pp. 1-10, 82-88, 1954; vol. 60, pp. 1-5, 75-79. 1955.

MACCARTHY. The Pedigree and Succession of the House of MacCarthy Mór, with a map. By W. F. Butler. (22) vol. 51, pp. 32-48. 1921. (Genealogical chart, A. D. 950 to 1596.)

MACCARTHY. The Clann Carthaigh. By S. J. McCarthy. (13) vol. 1, pp. 160-208, 233-251, 320-338, 385-402, 457-466, 1908-1912; vol. 2, pp. 3-24, 53-74, 105-122, 181-202, 1912-1914; vol. 3, pp. 55-72, 123-139, 206-226, 271-292, 1914-1916; vol. 4, pp. 207-214, 1917.

MACDONALD. The MacDonalds of Mayo. By G. A. Hayes-McCoy. (8) vol. 17, pp. 65-82. 1936-1937.

MACDONNELL. The Macdonnells of Tinnakill Castle. By Lord Walter Fitzgerald. (14) vol. 4, pp. 205-215. 1903-1915.

MACDONNELL. Chiefs of the Antrim Macdonnells prior to Sorley Boy. By G. H. (23) vol. 7, pp. 247-259. 1859.

MACDONNELL. Notices of the Clan Iar Vór Clan Donnell Scots, especially of the branch which settled in Ireland. By the Rev. George Hill. (23) vol. 9, pp. 301-317. 1861-1862.

MACDONOGH. The Lords of Ella: The Macdonoghs of Dunhallow. By William F. Dennehy. (5) vol. 3, pp. 157-162. 1894.

MACEGAN. Two Irish Brehon Scripts, with notes on the MacEgan Family. By Martin F. Blake. (8) vol. 6, pp. 1-9. 1909-1910.

MACGILLYCUDDY. The MacGillycuddy Family. (13) vol. 3, pp. 176-185. 1915.

MACKENZIE. See Fitzgerald. (14) vol. 2, p. 269. 1896-1899.

MACLELLAND, MCCLELLAND. Maclelland Family, went from Kirkudbright, Scotland, during the Ulster Plantation. Member or members of the family settled in Chester County, Pennsylvania, prior to 1763 . . . (23) vol. 5, 2nd series, p. 58. 1898.

MACNAGHTEN. Gleanings in Family History from the Antrim Coast. The MacNaghtens and MacNeills. By the Rev. George Hill. (23) vol. 8, pp. 127-144. 1860.

MACNEILL. See MacNaghten.

MACQUILLAN. The Clan of the MacQuillans of Antrim. By M. Webb. (23) vol. 8, pp. 251-268. 1860.

MACQUILLAN. The MacQuillans of the Route. By the Rev. George Hill. (23) vol. 9, pp. 57-70. 1861-1862.

MAGENNIS. The Magennises of Clanconnell. By the Rev. E. D. Atkinson. (23) vol. 1, 2nd series, pp. 30-32. 1895.

MAGENNIS. Magennis of Iveagh. By Henry S. Guinness. (22) vol. 62, pp. 96-102. 1932.

MAGRATH. Family of: "The Castle and Territory of Termon Magrath". By the Earl of Belmore. (23) 2nd series, vol. 9, pp. 49-54, 97-111, 185-190. 1903.

MAGUIRE. The Maguires in Fermanagh; History of; Estates of; Pedigree (5 generations). By the Earl of Belmore. (23) 2nd series, vol. 3, pp. 53-54, 85-88, 174-186, 209-219. 1897.

MANSFIELD. See Lattin.

MARISCO. The Family of Marisco. By E. St. J. Brooks. (22) vol. 61, pp. 22-38, 89-112. 1931.

MARSHAL. The Marshal Pedigree. By Hamilton Hall. (22) vol. 43, pp. 1-29. 1913.

McKINLEY. The McKinleys of Conagher, County Antrim and their descendants. With notes about the President of the United States. By Thomas Camac. (23) 2nd series, vol. 3, pp. 167-170. 1897.

MERRY. The Waterford Merrys. (24) vol. 16, pp. 30-35. 1913.

MONTGOMERY. The Montgomery Family History (unpublished portion of the "Montgomery Manuscripts"). By the Rev. William MacIlwaine. (23) vol. 9, pp. 151-171, 278-293. 1861-1862.

MOORE. Sir Thomas Moore: His Descendants in the Male Line: The Moores of Moorehall, County Mayo. By Martin J. Blake. (22) vol. 36, pp. 224-230. 1906.

MORAN. The Morans and the Mulveys of South Leitrim. By the Very Rev. Joseph McGivney. (1) vol. 1, pp. 14-19. 1932.

MULVEY. See Moran.

NANGLE. Ballysax and the Nangle Family. By Omurethi. (14) vol. 6, pp. 96-100. 1909-1911.

NICHOLSON. See Lennon.

NUTTALL. The Nuttalls of County Kildare. By R. W. Smith, Jr. (14) vol. 8, pp. 180-184. 1915-1917.

O'BRENNAN. The O'Brennans and the Ancient Territory of Hy-Duach. By the Rev. Nicholas Murphy. (20) vol. 1, pp. 393-407. 1874-1879.

O'BRIEN. The Sept of Mac-I-Brien Ara. By the Rev. W. B. Steele. (5) 2nd series, vol. 3, pp. 10-21. 1897.

O'BRIEN. Carrigogunnell Castle and the O'Briens of Pubblebrian in the County of Limerick. By Thomas J. Westropp. (22) vol. 37, pp. 374-392, 1907; vol. 38, pp. 141-159, 1908.

O'BRIEN. The O'Briens in Munster after Clontarf. By the Rev. John Ryan. (18) vol. 2, pp. 141-152. 1941.

O'BRIEN. Family Register of the O'Briens of Newcastle, Ballyporeen, County Tipperary. By the Rev. Wallace Clare. (11) vol. 2, pp. 308-310.

O'CAHAN. The O'Cahans, a Notable Irish Military Family. By Dr. Richard Hayes. (12) vol. 1, pp. 14-18. 1949.

O'CALLAGHAN. The Chieftains of Pobul-I-Callaghan, County Cork. By Herbert Webb Gillman. (5) 2nd series, vol. 3, pp. 201-220. 1897.

O'CLERY. The Muintier Cleirigh of Tirawkley. By A. B. Clery. (22) vol. 75, pp. 70-75. 1945.

O'CROWLEY. A Defeated Clan. By Michael Crowley. (5) 2nd series, vol. 26, pp. 24-28. 1920.

O'CROWLEY. O'CROWLEY Pedigree. Compiled from the Carew Manuscripts and other sources. By F. C. Long. (5) 2nd series, vol. 35, p. 89. 1930.

O'CROWLEY. The O'Crowleys of Coill-t-Sealbhaigh. By John T. Collins. (5) 2nd Series, vol. 56, pp. 91-94, 1951; vol. 57, pp. 1-6, 105-109, 1952; vol. 58, pp. 7-11, 1953.

O'DAVOREN. The O'Davorens of Cahermacnaughten, Burren, County Clare. By Dr. George U. Macnamara. (18) vol. 2, pp. 63-93, 149-164, 194-201. 1912-1913.

O'DEMPSEY. The O'Dempseys, Chiefs of Clanmaliere. By Lord Walter Fitzgerald. (14) vol. 4, pp. 396-431. 1903-1905.

O'DOHERTY. See Chamberlain.

O'DRISCOLL. The O'Driscolls and Other Septs of Corca Laidhe. By James M. Burke. (5) 2nd series, vol. 16, pp. 24-31. 1910.

O'FLAHERTY. The Flight of the O'Flahertys, Lords of Moy Soela, to Iar Connaught. By the Very Rev. J. Fahy. (22) vol. 27, pp. 19-27. 1897.

O'FLYNN. The O'Flynns of Ardagh. By J. M. Burke. (5) 2nd series, vol. 11, pp. 99-101. 1905.

O'HANLON. Redmond, Count O'Hanlon's Descendants. (17) vol. 2, p. 61. 1908-1911.

O'HEAS. The O'Heas of South West Cork. By John T. Collins. (5) 2nd series, vol. 51, pp. 97-107.

O'HEGERTYS. The O'Hegertys of Ulster. By the Rev. Walter Hegerty. (6) vol. 1, pp. 86-92. 1948.

O'HURLEY. Some Account of the Family of O'Hurly. (5) 2nd series, vol. 11, pp. 105-123, 177-183, 1905; vol. 12, pp. 26-33, 76-88, 1906.

O'KANE. Some Account of the Sept of the O'Cathains of Ciannachta Glinne-Geinhin. Now the O'Kane's of the County of Londonderry. By J. Scott Parker. (23) vol. 3, pp. 1-8, 265-272, 1855; vol. 4, pp. 139-148, 1856.

O'KELLY. The O'Kellys of Gallagh, Counts of the Holy Roman Empire. By Richard J. Kelly. (8) vol. 3, pp. 180-185. 1903-1904.

O'KELLY. Notes on the Family of O'Kelly. By Richard J. Kelly. (8) vol. 4, pp. 92-96. 1905-1906.

O'KELLY. The Pedigree of Maria Anna O'Kelly, Countess of Marcolini. (8) vol. 4, pp. 108-110. 1905-1906.

O'KELLY. Notes on the O'Kelly Family. By E. Festus Kelly. (8) vol. 16, pp. 140-143. 1934-1935.

O'MADDEN. The O'Maddens of Silanchia or Siol Anmachadha and their Descendants, from the Milesian Invasion of Ireland to the Present Time. By Thomas More Madden. (8) vol. 1, pp. 184-195, 1900-1901; vol. 2, pp. 21-33. 1902.

O'MAHONY. A History of the O'Mahony Septs in Kinelmeky and Ivagha and the Kerry branch. By the Rev. Canon John B. O'Mahony. (5) 2nd series, vol. 12, pp. 183-195, 1906-1910; vol. 13, pp. 27-36, 73-80, 105-115, 182-192; vol. 14, pp. 12-21, 74-81, 127-141, 189-199; vol. 15, pp. 7-18, 63-75, 118-126, 184-196; vol. 16, pp. 9-24, 97-113.

O'MAHONY (MAHONY). The Mahonys of Kerry. (13) vol. 4, pp. 171-190, 223-255. 1917-1918.

O'MALLEY. Note on the O'Malley Lordship, at the close of the Sixteenth Century. By Sir Owen O'Malley. (8) vol. 24, pp. 27-57. 1950-1951.

O'MALLEY. The O'Malleys between 1651 and 1725. By Sir Owen O'Malley. (8) vol. 25, pp. 28-31. 1952-1954.

O'MAOLCONAIRE. The O'Maolconaire Family: A Note. By E. de Lacy Staunton. (8) vol. 20, pp. 82-88.

O'MORE. Notes on an Old Pedigree of the O'More Family of Leix. By Sir Edmund T. Bewley. (22) vol. 35, pp. 53-59. 1905.

O'MORE. Historical Notes on the O'Mores and their Territory of Leix, to the end of the Sixteenth Century. By Lord Walter Fitzgerald. (14) vol. 16, pp. 1-88. 1909-1911.

O'MORE. The O'More Family of Balyna in the County of Kildare. By James More of Balyna, *ca.* 1774. (14) vol. 9, pp. 277-291, 318-330. 1918-1921.

O'MULCONRY. The O'Maolconaire Family. Edited by Edmund Curtis. (8) vol. 19, pp. 118-146. 1940-1941.

O'MULCONRY. The O'Maolconaire Family. A Note. By E. de Lacy Staunton. (8) vol. 20, pp. 82-88. 1942-1943.

O'MULLANE. The O'Mullanes and Whitechurch. By Sir Henry Blackall. (5) 2nd series, vol. 58, pp. 20-21. 1953.

ONSELEY. The Name and Family of Onseley. By Richard J. Kelly. (22) vol. 40, pp. 132-146. 1910.

O'Reilly. The Descendants of Col. Myles O'Reilly in County Leitrim (1650-1830), from tradition. By Thomas O'Reilly. (3) vol. 2, pp. i, 15-19. 1923.

O'SHAUGHNESSY. O'Shaughnessy of Gort (1543-1783) : Tabular Pedigree. By M. J. Blake. (8) vol. 7, p. 53. 1911-1912.

O'SHEIL. The Irish Medical Family of O'Sheil. By the Rev. John Brady. In the *Irish Book Lover,* vol. 30, pp. 50-51.

PALLISER. See Codd.

PARKINSON. Some Notes on the Family of Parkinson of Redhouse, or Red House, Ardee. (17) vol. 10, pp. 255-256.

PENN. Admiral Penn, William Penn, and their Descendants in the County Cork. By J. C. (5) 2nd series, vol. 14, pp. 105-114, 177-189. 1908.

PEYTON. See Lennon.

PHAIRE. Col. Robert Phaire, "Regicide". His ancestry, history and descendants. By W. H. Welply. (5) 2nd series, vol. 29, pp. 76-80, 1924; vol. 30, pp. 20-26, 1925; vol. 31, pp. 31-36, 1926; vol. 32, pp. 24-32, 1927.

PHIBBS. See Lennon.

PHILPOTTS. See Kells.

PILCHARDS. Pilchards in the South of Ireland. By A. E. J. Went. (5) 2nd series, vol. 51, pp. 137-157. 1946.

PONSONBY. Bishopscourt and its Owners. By the late Capt. Gerald Ponsonby. (14) vol. 8, pp. 3-29. 1915-1917.

POWER. The Powers of Clashmore, County Waterford. By Matthew Butler. (5) 2nd series, vol. 47, pp. 121-122. 1942.

PUNCH. The Punch Family of the City and County of Cork. (5) 2nd series, vol. 33, p. 106. 1928.

PURCELL. Family Papers belonging to the Purcells of Loughmoe, County Tipperary. By the Rev. St. John D. Seymour. (18) vol. 3, pp. 124-129, 191-203. 1914.

REYNOLDS. Notes on the MacRannals of Leitrim and their Country; being introductory to a diary of James Reynolds, Lough Scur, County Leitrim, for the years 1658-1660. By the Rev. Joseph Meehan. (22) vol. 35, pp. 139-151. 1905.

ROBERTS. The Roberts Family of Waterford. By William T. Bayly. (24) vol. 2, pp. 98-103. 1896.

ROBERTS. Some Account of the Roberts Family of Kilmoney. By Bessie Garvey. (5) 2nd series, vol. 34, pp. 107-110. 1929.

ROCHE. The Roches, Lords of Fermoy. By Eithne Donnelly. (5) 2nd series, vol. 38, pp. 86-91, 1933; vol. 39, pp. 38-40, 57-68, 1934; vol. 40, pp. 37-42, 63-73, 1935; vol. 41, pp. 20-28, 78-84, 1936; vol. 42, pp. 40-52, 1937.

ROCHFORD. A Cork Branch of the Rochford Family. By James Buckley. (5) 2nd series, vol. 21, pp. 112-120. 1915.

RONAYNE. Notes on the Family of Ronayne, or Ronan, of Counties Cork and Waterford. By Frederick W. Knight. (5) 2nd series, vol. 22, pp. 56-63, 109-114, 178-185, 1916; vol. 23, pp. 93-104, 142-152, 1917.

RONAYNE. Some Desmond Incidents and Notes on the Ronayne Family. By E. C. R. (5) 2nd series, vol. 23, pp. 104-107. 1917.

ROPER. See Englefield.

ROTHE. The Family of Rothe of Kilkenny. By George Dames Burtchall. (22) vol. 17, pp. 501-537, 620-654. 1886.

ROWAN. Some Kerry Records, chiefly concerned with the Rowan family. (13) pp. 18-32. 1939.

RUMLEY. The Rumley Family of Cork. "Supposed descendants of the Huguenot settlers." (Genealogical chart of three generations.) (5) 2nd series, vol. 7, p. 127. 1901.

RYLAND. Pedigree of Ryland of Dungarvan and Waterford. (22) vol. 15, pp. 562-565. 1881.

ST. LAWRENCE. Notes on the St. Lawrences, Lords of Howth, from the end of the 12th to the middle of the 16th century. By Lord Walter Fitzgerald. (22) vol. 37, pp. 349-359. 1907.

SARSFIELD. Patrick Sarsfield, Earl of Lucan; with an account of his family and their connection with Lucan and Tully. By Lord Walter Fitzgerald. (14) vol. 4, pp. 114-147. 1903-1905.

SARSFIELD. Dr. Caulfield's Records of the Sarsfield Family of the County of Cork. By J. C. (5) 2nd series, vol. 21, pp. 82-91, 131-136. 1915.

SARSFIELD. The Sarsfields of County Clare. By R. W. Twigge. (18) vol. 3, pp. 92-107, 132-143, 170-190. 1914-1915.

SAUNDERS. The Family of Saunders of Saunders Grove, County Wicklow. By T. U. Sadleir. (14) vol. 9, pp. 125-133. 1918-1921.

SEAVER. The Seavers of Lusk and Rogerstown, County Dublin. By the Rev. George Seaver. (22) vol. 72, pp. 14-28. 1943.

SHAW. Some Notes on the Shaw Family of Monkstown Castle. By James B. Fox. (5) 2nd series, vol. 37, pp. 93-95, 1932; vol. 40, pp. 53-54, 1935.

SHERLOCK. Notes on the Family of Sherlock; from State Papers and Official Documents. By the Rev. J. F. M. ffrench. (14) vol. 2, pp. 33-47. 1896-1899.

SHERLOCK. Distinguished Waterford Families. (24) vol. 9, pp. 120-128, 171-175, 1906; vol. 10, pp. 42-44, 171-183, 1907.

SHERLOCK. Extract from the Pedigree of Sherlock of Mitchelstown, County Cork. 1660-1814. By W. Devereux. (5) 2nd series, vol. 12, pp. 50-51. 1906.

SITLINGTON. The Sitlington Family of Dunagorr, County Antrim. By Edmund Getty. (23) 2nd series, vol. 15, pp. 161-172. 1909.

SKERRETT. Some Records of the Skerrett Family. By Philip Crossle. (8) vol. 15, pp. 33-72. 1931-1933.

SOMERVILLE. The Somerville Family of County Cork. By P. S. O'Hegarty. (5) 2nd series, vol. 47, pp. 30-33. 1942.

SPENSER. Pedigree of the Poet Spenser's Family. (5) 2nd series, vol. 11, facing p. 196. 1905.

SPENSER. Memorials of Edmund Spenser, the Poet, and His Descendants in the County of Cork, from the Public Records of Ireland. By J. C. (5) 2nd series, vol. 14, pp. 39-43. 1908.

SPENSER. Spenser's Pedigree. By William Devereux. (5) 2nd series, vol. 15, pp. 101-102. 1909.

SPENSER. The Family and Descendants of Edmund Spenser. By W. H. Welply. (5) 2nd series, vol. 28, pp. 22-34, 49-61. 1922.

STEWART. The Stewarts of Ballintoy; with notices of other families in the district in the 17th Century. By the Rev. George Hill. (23) 2nd series, vol. 6, pp. 17-23, 78-89, 142-161, 218-223, 1900; vol. 7, pp. 9-17, 1901.

STEWART. Pedigrees of the Stewarts of Ballylawn, County Donegal, now Marquesses of Londonderry. By W. A. Stewart. (11) vol. 7, pp. 302-309. 1936.

STOUT. The Old Youghal Family of Stout. By Henry F. Berry. (5) 2nd series, vol. 23, pp. 19-29. 1917.

STUART. The Connection between the Stuarts of Castlestuart and the O'Neills. By the Very Rev. R. S. S. King. (11) vol. 1, pp. 14-15.

SWEETMAN. Notes on the Sweetman Family. By the Rev. Canon Sherlock. (14) vol. 3, pp. 389-390. 1899-1902.

TERRY. Terry Pedigree. By J. F. Fuller. (5) 2nd series, vol. 9, pp. 274-276. 1903.

THOMSON. See Burnside.

TIERNEY. The Tierneys and the Egmont Estates. By M. J. Bourke. (5) 2nd series, vol. 27, pp. 10-14. 1921.

TOBIN. The Genealogy of Walter Tobin and His Family. Presented by Mr. Thomas Shelly. (20) pp. 92-95. 1880-1883.

TONE. The Family of Tone. By T. U. Sadleir. (14) vol. 12, pp. 326-329. 1935-1945.

TRANT. The Trant Family. By S. M. (13) vol. 2, pp. 237-262, 1914; vol. 3, pp. 20-38, 1914.

TRANT. The Trant Family. By J. F. Fuller. (13) vol. 5, pp. 18-26. 1919.

TRAVERS. Hollywood, County Wicklow; with an account of its owners, to the commencement of the 17th Century. By Lord Walter Fitzgerald. (14) vol. 8, pp. 185-196. 1915-1917.

TYNTE. Some Notes on the Tynte Family. By H. T. Fleming. (5) 2nd series, vol. 9, pp. 156-157. 1903.

TYRRELL. The Tyrels of Castleknock. By E. St. John Brooks. (22) vol. 76, pp. 151-154. 1946.

WADDING. See Dobbyn.

WALKER. Walker of Derry. By the Very Rev. W. S. Kerr. (16) Sentinel, 1938, p. 144.

WALSH. Notes on the Norman-Welsh Family of Walsh in Ireland, France and Austria. (22) vol. 75, pp. 32-44. 1945.

WARREN. Some Notes on the Family of Warren of Warrenstown, County Louth. By the Hon. Mrs. Richard Bellow. (17) vol. 4, pp. 26-34. 1916.

WATERS. The Waters Family of Cork. By Eaton W. Waters. (5) 2nd series, vol. 31, pp. 71-78, 1926; vol. 32, pp. 17-23, 104-113, 1927; vol. 33, pp. 35-41, 1928; vol. 34, pp. 36-42, 97-105, 1929; vol. 35, pp. 36-43, 102-113, 1930; vol. 36, pp. 26-38, 76-86, 1931; vol. 37, pp. 35-41, 1932.

WEST. The Wests of Ballydugan, County Down; the Rock, County Wicklow; and Ashwood, County Wexford. By Edward Parkinson and Capt. E. E. West. (23) 2nd series, vol. 12, pp. 135-141, 159-165. 1906.

WHITE. The Whites of Dufferin and their Connections. By Maj. R. G. Berry. (23) 2nd series, vol. 12, pp. 117-125, 169-174, 1906; vol. 13, pp. 89-95, 125-132, 1907.

WILDMAN (WILEMAN). See Englefield.

WILDRIDGE. Wildridge of Killahoman, County Monaghan. By Henry F. Reynolds. (19) vol. 180, pp. 5-8.

WOLFE. The Wolfe Family of County Kildare. By George Wolfe. (14) vol. 3, pp. 361-367. 1899-1902.

WYSE. Ancient and Illustrious Waterford Families. The Wyses of the Manor of St. Johns, Waterford. By P. Higgins. (24) vol. 5, pp. 199-206. 1899.

CHAPTER VI

A SELECT LIST OF HISTORICAL WORKS CONTAINING MATERIAL FOR FAMILY HISTORY

This chapter will be divided into three sections; namely, county and town histories, diocesan and parish histories and histories of Ireland.

Irish county and town histories are, for the most part, better documented than similar histories in the United States and, on the whole, are more reliable. Diocesan and parish histories are usually based on church or local documents. The majority of the histories listed herein are devoted to seventeenth, eighteenth, and early nineteenth century records. They vary in quantity and classes of records. Some are rich in family history, genealogy, pedigrees, and brief genealogical notes of from one to several generations. Some contain transcripts of wills, marriage records, cemetery records, early and later tax records, rent rolls, muster rolls, freeman rolls, county lists of officers, etc., copied from original documents. A classic example which includes such records is found in *The History of County Monaghan,* by Evelyn Philip Shirley. London, 1879.

The National Library of Ireland has the most complete collection of histories of all classes. The Public Record Office of Northern Ireland has an excellent collection. The University libraries have good selections. The County libraries tend to specialize in their local areas. The larger American genealogical libraries have fairly good collections of the better county histories. The American Irish Historical Society in New York City has an excellent selection of county, town, diocesan and parish histories. The larger Irish book shops, such as Hodges Figgis in Dublin, and the Cathedral Book Shop in Belfast, carry a good selection.

COUNTY AND TOWN HISTORIES

(Arranged by County)

ANTRIM:

BALLYMENA: Old Ballymena; a history of Ballymena during the 1798 Rebellion. Published in the *Ballymena Observer,* in 1857, under the title, "Walks about Ballymena". Book published in 1938.

BASSETT, GEORGE H. The Book of Antrim. 1888.

BENN, GEORGE. A History of the Town of Belfast. 2 vols. London, 1877-80.

CLARKE, REV. H. J. ST. J. Thirty Centuries in South East Antrim. 1938.

HILL, GEORGE. The Macdonnells of Antrim. Belfast, 1877.

JOY, HENRY. Historical Collections relative to the Town of Belfast. Belfast, 1817.

MCSKIMIN, SAMUEL. The History and Antiquities of the County of the Town of Carrickfergus, 1318-1839. 2nd edition, with Notes and Appendix, by E. J. McCrum. Belfast, 1909.

MILLIN, S. SHANNON. Sidelights on Belfast History. 1932.

OWEN, J. D. History of Belfast. 2 vols. Belfast, 1921.

SHAW, WILLIAM. Cullybackey, the Story of an Ulster Village. 1913.

SIBBETT, R. M. On the Shining Ban; Records of an Ulster Manor. Belfast, 1928.

YOUNG, ROBERT M. Historical Notices of Old Belfast, and its Vicinity. 1896. Maps.

YOUNG, ROBERT M. The Town Book of the Corporation of Belfast, 1613-1816. 1892. Maps.

ARMAGH:

DONALDSON, JOHN. A Historical and Statistical Account of the Barony of Upper Fews (Armagh).

MARSHALL, J. J. The History of Charlemont Fort and the Borough in the County Armagh and of Mountjoy Fort in County Tyrone. 1921.

STEWART, JAMES. Historical Memoirs of the City of Armagh. New edition, edited by Rev. Ambrose Coleman. Dublin, 1900.

CARLOW:

BROPHY, MICHAEL. Carlow Past and Present,—with a short account of the Dalcassian families. 1888.

COYLE, JAMES. The Antiquities of Leighlin (Co. Carlow).

HORE, H. J. The Social State of the Southern and Eastern Counties of Ireland in the Sixteenth Century; being the presentments of gentlemen, commonalty and citizens of Carlow, Cork, Kilkenny, Tipperary, Waterford, and Wexford, made in the Reigns of Henry VIII and Elizabeth (records from the Public Record Office, London). 1870.

RYAN, JOHN. The History and Antiquities of the County of Carlow. Dublin, 1833.

CAVAN:

SMITH, T. S. The Civic History of the Town of Cavan. 3rd edition. Dublin, 1938.

ANOMYMOUS. The Highlands of Cavan. Belfast, 1856. (Only general.)

CLARE:

FROST, JAMES. The History and Topography of the County of Clare. Dublin, 1893.

WHITE, REV. P. History of Clare and the Dalcassian Clans of Tipperary, Limerick and Galway. Dublin, 1893.

CORK:

BENNETT, GEORGE. The History of Bandon and the Principal Towns in the West Riding of County Cork. 2nd edition. Cork, 1869.

CAULFIELD, RICHARD, *Ed.* The Council Book of the Corporation of Cork, from 1609-1643; 1690-1800. Guilford, Surrey, 1876.

CAULFIELD, RICHARD, *Ed.* The Council Book of the Corporation of Kinsale. Guilford, Surrey, 1879.

CAULFIELD, RICHARD, *Ed.* The Council Book of the Corporation of Youghal, from 1610-1659; 1666-1687; 1690-1800. Guilford, Surrey, 1878.

CUSACK, MARY FRANCES. A History of the City and County of Cork. Dublin, 1875.

DENNEHY, THE VENERABLE ARCHDEACON. History of—Queenstown, Cork. Cork, 1923.

GIBSON, REV. C. B. The History of the County and City of Cork. 2 vols. London, 1861.

HARTNETT, P. J. Cork City, its History and Antiquities. 1943.

HAYMAN, REV. SAMUEL. Guide to Youghal, Ardmore and the Black Water. 1860.

HORE, H. J. (See under Co. Carlow.)

O'SULLIVAN, FLORENCE. The History of Kinsale. Dublin, 1916.

POWER, PATRICK. Place-Names and Antiquities of Barrymore (Barony), County Cork. 1923.

SMITH, CHARLES. The Ancient and Present State of the County and City of Cork. 2 vols. 1st edition, 1750; 2nd edition, 1815; new edition, revised and enlarged by Robert Day and W. A. Coppinger. Cork, 1893-4.

TUCKY, FRANCIS H. The County and City of Cork Remembrancer. n. d.

VON KARTOFFEL and others, letters of. (Germans in Cork.)

WHITE, COL. JAMES GROVE. Historical and Topographical Notes, etc., on Buttevant, Castletownroche, Doneraile, Mallow, and places in their Vicinity. 4 vols. Cork, 1905-16. (This is filled with family history, genealogy and pedigrees, by a great genealogist.)

WHITE, COL. JAMES GROVE. History of Kilbyrne, Doneraile, Cork. Cork, 1915.

DONEGAL:

ALLINGHAM, HUGH. Ballyshannon: its History and Antiquities. Londonderry, 1879.

DOHERTY, W. J. Inis-Owen and Tirconnell. Being some account of the Antiquities and Writers of County Donegal. Second series. Dublin, 1895.

HARKIN, WILLIAM. Scenery and Antiquities of North West Donegal. 1893.

HILL, GEORGE. Facts from Gweedore. Dublin, 1854.
SWAN, H. P. The Book of Inishowen. Buncrana, 1938.
YOUNG, AMY. Three Hundred Years in Inishowen. Belfast, 1929.

DOWN:

CROSSLE, FRANCIS C. Local Jottings of Newry Collected and Transcribed. (Vols. 1-34.) Newry, 1890-1910.

HARRIS, WALTER. The Ancient and Present State of the County of Down. Dublin, 1744.

HILL, REV. GEORGE. Montgomery Manuscripts, 1603-1706, compiled from Family Papers. Belfast, 1869.

KNOX, ALEXANDER. History of the County Down. Dublin, 1875.

LINN, CAPT. RICHARD. A History of Banbridge. Edited by W. S. Kerr. Belfast, 1935. (Includes Tullylish.)

LOWREY, T. K. The Hamilton Manuscripts. Compiled and edited by T. K. Lowrey. Belfast, 1867.

PARKINSON, EDWARD. The City of Down from its Earliest Days. Belfast, 1928.

STEVENSON, JOHN. Two Centuries of Life in Down, 1600-1800. Belfast, 1920.

WILLIAMSON, W. The Ancient and Present State of the County Down. 1757. (Ascribed both to Walter Harris and Charles Smith.)

DUBLIN:

BALL, FRANCIS EBRINGTON. A History of the County Dublin. 6 parts. Dublin, 1902-20.

CRAIG, MAURICE. Dublin, 1660-1860. Dublin, London, 1952.

GILBERT, SIR JOHN T. A History of the City of Dublin. 3 vols. Dublin, 1854-9.

HARRIS, WALTER. The History and Antiquities of the City of Dublin, from the Earliest Accounts. Dublin, 1766.

PHADRAIG, BRIAN MacGIOLLA. History of Terenure. (A townland in the parish of Rathfarnham, Co. Dublin.) Dublin, 1954.

WARBURTON, JOHN; JAMES WHITLAW and ROBERT WALSH. History of the City of Dublin. 2 vols. London, 1818.

FERMANAGH:

BELMORE, EARL OF. Parliamentary Memoirs of Fermanagh, 1613-1885. Dublin, 1887.

DUNDAS, W. H. Enniskillen, Parish and Town. Dundalk, 1913.

GRAHAM, REV. JOHN. Derriana, consisting of a History of the Siege of Derry and the Defense of Enniskillen in 1688 and 1689, with — and Biographical Notes. 1823.

TRIMBLE, W. C. The History of Enniskillen, with some Manors of Fermanagh. 3 vols. Enniskillen, 1919-21.

GALWAY:

HARDIMAN, JAMES. History of the Town and County of the Town of Galway. Dublin, 1820. Reprint by the Connacht Tribune, Galway, 1926.

HISTORY OF GALWAY. Galway: Connacht Tribune. 1926.

O'SULLIVAN, M. D. Old Galway; the History of a Norman Colony in Ireland. Cambridge, 1942.

WHITE, REV. P. See Co. Clare.

KERRY:

BRADY, W. MAZIERE. The McGellycuddy Papers. London, 1867.

CUSACK, M. F. History of the Kingdom of Kerry. London, 1871.

DONOVAN, T. M. A Popular History of East Kerry. 1931.

HICKSON, MARY A. Selections from Old Kerry Records, Historical and Genealogical. 2 vols. London, 1872-4.

KING, JEREMIAH. County Kerry, Past and Present. Handbook to Local and Family History. Dublin, 1931.

SMITH, CHARLES. The Ancient and Present State of the County of Kerry. Dublin, 1756.

KILDARE:

COMERFORD, REV. M. Collections Relating to Kildare and Leighlin. 3 vols. 1883.

HEALY, REV. WILLIAM. History and Antiquities of Kilkenny, County and City. Vol. I (all published). Kilkenny, 1893.

HOGAN, JOHN. Kilkenny, the Ancient City of Ossory. Kilkenny, 1884.

HORE, H. J. See Co. Carlow.

KING'S: See Offaly (now Co. Offaly).

LAOIGHIS: See Queen's Co. (now Laoighis).

LEITRIM: None.

LIMERICK:

DOWD, REV. JAMES. Limerick and its Sieges. Limerick, 1896.

FERRAR, JOHN. A History of the City of Limerick. Limerick, 1767.

FERRAR, JOHN. The History of Limerick, Ecclesiastical, Civil and Military, from the Earliest Records to the Year 1787. Limerick, 1787.

FITZGERALD, P. and J. J. MCGREGOR. The History, Topography and Antiquities of the County and City of Limerick. 2 vols. Dublin, 1826-7.

HAYES, RICHARD. The German Colony in County Limerick. Reprint, from the *North Munster Antiquarian Society Journal*. Limerick, 1937.

LENIHAN, MAURICE. Limerick; its History and Antiquities. Dublin, 1866.

MAC CAFFREY, JAMES. The Black Book of Limerick. With Introduction and Notes. 1907.

WHITE, REV. P. See Co. Clare.

LONDONDERRY:

BERNARD, NICHOLAS, *Ed.* The Whole Proceedings of the Siege of Drogheda, to which is added a true account of the Siege of Londonderry, by the Rev. George Walker, late Governor of Derry. Dublin, 1736.

FERGUSON, REV. SAMUEL. Some Items of Historic Interest about Waterside (with tables of householders in Glendermott Parish, 1663, 1740). Londonderry, 1902.

GRAHAM, REV. JOHN. A History of the Siege of Londonderry and the Defense of Enniskillen in 1688 and 1689. 1829.

KERNOHAN, J. W. The County of Londonderry in Three Centuries. Belfast, 1921.

KING, VERY REV. R. G. Londonderry: A Particular of the "Howses and Famyleys" in Londonderry, May 15, 1628. Londonderry, 1936.

MARTIN, SAMUEL. Historical Gleanings from County Derry. Dublin, 1955.

MOODY, T. W. *Ed.* The Londonderry Plantation, 1609-41. The City of London and the Plantation in Ulster. Maps and Plan. Belfast, 1939.

PHILLIPS, SIR THOMAS. Londonderry and the London Companies, 1609-1629. Being a Survey and other Documents, submitted to King Charles I, by Thomas Phillips. Published for the Public Record Office, Northern Ireland. Belfast, 1928.

WITHEROW, THOMAS. Derry and Enniskillen, in the Year 1689. 1873, 1885.

WITHEROW, THOMAS, *Ed.* A True Relation of the Twenty Weeks Siege of Londonderry, by the Scotch, Irish, and the disaffected English,—. London, 1649. (Copied by his son from a copy taken by Rev. Robert Sewell, in the British Museum, 1878.)

YOUNG, WILLIAM R. Fighters of Derry, their Deeds and Descendants. With an Introduction by Thomas U. Sadleir. 1932.

LONGFORD:

BUTLER, H. T. and H. E. BUTLER. The Black Book of Edgeworthstown, and other Edgeworth memories, 1585-1817. 1927.

FARRELL, JAMES P. Historical Notes and Stories of the County Longford. 1886. 2nd edition, 1891.

LOUTH:

BERNARD, NICHOLAS. The Whole Proceedings of the Siege of Drogheda, to which is added a True Account of the Siege of Londonderry, by the Rev. George Walker, late Governor of Derry. Dublin, 1736.

D'ALTON, JOHN. History of Drogheda, with its environs. 2 vols. Dublin, 1844.

D'ALTON, JOHN, and J. R. O'FLANAGAN. The History of Dundalk. Dundalk, 1864.

WITHEROW, THOMAS. The Boyne and the Aghrim. 1879.

ANONYMOUS. Drogheda, The Siege of: or Reminiscences of the Families of Ireland.

MAYO:

KNOX, HUBERT THOMAS. The History of County Mayo, to the Close of the Sixteenth Century. Dublin, 1908.

STOCK, JOSEPH. A Narrative of what passed at Killala, in the County of Mayo, in the Summer of 1798. London, 1800.

MEATH:

D'ALTON, JOHN. Antiquities of the County of Meath, with Illustrations of the Principal Abbeys, Castles, etc., by the late Francis Grose, Esq. To which is prefixed a Brief View of the Annals and Records of the County. Dublin, 1833.

MONAGHAN:

RUSHE, DENIS CAROLAN. History of Monaghan for Two Hundred Years, 1660-1860. Dundalk, 1921.

SHIRLEY, EVELYN PHILIP. The History of the County of Monaghan. London, 1879.

SHIRLEY, EVELYN PHILIP. Some Account of the Territory and Dominion of Farney, in the Province and Earldom of Ulster. London, n. d.

OFFALY (KING'S CO.):

COOKE, THOMAS L. The Early History of the Town of Birr, or Parsonstown (and celebrated places of the surrounding country). Dublin, 1875.

HITCHCOCK, F. R. M. The Midland Septs and the Pale. An account of the Early Septs and Later Settlers of King's County and of Life in the English Pale. Dublin, 1908.

QUEEN'S CO., now LAOIGHIS:

O'BYRNE, DANIEL. The History of Queen's County. Also an account of Some Noble Families of English Extraction. Dublin, 1856.

O'BYRNE, DANIEL. The History of Queen's County. 1856.

O'HANLON, J. History of Queen's County. By J. O'Hanlon and E. O'Leary. 2 vols. Dublin, 1907-14.

ROSCOMMON:

BECKETT, REV. M. Facts and Fictions of Local History. With reference chiefly to the District of Killultagh. 1929.

SLIGO:

O'RORKE, T. The History of Sligo, Town and County. 2 vols. Dublin, 1889.

WOOD-MARTIN, W. G. The History of Sligo, County and Town, from the Earliest Ages to the Present Time. 3 vols. Dublin, 1882-92.

WOOD-MARTIN, W. G. Sligo and the Enniskilleners, from 1688-1691. Dublin, 1882.

TIPPERARY:

BURKE, WILLIAM P. History of Clonmel. Waterford, 1907.

COTTER, JAMES. Tipperary. New York, 1929.

FLYNN, PAUL J. The Book of the Galtees and the Golden Vein. A Border History of Tipperary, Limerick and Cork. Dublin, 1926.

GLEESON, D. F. The Last Lords of Ormond. London, 1938.

GLEESON, J. Cashel of the Kings. Dublin, 1927.

HEMPHILL, W. DESPARD. Clonmel and the Surrounding Country. 1860.

MCILROY, M. Gleanings from Garrymore (Townland) n.d.

SHEEHAN, E. H. Nenagh (Co. Tipperary) and its Neighborhood. (Includes many family records.) n.d.

WHITE, JAMES, *Ed.* My Clonmel Scrap Book, n. d.

WHITE, REV. P. History of Clare and the Dalcassian Clans of Tipperary, Limerick and Galway. 1893.

TYRONE:

HUTCHINSON, W. R. Tyrone Precinct. Belfast, 1951.

WATERFORD:

BUTLER, M. The Barony of Gaultier, n. d.

DOWNEY, E. The Story of Waterford. 1914.

EGAN, P. M. History and Directory of County and City of Waterford. Kilkenny, n. d.

FITZPATRICK, THOMAS. Waterford during the Civil War, 1641-1653. 1912.

OCHILLE, F. The Holy City of Ardmore, Co. Waterford. Youghal, n. d.

POWER, REV. PATRICK. History of the County of Waterford. Waterford, 1933.

RYLAND, R. H. The History, Topography and Antiquities of the County and City of Waterford. London, 1824.

SMITH, CHARLES. The Ancient and Present State of the County and City of Waterford. 2nd edition. Dublin, 1774.

WESTMEATH:

WOODS, J. The Annals of Westmeath, Ancient and Modern. Dublin, 1907.

WEXFORD:

DOYLE, LYNN. Ballygullion, County Wexford. 1945.

DOYLE, MARTIN. Notes and Gleanings Relating to the County of Wexford. Dublin, 1868.

FLOOD, W. H. GRATTAN. History of Enniscorthy, County Wexford. n. d.

HAY, EDWARD. History of the Insurrection of County Wexford, in 1798. Dublin, 1803.

HORE, H. J. See County Carlow.

HORE, PHILIP HERBERT. History of the Town and County of Wexford, with notes of some parishes. 6 vols. London, 1900-1911.

WICKLOW:

ANOMYMOUS. Bray: A Hundred Years of Bray and its Neighborhood, from 1770 to 1870. By an old inhabitant. 1907.

DIOCESAN AND PARISH HISTORIES

(ARRANGED BY AUTHOR)

ADAMS, B. N. History and Description of Santry and Clogran Parishes, Co. Dublin. Dublin, 1883.

ALLINGHAM, HUGH. Ballyshannon, its History and Antiquities. Londonderry, 1879. (In Co. Donegal.)

ATKINSON, EDWARD D. An Ulster Parish: Being a History of Donaghcloney. 1898. (Warringstown, Co. Down.)

ATKINSON, E. D. Dromore, an Ulster Diocese. Dundalk, 1925.

BALL, FRANCIS ELRINGTON and EVERARD HAMILTON. The Parish of Taney: A History of Dundrum, near Dublin, and its Neighborhood. Dublin, 1895.

BEGLEY, JOHN (ARCHDEACON). The Diocese of Limerick, from 1691 to the Present Time. 1938.

BERRY, J. FLEETWOOD. The Story of St. Nicholas Collegiate Church, Galway. Galway, 1912.

BLACKER, REV. BEAVER H. Brief Sketches of the Parishes of Booterstown and Donnybrook, in the County of Dublin. In 4 parts. 1860-1874.

BOYD, H. A. A History of the Church of Ireland in Ramoan Parish. 1930. (In Co. Antrim.)

BRADSHAW, W. H. Enniskillen Long Ago; an Historic Sketch of the Parish of "Iniskeene in Lacu Ernensi". 1878. (In Co. Fermanagh.)

BRADY, W. MAZIERE. Clerical and Parochial Records of Cork, Cloyne and Ross; taken from Diocesan and Parish Registries, Manuscripts in the Principal Libraries and Public Record Offices of Oxford, Dublin and London, and from private family papers. 3 vols. London, 1864.

BROIN, LEAM UA. Traditions of Drimnagh, County Dublin and its Neighborhood. (In the *Journal of the Royal Society of Antiquaries of Ireland,* vol. 72.)

BURKE, FRANCIS. Loch Ce' and its Annals; North Roscommon and the Diocese of Elphin. Dublin, 1895.

CARMODY, THE VERY REV. W. P. Lisburn Cathedral and its Past Rectors. 1926.

CARRIGAN, REV. WILLIAM. The History and Antiquities of the Diocese of Ossory. 4 vols. Dublin, 1905.

CARROLL, W. G. The Succession of Clergy in the Parishes of S. Bride, S. Michael le Pole and S. Stephen. Dublin, 1884.

CAULFIELD, RICHARD, *Ed.* The Parish Registers of Holy Trinity, Cork, 1643-68. 1877.

CAULFIELD, RICHARD. Annals of St. Fin Barres Cathedral, Cork. 1871.

CLARKE, REV. H. J. ST.J. Three Centuries in South East Antrim; the Parish of Coole or Carnmoney. Belfast, 1938.

COGAN, REV. A. The Diocese of Meath, Ancient and Modern. 3 vols. Dublin, 1862.

COLE, REV. J. H. Church and Parish Records of the United Diocese of Cork, Cloyne and Ross. Cork, 1903. (A continuation or supplement to Brady's 3 vols.)

COMERFORD, REV. M. Collections Relating to the Dioceses of Kildare and Leighlin. 3 vols. Dublin, 1883.

COTTON, HENRY. Fasti Ecclesiae Hibernicae: Diocese of Waterford; Diocese of Cashel and Emly. Dublin, 1845.

COWAN, J. DAVISON. An Ancient Parish, Past and Present; being the Parish of Donaghmore, County Down. London, 1914.

D'ALTON, RT. REV. MONSIGNOR. The History of the Archdiocese of Tuam. 2 vols. Dublin, 1928.

DARLING, JOHN. St. Multose Church, Kinsale,—. Cork, 1895.

DOWD, JAMES. St. Mary's Cathedral, Limerick (A History of). 1936.

DUNDAS, W. H. Enniskillen, Parish and Town. 1913. (In Co. Fermanagh)

DWYER, PHILIP. The Diocese of Killaloe, from the Reformation to the Close of the Eighteenth Century. Dublin, 1878.

FAHEY, J. The History and Antiquities of the Diocese of Kilmacduagh. Dublin, 1893.

GALLOGLY, JOHN. The History of St. Patrick's Cathedral, Armagh. 1880.

HADDOCK, JOSIAH. A Parish Miscellany, Donaghcloney. (In Co. Down.)

HEALY, JOHN. History of the Diocese of Meath. 2 vols. Dublin, 1908.

HENRY, SAMUEL. The Story of St. Patrick's Church, Coleraine. n. d.

HOGG, REV. M. B. Keady Parish; A Short History of its Church and People. 1928. (In Co. Armagh.)

HOLLAND, REV. W. History of West Cork and the Diocese of Ross. Skibbereen, 1949.

HUGHES, THOMAS. The History of Tynan Parish, County Armagh. 1910.

HURLEY, REV. TIMOTHY. St. Patrick and the Parish of Kilkeeran. Vol. I. (All published.) (In Co. Mayo.)

INNES, R. Natural History of Magilligan Parish (in 1725). (In Co. Londonderry.)

KEENAN, PADRAIC. Clonallon Parish: Its Annals and Antiquities. In the *Journal of the County Louth Archaeological Society*. Vol. X.

KEENAN, PADRAIC. Diocese of Dromore: Brief Historical Sketch of the Parish of Clonduff. Newry, 1941.

KINGSTON, REV. JOHN. The Parish of Fairview: including the present parishes of Corpus Christi, Glasnevin, Larkhill, Marino, and Donnycarney. Dundalk, 1953.

KNOX, H. T. Notes on the Early History of the Dioceses of Tuam, Killala, and Achonry. Dublin, 1904.

LAHERT, RICHARD. The History and Antiquities of the Parish of Dunnamaggan. Tralee, 1956.

LAWLER, HUGH J. The Fasti of St. Patrick's, Dublin. 1930.

LEATHEM, W. S. A History of the Church of Ireland in St. Mary Magdalene Parish. Belfast, 1939.

LEDWICH, EDWARD. A Statistical Account of the Parish of Aghaboe, in Queen's County. 1796.

LEE, REV. DR. C. Certain Statistics from the United Parishes of Knockainy and Patrickswell (Diocese of Emly), County Limerick, for the Years 1819-1941. In the *Journal of the Cork Historical and Archaeological Society.* Vol. 47, no. 165.

LEE, REV. W. H. A. St. Colmanell, Ahoghill: A History of its Parish. 1865. (In Co. Antrim.)

LESLIE, REV. JAMES B. Ardfert and Aghadoe; Clergy and Parishes—from the earliest period, with historical notices of the several parishes, churches, etc. Dublin, 1940.

LESLIE, REV. JAMES B. Armagh Clergy and Parishes. 1911.

LESLIE, REV. JAMES B. Clogher Clergy and Parishes. 1908.

LESLIE, REV. JAMES B. Derry Clergy and Parishes,—with historical notices of the several parishes, churches, etc. Enniskillen, 1937.

LESLIE, REV. JAMES B. Ferns Clergy and Parishes. 1936.

LESLIE, REV. JAMES B. History of Kilsaran Union of Parishes, County Louth; being a history of the parishes of Kilsaran, Gernonstown, Stabannon, Manfieldstown and Dromiskin. Dundalk, 1908.

LESLIE, REV. JAMES B. Ossory Clergy and Parishes. 1933.

LESLIE, REV. JAMES B. Raphoe Clergy and Parishes. Enniskillen, 1940.

LESLIE, REV. JAMES B. and THE VERY REV. H. B. SWANZY. Biographical Lists of the Clergy of the Diocese of Down. 1936.

MACNAMEE, JAMES J. History of the Diocese of Ardagh. Dublin, 1954.

MACSORLEY, CATHARINE M. The Story of Our Parish; St. Peter's, Dublin. Dublin, 1917.

MAGUIRE, THE VERY REV. CANON. The History of the Diocese of Raphoe. 2 vols. Dublin, 1920.

MAITLAND, W. H. The History of Magherafelt. Cookstown, 1916.

MARSHALL, REV. H. C. The Parish of Lambeg. 1933. (In Co. Antrim.)

MARSHALL, JOHN J. Vestry Records of the Church of St. John, Parish of Aghalow (Caledon, Co. Tyrone).

MARSHALL, J. J. History of the Parish of Tynan, Co. Armagh. 1932.

MASON, WILLIAM MONK. The History and Antiquities of the Collegiate Cathedral Church of St. Patrick, near Dublin, from its foundation in 1190, to the year 1819. Dublin, 1820.

MASON, WILLIAM SHAW. A Statistical Account or Parochial Survey of Ireland, Drawn from Communications of the Clergy. 3 vols. Dublin, 1814.

McILROY, MARY. Gleanings from Garrymore.

MEREDYTH, FRANCIS. A Descriptive and Historic Guide through St. Mary's Cathedral, Limerick. (Tombstone records and family notes.) Limerick, 1887.

MONAHAN, REV. J. Records Relating to the Diocese of Ardagh and Clonmacnoise. 1886.

MURRAY, REV. LAWRENCE P. History of the Parish of Creggan, in the Seventeenth and Eighteenth Centuries. Dundalk, 1940. (In Co. Londonderry.)

O'CONNELL, PHILIP. The Diocese of Kilmore; its History and Antiquities. Dublin, 1937.

O'LAVERTY, REV. JAMES. An Historical Account of the Diocese of Down and Connor. 4 vols. Dublin, 1878-1889.

O'LAVERTY, J. O. The History of the Parish of Holywood, from the earliest times. (In Co. Down.)

O'RORKE, T. History, Antiquities and Present State of the Parishes of Ballysadare and Kilvarnet, in County Sligo. Dublin, n. d.

POOLER, L. A. Down and its Parishes. 1907.

POWER, VERY REV. P. Waterford and Lismore: a Compendious History of the United Dioceses. Cork, 1937.

REEDY, REV. DONAL A. The Diocese of Kerry (formerly Ardfert), with special sections on Innisfallen, Muckross, Friary and St. Mary's Cathedral. Killarney.

REEVES, WILLIAM. Ecclesiastical Antiquities of Down, Connor and Dromore. 1847.

RENNISON, WILLIAM H. Succession List of Bishops and Clergy of the Dioceses of Waterford and Lismore. Waterford, 1922.

RESIDE, S. W. St. Mary's Church, Newry; its History. 1933. (In Co. Down.)

SEYMOUR, ST. JOHN D. The Diocese of Emly. Dublin, 1913.

SHIRLEY, REV. EVELYN PHILIP. Lough Fea. 2 vols. London, 1859. 2nd edition, 1869. (In Co. Monaghan.)

STEELE, REV. W. B. The Parish of Devenish, County Fermanagh. Enniskillen, 1937.

STEWART, REV. DAVID (?). Tullylish, Parish of; Historical Notes. (In Co. Down.)

SWANZY, HENRY B. Biographical Succession Lists of the Diocese of Dromore. Edited by Canon James B. Leslie. Belfast, 1933.

SWAYNE, JOHN. The Register of John Swayne, Archbishop of Armagh and Primate of Ireland, 1418-1439. 1935.

TEMPEST. Tempest's Annual. (Contains Minutes of the Vestry of the Parish of Dundalk, Co. Louth.) 1936-1942.

WATSON, CHARLES. Glenavy, Camlin and Tullyrusk; the Story of the United Parishes of. 1892.

WEBSTER, CHARLES A. The Diocese of Cork. Cork, 1920.

WEBSTER, CHARLES. The Diocese of Ross. Reprint from the *Journal of the Cork Historical and Archaeological Society.* 1924.

ANONYMOUS. Templecorran and Islandmagee, History of the Parishes of.

HISTORIES OF IRELAND

No attempt is made by this compiler to present a lengthy bibliography of the works of Irish historians. It would only result in obscuring the few works which present material of use to the genealogist. A genealogist must have a good working knowledge of Irish history in order to understand the causes and effects which produced the records, and the various classes of records. Therefore, familiarity with certain works will teach the genealogist not only what happened to the Irish, the Anglo-Irish and the Scotch-Irish during the turbulent centuries before the mid-nineteenth century, but will also call attention to various collections of records which aid in compiling family history and genealogy.

BIGGER, FRANCIS JOSEPH. The Ulster Land War. Dublin. 1910.

CARTY, JAMES. Ireland from the Flight of the Earls to Grattan's Parliament, 1607-1782. Dublin, 1949.

CARTY, JAMES. Ireland from Grattan's Parliament of the Great Famine, 1783-1850. Dublin, 1949.

CARTY, JAMES. Ireland from the Great Famine to the Treaty, 1851-1921. Dublin, 1951.

CHART, D. A. A History of Northern Ireland. Belfast, 1927.

CURTIS, EDMUND. A History of Ireland. 6th ed. London, 1950.

DUNLOP, ROBERT. Ireland Under the Commonwealth; Being a Selection of Documents Relating to the Government of Ireland from 1651-1659. Manchester, 1913.

FITZGERALD, BRIAN. The Anglo-Irish. London, 1952.

FITZGERALD, T. W. H. Ireland and Her People. n. d.

FROUDE, JAMES ANTHONY. The English in Ireland in the Eighteenth Century. 3 vols. 1887.

GILBERT, JOHN T. Contemporary History of Affairs in Ireland from 1641 to 1652. 6 vols. 1879. (With Appendix of original letters and documents.)

HARRISON, JOHN. The Scot in Ulster. Edinburgh & London, 1888.

HAYES, RICHARD. The Last Invasion of Ireland when Connacht Rose. Dublin, 1937.

HENNESSY, WILLIAM M., and B. MACCARTHY. Annals of Ulster, A. D. 431-1541. 4 vols. Dublin, 1887, 1893, 1895, 1901.

HILL, REV. GEORGE, *Ed.* The Plantation of Ulster, 1608-1620.

MORAN, HIS EMINENCE, PATRICK FRANCIS. Historical Sketch of the Persecutions Suffered by the Catholics of Ireland, under the Rule of Cromwell and the Puritans. Dublin.

PRENDERGAST, JOHN P. The Cromwellian Settlement of Ireland. 2nd edition. Dublin, 1875. Reprint, 1922.

SIMMS, J. G. The Williamite Confiscation in Ireland. London, 1956.

STAFFORD, THOMAS. Pacata Hibernia; or a History of the Wars in Ireland during the Reign of Queen Elizabeth. Edited by Standish O'Grady. London, 1896.

YOUNG, ARTHUR. A Tour of Ireland (1776-1779). Edited with introduction and notes by A. W. Hutton. London, 1892. Cambridge, 1925.

CHAPTER VII

PUBLICATIONS OF THE IRISH MANUSCRIPTS COMMISSION WHICH RELATE TO GENEALOGY

The Irish Manuscripts Commission, through its publications, has performed a great service to genealogists. Among those described herein are two volumes containing abstracts of 1,464 wills, 1708 to 1785, which relate to land matters and are, therefore, deposited in the Registry of Deeds, Dublin. Another publication contains the abstracts of 224 early Quaker wills. A valuable aid to genealogists has been provided with the publication of the index to some 7,200 will abstracts which are in various manuscript collections in the Genealogical Office, Dublin Castle, Dublin. The Commission has also published collections of early Irish genealogies and much other material of a genealogical nature. For this reason, it is important to understand the history, the purpose and the scope of the work of the Irish Manuscripts Commission.

A Government Warrant of October, 1928, established the Irish Manuscripts Commission, its chosen personnel being historians, archivists, and literary men of the highest order. Among the distinguished members of the Commission are Mr. D. A. Chart, Past Deputy Keeper of the Public Records of Northern Ireland, and Dr. Richard J. Hayes, Director of the National Library of Ireland, both of whom have given long service. Dr. Edward MacLysaght, formerly Chief Herald of Ireland and Keeper of the Manuscripts in the National Library, was Chairman of the Commission in 1957, and Dr. James Hogan has been its Editor.

The purpose of the Commission is to search public repositories and private archives in England, Scotland, Wales, Ireland, and also certain ones abroad, for collections of manuscripts, documents and extremely rare printed works of historical, genealogical, literary and other interest pertaining to Ireland. The further purpose of the Commission has been to make selections from this material and to transcribe and edit for publication chosen collections of papers, manuscripts, etc., dating from the Middle Ages to the nineteenth century.

The Irish Manuscripts Commission has, since 1930, issued a journal from time to time entitled *Analecta Hibernica.* The purpose of the journal is to publish selected material which is not of sufficient length for separate volumes. The various numbers of *Analecta Hibernica* include reports on manuscript collections and abstracts of documents; also lists and indexes of record collections.

Much of the published material in the volumes and in the journal is of a genealogical nature. Therefore, genealogists will be interested in all of the following items, selected by this compiler from the full list of publications. Any of these may be purchased through the Dublin Stationery Office (Government Publications Sale Office), at 3 College Street, Dublin. A descriptive catalogue of all publications of the Irish Manuscripts Commission will be furnished upon request.

THE ANNALS OF LOCH CÉ, 1014-1636. 2 vols. 1939. Reproduction of the edition of 1871, prepared by W. M. Hennessy for the Rolls Series of Chronicles and Memorials of Great Britain and Ireland during the Middle Ages. 2 vols. The original manuscript, copied in 1588 by a scribe called Philip Bradley, for members of the MacDermot Family.

THE BOOK OF FENAGH. 1939. Reproduction of the edition by W. M. Hennessy and D. H. Kelly, 1875.

THE BOOK OF LECAN. A collotype facsimile (1937), with Foreword by Eoin MacNeill and Descriptive Introduction and Indexes by Kathleen Mulchrone. The original *Great Book of Lecan,* a treasured vellum manuscript in the Royal Irish Academy, is one of the earliest and most authoritative compilations of Irish genealogical material extant. It contains fifteenth century pedigrees of D'Arcy, De Cusack, Higgins, Keating, O'Keefe, Lynch, MacCartan, MacDonald, Macnamara, Maguire, Meginis, Middleton, Oglethorpe, O'Mahony, Porter, Power, Ryan, Sandilands, Williamson, with Appendix records of Naturalizations and Extracts from Registers.

THE BOOK OF UÍ MAINE. A collotype facsimile (1942), with Introduction and Indexes by R.A.S. Macalister. This is a fourteenth century manuscript, known as the Book of the O'Kellys. The contents are genealogical, romantic, metrical, etc.

A CENSUS OF IRELAND (*ca.* 1659). Edited by Séamus Pender. 1939. This is printed from the manuscript collection; copies of the original townland Census Returns of the inhabitants of Ireland, compiled under the direction of Sir William Petty. The Returns are listed geographically by counties, baronies, parishes and townlands. In cities, they are listed by parishes and streets. Under each townland and each city street, the number of English, Scotch and Irish inhabitants is stated. The Census Returns for the counties of Cavan, Galway, Mayo, Tyrone and Wicklow are missing, as are those for four baronies of County Cork and nine baronies of County Meath. Supplementary records taken from the Poll Money Ordinances, 1660-61, are supplied from manuscripts now in Marsh's Library, Dublin, and appear in Appendices.

THE CIVIL SURVEY (A. D. 1654-1656). Edited by Robert C. Simington.

VOL. I (Tipperary E. & S.) 1931.

VOL. II (Tipperary W. & N.) 1934.

VOL. III (Donegal, Derry & Tyrone). 1937.

VOL. IV (Limerick). 1938.

VOL. V (Meath). 1940.

VOL. VI (Waterford, Muskerry Barony (Co. Cork), and Kilkenny City. Valuations, *ca.* 1663-1664, for Cork and Waterford Cities). 1942.

VOL. VII (Dublin County). 1945.

VOL. VIII (County Kildare). 1952.

VOL. IX (County Wexford). 1952.

The records of the Civil Survey were written, 1654-1656, from the information and evidence supplied by "the most able and ancient inhabitants of the country". The testimony was supplied by local juries in all parts of the country, being descriptions and records of the land and its owners in 1640, before the Catholic Revolution. The Civil Survey enumerated, by name and description, every estate of every proprietor of land in twenty-seven Irish counties. Also Gaelic and Norman ancestral records of tenure and titles acquired by patent from the Crown were set forth. Local information for each townland included the name and residence of the owner, the homes of the tenants, estimates of their value, acreage under cultivation and pasture, etc., and antiquities and valuable notes of information about the families. Particulars of deeds and wills were frequently given. The surveys of the counties vary in the wealth of detail. In Vol. III, the Survey sets forth the owners established after the Plantation of Ulster and also includes the properties of minor freeholders. Vol. V includes a section of the Survey descriptive of the tithes of every parish of County Meath, the landowners and the values in 1640. Vol. VI gives the valuations, *ca.* 1663-1664, naming the proprietors of Cork and Waterford cities in 1640, and their tenants or possessors some twenty years later. The purpose of the Civil Survey was to inform the English Government. Parliament was responsible for heavy debts incurred to finance the English armies in Ireland. The Cromwellian Government planned to confiscate the lands of Catholic revolutionaries and raised money by previous sale of Irish lands to English "Adventurers." The Commonwealth Government also needed to satisfy its own officers and soldiers for arrears in pay with allotments of Irish land. Thus, the Government needed to know all of the particulars regarding Irish landowners and tenants in preparation for a mass confiscation. In so doing, a wealth of genealogical information was preserved.

THE COMPOSSICION BOOKE OF CONOUGHT. Edited by A. Martin Freeman. 1936. This book sets forth the details of the agreement of October, 1585, between the great lords of the Western Province of Ireland and the Royal Commission for a resettlement of the Province under feudal plan. Beginning with County Clare and on northwards, the property was enumerated by records of assignments to the great chiefs as tenants of the Crown and to the lesser men as their vassals. This book has especial value in regard to County Connaught and County Clare families.

DOWDALL AND PEPPARD DEEDS. 2 vols. Edited by Charles McNeill, A. Gwynn, and A. J. Otway-Ruthven. 1951. The collection of original Dowdall and Peppard Deeds is now in the National Library. It forms a complete series of deeds of one family, dating from the early thirteenth century down to the mid-seventeenth century. With other miscellaneous records, the collection mainly concerns the family of Douedale (now Dowdall) and their estates located in and near Dundalk, Co. Louth. Documents show that this family acted as legal representatives for other families. They show evidence of family descent, inheritance of the land in English Oriel (Co. Louth), and illustrate the legal methods from the beginning of the English occupation. The Peppard family of Drogheda has owned most of the collection since the time of Cromwell, and from this time, for some years, their legal papers, etc., were added to the earlier documents. Aside from the Ormond archives, no other family collection is as complete in Ireland, for the span of time. The editors have compiled a complete calendar of abstracts of the documents, arranged in chronological order, with an index of personal and place names.

THE KENMARE MANUSCRIPTS. Edited by Edward MacLysaght. 1942. This manuscript collection has been edited and printed by permission of the Earl of Kenmare, Killarney. The documents tell the story of the fall of a powerful Catholic family after supporting the cause of James II, who was defeated in Ireland by William of Orange. The Kenmare estates were confiscated under William III but, in time, the family regained its extensive lands in counties Kerry, Limerick and Cork and held them through the worst years of Catholic persecution. The collection includes the rental books of the Kerry estates which aid in tracing Co. Kerry families from the present time back to dates between 1600-1650. Letters, diaries, etc., add much detail of the times. The documents date mainly from 1588-1795.

THE KING'S INNS ADMISSION PAPERS: 1607-1867. Edited

by Thomas U. Sadleir. 1952. The Registers of the Honorable Society of the King's Inns, Dublin, concern the records of barristers and solicitors and students of law in Dublin. The seventeenth century entries usually are lacking records of parentage and age, residence, etc., such as appear in the Registers of Trinity College, Dublin. However, as Irish law students were required to complete their studies in one of the English Inns of Court in London, the Registers of the Inner Temple, the Middle Temple, Gray's Inn, or Lincoln's Inn, usually supply the lack for Irish law students who completed their work in London. Beginning about 1720, the Registers of King's Inns usually contain the records of parentage. The nineteenth century entries supply such items as parentage, place of education, mother's maiden name, etc., based on an application made at age 16 by the student and an affidavit signed by a friend or relative.

KNIGHTS' FEES IN COUNTIES WEXFORD, CARLOW AND KILKENNY. Edited by E. St. John Brooks. 1950. This is an account of the Knights' fees, recorded for the three counties, upon the death of the last Earl Marshall, Lord of Leinster, in the year 1247. Later lists record family descents with identification of place names.

("THE MUNSTER BOOK") AN LEABHAR MUIMHNEACH. Edited by Tadhg óDonnchadha. 1940. The genealogies of many Irish families of the Province of Munster are set forth in this book which includes also the genealogies of the leading Gaelic families of Ireland and of many early families tracing to Norman origin. The genealogies dating from ancient times are in many cases brought down to later than 1700. Records of the Munster families include land holdings. The original work was compiled, *ca.* 1750, in two manuscripts which drew upon ancient sources. This is in the Royal Irish Academy, MS. 23 E. 26.

CALENDAR OF ORMOND DEEDS, 1172-1603. 6 vols. Edited by E. Curtis. 1932-43. The collection of Ormond Deeds belonging to the Ormond family, long preserved in Kilkenny Castle, ranks as the largest family collection of medieval records in Ireland. Later documents of this family, 1603 onwards, have been calendared by the English Historical

Manuscripts Commission. The Calendar, 1172-1603, regarding deeds and other records, mostly of the Butler family, was made while the documents were loaned by the Earl of Ossory (later Marquess of Ormonde). Among several thousands of deeds and other records, great numbers relate to the Anglo-Norman families as well as to the Butler family, in the counties of Carlow, Kilkenny, Tipperary, Waterford, and some other locations. Much information is given for pedigrees of important county families.

THE RED BOOK OF ORMOND. Edited by Newport B. White. 1932. This is a transcript of the original register belonging to the Butler family, once preserved in Kilkenny Castle and now deposited in the Bodleian Library, Oxford. It records the rentals of many manors and properties, mostly in Counties Kildare, Kilkenny and Tipperary, largely in the fourteenth century, a few in the fifteenth, and one in the sixteenth century. Rentals throw light on family land tenures through the generations.

IRISH MONASTIC AND EPISCOPAL DEEDS FROM THE ORMOND COLLECTION. Edited by Newport B. White. 1936. Transcripts of over 150 deeds, charters, and some documents, including matrimonial causes, questions of legitimacy, inheritance, etc., are calendared in this volume. Over sixty documents are dated in the thirteenth, fourteenth and fifteenth centuries and the remainder later than 1500.

CALENDAR OF THE ORRERY PAPERS. Edited by Edward MacLysaght. 1941. The original documents preserved in the National Library relate to the Orrery family during the thirty year period from the Restoration, *ca.* 1659, to the Williamite War, *ca.* 1689. The documents consist of rent rolls, leases, marriage settlements, wills, etc. Many letters in the collection concern family affairs, disagreements, etc.; others deal with the family estates in Counties Cork and Limerick.

INDEX OF PARISHES AND TOWNLANDS OF IRELAND FROM SEVENTEENTH CENTURY MAPS. Edited by Y. M. Goblet. 1932. This is the first published index of seventeenth century Irish place names, recorded on old maps. The Down

Survey and the Manuscript Barony maps prepared by Sir William Petty, *ca.* 1655-59, were used by Dr. Goblet. The names of some 25,000 townlands are arranged alphabetically, showing the parish and county where each is located. A second indexed list of about 2,000 names of parishes, arranged alphabetically, places each parish in its respective barony and county.

QUAKER RECORDS, DUBLIN, ABSTRACTS OF WILLS. Edited by P. Beryl Eustace and Olive C. Goodbody. 1957. This volume contains abstracts of 224 Quaker wills, arranged alphabetically by name of the testators. Some are dated before 1700, but most are of the early eighteenth century. They give the name of the testator, occupation or condition (widow, etc.), place of residence, date of will, occasionally the date and place of probate, the names of legatees with descriptions of relationship, property specified, and often the place of burial. These abstracts are based upon six manuscript collections of wills preserved at the Meeting House of the Society of Friends, Eustace Street, Dublin. Appendix I gives an alphabetical list of the wills preserved in the Records of the Ulster Quarterly Meeting at The Meeting House, Railway Street, Lisburn. This shows the name of the testator, address, some dates of death, date of will, and some dates of inventory. Appendix II gives a list of full copies of wills (some original), deposited in the library of Friends House, Dublin.

THE SHAPLAND CAREW PAPERS. Edited by A. K. Longfield. 1946. This volume is a calendar of a collection of papers relating to the Carew family, whose estates lay in Counties Wexford and Waterford. The documents are dated 1740-1822, a few being dated from the seventeenth century. Four books of rentals show tenancies and tenures. This is not a complete family collection.

BOOKS OF SURVEY AND DISTRIBUTION. Edited by R. C. Simington. Vol. I. County Roscommon. 1949. Vol. II. County Mayo. 1951. The Public Record Office, Dublin, has a complete set of Manuscript Books of Survey and Distribution for all counties, sent in from the Quit Rent Office. Because of the general scarcity of records for the above two counties, these two volumes have been published to supply valuable records of land ownership in every parish and barony prior to and following the forfeitures of land under Cromwell and William III. These provide the names of the original owners before the forfeitures, the description and extent of the lands forfeited, and the lands distributed to the new [Protestant, usually English and some Huguenot] owners.

ABSTRACTS OF WILLS AT THE REGISTRY OF DEEDS, DUBLIN. Edited by P. Beryl Eustace. Vol. I, 1708-1745; Vol. II, 1746-1785. 1954, 1956. Some years ago, Miss P. Beryl Eustace began this work by compiling an index to over two thousand wills which, because of their significance in land matters, were deposited in the Registry of Deeds. The work was continued with the compiling of abstracts of 738 registered wills, 1708-1745, for Vol. I. Vol. II contains the abstracts of 726 registered wills, 1746-1785. Over seven hundred abstracts may appear in a third volume. These abstracts provide the name of the testator, address, occupation or condition (such as title, Esq., gent., widow, etc.), date of will, date of registration, names and relationships and addresses (where stated) of all legatees, property devised, witnesses at the signing and at registration. Notes describe the length, etc., of the will, and the reference to the book and page number of the copy of memorial in the Registry of Deeds; also the number by which the original memorial is filed in this repository. These provide the necessary numbers for ordering copies for more detailed study. The volumes of the above abstracts are indexed with the names of the testators in bold print and the names of all others mentioned in the wills in light print.

ANALECTA HIBERNICA (The Journal of the Irish Manuscripts Commission). Only the numbers which contain records of particular interest to the genealogist are listed.

ANALECTA HIBERNICA, No. 3. 1931. Eoin MacNéill and Cormac ÓCadhla have edited and presented a collection of rare Ulster genealogies, set forth in a manuscript book in the library of St. Colman's College, Fermoy. These include the pedigrees, forming a valuable supplement to pedigrees in the Annals of Ulster, 1300-1588 (in some cases brought down later than 1700), chiefly of County Fermanagh families. The records are given in great detail for the families of: MagUidhir (Maguire); MacMaghnusa (MacManus); MacDomhnaill (MacDonnell); MacGothraidh (MacCorry, or Corry); MacCába (MacCabe); MacGafraidh (MacCaffrey, Caffrey); ÓFlannagáin, MagRaith (Magrath); MacMathghamhna (MacMahon, or Matthews); Mac an Mhaighister (MacMaster, Masterson); MacMoruinn (Morrin); ÓCaiside (Cassidy); Mag Aodha (Magee, MacHugh, Hughes); ÓManacháin (Monahan); ÓTréasaigh (Tracey); ÓBanáin (Bannon), etc. Also in this number, Dr. James Hogan has edited and presented (from Rawlinson MS. A. 237, Bodleian Library, Oxford), the text of the Barony and Townland Survey of the six escheated counties of Ulster, made in 1608, in preparation for the Plantation of Ulster.

ANALECTA HIBERNICA No. 4. 1932. This number presents a collection of documents, edited and compiled chronologically by the Rev. Fr. Aubrey Gwynn, relative to the Irish settlers in the West Indies in the seventeenth century, having been driven there by their misfortunes and forfeitures, after the Catholic Rebellion of 1641, and by the Cromwellian confiscations. Some documents refer to the first Irish settlements in Virginia.

ANALECTA HIBERNICA No. 5. 1934. Index to Numbers 1-4. Prepared by Newport B. White.

ANALECTA HIBERNICA No. 7. A Guide to Irish Genealogical Collections. By Séamus Pender. 1935. This is an introductory guide to material in early Irish manuscripts. A table of references is presented for the following: The Book of Leinster (Rawlinson B 502); the Book of Ballymote (Bodleian MS. Laud 610); the Leabhar Breac; the Yellow Book of Lecan; the Book of Lecan; the Book of Uí Maine; MacFirbis's Book of Genealogies; the O'Clery Book of Genealogies. References are made to further works in genealogical manuscripts preserved in the British Museum, King's Inns (Dublin), Advocates (Edinburgh), Franciscan

Convent (Merchants' Quay, Dublin), the Royal Irish Academy, and Trinity College Library (Dublin).

ANALECTA HIBERNICA No. 8. 1938. This contains items such as the Ulster Plantation Papers, 1608-13, edited by Dr. T. W. Moody from a manuscript in the library of Trinity College, Dublin. It also contains the O'Clery MS. (23 D. 17, Royal Irish Academy), edited by the late Rev. Fr. Paul Walsh. This sets forth the O'Donnell Genealogies (13th-17th centuries).

ANALECTA HIBERNICA No. 9. 1940. Indexes to Numbers 6 and 8, prepared by Newport B. White.

ANALECTA HIBERNICA No. 10. 1941. In this number, among other records, is the contribution of the late Rev. Fr. Paul Walsh. He has transcribed the *Adams Rental* from the manuscript in the National Library, accompanied by nine maps which set forth the formation of a great post-Cromwellian estate in Co. Westmeath.

ANALECTA HIBERNICA No. 13, 1944. Index to Numbers 10 and 12, prepared by Newport B. White.

ANALECTA HIBERNICA No. 14. 1944. Dr. Edward MacLysaght, formerly Chief Herald of Ireland and, in 1957, Chairman of the Irish Manuscripts Commission, presents a calendar of important material for a diocesan history of the Co. Galway area, which is of value to genealogists interested in Galway.

ANALECTA HIBERNICA No. 16. 1946. Dr. R. C. Simington contributes a description of the Annesley collection, Castlewellan, Co. Down, which comprises a great many manuscript volumes. An important part of this collection, which was photographed by the National Library, is the set of Books of Survey and Distribution for all Irish counties, except one. Two Books of Survey and Distribution, for Counties Mayo and Roscommon, have been transcribed, edited and published by the Irish Manuscripts Commission. These are described among their published books, and their genealogical value which pertains to all such works, has been noted. Also, in the Annesley collection are the 1700-3

Proceedings of the Council of Trustees, appointed to dispose by sale of the estates [of Catholics] forfeited in 1688. These are set forth in thirty-two documents which include "Outlawrys", petitions, depositions, rent rolls, and accounts of valuations of estates with the names of former owners and purchasers. No duplicate of this series was in the Public Record Office, Dublin, before 1922. They contain much genealogical information.

ANALECTA HIBERNICA No. 17. 1949. This number should be in constant use by genealogists. It contains (pp. 149-348) the Index of the Will Abstracts in the Genealogical Office, Dublin, presented by Miss P. Beryl Eustace. Some 7,500 will abstracts are listed. The Index shows the name and address of each testator, the year of probate (almost entirely seventeenth and eighteenth century), description, by profession or rank, and a key to the manuscript collection in which the will abstract may be located. See VOLUME I, CHAPTER IV, for further details.

PART TWO

UNPUBLISHED FAMILY RECORDS

A SELECTED BIBLIOGRAPHY AND FAMILY INDEX OF GENEALOGY, FAMILY HISTORY, PEDIGREES, NOTES, AND COLLECTIONS OF FAMILY DOCUMENTS

CHAPTER I

MANUSCRIPTS IN THE PUBLIC RECORD OFFICE OF NORTHERN IRELAND*

Following is a family index to some important manuscripts deposited in the Public Record Office of Northern Ireland, located in the Law Courts Building, May Street, Belfast. Mr. Kenneth Darwin, M. A., is the Deputy Keeper of the Records. Included are pedigrees, family history, genealogical records, and collections of family documents.

This list has been compiled as a representative selection from the many thousands of records of a genealogical nature which are calendared in the *Reports of the Deputy Keeper of the Public Records of Northern Ireland,* 1924-53.** These *Reports* are, in fact, catalogues of a large part of the records in this office. They are fully described in VOLUME I, PART TWO, CHAPTER VI, which is devoted to the accession lists in the Public Record Office of Northern Ireland.

The manuscript records vary from a single pedigree, brief family history, genealogical chart, compiled genealogy, etc., to collections of a few or many wills, marriage records, deeds, leases and other classes of records which may be used for compiling genealogy.

Some of the largest collections in the Public Record Office of Northern Ireland represent the life work of a famous genealogist, the collections of legal or personal documents during many generations in a family, or the wills, marriage settlements, deeds, etc., accumulated over centuries in a solicitor's office. One fairly recent gift of records, which were original legal documents dating from the seventeenth century, weighed over two tons.

The very large collections are described in detail in the *Reports* and are self-indexed as the items are too numerous for inclusion in the name index of the *Reports.* These are noted by this compiler in VOLUME I, PART TWO, CHAPTER VI.

One of these collections comprises forty-two large volumes

*Now located at 66 Balmoral Avenue, Belfast BT9 6NY. The staff, of course, has changed since this book was first published.

**Three further *Deputy Keeper's Reports* have been published since Mrs. Falley's work first appeared.

of pedigree charts, copied by or for Sir Bernard Burke, from Sir William Betham's 39-volume collection which he made from his own abstracts of all the Prerogative Wills of Ireland, 1536-1800. One of Burke's volumes contains pedigree charts from Prerogative Grants of Administration, 1595-1800. These pedigree charts range in length from two to many generations. The longer charts have been compiled from more than one will in a family and, in some cases, from additional sources. Microfilms of Sir William Betham's collections are in the United States; see PART FOUR of this volume.

The family manuscript collections and documents in the Public Record Office of Northern Ireland largely concern those families which lived in one or more of the nine original counties of the Province of Ulster. However, there are some notable exceptions to this rule, as some large genealogical collections which have been acquired contain documents (transcripts or abstracts) concerning individuals or families of the southern counties of Ireland. The greater portion of the families of English or Scottish origin which settled in Ulster, came there in the seventeenth century. Many of the pedigrees, etc., listed below, trace these families to the places of their origin. There are, however, many families of ancient Gaelic or Norman origin, particularly in counties Donegal, Fermanagh, and Monaghan, which have been there since early times. There are also many families of this origin which settled in ancient times in one of the three southern provinces and then, during the late seventeenth or early eighteenth century, removed to one of the nine original counties of Ulster. Since 1922, three of these original counties of Ulster, namely, Cavan, Donegal, and Monaghan, have been embraced in the Republic of Ireland.

Each family listing will be followed by a date (year) and a page number in parentheses. These represent the year of the *Report of the Deputy Keeper of the Public Records of Northern Ireland*, and the page number of the printed index of the *Report* where the item is listed. These dates and page numbers are for the convenience of the person who may wish to order photostats or copies of the records. Thus, in giving the order, one can signify where the item is calendared in a specific *Report*, and so identify the desired record. For further instructions regarding the ordering of records and the price lists, see VOLUME I, PART TWO, CHAPTER VI, concerning this repository. Let us suppose that a genealogist wishes to order the first item listed by requesting a photostatic copy of the "Acheson Family Pedigree and Notes, 1692-1938. (1938-45, p. 15.)" In sending the order, he will give the title of the manuscript and, for identification, will state that it is listed in the *Report of the Deputy Keeper of the Public Records of Northern Ireland,* 1938-1945, on page 15. A money* order for $6.00 is now required as a registration fee and deposit. An estimate of any additional charges for the photostating should be requested. These charges are reasonable.

* * * * *

ACHESON. Acheson Family Pedigree and Notes, 1692-1838. (1938-45, p. 15.)

ADAIR. Adair Family of Kilhilt, Ballymena, County Antrim and Wigtonshire; Genealogical Notes, 1626-1655. (1946-47, p. 14.)

ADAIR. Pedigrees of the Allen and Adair Families, 1616-1934. (1935, p. 8.)

ADAIR. Adair Family of Loughanmore, County Antrim. Pedigree, 1685-1931. (1935, p. 27.)

ADAMS. Adams Family (Quaker Records), County Armagh, 1695-1800. (1951-53, p. 30.)

AGNEW. Agnew Family (Quaker Records), Counties Antrim and Armagh, 1676-1730. (1951-53, p. 31.)

AGNEW. Agnew Family, County Down, 1536-1799; Notes of Prerogative and Down Wills, Grants, Administration Bonds. (1924, p. 10.)

AGNEW. Agnew Documents; 161 documents, leases, testamentary papers, etc., 1637-1903 (principal names: Agnew, Donaldson, Hamilton, Moore). (1929, p. 10.)

AGNEW. Agnew, Blair, Daly, McCulloch, Shaw; 71 documents, 1692-1908. (1929, p. 10.)

*Orders are now quoted for when they have been assessed. A registration fee of $20.00 is required for a genealogical search, providing the search is accepted by the Ulster Historical Foundation.

AGNEW. Agnew, Andrew (s), Brown, Graham, Law, McCammon, McCance, Napier, Neeper, Stephenson, Watson, Wilson documents; Down Wills, Grants of Administration; 111 copies or abstracts, 1718-1830. (Crosslé Mss.) (1925 p. 8.)

AIKEN. Aiken, Bird, Campbell, Johnston; 56 Bonds, Conveyances, Grants of Probate, Leases, Marriage Settlements, etc., 1738-1917, from County Fermanagh. (1928, p. 8.)

ALDWORTH. Aldworth Family Pedigree, Extract, 1617-1674. (1949-50, p. 20.)

ALEXANDER. Alexander Family, County Tyrone, Genealogical Chart, 1688-1800. (1951-53, p. 31.)

ALEXANDER. Family of James Alexander, Sizehill, County Antrim, 1708-1769 (McKinney Note Book). (1949-50, p. 21.)

ALEXANDER. Alexander Family Pedigree, 1618-1859. From County Fermanagh. (1933, p. 10.)

ALLEN. Allen Family (Quaker Records), 1698-1800, County Armagh. (1951-53, p. 32.)

ALLEN. Allen Family History, of Lisconnan, County Antrim. Pedigree of the Allen and Adair Families, 1616-1934; 72 Documents, Leases, Wills, Chancery Decrees, etc. (1935, p. 8.)

ANDERSON. Anderson, Barklie, Baxter, Boyd, Carothers, Cox, Crookshank, Galt, McElfatrick, McPhall, Wilson, 25 documents, affidavits, leases, wills, etc., 1789-1911. (1951-53, p. 18.)

ANDERSON. Anderson, Andrews, Davidson, McMurray, Young Genealogical Notes—extracts from Wills, Chancery and Exchequer Bills, 1671-1858. (Crosslé Mss.) (1937, p. 8.)

ANDERSON. Anderson Family (Quaker Records), Counties Armagh, Down, Tyrone, pre-1634—*ca.* 1775. (1951-53, p. 33.)

ANDERSON. Connor Wills and Grants of Administration; 168 copies or abstracts for Anderson, Andrews, Cunningham, Finlay, Hayes, Law, McCammon, McCance, McClelland, Mulligan, Russel, Stinson, Stouppe, Watson, Wilson, 1672-1847. (Crosslé Mss.) (1925, p. 8.)

ANDREWS. Prerogative Wills, Grants of Administration; 107 copies or abstracts, for Andrews, Charley, Law, McCammon, McCance, Murray, Stephenson, Stouppe, Watson, Wilson, 1668-1855. (Crosslé Mss.) (1925, p. 7.)

ANDREWS. Andrews Family (Quaker Records), Counties Armagh and Antrim, 1711-1782. (1951-53, p. 33.)

ANDREWS. See Anderson and other family documents, 1672-1847. (1925, p. 8.)

ANDREWS. See Anderson and other family documents, 1671-1858. (1937, p. 8.)

ANDREWS. See Agnew and other family documents, 1718-1830. (1925, p. 8.)

ANDREWS. Dromore Wills, Grants, etc., 129 copies or abstracts for Andrew(s), Blizard, Law, McCance, Murray, Wallace, Waterson, Watson, 1728-1852. (Crosslé Mss.) (1925, p. 8.)

ANTRIM. Antrim Family Papers. (1925, pp. 16, 17; 1928, p. 13.)

ARCHDALE. Archdale Family Papers, County Fermanagh, 1537-1909. Wills, Grants, Parish Records and Family Notes, Counties Armagh and Londonderry, 1729-1864; principal names included: Archdale, Blackwood, Blennerhassett, Dobson, Dunbar, Humphrys, Mervyn, Montgomery, Price, Sexton. (1927, pp. 4, 8, 24.)

ARCHDALE, ARCHDALL, ARCHDAELLE. Archdall (Archdaelle) Family, County Fermanagh Pedigree, 1451-1821. (1951-53, p. 34.)

ARDKEEN. Ardkeen, Savage Family of County Down, Pedigree; Memo, 1197-1800. (1951-53, p. 34.)

ARMSTRONG. Armstrong Family Genealogical Notes and Registry of Deeds extracts, 1700-1800. Also Armstrong Family (Quaker Records), 1695-1772. (1951-53, p. 35.)

ARMSTRONG. Genealogical Notes on the Armstrong Family, extracted from Bible dated 1716. Also Wills, etc., 1628-1816; 38 documents, Savage-Armstrong. (1951-53, p. 17.)

ARMSTRONG. 196 Prerogative and Principal Registry (Dublin) Wills and Grants; principal names included: Armstrong, Beatty, Corry, Cuppage, Fleming, Hamilton, Higinbothem, Johnston, Knipe, Nixon, Noble, Ovens, Richardson, Rogers, Spencer, Stamford, Swanzy, Vincent, Young; all in Counties Cavan, Armagh, Monaghan, Fermanagh, 1666-1859. (1924, p. 10.)

ARMSTRONG. 38 Kilmore Wills, Marriage Licences; principal names included: Armstrong, Beatty, Burroughs, Harmon, Nixon, Young, 1694-1806. (Swanzy Mss.) (1924, p. 10.)

ARMSTRONG. Armstrong, Burns, Cole, Trotter, Vaughan, Wills and Leases, County Fermanagh, 1731-1878. (1927, p. 8.)

ARUNDELL. Abstracts of Wills, Bonds, Marriage Licences for Arundell, Babington, Best, Ecles, Leslie, Madden, Paterson, Stewart, Walsh, Wray, Wilkin, from County Fermanagh, 1646-1846. (1926, p. 9.)

ASH. History of the Ash Family of County Londonderry, *ca.* 1671-1735. (1948, p. 21.)

ATKINSON. Atkinson Family (Quaker Records), Counties Armagh and Tyrone, dated between 1680-1784. (1951-53, p. 37.)

ATKINSON. Atkinson Family, Mullartown, County Down; Pedigree dated 1730. (1934, p. 28.)

ATKINSON. Note Book containing Will extracts, etc., 1722-1824. (Crosslé Mss.) (1933, p. 27.)

AUCHMUTY. Auchmuty Family Genealogical memorandum 1600-1800. (1951-53, p. 38.)

AULD. Auld Family of Ballyhone, County Antrim, pre-1776-1892. (1949-50, p. 26.)

BABINGTON. See Arundell and other family documents, 1646-1846. (1926, p. 9.)

BACON. The Bacon Family, County Londonderry, Genealogical Notes, *ca.* 1684-1792. (1951-53, p. 38.)

BACON. Bacon, Lane, Sterling, Suxberry; extracts from Prerogative and Diocesan Wills, 1623-1943. (1949-50, p. 5.)

BA(E)C(K)HOUS(E). Ba(e)c(k)hous(e) Family Quaker Records, dated between 1718-1763. (1951-53, p. 38.)

BAILIE. Family of Bailie; Note Book containing Will extracts, etc., 1696-1815. (Crosslé Mss.) (1933, p. 27.)

BAILEY, BAILLIE. Family of Hugh and Jane (Simpson) Bailey (Baillie), Carnmoney Parish, County Antrim, 1767-1806. (McKinney Note Book.) (1949-50, p. 26.)

BAILLIE. Baillie Family Genealogical Notes, *ca.* 1600-1800. (1951-53, p. 39.)

BAIRD. See Baskerville. (1931, p. 15.)

BAKER. Baker Family Genealogical Notes, *ca.* 1600-1800. (1951-53, p. 39.)

BALL(A)ENTINE. Ball(a)entine Family (Quaker Records), dated between 1698-1788. (1951-53, p. 40.)

BARCLAY. Barclay Family, Ardrossan, Scotland, Genealogical Notes, *ca.* 1100-1800. (1951-53, p. 41.)

BARKLIE. See Anderson, etc., documents, 1789-1911.

BARQUHOIS or BARCOSH. Barquhois or Barcosh Genealogical Notes, 1100-1800. (1951-53, p. 42.)

BARTON. Barton, Jackson, Ogle family documents, 1612-1860; 22 documents, Wills, Patent Grant, Leases, Rentals. (1930, p. 10.)

BARTON. Barton, Jackson, Noell, Ogle family documents, 1611-1867; 145 documents, Assignments, Leases, Rentals. (1930, p. 9.)

BASKERVILLE. Genealogical Tables and Notes on the families of Baskerville, Sproulle, Crowther, Bowden, Maginniss, Holmes, Baird, Cuthbert, Davenport, Perrott. (1931, p. 15.)

BATT. Notes on the Families of Holmes and Batt, 1622-1859. (1951-53, p. 19.)

BAXTER. See Anderson, etc., documents, 1789-1911.

BEATTY. See Armstrong and other family records, 1694-1806. (1924, p. 10.)

BEATY. See Armstrong and other family documents, 1666-1859. (1924, p. 10.)

BECK. Beck Family Pedigree, 1630-1930. (1930, p. 26.)

BECK. Beck Family Pedigree, 1783-1842; also 18 documents, Assignments, Bonds, Leases. (1930, p. 10.)

BECK. Beck, Bullick, Bullock family documents; Abstracts of Wills, Census Returns, Freeholders Registers, Parish Registers, etc., 1514-1902. (1928, pp. 9, 31.)

BECKER. Becker Family Genealogical Notes, *ca.* 1600-1800. (1951-53, p. 44.)

BELL. Bell Family Genealogical Notes, *ca.* 1600-1800. (1951-53, p. 45.)

BELL. Bell Family Historical Sketch; also many documents, 17th-18th Centuries. (1926, p. 12.)

BELLEW. Bellew Family Pedigree. (1951-53, p. 46.)

BELLINGHAM. Bellingham Family Genealogical Notes, *ca.* 1600-1800. (1951-53, p. 46.)

BELMORE. Belmore Family, Enniskillen, County Fermanagh; Genealogical Notes, *ca.* 1600-1800. (1951-53, p. 47.)

BENSON. Benson Family Genealogical Notes, *ca.* 1600-1800. (1951-53, p. 47.)

BENSON. Benson, Rogers; copies of Down and Connor Wills, 1741-1811. (1926, p. 9.)

BERESFORD. Beresford Family Genealogies; fragmentary, with map of Walworth Manor, County Londonderry, 1732. (1936-45, p. 13.)

BERESFORD. Beresford Family Notes on births and marriages, of Walworth and Learmount, County Londonderry (Family Bible entries), 1812-1886. (1938-45, p. 18.)

BERKELEY. Genealogical extracts; Berkeley and Dawson families, 18th Century. (1951-53, p. 47.)

BERRY. Berry Families, King's County, Cavan, Westmeath, etc.; genealogical notes, Irish Newspaper extracts, 1664-1800. (1951-53, p. 48.)

BEST. See Arundell and other family documents, 1646-1846. (1926, p. 9.)

BICKERTON. Bickerton Family Notes, *ca.* 1600-1800. (1951-53, p. 50.)

BIGGER. Bigger Family of Mallusk, County Antrim, Family Records, 1687-1796. (1949-50, p. 35.)

BIGGER. Bigger Family Records, 1687-1853. (1949-50, p. 351.)

BIRD. Bird Family Genealogical Notes, *ca.* 1600-1800. (1951-53, p. 50.)

BIRD. See Aiken and other family documents, 1738-1917. (1928, p. 8.)

BLACK. Black Family, Belfast and Bordeaux; Arms, Motto, Seal of; Genealogical Notes, 1716-1800. (1951-53, p. 51.)

BLACKWOOD. Blackwood Family Genealogical Tree, 1663-1910. (1948, p. 28.)

BLACKWOOD. Blackwood Pedigree, 1663-1910. (1938-45, p. 19.)

BLACKWOOD. Short Account of the Family of Blackwood, 1703-1830. (1927, p. 29.)

BLACKWOOD. See Archdale documents, 1729-1864. (1927, p. 8.)

BLAIR. See Agnew and other family documents, 1692-1908. (1929, p. 10.)

BLENNERHASSETT. Short Account of the Family of Blennerhasset, 1611-1663. (1927, p. 29.)

BLENNERHASSETT. See Archdale documents, 1729-1864. (1927, p. 8.)

BLIZARD. See Andrews and other family documents, 1728-1852. (1925, p. 8.)

BOLTON. Bolton Family of County Londonderry, County Antrim and U. S. A. Copy of Testamentary Papers, 1604-1821. (1926, p. 8.)

BOLTON. Bolton of Knock, County Louth; Massereene Papers. (1949-50, p. 14.)

BOND. The Bond Family Pedigree, of County Armagh, extracted from Chancery Bill, 1763. (1948, p. 29.)

BOOTH. Booth Family Genealogical Notes, 1600-1800. (1951-53, p. 53.)

BOURNE. References to Bourne families, extracts from Irish newspapers, 1742-1800. (1951-53, p. 54.)

BOWDEN. See Baskerville. (1931, p. 15.)

BOYD. See Anderson, etc., documents, 1789-1911.

BOYD. Boyd family of Ballycastle, County Antrim, 1700-1850; from letter, 1859; Rev. George Hill to Mrs. Boyd. (1938-45, p. 13.)

BOYD. Families of Boyd, Bruce, Hamilton, Hutcheson, Hutchinson, McRobert, Nevin, Price, Savage, Walker, Wallace, Weld, 1660-1811; 87 abstracts of Prerogative Wills; 28 abstracts of Down Wills. (1926, p. 9.)

BOYDE. Boyde Family Genealogical Notes; extracts from the Registry of Deeds. (1951-53, p. 55.)

BRABAZON. Brabazon Family Genealogical Notes, 1600-1800. (1951-53, p. 56.)

BRADSHAW. Bradshaw Families (Quaker Records), County Armagh, dated between 1619-1782. Also Bradshaw Family Genealogical Notes, 1600-1800. (1951-53, p. 57.)

BRADY. Brady Family (Quaker Records), County Antrim, dated between 1695-1784. (1951-53, p. 57.)

BRASSINGTON. Brassington Family Genealogical Notes, 1600-1800. (1951-53, p. 58.)

BREDEN. Breden Family Genealogical Notes, 1600-1800. (1951-53, p. 58.)

BRISTOW. Bristow Family Genealogical Notes, 1600-1800. (1951-53, p. 58.)

BROAD-STAINE. Broad-Staine Family Genealogical Notes, 1100-. (1951-53, p. 59.)

BROWN. Brown Family (Quaker Records), County Armagh, dated between 1691-1773. (1951-53, p. 60.)

BROWN. See Agnew and other family documents, 1718-1830. (1925, p. 8.)

BRUCE. See Boyd and other family documents, 1660-1811. (1926, p. 9.)

BRUNKER. Brunker Family Genealogical Notes, 1600-1800. (1951-53, p. 61.)

BULLOCK. Bullock Family (Quaker Records), County Armagh, dated between 1661-1797. (1951-53, p. 62.)

BULLOCK, BULLICK. See Beck family documents, 1514-1902. (1928, p. 36.)

BULLOCK, BULLICK. See Beck family documents, 1514-1902. Wills, Leases, Bonds, etc. (1928, pp. 9, 10.)

BULTEEL. Bulteel Family Genealogical Notes, *ca.* 1600-1800. (1951-53, p. 63.)

BURGOYNE. Notes on the Burgoyne Family of County Tyrone, *ca.* 1775- *ca.* 1924.

BURGOYNE. Burgoyne Genealogy, 1755-1800. (Chesney Diary.) (1951-53, p. 63.)

BURNS. See Armstrong documents, 1731-1878. (1927, p. 24.)

BURROUGHS. See Armstrong and other families, 1694-1806. (1924, p. 10.)

BURROWES. Burrowes Family Genealogical Notes *ca.* 1600-1800. (1951-53, p. 64.)

BURY. Bury Families; Irish Newspaper Extracts, 1731-1800. (1951-53, p. 64.)

BUTLER. Butler Family, Counties Meath and Kerry; Genealogical Notes. (1951-53, p. 65.)

CALDWELL. Notes on the families of Caldwell, Despard, King, Harkness, McCulloch, Sanderson, Twigg, 17th-19th Centuries. (1951-53, p. 18.)

CALDWELL. See Elizabeth Sproule, wife of Matthew Caldwell. (1951-53, p. 10.)

CALVERT. Calvert Family (Quaker Records), County Armagh, dated between 1648-1787. (1951-53, p. 66.)

CAMPBELL. See Aiken and other family documents, 1738-1917. (1928, p. 8.)

CARLILE. Carlile Pedigree of Ashgrove, County Armagh, 1699-1925; from Curator of the County Museum, Armagh. (1936, p. 8.)

CARLOW. Carlow Family Genealogical Notes, *ca.* 1600-1800. (1951-53, p. 69.)

CARMICHAEL - CARMICHAILLE. Carmichael - Carmichaille Family, Irish Newspaper extracts, 1758-1800. Also Quaker Records, County Armagh, 1734-1776. (1951-53, p. 69.)

CAROTHERS. See Anderson, etc., documents, 1789-1911.

CARSON. The Carsons of Monanton, Ballybay, County Monaghan. By James Carson, Springfield, County Down, 1907. (1931, p. 15.)

CARY. Cary Family, Dungiven, County Londonderry, Pedigree. n. d. (1951-53, p. 71.)

CATHCART. Cathcart, Corry, Crawford, Dane, Hamilton, Leslie families of Counties Monaghan, Fermanagh and Tyrone; 90 copies and extracts of Prerogative and Clogher Diocesan Wills and Administrations, 1624-1830. (1927, p. 7.)

CAULFIELD. Caulfield Genealogical Extracts, *ca.* 1604-1725. (1951-53, p. 72.)

CECIL. William Cecil, Lord Burghley, Genealogical Notes, *ca.* 1500-1800. (1951-53, p. 72.)

CHAMBERS. Chambers Family (Quaker Records), County Armagh, dated between 1646-1793. Also Chambre Family, 1792-1800; Irish Newspaper extracts. (1951-53, p. 72.)

CHAPMAN. Chapman Family (Quaker Records), County Armagh, dated between 1685-1789. (1951-53, p. 73.)

CHARLEY. See Andrews and other family documents, 1668-1855. (1925, p. 8.)

CHERRY. Cherry Family (Quaker Records), County Armagh, dated between 1685-1787; County Down, dated between 1685-1756. (1951-53, p. 73.)

CHESNEY. Chesney Family, Counties Antrim, Down, and South Carolina; Pedigree, 1641-1800. (Chesney Diary.) (1951-53, p. 74.)

CHESNEY. Chesney Family Memoirs. (1935, p. 19.)

CHETWODE. Chetwode, Langtry, Waddell Families, etc., Pedigrees and Notes, 1222-1878. (1938-45, p. 17.)

CHRISTY. Christy Family (Quaker Records), County Down, dated between 1674-1809; 1682-1800. Also in County Armagh, dated between 1685-1800. (1951-53, p. 74.)

CHUTE. Chute Family, County Kerry, Genealogical Notes. (1951-53, p. 75.)

CLARKE. Clarke Family Genealogical Notes, 1600-1800. Also Quaker Records, County Antrim, dated between 1690-1789; County Armagh, dated between 1700-1746. (1951-53, p. 75.)

CLELAND. Cleland, Digby, Graham, Gribben, King, McParlon, Molyneaux, Stanley, Thompson families; 46 documents, County Tyrone, emigration list, rentals, will, 1682-1905. (1951-53, p. 16.)

CLEMENTS. Clements Family Genealogical Notes. n. d. (1951-53, p. 76.)

COANE. Coane Family Genealogical Notes, *ca.* 1600-1800. (1951-53, p. 78.)

COLE. See Armstrong documents, 1731-1878. (1927, p. 24.)

COLLEY. Colley or Cowley Family Pedigree, 1460-1880. (1934, p. 9.)

COLVILL. Colvill, Graham, Kennedy, Moffett, O'Donnell, Osborne, Speer family records, 1603-1870; abstracts of Prerogative Wills, Diocesan Wills of Armagh, Connor, Derry, Down, Raphoe, etc.; abstracts of Parish Records, and Deeds, Census Records, etc., all extensive family notes from original records. (1927, pp. 4, 8.)

COLVIN. Colvin Family (Quaker Records), County Armagh, dated between 1714-1800. (1951-53, p. 79.)

CONNELL. Connell Family, Castle Lyons, County Cork; Genealogical Notes. (1951-53, p. 80.)

CONYNGHAM - LENOX. Lenox - Conyngham Family, County Fermanagh, Papers, Part I, 1630-1759 (1927, p. 25); 1722-1739 (1926, p. 20); 1719-1852 (1929, p. 17).

COOKE. Cooke Family (Quaker Records), County Armagh, dated between 1698-1788. Also records of Cooke family to Pennsylvania and South Carolina, 1755-1800 (Chesney Diary). (1951-53, p. 82.)

COOPER. Cooper Family (Quaker Records), County Armagh, dated between 1674-1785. (1951-53, p. 82.)

COPE. Cope Family (Quaker Records), County Armagh, dated between 1692-1758. (1951-53, p. 82.)

COPELAND, COPLAND. Copeland, Copland Family Genealogical Notes, *ca.* 1600-1800. (1951-53, p. 82.)

CORRY. Corry Family, Rockcorry, County Monaghan and Newry, County Down; Genealogical Notes. (1951-53, p. 84.)

CORRY. See Armstrong and other family documents, 1666-1859. (1924, p. 10.)

CORRY. See Cathcart and other family documents, 1624-1830. (1927, p. 7.)

COURTENAY. Pedigree of Courtenay and Parsons Families, 1689-1873. (1935, p. 8.)

COURTENAY. Family of Courtenay; Note Book containing Wills Extracts, etc., 1640-1825. (Crosslé Mss.) (1933, p. 34.)

COURTNEY. Courtney Family (Quaker Records), County Armagh, dated between 1687-1800; County Tyrone, dated between 1702-1778; County Down, dated between 1722-1778. (1951-53, pp. 84, 85.)

COX. See Anderson and other family documents, 1789-1911. (1951-53, p. 18.)

CRAWFORD. See Cathcart and other family documents, 1624-1830. (1927, p. 7.)

CRAWFORD. The Rev. Thomas and Janet (Stewart) Crawford, Family of, Ayreshire, Scotland and Donegore, County Antrim, 1625-1703 (McKinney Note Book). (1949-50, p. 70.)

CRAWFORD. The Rev. Andrew Crawford, Family of, Carnmoney, County Antrim, 1696-1790 (McKinney Note Book). (1949-50, p. 69.)

CROOKSHANK. See Anderson, etc., documents, 1789-1911.

CROW, CROWE. Crow or Crowe Family Genealogical Notes, Prerogative Will extracts, etc., 1515-1726. Also the Crowe or Crow families of King's and Galway Counties, Genealogical Notes, 1582-1800. (1951-53, p. 88.)

CROWTHER. See Baskerville. (1931, p. 15.)

CROZIER. Crozier, Forster, Hassard, Johnston, Nixon, Noble, Thompson family records; 63 Clogher Wills, Grants, and Marriage Licences, 1697-1832. (Swanzy Mss.) (1924, p. 10.)

CUNINGHAM, CUNNINGHAM. Cunningham, Drennan, Duffin, Grimshaw, Hincks, Johnston, Swanwick, Taylor, Yardell families; 55 documents, including pedigrees and genealogical notes, letters, wills, etc., *ca.* 1600-1935. (1951-53, p. 19.)

CUNNINGHAM, CUNINGHAM. Cuningham Family of Aughlyard, County Donegal, genealogy, 1100-1800. (1951-53, pp. 10, 90.)

CUNNINGHAM. The Cunningham Family in Scotland and Ireland, 1609-1697; includes notes from Scottish Record Office, 1609-1697; also includes Pedigree of the Family of Counties Armagh and Down, with notes, 1690-1896. (1932, pp. 8, 25.)

CUNNINGHAM. See Anderson and other family documents, 1672-1847. (1925, p. 8.)

CUNNINGHAM. Descendants of Robert Cunningham (Ms., 1917.) (1933, p. 15.)

CUPPAGE. See Armstrong and other family documents, 1666-1859. (1924, p. 10.)

CUPPAIGE, CUPPAIDGE. Cuppaige, Cuppaidge Family Genealogical Notes, n. d. (1951-53, p. 90.)

CUTHBERT. See Baskerville. (1931, p. 15.)

DALY. See Agnew and other family documents, 1692-1908. (1929, p. 10.)

DANCY. Dancy Family Genealogical Notes, *ca.* 1600-1800. (1951-53, p. 92.)

DANE. See Cathcart and other family documents, 1624-1830. (1927, p. 7.)

DANIEL. Daniel Family (Quaker Records), County Armagh, dated between 1682-1797. (1951-53, p. 92.)

DARLEY. George Darley, Pedigree and Descendants of, 1730-1820. (1926, p. 31.)

DAVENPORT. Davenport Family Genealogical Notes, *ca.* 1600-1800. (1951-53, p. 92.)

DAVENPORT. See Baskerville. (1931, p. 15.)

DAVIDSON. Davidson Family, Killyleagh, County Down, Pedigree, *ca.* 1660-1866. (1938-45, p. 47.)

DAVIDSON. See Anderson and other family documents, 1671-1858. (1937, p. 8.)

DAVIDSON. Davidson, Frackleton, McCreery, Stannus Genealogies; 8 documents, 17th Century to 1930. (1938-45, p. 16.)

DAVIS. Davis Family, County Cork, Genealogical Notes. (1951-53, p. 93.)

DAVIS. Davis Family (Quaker Records), County Armagh, dated between 1771-1800. (1951-53, p. 93.)

DAWSON. Dawson Family of Bellaghy, County Londonderry, Genealogical Notes, (Castledawson), 1170-1800. (1951-53, p. 93.)

DAWSON. Dawson Family (Quaker Records), County Armagh, also Counties Cavan and Tyrone, etc., dated between 1695-1800. (1951-53, p. 93.)

DAWSON. See Berkeley. (1951-53, p. 47.)

DEACON. Deacon or Deighan, Family of, County Armagh, Genealogical Notes, 1641-1850. (1949-50, p. 75.)

DEACON. Deacon, Dobbin, Gillespie, King, mainly of County Armagh; genealogical notes, *ca.* 1664-1850. (1938-45, p. 15.)

DEAN, DEANE. Dean or Deane Family (Quaker Records), County Antrim, dated between 1713-1759; County Armagh, dated between 1701-1787. (1951-53, p. 94.)

DEBARKLEY. DeBarkley Family of Ardrossan, Ayr; Genealogical Notes, 1100-1800. (1951-53, p. 94.)

DELAFIELD. Delafield Family, Irish Rolls, from Medieval Times. (1924, p. 54; 1934, pp. 5, 17.)

DELAFIELD. Delafield Family History. (1946-47, p. 9.)

DELAP. Delap Family, County Tyrone (Quaker Records), dated between 1700-1784; County Armagh, dated between 1690-1782. (1951-53, p. 95.)

DELIUS. Delius Family, Westphalia, Germany, pedigrees, *ca.* 1600-1800. (1951-53, p. 95.)

DEMONTGOMERY. DeMontgomery Genealogical Notes, A. D. 900-1800. (1951-53, p. 95.)

DENEGRIS. DeNegris, Francis, Genealogical Notes, 1600-1800. (1951-53, p. 95.)

DESPARD. Despard Family Genealogical Notes, *ca.* 1600-1800. (1951-53, pp. 18, 96.)

DICKSON, DIX(S)ON. Dickson, Dixson, Dixon, Family (Quaker Records), County Armagh, dated between 1671-1793; County Down, dated between 1698-1781; County Londonderry, 1763. (1951-53, pp. 96, 97.)

DIGBY. See Cleland and other family documents, 1682-1905. (1951-53, p. 16.)

DILL. Dill Family History; Notes on; 1668-1924. (1932, p. 8.)

DILLON. Dillon Family Genealogical Notes, 1600-1800. (1951-53, p. 97.)

DILLON. Dillon, Viscounts of, Pedigree, dated 1912.

DOBBIN. Family of Dobbin, Counties Armagh and Down, Genealogical Notes, 1673-1900. (1949-50, p. 78.)

DOBBIN. See Deacon, 1664-1850. (1938-45, p. 15.)

DOBBIN. Dobbin Family of Carrickfergus, County Antrim and elsewhere; Memoir, 17th-19th Centuries; much biographical detail; includes allied families of Reynell, Edgar, and Kane. (1926, pp. 9, 25.)

DOBBS. Dobbs Family of Carrickfergus, County Antrim, Genealogical Notes, *ca.* 1600-1800. (1951-53, p. 98.)

DOBBS. Dobbs Family (Quaker Records), County Armagh, dated between 1687-1734. (1951-53, p. 98.)

DOBBS. Dobbs Family Papers; Correspondence of Arthur Dobbs, Governor of North Carolina, 1694-1775. (1925, p. 13; 1927, p. 17; 1936, p. 23.)

DOBSON. Short account of the family of Dobson, 1689. (1927, p. 35.)

DOBSON. See Archdale documents, 1729-1864. (1927, p. 8.)

DONALDSON. See Agnew and other family documents, 1637-1903. (1929, p. 10.)

DOUGLAS. Family (Quaker Records). For the following counties and between dates of: Armagh, 1714-1797; Tyrone, 1723-1800; Cavan, 1739-1797; Antrim, 1766-1774. (1951-53, p. 100.)

DOUGLASS. See Hazelton and other family documents, 1802-1851. (1951-53, p. 13.)

DOWNING. Squire Downing, Bellaghy, County Londonderry, Pedigree, date, *ca.* 1800. 1951-53, p. 101.)

DOWSE. Dowse Family History. (1927, p. 10.)

DRENNAN. Drennan and McTier Families, Belfast; Notes regarding, 1672-1879. (1929, pp. 10, 28.)

DRENNAN. Drennan Family Deeds, 1726-1886. (1928, p. 8.)

DRENNAN. See Cunningham, (Cuningham) and other family pedigrees, *ca.* 1600-1935. (1951-53, p. 19.)

DRENNAN. William Drennan Family Letters, 1775-1819. (1928, p. 9.)

DROPE. Drope Family Genealogical Notes, *ca.* 1600-1800. (1951-53, p. 102.)

DROUGHT. Drought Family Documents; 63 documents, Prerogative and Connor Diocesan Will extracts, also Pedigree, 1683-1904. (1938-45, p. 15.)

DRUIT. Druit or Druitt Family (Quaker Records), County Armagh, 1743-1800. (1951-53, p. 102.)

DRURY. Drury Family Pedigree, 1535-1922; including allied families of Girdwood, Macoubry, Mahony. (1932, p. 9.)

DUFFIN. Duffin Family Connections, 1794-1852; 13 documents, Wills, Letters, Notes. (1936, p. 9.)

DUFFIN. See Cuningham Pedigree, etc., 1600-1935. (1951-53, p. 19.)

DUNBAR. Dunbar Family, County Fermanagh, Genealogical Notes, *ca.* 1615-1722. (1951-53, p. 103.)

DUNBAR. Dunbar Family Genealogical Extracts from Chancery Bill, A. D. 900-1870. (1951-53, p. 103.)

DUNBAR. Dunbar Family (Quaker Records), County Armagh, dated between 1684-1710. (1951-53, p. 103.)

DUNBAR. Dunbar Family, Cumnok, Ayrshire, Register of Acts and Decreets Search, 1602-1654. (1951-53, p. 103.)

DUNBAR. Short Account of the Dunbar Family, 1680-1858. (1927, p. 36.)

DUNBAR. See Archdale and other family documents, 1729-1864. (1927, p. 8.)

DUNGANNON. Pedigree of the Dungannon Family, *ca.* 1630-1894.

EAMES. Eames Family Genealogical Notes, *ca.* 1600-1800. (1951-53, p. 105.)

ECHLIN. Echlin Family, Fifeshire, Genealogical Notes, 1100-1800. (1951-53, p. 106.)

ECLES. See Arundell and other family documents, 1646-1846. (1926, p. 9.)

EDGAR. See Dobbin Family Memoir, 17th-19th Centuries. (1926, pp. 9, 25.)

EDMONDSTONE. Edmonstone Family, Red Hall, County Antrim; Letters, Deeds, 1769-1780; Rent Roll, 1777. (1927, p. 6.)

EDWARDS. Hugh Edwards Pedigree, Londonderry, 1640-1881. (1936, p. 9.)

EGLINTO(W)N(E). Eglinto(w)n(e) Family Genealogical Notes, *ca.* 1066-1800. (1951-53, p. 106.)

ELDER. Andrew Elder of Roughan, County Donegal, Pedigree, 18th-19th Centuries. (1951-53, pp. 10, 107.)

ELLIS. Ellis Family Genealogical Notes. (1951-53, p. 107.)

ELMLEY. Elmley, Worcestershire, Savage, Family of. Pedigree. 1545-1766. (1951-53, p. 107.)

EMISON. The Emison Families. With partial genealogies of collateral families. Indiana, 1947. (1946-47, p. 9.)

ERWIN. Erwin Family (Quaker Records), County Antrim, dated between 1675-1758. (1951-53, pp. 108, 109.)

EVANS. Evans, Glen, Hearn, Hillis, Houston, James, Kisby, Lyttle, Moore, French, Wilson; extracts from Wills, Administrations, etc., 1620-1856. (1926, p. 9.)

EVANSON. Evanson Family Genealogical Notes. (1951-53, p. 109.)

EWARTS. Ewarts of Northern Ireland; Genealogical Table, 1716-1928. (1930, p. 10.)

FARIS. Faris Family Genealogical Notes, *ca.* 1600-1800. (1951-53, p. 110.)

FAWCET(T). Fawcet(t) Family (Quaker Records), County Antrim, dated between 1695-1777; County Armagh, dated between 1682-1731. (1951-53, p. 111.)

FELLENBERG. Fellenberg Family Genealogical Notes, 1100-1800. (1951-53, p. 111.)

FERRARD. See Massereene and Ferrard Family and State Papers, 1539-1822. (1926, p. 8.)

FETHERSTONE. Fetherstone Family; Irish Newspaper Extracts, 1731-1800. (1951-53, p. 113.)

FINLAY. See Anderson and other family documents, 1672-1847. (1925, p. 8.)

FINNIS. Finnis Family Genealogical Notes, ca. 1600-1800. (1951-53, p. 113.)

FISHER. Fisher Family (Quaker Records), County Armagh, dated between 1678-1732. (1951-53, p. 114.)

FITCH. Fitch Family Genealogical Notes, *ca.* 1600-1800. (1951-53, p. 114.)

FLEETWOOD. Fleetwood Family. Irish Newspaper extracts, 1757-1800. (1951-53, p. 115.)

FLEMING. See Armstrong and other family documents, 1666-1859. (1924, p. 10.)

FLEMMING, FLEMENG. Flemming, Flemeng Family Pedigree, Genealogical Notes, 1518-1708. (1951-53, p. 115.)

FLETCHER. Fletcher Family (Quaker Records). For the following counties and between dates of: Antrim, 1693-1732; Armagh, 1696-1786; Down, 1715-1786; Tyrone, 1713-1800. (1951-53, pp. 115, 116.)

FOLVIL. Folvil Family Genealogical Notes. *ca.* 1600-1800. (1951-53, p. 116.)

FORBES. Forbes Family (Quaker Records), County Antrim, dated between 1703-1754; County Armagh, 1720-1788. (1951-53, p. 116.)

FORD(E). Ford(e) Family (Quaker Records), County Armagh, dated between 1739-1767; County Tyrone, 1685-1741. (1951-53, p. 117.)

FORSTER. Forster Family, Tullaghan, County Monaghan, Genealogical Notes, 1451-1800. (1951-53, p. 117.)

FORSTER. See Crozier and other family documents, 1697-1832. (1924, p. 10.)

FORSYTH(E). Forsyth(e) Family of Artikelly, County Londonderry, Genealogical Notes, 1686-1800. (1951-53, p. 117.)

FORSYTH(E). Forsyth(e) Family; Irish Newspaper extracts, 1738-1800. (1951-53, p. 117.)

FORSYTH(E). Forsyth(e) Family of Lurgan, County Armagh (Quaker Records) dated between 1752-1791. (1951-53, p. 117.)

FOS(S)TER. Fos(s)ter Family (Quaker Records), County Antrim, 1684-1778. (1951-53, p. 118.)

FOSTER. Foster Family (Massereene Papers), Dunleer, County Louth, *ca.* 1650-. Allied families of: Burghs, County Kildare; Moore, County Monaghan; Tennison, County Louth; Hamilton, County Down; also Edwards, Kenmare, Ludlow, Granard, Waldon of Cashel, and Baltinglass. (1948, p. 14.)

FOSTER. Foster; see Massereene Family Papers.

FOULKE. Foulke Family Genealogical Notes, *ca.* 1600-1800. (1951-53, p. 118.)

FOX. Fox Family Genealogical Notes, *ca.* 1600-1800. (1951-53, p. 118.)

FOX. Fox Family (Quaker Records), County Armagh, 1664-1791. (1951-53, p. 118.)

FRACKLETON. Frackleton; see Davidson and other family genealogies, 17th Century-1930. (1938-45, p. 16.)

FRANCIS. Francis Family (Quaker Records). For the following counties and between dates of: Armagh, 1700-1792; Londonderry, 1673-1685; Tyrone, 1673-1707. (1951-53, p. 119.)

FRENCH. See Evans and other family documents, 1620-1856. (1926, p. 9.)

FREW. Connor Diocesan Wills for: David Frew, 1699; Alexander Frew, 1732; Alexander Frew, 1778; also 119 Memorials of Deeds. (Crosslé Mss.) (1938-45, p. 15.)

FRITH. Frith Family Genealogical Notes, *ca.* 1600-1800. (1951-53, p. 120.)

GAILEYS. Family Records of the Gaileys and some of their Connections, 18th-20th Centuries. (1951-53, p. 21.)

GALT. See Anderson, etc., documents, 1789-1911.

GARNET(T). Garnet(t) Family (Quaker Records), County Armagh, dated between 1702-1760; County Tyrone, dated between 1685-1743. (1951-53, p. 122.)

GETTY. Getty Family, Belfast. Bible with genealogical entries, 1793-1800. (1951-53, p. 123.)

GIBSON. Gibson Family (Quaker Records), County Armagh, dated between 1662-1775; County Down, dated between 1756-1769. (1951-53, p. 123.)

GILBERT(S). Gilbert(s) Family (Quaker Records), County Armagh, 1698-1732. (1951-53, p. 123.)

GILLESPIE. See Deacon and other family genealogical notes, *ca.* 1664-1850. (1938-45, p. 15.)

GILLESPY. Gillespy, Martha, Matthew, South Carolina (Chesney Diary), 1755-1800. (1951-53, p. 124.)

GILMORE, GILLMER. Gilmore (Gillmer) Family (Quaker Records), County Armagh, 1729-1773. Also, Pedigree (Mary Gilmore of Brackville, Canada, dated 1746). (1951-53, p. 124.)

GIL(L)PIN. Gil(l)pin Family. (Quaker Records), County Armagh, dated between 1685-1759; County Tyrone, dated between 1734-1773.) (1951-53, p. 124.)

GIRDWOOD. See Drury Family Pedigree, 1535-1922. (1932, p. 9.)

GLEN. See Evans and other family documents, 1620-1856. (1926, p. 9.)

GOODLATT. Goodlatt Family, County Tyrone, Genealogical Notes, *ca.* 1627-1722. Also Tombstone Extracts, 1641-1716. (1951-53, p. 126.)

GORDON. The Gordon Clan of Antrim. (1935, p. 12.)

GOSSELIN. Gosselin Family Genealogical Notes, *ca.* 1600-1800. (1951-53, p. 127.)

GOULDSBURY. Gouldsbury Family Genealogical Notes, *ca.* 1600-1800. (1951-53, p. 127.)

GRAHAM. See Agnew and other family documents, 1718-1830. (1925, p. 8.)

GRAHAM. See Cleland and other family documents, 1682-1905. (1951-53, p. 16.)

GRAHAM. Graham Family of Drumogher and Jackson Family of County Armagh (Pillow Mss.) ; see Jackson. (1934, p. 5.)

GRAHAM. Graham Family of Drumogher; Notes on, 1770. (1934, p. 56.)

GRAHAM. See Colvill and other family documents, 1603-1870. (1927, p. 8.)

GRAVES. Graves, Greer, Grierson, Hooper, Morton, Whittsite families; 25 extracts from Wills, 1728-1776. (1951-53, p. 17.)

GRAY. Gray (Grey) Family (Quaker Records), County Antrim, dated between 1675-1787; County Armagh, dated between 1690-1789. (1951-53, p. 129.)

GREEN(E). Green(e) Family (Quaker Records), County Antrim, dated between 1697-1800; County Armagh, dated between 1718-1800. (1951-53, p. 129.)

GREER, GRIER, GREAR. Greer, Grier, Grear Family (Quaker Records). For the following counties and between dates of: Antrim, 1675-1784; Armagh, 1633-1800; Cavan, 1718-1800; Tyrone, 1630-1800. Also for Northumberland, 1623-1693. (1951-53, pp. 130, 131.)

GREER. See Graves (Wills, 1728-76). (1951-53, p. 17.)

GREEVES, GRIEVE(S). Greeves, Grieve(s) Family (Quaker Records). For the following counties and between dates of: Antrim, 1774-1783; Armagh, 1694-1775; Down, 1780-1790; Tyrone and America, 1708-1800. (1951-53, pp. 131-132.)

GREEVES. See Hazelton and other family documents. (1951-53, p. 13.)

GREGG. Gregg Family (Quaker Records). County Londonderry, dated between 1694-1774; County Antrim, dated between 1709-1784. (1951-53, p. 132.)

GRIBBEN. Gribben; see Cleland and other family documents, 1682-1905. (1951-53, p. 16.)

GRIERSON. Grierson Families of Scotland and Ireland, *ca.* 1451-1800. (1951-53, p. 132.)

GRIERSON. Notes on the History of the Grierson Family, by G. A. Grierson, edited with notes by J. H. G(reeves). (1951-53, p. 20.)

GRIERSON. See Graves (Wills, 1728-1776). (1951-53, p. 17.)

GRIMSHAW. See Cuningham (Pedigree, etc., 1600-1935). (1951-53, p. 19.)

HAD(D)OCK, HAYDOCK. Had(d)ock, Haydock Family (Quaker Records), for the counties and between dates: Antrim, 1675-1800; Armagh, 1683-1800; Tyrone, 1698-1800. (1951-53, p. 134.)

HAGAN. Hagan Family (Quaker Records), County Armagh, 1702-1800. (1951-53, p. 134.)

HALL. Hall Family (Quaker Records). For the following counties and between dates of: Antrim, 1741-1785; Armagh, 1685-1785; Monaghan, 1733-1767. (1951-53, p. 135.)

HALLADAY. Halladay, Halliday, Halloday, Holliday, Hollyday, Family (Quaker Records), County Armagh, dated between 1675-1783. (1951-53, p. 135.)

HALLOW(E)S. Hallow(e)s Family, Irish Newspaper extracts, 1742-1800. (1951-53, p. 136.)

HAMILTON. Hamilton Family, Scotland, Pedigree, 1290-1608. (1948, p. 60.)

HAMILTON. Hamilton Family Genealogical Notes, 1670-1725. (1951-53, p. 136.)

HAMILTON. Hamilton Family Genealogical Notes from Chancery Bill, 1670-1725. (1951-53, p. 137.)

HAMILTON. Hamilton Family (Quaker Records). For the following counties and between dates of: Armagh, 1690-1749; Down, 1749-1784; Tyrone, 1700-1747. (1951-53, p. 137.)

HAMILTON. Many Hamilton family extracts from Registry of Deeds, Dublin; Chancery Bills, Wills, 1622-1932. (1938-45, p. 16.)

HAMILTON. See Agnew and other family documents, 1637-1903. (1929, p. 10.)

HAMILTON. See Armstrong and other family documents, 1666-1859. (1924, p. 10.)

HAMILTON. See Boyd and other family documents, 1660-1811. (1926, p. 9.)

HAMILTON. Pedigree of the Hamilton and McCurdy Families, 1727-1932. (1935, p. 8.)

HAMILTON. Rev. Hans Hamilton, 1536-1936 Pedigree. (1936, p. 9.)

HAMILTON. 94 Deeds relating to the Hamilton family. (1925, p. 15.)

HAMPTON. Hampton (Quaker Records), County Armagh, dated between 1697-1756. (1951-53, p. 137.)

HAN(D)CO(C)K. Han(d)co(c)k Family (Quaker Records). For the following counties and between dates of: Antrim, 1676-1786; Armagh, 1682-1800; Down, 1741-1782. (1951-53, p. 138.)

HANNA. Hanna Genealogical Tree of the Rev. John and Matilda, 1734-1944. (1946-47, p. 6.)

HANNAH, HANA. Hannah (Hana) Family (Quaker Records), County Armagh, 1708-1755. Also Irish Newspaper extracts and Census Returns, 1753-1851. (1951-53, p. 138.)

HARCO(U)RT. Harco(u)rt Family (Quaker Records), County Armagh, dated between 1756-1785. (1951-53, p. 139.)

HARDINGE. Hardinge Family (Quaker Records), County Antrim, dated between 1696-1705; County Armagh, dated between 1649-1774. (1951-53, p. 139.)

HARE. Hare Family, Genealogical Notes, *ca.* 1600-1800. (1951-53, p. 139.)

HARKNESS. Harkness Family, Genealogical Notes, *ca.* 1600-1800. (1951-53, pp. 10, 140.)

HARLAN(D). Harlan(d) Family (Quaker Records), County Armagh, dated between 1671-1792; County Down, dated between 1678-1785. (1951-53, p. 140.)

HARMAN. Harman Family, Genealogical Notes, *ca.* 1600-1800. (1951-53, p. 140.)

HARMAN. See Armstrong and other family records, 1694-1806. (1924, p. 10.)

HARPER. Robert Harper of Charleston, South Carolina (Chesney Diary), 1755-1800. (1951-53, p. 140.)

HAR(R)ISON. Har(r)ison Family (Quaker Records), County Armagh, 1672-1733. (1951-53, p. 141.)

HART(E). Hart(e). Family Genealogy (notes), *ca.* 1600-1800. (1951-53, p. 141.)

HARTL(E)Y. Hartl(e)y Family (Quaker Records). For the following counties and between dates of: Antrim, 1714-1744; Armagh, 1682-1782; Down, 1786-1790. (1951-53, p. 141.)

HASLET(T). Haslet(t) Family. Irish Newspaper extracts, 1770-1800. (1951-53, pp. 141, 142.)

HASSARD. See Crozier and other family documents, 1697-1832. (1924, p. 10.)

HAUGHTON. Haughton Family (Quaker Records). For the following counties and between dates of: Antrim, 1763-1785; Armagh, 1795; Kildare, 1730-1780. (1951-53, p. 142.)

HAY. Hay Family (Quaker Records). County Antrim, dated between 1699-1704; County Armagh, dated between 1702-1726. (1951-53, p. 143.)

HAYDO(C)K. Haydo(c)k Family (Quaker Records). For the following counties and between dates of: Antrim, 1682-1714; Armagh, 1735-1800; Tyrone, 1734-1800. Also to North Carolina, 1800. (1951-53, p. 143.)

HAYS. Hays, Murray, Watson, family documents, 1697-1819. Wills, Grants, etc., County Armagh. 22 copies. (1925, p. 7.) See also Anderson, for Hayes (1925, p. 8).

HAZELTON. Hazelton Family (Quaker Records), County Tyrone, pre-1747. (1951-53, p. 143.)

HAZELTON. Families of Hazelton, Heather, Greeves, Douglass and Williams, residing near Dungannon, County Tyrone and also U. S. A. and Canada, 94 documents, 1802-1851. (1951-53, p. 13.)

HEARN. Hearn Family Genealogical Notes, *ca.* 1600-1800. (1951-53, p. 144.)

HEARN. See Evans and other family Wills, Administrations, 1620-1856. (1926, p. 9.)

HEATHER. Pedigree of William and Mary (Gilmore) Heather of Killyman, County Tyrone and Brackville, Canada, dated 1746. (1951-53, pp. 13, 144.)

HEATHER. Heather: see Hazelton and other family documents. (1951-53, p. 13.)

HENDERSON. Henderson Family Pedigree, 1712-1751; families of Counties Donegal, Down, Fermanagh, Monaghan, and also the City of Belfast. (1927, p. 7.)

HENDERSON. Henderson Family (Quaker Records). For the following counties and between dates of: Antrim, 1704-1765; Armagh, 1682-1766; Londonderry, 1698-1725. (1951-53, p. 144.)

HENDERSON. Henderson Family Pedigree (n. d.). (1927, p. 41.)

HEN(E)RY. Hen(e)ry Family Genealogical Notes. The Rev. Samuel Henry of Sligo and County Kilkenny, Genealogical Notes; Ossory Diocesan Will, etc., 1671-1769. (1951-53, p. 145.)

HETHERINGTON. Hetherington Family (Quaker Records). County Antrim, dated between 1685-1719; County Armagh, dated between 1700-1746. (1951-53, p. 146.)

HEWET(T), HEWIT(T). Hewet(t), or Hewit(t) Family (Quaker Records), County Antrim, dated between 1719-1733; County Armagh, dated between 1682-1800. (1951-53, p. 146.)

HIGENBOTHEM. Higenbothem: see Armstrong and other family documents, 1666-1859. (1924, p. 10.)

HIGGENBOTHAM. Higgenbotham Family Genealogical Notes; Pedigree, 1735-1807. (1948, p. 63.)

HIGGINBOTHAM. Higginbotham Wills: John, 1656; Rev. John, 1687; John, 1699; Paul, 1614; John, 1748, Henry, 1783. (1933, p. 11.)

HIG(G)IN(G)BOTHAM. Hig(g)in(g)botham Family (Quaker Records), County Antrim, dated between 1692-1730; County Armagh, dated between 1716-1727. (1951-53, p. 147.)

HIG(G)INSON. (Hig(g)inson Family (Quaker Records), County Antrim, dated between 1677-1767. (1951-53, p. 147.)

HILL. Hill Family (Quaker Records). For the following counties and between dates of: Antrim, 1675-1781; Armagh, 1706-1794; Down, 1724-1794. (1951-53, p. 148.)

HILL. Hill Family Documents; extracts of Prerogative and Diocesan Wills, Grants. 128 documents. (1932, p. 8.)

HILLARY, HILLERY. Hillary, Hillery Family (Quaker Records), for Yorkshire, County Armagh and County Down, dated between 1650-1694. (1951-53, p. 148.)

HILLIS. See Evans and other family documents, 1620-1856. (1926, p. 9.)

HINCKS. See Cuningham Pedigree etc., 1600-1935. (1951-53, p. 19.)

HIN(D)SHAW. Hindshaw Family (Quaker Records), County Tyrone, 1708-1783. (1951-53, p. 149.)

HOBSON. Hobson Family (Quaker Records). For the following counties and between dates of: Antrim, 1692-1782; Armagh, 1692-1787; Tyrone, 1685-1800. (1951-53, p. 150.)

HODGKINSON. Hodgkinson Family (Quaker Records), Lancashire, 1638-1720. (1951-53, p. 150.)

HODS(H)ON. Hods(h)on Family (Quaker Records), County Armagh, dated between 1668-1744. (1951-53, p. 150.)

HOFFMEISTER. Hoffmeister Family, Germany; Genealogical Notes, *ca.* 1600-1800. (1951-53, p. 150.)

HOG(G). Hog(g) Family (Quaker Records), County Antrim, dated between 1727-1782; County Armagh, dated between 1698-1796. (1951-53, p. 150, 151.)

HOL(L)IN(G)(S)WORTH. Hol(l)in(g)(s)worth Family (Quaker Records), County Armagh, dated between 1628-1686. Henry and Lydia to Pennsylvania, America, 1688. (1951-53, p. 151.)

HOLME. Holme (Quaker Record); Benjamin Holme to Virginia-Maryland, 1709-1736.

HOLMES. Holmes Family (Quaker Records). For the following counties and between dates of: Antrim, 1705-1738; Armagh, 1731-1773; Londonderry, 1737-1779. (1951-53, p. 151.)

HOLMES. Notes on the Families of Holmes and Batt, 1622-1859. (1951-53, p. 19.)

HOLMES. See Baskerville, and other family genealogies. (1931, p. 15.)

HOOPER. See Graves Wills, 1728-1776. (1951-53, p. 17.)

HOOP(E)(S). Hoop(e)(s) Family (Quaker Records). For the following counties and between dates of: Antrim, 1682-1706; Armagh, 1638-1786; Down, 1703-1786. (1951-53, p. 152.)

HOPKINS. Hopkins Family, Genealogical Notes. (1951-53, p. 153.)

HOUSTON. Houston Family, Notes of Settlement in North Carolina, 1736-37; John Houston of Templepatrick, County Antrim (transcript of Templeton Rent Rolls); Robert Houston (Conyngham Mss., 21 Nov. 1699). McCulloch, Henry, "Notes regarding Ulster Emigrants to North Carolina, 1736-37." (1927, p. 41.)

HOUSTON. Notes of Emigration from Ulster to North Carolina, etc., from papers of the late W. C. Houston, Philadelphia, U. S. A. (1927, p. 7.)

HOUSTON. See Evans and other family Wills, etc., 1620-1856. (1926, p. 9.)

HOUSTON. Notes of births and deaths of Houston family, 1771-1828. (1951-53, p. 19.)

HUDSON. Hudson Family, County Louth. Genealogical Notes. Also Hudson Family (Quaker Records), County Antrim, dated between 1695-1743; County Armagh, dated between 1683-1750. (1951-53, p. 154.)

HUGHES, HUGHS. Hughes, Hughs Family (Quaker Records), County Antrim, dated between 1741-1784. (1951-53, p. 155.)

HUGHES. Hughes Family Genealogy (chart). 1649-1874. (1932, p. 9.)

HULL (HOOLE). Hull (Hoole) Copies of Prerogative Wills. Also Down and Connor Diocesan Wills, 1667-1779. (1925, p. 9.)

HULL. The Hull Family of County Down. 1932. (1932, p. 12.)

HUME. Patrick Hume Genealogical Notes, *ca.* 1599-1700. (1951-53, p. 155.)

HUMPHRYS. See Archdale documents, 1729-1864. (1927, p. 8.)

HUNTER. Hunter Family (Quaker Records). For the following counties and between dates of: Antrim, 1675-1784; Armagh, 1697-1798; Down, 1701-1788. (1951-53, p. 155.)

HUSSEY. Hussey Family, Ireland Pedigree, 1205- n. d. (1951-53, p. 156.)

HUTCHESON. See Boyd and other family documents, 1660-1811. (1926, p. 9.)

HUTCHINSON. See Boyd and other family documents, 1660-1811. (1926, p. 9.)

IRVINE. Irvine Pedigree; Grant of Arms (Scottish). 24 documents, including Account of the Irvines and their settlement in Ireland (names included, Irvine, Towers), 1673-1853. (1951-53, p. 20.)

IRWIN. Irwin Family and estate of Carnagh, County Armagh, 1737-1888. (1929, p. 17.)

IRWIN (E). Irwin (e) Family (Quaker Records), County Antrim, 1697-1769. (1951-53, p. 158.)

JACKSON. Genealogy of the Jackson Family, 1631-1874. (1951-53, p. 20.)

JACKSON. Jackson Family (Quaker Records), County Armagh, dated between 1647-1785. Also Genealogical Notes, 1631-1800. (1951-53, p. 159.)

JACKSON. Jackson documents; see Barton, 1611-1867. (1930, p. 9.)

JACKSON. Jackson documents; see Barton, 1612-1860. (1930, p. 10.)

JACKSON. Jackson Family Pedigree, 1681-1933. (1933, p. 11.)

JACKSON. Jackson Family of County Armagh and the Graham Family of Drumogher. (Pillow Mss.) (1934, p. 5.)

JAMES. See Evans and other family documents, 1620-1856. (1926, p. 9.)

JELLET(T). Jellet(t) Family Genealogical Notes, *ca.* 1600-1800. (1951-53, p. 160.)

JOHNSTON. See Aiken and other family documents, 1738-1917. (1928, p. 8.)

JOHNSON, JOHNSTON. Johnson or Johnston Family of Dumfriesshire, Scotland and County Monaghan, also County Down, Genealogical Notes, 1066-1840. (1946-47, p. 68.)

JOHNSON, JOHNSTON. Johnston Family of Ramoran, County Fermanagh, Genealogical Notes, 1693. (1948, p. 67.)

JOHNSTON. Ancestry and Genealogical notes on Mary Johnston, wife of Archibald Hamilton, of Lillyleagh, *ca.* 1721. (1938-45, p. 16.)

JOHNSTON. See Armstrong and other family documents, 1666-1859. (1924, p. 10.)

JOHNSTON. See Crozier and other family records, 1697-1832. (1924, p. 10.)

JOHNSTON. See Cuningham Pedigree, etc., 1600-1935. (1951-53, p. 19.)

JOHNS(T)ON(E). Johns(t)on(e) Family (Quaker Records). For the following counties and between dates of: Antrim, 1683-1781; Armagh, 1688-1799; Down, 1694-1795. (1951-53, pp. 161, 162.)

JOHNSTONE. Johnstone Family, of Gilford, County Down, *ca.* 1500-1700. (1928, p. 65.)

JONES. Jones Family Genealogical Notes, 1600-1800. (1951-53, p. 163.)

JO(O)NES. Jo(o)nes Family (Quaker Records). For the following counties and between dates of: Antrim, 1676-1782; Armagh, 1685-1772; Cavan, 1708-1772; Londonderry, 1659-1660. (1951-53, p. 163.)

KANE. See Dobbin Family Memoir, 17th-19th Centuries. (1926, p. 25.)

KEATING. Keating Family Genealogical Notes, *ca.* 1600-1800. (1951-53, p. 164.)

KELLETT. Kellett Genealogical Notes, *ca.* 1680-1800. (1951-53, p. 165.)

KELLY. Kelly Family Genealogical Notes, *ca.* 1600-1800. (1951-53, p. 165.)

KENAH. Kenah Family Genealogical Notes. (1951-53, p. 166.)

KEN(N)A(E)D(A)Y. Kennedy, etc., Family (Quaker Records), County Armagh, dated between 1723-1796; County Down, dated between 1715-1793. (1951-53, p. 166.)

KENNEDY. Kennedy Family of Clogher and Londonderry, *ca.* 1600-1938. Ayrshire family settled at Clogher, 1650; one at Derry, 1654. Two genealogical charts. (1938-45, p. 16.)

KENNEDY. See Colvill and other family documents, 1603-1870. (1927, p. 8.)

KERR. Kerr Family Genealogical Notes, 1100-1800. (1951-53, p. 167.)

KER(R). Ker or Kerr Family (Quaker Records), County Armagh, dated between 1694-1783; County Tyrone, dated between 1694-1800. (1951-53, p. 167.)

KERR. Pedigree of Robert Kerr, Strabane, County Tyrone, 1748-1947. (1951-53, p. 17.)

KILPATRICK. Kilpatrick of Argrey Hill, Raphoe, County Donegal and U. S. A. Family Genealogy, 18th and 19th Centuries. (1951-53, p. 10.)

KING. King Family Genealogical Notes, *ca.* 1600-1800. (1951-53, pp. 168, 169.)

KING. King Family (Quaker Records), County Armagh, dated between 1699-1783; County Tyrone, 1715-1800. (1951-53, pp. 168, 169.)

KING. Notes on the Family of King, 17th-19th Centuries. (1951-53, p. 18.)

KING. See Cleland and other Family documents, 1682-1905. (1951-53, p. 16.)

KING. See Deacon and other family genealogical notes, 1664-1850. (1938-45, p. 15.)

KINGSLEY. Kingsley Family Genealogical Notes, *ca.* 1600-1800. (1951-53, p. 169.)

KINGSTON. The Kingston Family in West Cork. (1929, p. 13.)

KIRK. Jacob Kirk, County Antrim and Pennsylvania, 1728-1772. (1951-53, p. 170.)

KIRK(E). Kirk(e) Family (Quaker Records), County Antrim, dated between 1704-1716; County Armagh, dated between 1645-1797. (1951-53, p. 170.)

KIRKPATRICK. Kirkpatrick Family, Scotland and Ireland. Pedigree, 1280-1800. (1951-53, p. 170.)

KISBY. Kisby: see Evans and other family documents, 1620-1856. (1926, p. 9.)

KNIGHT. Knight Family Genealogical Notes, 1600-1800. (1951-53, p. 170.)

KNIPE. Knipe Family Genealogical Notes, *ca.* 1600-1800. (1951-53, p. 170.)

KNIPE. See Armstrong and other family documents, 1666-1859. (1924, p. 10.)

KNOX. John Knox Descendants, 1505-1947. (1948, p. 6.)

LAMB(E). Lamb(e) Family (Quaker Records), County Antrim, dated between 1704-1781. (1951-53, p. 171.)

LAMBERT. George Lambert, Downpatrick, Prerogative Will; also Montague of Dublin; Robert of Dunlady, County Down; Ralph of Dublin. Prerogative Wills, 1723-1762. (1929, p. 11.)

LAMBERT(E). Lambert(e) Family Genealogical Notes, *ca.* 1600-1800. (1951-53, p. 172.)

LANE. Lane Family, Ballycarton, County Londonderry, Genealogical Notes, *ca.* 1661-1800. Also Lane Family Irish Newspaper extracts, 1778-1800. (1951-53, p. 172.)

LANGTRE(E). Langtre(e) Family (Quaker Records), County Armagh, dated between 1679-1777. (1951-53, p. 172.)

LANGTRY. See Chetwood or Chetwode and other family pedigrees, 1222-1878. (1938-45, p. 17.)

LAW. See Agnew and other family documents, 1718-1830. (1925, p. 8.)

LAW. See Anderson and other family documents, 1672-1847. (1925, p. 8.)

LAW. See Andrews and other family documents, 1668-1855. (1925, p. 7.)

LAW. See Andrews and other family documents, 1728-1852. (1925, p. 8.)

LAWRENCE. Pedigree of Thomas Edward Lawrence (of Arabia), 1733-1888. (1949-50, p. 5.)

LECKY. Lecky Family of County Donegal, Family Genealogy, 18th and 19th Centuries. (1951-53, p. 10.)

LESLIE. Leslie Family Pedigree, 1067-1800. (1951-53, p. 176.)

LESLIE. See Arundell and other family documents. (1926, p. 9.)

LEWIS. Lewis Family Records, extracted from Family Bible, 1763; also Lewis Family Records, 1721. (1938-45, p. 15.)

LINDSAY. The Lindsay Memoirs. A record of the Lisnacrieve and Belfast branch . . . . during the last two hundred years. By J. C. and J. A. Lindsay, 1884. (1927, p. 11.)

LINDSAY, LINDESAY. The Lindesays of Loughry and Tullahoge, *ca.* 1588-1781. (1938-45, p. 13.)

LITTLE. Abstracts from Armagh and Derry Wills of the Little Family, 1715-1833; also Parish Register extracts, of Ardstraw, County Tyrone. (1927, p. 8.)

LOMBARD. Lombard Family Genealogical Notes, *ca.* 1600-1800. (1951-53, p. 180.)

LOWDAN, LOWDEN, LOWDON. Lowdan, etc., Family (Quaker Records), County Antrim, dated between 1699-1744; County Armagh, dated between 1698-1700. (1951-53, p. 181.)

LOWRY. Lowry Family Genealogy, 1610-1917. (1931, p. 13.)

LUKE. Luke Family Genealogical Notes, 1783-1800. (1951-53, p. 182.)

LURTING. Lurting Family, Magilligan, County Londonderry, Genealogical Notes; Census Returns (extracts). 1625-1949. (1951-53, p. 182.)

LUTHER. Luther Family Genealogical Notes, *ca.* 1600-1800. (1951-53, p. 182.)

LYNAS(S), LINAS, LINNAS, LYNAS, LYNUS. Lynas, etc., Family (Quaker Records), of Easington, Yorkshire, 1654; County Armagh, 1654, 1694, 1703, 1795. (1951-53, pp. 178, 182.)

LYTTLE. See Evans and other family documents, 1620-1856. (1926, p. 9.)

MACDONALD. MacDonald Family, Glenco, Scotland and Drumbohena, County Fermanagh, Pedigree Extract, 1745-1926. (1938-45, p. 60.)

MACDONALDS, MACDONNELLS. Manuscript History. (1934, pp. 20, 21.)

MA(C)K(I)E(Y). Ma(c)k(i)e(y) Family (Quaker Records). County Armagh, 1692-1789. (1951-53, p. 193.)

MACNEILL. MacNeill: Pedigree of Col. James Graham Douglas MacNeill, 1380-1896. (1951-53, p. 21.)

MACOUBRY. See Drury and allied families pedigree, 1535-1922. (1932, p. 9.)

MADDEN. See Arundell and other family documents, 1646-1846. (1926, p. 9.)

MAGENIS. Magenis, McGennis, McGinnis, Meginnis, etc., Family Pedigree. (1951-53, p. 199.)

MAGENNIS. Notes relating to Magennis of Iveagh, and Stephenson of Hillsborough, 1500-1758. (1937, p. 8.)

MAGENNIS. Notes and Pedigree of the Magennis Family of Iveagh, 1542-1744. (1932, p. 9.)

MAGINNIS. Maginnis Family documents; 58 copies of Wills, Extracts from Wills, Grants, Bonds, Chancery Bills, Petitions, Marriage Settlements, Leases, Deeds, dated between 1629-1831. (1924, p. 10.)

MAGINNISS. See Baskerville and other family genealogical Tables, etc. (1931, p. 15.)

MAGRATH. Magrath Family Genealogical Notes, 1600-1800. (1951-53, p. 199.)

MAHONY. See Drury and allied families pedigree, 1535-1922. (1932, p. 9.)

MA(I)SON, MAYSON, MEASON. Mason, Maison, etc., Family (Quaker Records), County Armagh, dated between 1688-1739. (1951-53, p. 200.)

MAITLAND. Maitland Family, Newry, County Down, Pedigree, 1771-1850. (1938-45, p. 6.)

MAJOR. Major Family Genealogical Notes, 1600-1800. (1951-53, p. 201.)

MALCOMSON. Malcomson: copies of Family Pedigree, Wills, etc., 1727-1749. (1926, p. 9.)

MARSH. Marsh Family (Quaker Records), 1694-1788. (1951-53, p. 202.)

MARSHAL(L). Marshal or Marshall Family (Quaker Records), County Antrim, dated between 1684-1732; County Armagh, dated between 1685-1799. (1951-53, p. 203.)

MASSEREENE. Massereene Family documents, 1539-1799. (1926, p. 15.)

MASSEREENE. Massereene and Ferrard Family and State Papers, 1539-1822. (1926, p. 8.)

MASSEREENE. Massereene-Foster Family Papers, County Louth and County Antrim, 1650-1757. (1949-50, p. 5.)

MATHEWSON. Mathewson Family of Ardstraw, County Tyrone; genealogy, 1700-1800. (1951-53, pp. 10, 204.)

MAT(T)HEW(S). Mat(t)hew(s) Family (Quaker Records). For the following counties and between dates of: Antrim, 1645-1683; Armagh, 1645-1788; Down, 1649-1683, 1789-1800. (1951-53, pp. 204, 205.)

MATTHEWS. Matthews Pedigree Extract, 1848. (1938-45, p. 16.)

MCADAM. McAdam and Shipboy Families, 1762-1874. 52 documents, wills, letters, leases, bills of exchange. (1946-47, p. 6.)

MCASKIE. McAskie Family (Quaker Records), Genealogical Notes, 1700-1800. (1951-53, p. 184.)

MCBRIDE. McBride Family (Quaker Records), County Armagh, dated between 1677-1709. (1951-53, p. 184.)

McCAIN and McKay Families of Meenahoney and Ballindrait, County Donegal, and U. S. A. Family Genealogies, 18th and 19th Centuries. (1951-53, pp. 10, 184.)

McCALLY. McCally Family, Genealogical Notes, *ca.* 1600-1800. (1951-53, p. 185.)

McCAMMON. McCammon: See Agnew and other family documents, 1718-1830. (1925, p. 8.)

McCAMMON. See Anderson and other family documents, 1672-1847. (1925, p. 8.)

McCAMMON. See Andrews and other family documents, 1668-1855. (1925, p. 7.)

McCANCE. See Agnew and other family documents, 1718-1830. (1925, p. 8.)

McCANCE. See Anderson and other family documents, 1672-1847. (1925, p. 8.)

McCANCE. See Andrews and other family documents, 1668-1855. (1925, p. 7.)

McCANCE. See Andrews and other family documents, 1728-1852. (1925, p. 8.)

McCANCE. McCance and Stouppe Families, 1660-1902; extracts from Note Book of Births and Deaths. Will of William McCance, 1809; Will of William McCance, 1835. Extracts from Diary of John McCance, 1827-1856. (1938-45, p. 18.)

McCA(U)SLAND. McCa(u)sland Family; Irish Newspaper extracts, 1795-1800. (1951-53, p. 185.)

McCLELLAND. See Anderson and other family documents, 1672-1847. (1925, p. 8.)

McCREADY (McCREERY). McCready (McCreery) family, County Down: Genealogical Table, 1700-1926. (1930, p. 10.)

McCREERY. See Davidson, 17th Century documents. (1938-45, p. 16.)

McCULLOCH. See Agnew and other family documents, 1692-1908. (1929, p. 10.)

McCULLOCH. Notes on the Family of McCulloch, 17th-19th Centuries. (1951-53, p. 18.)

McCULLOUGH, McCULLAGH, Mc CULLACH, etc. McCullough, etc., Family of County Antrim, Pedigree, 1682. (1951-53, p. 188.)

McDONALD, Mc DON(N)EL(L). McDonald, McDon(n)el(l) Family (Quaker Records), County Armagh, dated between 1733-1800. (1951-53, p. 189.)

McDOWELL. McDowell Family; Irish Newspaper Extracts, 1738-1800. (1951-53, p. 189.)

McELFATRICK. See Anderson, etc., documents, 1789-1911.

McGUSTY. McGusty Family Genealogical Notes, *ca.* 1600-1800. (1951-53, p. 192.)

McKAY. McKay and McCain Families; Genealogical Notes, n. d.-1800. (1951-53, p. 192.)

McMAHON. McMahon Family Genealogical Notes, *ca.* 1600-1800. (1951-53, p. 194.)

McMO(U)R(R)A(I)N. McMo(u)r(r)a(i)n Family, County Down and County Monaghan; Newspaper Extracts; Genealogical Notes, 1734-1800. (1951-53, p. 195.)

McMURRAY. McMurray; see Anderson and other family documents, 1671-1858. (1937, p. 8.)

McNEIL, McNEILE, McNEAL, etc. McNeil, etc., Family of Scotland and Ireland, Genealogical Notes, 1380-1800. (1951-53, p. 196.)

McPARLON. See Cleland and other family documents, 1682-1905. (1951-53, p. 16.)

McPHALL. See Anderson, etc., documents, 1789-1911.

McROBERT. See Boyd and other family documents, 1660-1811. (1926, p. 9.)

McTIER. See Drennan and McTier, Belfast, Family Notes, 1672-1879. (1929, pp. 10, 28.)

MEGINNIS. Meginnis Family of Iveagh; Pedigree, 1542-1744. (1932, p. 9.)

MERCER. Mercer Family (Quaker Records) of: County Antrim, dated between 1699-1784; County Armagh, 1683-1695, 1715-1780; County Down, 1682-1784. (1951-53, p. 207.)

MEREDITH. Meredith Family (Quaker Records) of: County Antrim, between 1725-1766; County Down, 1737-1766. (1951-53, p. 207.)

MERVYN. Short Account of the Mervyn Family, 1657-1882. (1927, p. 50.)

MERVYN. See Archdale documents, 1729-1864. (1927, p. 8.)

MILLER. Miller Family (Quaker Records) of: County Armagh, dated between 1737-1792; County Fermanagh, 1769-1787; County Londonderry, 1699-1708; County Tyrone, 1698-1701. Irish Newspaper Extracts, 1738-1800. (1951-53, p. 209.)

MIL(L)HOUS(E). Mil(l)hous(e) Family (Quaker Records), County Antrim, dated between 1695-1729; County Armagh, 1699-1766. (1951-53, p. 209.)

MILLIKIN, MILLIKEN. Millikin, Milliken Family (Quaker Records) of: County Armagh, dated between 1671-1729; County Down, 1671-1724. (1951-53, p. 210.)

MILLS. Mills Family Genealogical Notes (Quaker Records), County Armagh, dated between 1698-1787. (1951-53, p. 210.)

MITTEN, MYTON. Mitten, Myton Family (Quaker Records), County Armagh, dated between 1728-1800; County Cavan, 1703-1796. (1951-53, p. 211.)

MOFFETT. See Colvill and other family documents, 1603-1870. (1927, p. 8.)

MOLYNEAUX. See Cleland and other family documents, 1682-1905. (1951-53, p. 16.)

MONTGOMERY. Montgomery Family; Adam, of Braidstones, Scotland, Genealogical Notes, *ca.* 1550-1800; Sir Alex., Genealogical Notes, *ca.* 1450-1800; Family Pedigree and sketches of Shields of Arms, A. D. 900-1800; Family Genealogical Notes, Blessingbourne, County Tyrone, *ca.* 900-1800; Family Tombstone Inscriptions at Derrybrusk, County Fermanagh, *ca.* 1640-1720; Hugh of Derrybrook, County Tyrone, Genealogical Notes, *ca.* 1600-1800; Hugh of Hessilhead, Scotland, Genealogical Notes, *ca.* 1500-1750; Sir Hugh, Genealogical Notes, *ca.* 1380-1800. (1951-53, pp. 212, 213.)

MONTGOMERY. Montgomery Family of Blessingbourne, County Tyrone, Pedigree, 1618-. (1946-47, p. 95.)

MONTGOMERY. Montgomery Family in Europe; Pedigree, *ca.* 1100-present day. (1938-45, p. 16.)

MONTGOMERY. See Archdale documents, 1729-1864. (1927, p. 8.)

MONTGOMERY. Family of Alexander Montgomery of Dundesert, County Antrim; Family Bible, records of births, etc., 1811-1905. (1938-45, p. 17.)

MOORE. See Agnew and other family documents, 1637-1903. (1929, p. 10.)

MOORE. See Evans and other family documents, 1620-1856. (1926, p. 9.)

MO(O)R(E). Mo(o)r(e) Family (Quaker Records) of: County Antrim, dated between 1682-1779; County Armagh, 1679-1779; County Londonderry, 1721-1773. Also Family Pedigree. (1951-53, p. 215.)

MOR(E)TON(E), MORTAN, MORTEN. Mor(e)ton(e), etc., Family (Quaker Records) of: County Antrim, dated between 1708-1785; County Armagh, 1656-1779; County Down, 1656-1795; County Tyrone, 1725-1800. Also County Tyrone Family Pedigree, 1724-1770. (1951-53, p. 216.)

MOR(R)ISON, MUR(R)ISON. Mor(r)ison, Mur(r)ison Family (Quaker Records) of: County Armagh, dated between 1723-1800; County Tyrone, 1789-1800. (1951-53, p. 217.)

MORTON. See Graves. Wills, 1728-1776. (1951-53, p. 17.)

MORTON. Pedigree of James and Sarah Morton of Moyallan, County Down, and of Grange, County Tyrone. (1951-53, p. 216.)

MOSTYNS. Mostyns Family History. (1926, p. 12.)

MULHOLLAND. Mulholland Family Genealogical Notes, *ca.* 1600-1800. (1951-53, p. 219.)

MULHOLLAND. Notes on the families of Mulholland, Sinclair, Rankin, and Thompson, 1679-1950. (1951-53, p. 21.)

MULLIGAN. See Anderson and other family documents, 1672-1847. (1925, p. 8.)

MULOCK. Mulock Family; Irish Newspaper extracts, 1767-1800. (1951-53, p. 219.)

MU(R)(A)(Y)(E), MORAY, MUREY. Mu(r)(a)(y)(e), etc., Family (Quaker Records), of: County Antrim, dated between 1700-1788; County Armagh, 1695, 1764-1787. (1951-53, p. 221.)

MURPH(E)Y, MURFHY, MURFY. Murph(e)y, etc., Family (Quaker Records), of: County Armagh, dated between 1702-1800; County Down, 1710-1800. (1951-53, p. 220.)

MURRAY. See Andrews and other family documents, 1668-1855. (1925, p. 7.)

MURRAY. See Andrews and other family documents, 1728-1852. (1925, p. 8.)

MURRAY. See Hays and other family documents, 1697-1819. (1925, p. 7.)

MURRAY. 25 copies or abstracts from Clogher Diocesan Wills, Grants, etc., principal name, Murray, 1720-1824. (1925, p. 8.)

NAPIER. See Agnew and other family documents, 1718-1830. (1925, p. 8.)

NEEPER. See Agnew and other family documents, 1718-1830. (1925, p. 8.)

NEIL(L)(E). Neil(l)(e) Family (Quaker Records) of: County Armagh, dated between 1685-1795; County Down, 1685-1799. (1951-53, p. 223.)

NESBIT, NESBITT. Nesbit, Nesbitt family; Genealogical Notes, *ca.* 1600-1800. (1951-53, p. 223.)

NEVIN. See Boyd and other family documents, 1660-1811. (1926, p. 9.)

NEVIN. Nevin family, Donaghadee district, 11 wills. (1936, p. 7.)

NICHOL(L)(S). Nichol(l)(s) Family Genealogical Notes. (1951-53, p. 225.)

NICHOLSON. Nicholson Family (Quaker Records), of: County Antrim, dated between 1687, 1703, 1786; County Armagh, 1682-1800; County Down, 1715-1800; County Dublin, 1734-1800; County Tyrone, 1701-1790. (1951-53, pp. 225, 226.)

NINCH. Ninch Family Genealogical Notes, *ca.* 1600-1800. (1951-53, p. 226.)

NIXON. Nixon Family Genealogical Notes. (1951-53, p. 226.)

NIXON. See Armstrong and other family documents, 1666-1859. (1924, p. 10.)

NIXON. See Armstrong and other family documents, 1694-1806. (1924, p. 10.)

NIXON. See Crozier and other family documents, 1697-1832. (1924, p. 10.)

NOBLE. Noble Family Genealogical Notes, *ca.* 1600-1800. (1951-53, p. 226.)

NOBLE. See Armstrong and other family documents, 1666-1859. (1924, p. 10.)

NOBLE. See Crozier and other family documents, 1697-1832. (1924, p. 10.)

NOELL. Noell documents, 1611-1867. See Barton. (1930, p. 9.)

NUGENT. Nugent family, Upper Ards Barony, County Down. 800 documents; Prerogative and Down Diocesan Wills, some 17th Century. 18th Century rentals of Portaferry; agreements, leases, etc., Upper Ards Barony, County Down. (1946-47, p. 4; 1949-50, p. 11.)

O'DONNELL. See Colvill and other family documents, 1603-1870. (1927, p. 8.)

OGLE. Ogle Family (Quaker Records), County Armagh, dated between 1698-1783. (1951-53, p. 229.)

OGLE. Ogle family documents, 1611-1867. See Barton. (1930, p. 9.)

OGLE. See Barton and other family documents, 1612-1860. (1930, p. 10.)

O'HANLON. See Tool. Pedigree of Tuathal or Tool-O'Hanlon Families. (1951-53, p. 18.)

O'HEGERTY. O'Hegerty Family Pedigree, 1622-1800. (1951-53, p. 229.)

O'HEGERTY. O'Hegerty Pedigree (French descendants of Denis O'Hegerty of Clunsullagh (Brookhill), County Donegal, 1622-1926. (1949-50, p. 5.)

O'NEIL(L)(E). O'Neil(l)(e) Family Genealogical Notes, *ca.* 1100-1800. (1951-53, p. 230.)

O'REILLY. O'Reilly Family Genealogical Notes, *ca.* 1600-1800. (1951-53, p. 230.)

OSBORNE. See Colvill and other family documents, 1603-1870. (1927, p. 8.)

OVENS. Ovens Family Genealogical Notes, *ca.* 1600-1800. (1951-53, p. 231.)

OVENS. See Armstrong and other family documents, 1666-1859. (1924, p. 10.)

PARKENSON. Parkenson Family of Ballygally. (1931, p. 13.)

PARKINSON. Parkinson Family Pedigree, of Ardee, County Louth. (1951-53, p. 233.)

PARSONS. Pedigree of the Parsons and Courtnay Families, etc., 1689-1873. (Crossle Mss.) (1935, p. 8.)

PATERSON. See Arundell and other family documents, 1646-1846. (1926, p. 9.)

PAT(T)ERSON. Pat(t)erson Family (Quaker Records). For the following counties and between dates of: Antrim, 1657, 1682-1778; Armagh, 1657-1679; Tyrone, 1700-1764. (1951-53, p. 234.)

PEARSON. Pearson Family (Quaker Records), County Armagh, dated between 1670-1800; County Tyrone, 1747-1800. (1951-53, p. 235.)

PEIRSON. Peirson Family (Quaker Records), County Armagh, dated between 1670-1775. (1951-53, p. 235.)

PENDLETON. Pendleton Family Genealogical Notes, *ca.* 1600-1800. (1951-53, p. 236.)

PERROTT. See Baskerville and other family documents. (1931, p. 15.)

PERSON. Person Family (Quaker Records), County Armagh, dated between 1702-1774. (1951-53, p. 237.)

PHELPS. Phelps Family (Quaker Records), County Down, 1750-1800. (1951-53, p. 237.)

PHILLIPS. Notes on descendants of Sir Thomas Phillips. (1927, p. 8.)

PHILLIPS. Sir Thomas Phillips of Newtown, Limavady, County Londonderry: Notes as to descendants of, 1635. (1927, p. 54.)

PI(D)GEON. Pi(d)geon Family (Quaker Records), County Monaghan, dated between 1720-1764; County Tyrone, 1709-1727. (1951-53, p. 237.)

PIERSON. Pierson Family (Quaker Records), County Armagh, dated between 1687-1797. (1951-53, p. 238.)

PILLAR. Pillar Family (Quaker Records), County Armagh, dated between 1717-1784; County Tyrone, 1686-1800. Also: William Pillar of Grange, County Tyrone and Baltimore, America. (1951-53, p. 238.)

PILLOW. Pillow Family Ms., County Armagh.

PILSON. Pilson Family Ms., Downpatrick.

PIM. Pim Family Pedigree, *ca.* 1650-1901. (1951-53, p. 17.)

PIM(M). Pim(m) Family Pedigree; England and Ireland, 1650-1800. (1951-53, p. 238.)

PLUNKET(T). Plunket(t) Family Pedigree, 1374- n. d. (1951-53, p. 239.)

POCKRICH. Pockrich Family Genealogical Notes, *ca.* 1600-1800. (1951-53, p. 239.)

PORTER. Porter Family (Quaker Records), Yorkshire and County Armagh, 1641-1704. (1951-53, p. 240.)

PORTER. Pedigree of the Porter and Rodgers Families, 1881-1917. (1948, p. 6.)

POYNTZ. Poyntz Family Genealogical Notes. (1951-53, p. 241.)

PRICE. Short Account of the Family of Price, 1649-1885.

PRICE. See Boyd and other family documents, 1660-1811. (1926, p. 9.)

PRICE. See Archdale and other family documents, 1729-1864. (1927, p. 8.)

PRINGLE. Pringle Family of Ballynahone, County Monaghan; Ms. notes on, 1646-1935. (1936, pp. 8, 9.)

PURDY. Purdy Family (Quaker Records) County Tyrone, dated between 1685-1761. (1951-53, p. 243.)

RADCLIFF(E). Radcliff(e) Family Genealogical Notes, 1600-1800. (1951-53, p. 244.)

RANKIN. See Mulholland and other family notes, 1679-1950. (1951-53, p. 21.)

RAY, REA, REAY, REE, REY. Ray, etc., Family (Quaker Records), County Down, dated between 1697-1763; County Armagh, *ca.* 1628-1739. (1951-53, pp. 245-7.)

READ(E), REED, REID. Read(e), etc., Family Genealogical Notes, *ca.* 1600-1800. Reed Family Genealogical Notes, *ca.* 1600-1800. Reid Family Genealogical Notes, 1717-1800. (1951-53, pp. 246, 247.)

REFORD, RAF(F)ORD. Reford, Raf(f)ord Family (Quaker Records), County Antrim, dated between 1693-1782. (1951-53, pp. 244, 247.)

REIL(L)(E)Y, REILY, RILEY. Reil(l)(e)y, etc., Family Genealogical Notes, *ca.* 1600-1800. (1951-53, p. 247.)

RENDELL. Rendell Family Pedigree, 1766-1902. Includes ffolliott family. Also extracts of Prerogative and Diocesan Wills and Administrations, 1655-1909. (1938-45, p. 17.)

RENDELL. Rendell Family Births and Deaths, 1775-1836. (1938-45, p. 19.)

RENNICK. Rennick Family Genealogical Notes, 1600-1800. (1951-53, p. 248.)

REYNELL. See Dobbin Family Memoir. (1926, pp. 9, 25.)

RICHARDSON. Richardson Family (Quaker Records) of: County Antrim, dated between 1675-1800; County Armagh, 1685-1800; County Cavan, 1695-1784; County Down, 1699-1800; County Tyrone, 1685-1782. (1951-53, pp. 248, 249.)

RICHARDSON. See Armstrong and other family documents, 1666-1859. (1924, p. 10.)

ROBINSON. Robinson Family (Quaker Records), County Armagh, dated between 1670-1793. (1951-53, p. 250.)

ROBSON. Robson Family (Quaker Records), of: Yorkshire, counties Down and Armagh, dated between 1607-1705. (1951-53, p. 251.)

RO(D)GER(S). Ro(d)ger(s) Family (Quaker Records), of: County Antrim, dated between 1732-1787; County Armagh, 1682-1800; County Down, and County Tyrone, 1740-1788. (1951-53, p. 252.)

ROGERS. See Armstrong and other family documents, 1666-1859. (1924, p. 10.)

ROGERS. See Benson. Wills, 1741-1811. (1926, p. 9.)

ROGERS. See Porter and Ro(d)gers families; Pedigree, 1881-1917. (1948, p. 6.)

ROLLO. Lord Rollo Genealogical Notes, *ca.* 1327-1800. (1951-53, p. 252.)

ROUSE. The Rouses of Rous Lench. (1933, p. 14.)

ROWAN. Rowan Family, County Antrim, Pedigree, *ca.* 1500-1921. (1938-45, p. 19.)

RUSSEL. See Anderson and other family documents, 1672-1847. (1925, p. 8.)

SA(U)NDERSON. Sa(u)nderson Family Genealogical Notes, *ca.* 1600-1800. (1951-53, pp. 18, 257.)

SAVA(D)G(E). Sava(d)g(e) Family, Arms of: English and American Branches of; Family Bible Extracts; Ardkeen Branch; Parish Register Extracts; Newspaper Extracts; Notes; Manuscripts; Pedigrees; Will Extracts; Tombstone Extracts. 1197-1800. (1951-53, p. 257.)

SAVAGE. Savage Family of Glastry and Ardkeen, County Down. Pedigree, 1197-1800. (1951-53, p. 125.)

SAVAGE. Savage Family Extracts from Comber Parish Registers, County Down, 1751-1800. (1951-53, p. 79.)

SAVAGE. Savage Family Pedigree, 1655-1930. Extracts, 4 documents; Prerogative and Down Diocesan Wills. (1937, p. 9.)

SAVAGE. See Boyd and other family documents, 1660-1811. (1926, p. 9.)

SAVAGE - ARMSTRONG. George Francis Savage - Armstrong, Manuscripts and Notes, 1100-1800. (1951-53, p. 257.)

SCHWARZ. Schwarz Family Genealogical Extracts, *ca.* 1600-1800. (1951-53, p. 258.)

SCOTS. Scots Family (Quaker Records), County Armagh, dated between 1677-1787; also Scots Family Genealogical Notes, 1600-1800. (1951-53, p. 258.)

SEAVER. Seaver Family Pedigree, 1596-1925. (1938-45, p. 17.)

SE(I)(D)G(E)(S)WICK. Se(i)(d)g(e)(s)wick Family (Quaker Records) of: County Antrim, dated between 1679-1772; County Armagh, 1701-1770. (1951-53, p. 259.)

SEXTON. See Archdale documents, 1729-1864. (1927, p. 8.)

SHARP. Sharp Family, extracts from Prerogative Wills, 1706-1781. (1926, p. 9.)

SHAW. See Agnew and other family documents, 1692-1908. (1929, p. 10.)

SHAW. Shaw Family of Ganaway, County Down, and Bush, County Antrim: Notes re, 1706-1785. (1946-47, p. 114.)

SHAW. Shaw Family of Glastry, County Down, Pedigree, 1766-1933. (1938-45, pp. 16, 17.)

SHAW. Shaw Family Tombstone Inscriptions, Greyabbey, County Down, 1740-1919. (1934, p. 9.)

SHAW(E). Shaw(e) Family (Quaker Records) of: County Antrim, dated between 1684-1787; County Armagh, 1690-1800; County Tyrone, 1740-1788. (1951-53, p. 260.)

SHIPBOY. See McAdam and Shipboy family documents, 1762-1874. (1946-47, p. 6.)

SHEP(P)(H)A(E)RD. Shep (p)(h)a(e)rd Family (Quaker Records) of: County Armagh, dated between 1698-1796; County Cavan, 1750-1776; County Monaghan, 1733-1799. (1951-53, p. 261.)

SHERIDAN. Sheridan Family Genealogical Notes, 1668-1800. (1951-53, p. 261.)

SHERIDAN. Sheridan Family Genealogical Notes, 1724-1828. (1948, p. 106.)

SHERIDAN. Three vols., containing notes of Wills, Bonds, Grants, etc., relating to the Sheridan family, etc., 1572-1861. (1949-50, p. 5.)

SHERINGHAM. Sheringham Family Genealogical Notes, *ca.* 1600-1800. (1951-53, p. 261.)

SINCLAIR. See Mulholland and other family notes, 1679-1950. (1951-53, p. 21.)

SINTON. Sinton Family (Quaker Records), County Armagh, dated between 1732-1800; County Down, 1732-1800. (1951-53, p. 263.)

SINTON. Sinton Family of Counties Armagh and Down; Notes for History of, 1730-1907. (1948, p. 107.) Same (1938-45, p. 19).

SIREE. Siree Family Genealogical Notes, *ca.* 1600-1800. (1951-53, p. 263.)

SKEL(L)TON. Skel(l)ton Family Genealogical Notes, *ca.* 1600-1800. (1951-53, p. 263.)

SMITH. Smith Family (Quaker Records), of: County Antrim, dated between 1675, 1737-1749; County Armagh, 1698-1733; County Down, 1705, 1740-1769; County Monaghan, 1706-1774. Also Smith Family Genealogical Notes, *ca.* 1600-1800. (1951-53, pp. 264, 265.)

SMITH-WAUGH. Smith-Waugh Family; Prerogative and Dromore Diocesan Wills, 1658-1832. (1927, p. 8.)

SMYTH. Smyth Family Pedigree; Quaker Records, County Antrim; miscellaneous documents; Genealogical Notes, 1572-1800. (1951-53, p. 265.)

SMYTH. Smyth Family Pedigree, 1572-1861; 25 documents, affidavits, wills, etc. (1949-50, p. 5.)

SOMERVIL(L)E. Somervil(l)e Family documents, Chancery Bills, Wills extracts, 1670-1725. (1951-53, p. 266.)

SPEER. See Colvill and other family documents, 1603-1870. (1927, p. 8.)

SPENCER. See Armstrong and other family documents, 1666-1859. (1924, p. 10.)

SPROULE. Sproule Family (Caldwell branch), Scotland and County Tyrone and U. S. A., Genealogical Notes, 1441-1800. Also genealogical notes re Elizabeth Sproule, wife of Matthew Caldwell, County Tyrone, *ca.* 1700-1800. (1951-53, pp. 10, 267, 268.)

SPROULE. See Baskerville and other family genealogical tables and notes. (1931, p. 15.)

STAFFORD. Stafford Family Genealogical Notes, 1100-1800. (1951-53, p. 268.)

STAFFORD. Stafford Family, notes of births, 1655-1739. (1948, p. 109.)

STAMFORD. Stamford: see Armstrong and other family documents, 1666-1859. (1924, p. 10.)

STANFORD. Stanford Family Genealogical Notes, *ca.* 1600-1800. (1951-53, p. 268.)

STANLEY. See Cleland and other family documents, 1682-1905. (1951-53, p. 16.)

STANNUS. Stannus Family Pedigree, 1616-1876. (1946-47, p. 6.)

STANNUS. Stannus Family, Moira, County Down, Pedigree, *ca.* 1710-1873. (1938-45, p. 69.)

STANNUS. See Davidson and other family documents, 17th Cent.-1930. (1938-45, p. 16.)

STE(A)ER(E). Ste(a)er(e) Family (Quaker Records), County Antrim, dated between 1694-1780; County Armagh, 1698-1759. (1951-53, p. 269.)

STEPHENS. Stephens Family (Quaker Records), County Armagh, dated between 1702-1798. (1951-53, p. 269.)

STEPHENSON. Stephenson Family, Cooladerry, County Donegal and U. S. A., Genealogical Notes, 18th and 19th Centuries. (1951-53, pp. 10, 269.)

STEPHENSON. See Andrews and other family documents, 1668-1855. (1925, p. 7.)

STEPHENSON. See Agnew and other family documents, 1718-1830. (1925, p. 8.)

STEPHENSON. See Magennis and Stephenson families, 1500-1758. (1937, p. 8.)

STERLING. Sterling Families of Counties Londonderry, Meath, Louth, and Dublin; also Scotland: Genealogical Notes and Irish Newspaper Extracts, 1600-1800. (1951-53, p. 269.)

STERLING. Edward Sterling of Waterford, Genealogical Notes, 1773-1800; Family Documents, 1671-1796. (1951-53, p. 269.)

STERL(Y)NG(E). Sterl(y)ng(e) Family (Quaker Records), Rental, 1698-1772. (1951-53, p. 270.)

STEVENSON. Stevenson Family (Quaker Records), County Armagh, 1675-1785. (1951-53, p. 270.)

STEWART. Stewart Family Genealogical Notes, 1600-1800. (1951-53, p. 271.)

STEWART. Stewart Family, County Tyrone and Ramelton, County Donegal; including several Stewart Wills, 1608-1879. (1932, p. 8.)

STEWART. Stewart Family Genealogical Notes. By Canon Grainger. *ca.* 1619-1819. (1946-47, p. 118.)

STEWART. Stewart Family Genealogy; Notebook. 1619-1791. (1938-45, p. 16.)

STEWART. Stewart Family Baptismal Records of Drumbo, Dundonald and Portaferry, 1642-1841 (Extracts); Population Returns, 1821; Census Return, 1841, etc. (1933, p. 11.)

STEWART. See Arundell and other family documents, 1646-1846. (1926, p. 9.)

STEWART. Stewarts of Irry (Eary), Pedigree and Letters, 1671-1720. (1938-45, p. 13.)

STEWART. Stewart Family of Irry (Eary), Co. Tyrone, Pedigree, 1719. (1946-47, p. 118.)

STINSON. See Anderson and other family documents, 1672-1847. (1925, p. 8.)

STIRLING. Stirling Family Genealogical Notes, 1600-1800. (1951-53, p. 271.)

STONE. Stone Family, England and Ireland. Pedigree; Account Book. 1388-1800. (1951-53, pp. 19, 271.)

STONE. Stone Family, Bromsberrow, Gloucestershire, 13th Cent.-1685. Ancestors of Samuel Stone who settled in County Londonderry in early 18th Century, married to Margaret Stewart of Londonderry and went to County Down. (1926, pp. 9, 26.)

STOTT. Stott Family (Quaker Records) of: County Antrim, dated between 1705-1766; County Armagh, 1732-1800; County Down, 1721-1784. (1951-53, p. 272.)

STOUPPE. See Anderson and other family documents, 1672-1847. (1925, p. 8.)

STOUPPE. See Andrews and other family documents, 1668-1855. (1925, p. 7.)

STOUPPE. See McCance and Stouppe Families, 1660-1902. (1938-45, p. 18.)

STUAR(D)T. Stuar(d)t Families, Mondooey and Roughan or Drumbuoy, County Donegal, Genealogical Notes, n.d.-1800. (1951-53, pp. 10, 273.)

SUTTCLIFF. Suttcliff Family (Quaker Records); Clogher Admon. Bond (extracts), 1713-1781. (1951-53, p. 273.)

SUXBERRY. Suxberry Family, Kinsale, County Cork, Genealogical Notes, 1655-1727. (1951-53, p. 274.)

SWANWICK. See Cuningham Pedigree, etc., 1600-1935. (1951-53, p. 19.)

SWANZY. Swanzy Family Registry of Deeds extracts; Genealogical Notes, 1600-1800. (1951-53, p. 274.)

SWANZY. See Armstrong and other family documents, 1666-1859. (1924, p. 10.)

SWENERTON, SWIN(N)ERTON. Swenerton, etc., Family (Quaker Records): County Armagh, dated between 1742-1796; County Tyrone, 1744-1800. (1951-53, p. 274.)

TAG(G)ART(T), TEGART. Tag(g)art(t), etc. Family (Quaker Records), County Armagh, dated between 1668-1793; County Down, 1668-1742, 1769, 1786-1795. (1951-53, pp. 275, 276.)

TANDY. Tandy Family Genealogical Notes, 1600-1800. (1951-53, p. 275.)

TAYLOR. Taylor Family (Quaker Records), of: County Antrim, dated between 1664, 1695-1726; County Armagh, 1715-1796; County Down, 1715, 1788-1794; County Dublin, 1698-1793. (1951-53, p. 276.)

TAYLOR. Taylor Family Documents, 1336-1718; exhaustive collection of 235 Wills, Bonds, Deeds, Leases, relating largely to this family and to Kilmainham, a suburb of Dublin. Indexed. (1937, pp. 4, 7.)

TAYLOR. See Cuningham Pedigree, etc., 1600-1935. (1951-53, p. 19.)

THOMPSON. Thompson Family, County Down, Pedigree, *ca.* 1720-. (1948, p. 113.)

THOMPSON. See Cleland and other family documents, 1682-1905. (1951-53, p. 16.)

THOMPSON. See Crozier and other family documents, 1697-1832. (1924, p. 10.)

THOMPSON. See Mulholland and other family notes, 1679-1950. (1951-53, p. 21.)

THOM(P)SON. Thom(p)son Family Genealogical Notes, *ca.* 1600-1800. Also Quaker Records for the following counties and between dates of: Antrim, 1709-1795; Armagh, 1691-1800; Cavan, 1750-1793; Down, 1753-1756. (1951-53, p. 278.)

TISDALL. Tisdall Family Pedigree, 1666-1940. (1948, p. 114.)

TOOL, TUATHAL. Pedigree of Tuathal or Tool-O'Hanlon Families. (1951-53, p. 18.)

TOPPIN. Toppin Family (Quaker Records). For the following counties and between dates of: Armagh, 1701-1786; Cavan, 1700-1741; Monaghan, 1730-1764. (1951-53, p. 281.)

TOULERTON. Toulerton Family (Quaker Records), County Armagh, 1677, 1703, 1731-1780. (1951-53, p. 282.)

TOWERS. See Irvine, 1673-1853. (1951-53, p. 20.)

TOWLE. Towle Family (Quaker Records), County Armagh, dated between 1684-1734. (1951-53, p. 282.)

TRAILL. Traill Family Records (extracts from), 1647-1868. (1925, p. 8.)

TRANCHELL. Tranchell Family Genealogical Notes, *ca.* 1600-1800. (1951-53, p. 282.)

TRAVER(S). Traver(s) Family Genealogical Notes, *ca.* 1600-1800. (1951-53, p. 283.)

TROTTER. See Armstrong documents, 1731-1878. (1927, p. 24.)

TRUEMAN, TREWMAN. Trueman, Trewman Family (Quaker Records), of: County Armagh, dated between 1698-1782; County Down, 1733-1777; County Dublin, 1688-1767. (1951-53, pp. 283, 284.)

TUCKER. Tucker and Armstrong Families; Genealogical Notes, (1951-53, p. 284.)

TURNER. Turner Family (Quaker Records), of: County Antrim, dated between 1701-1744; County Armagh, 1618, 1768-1793; County Down, 1618-1673; 1703-1714. (1951-53, p. 285.)

TWEGG, TWIGG. See Caldwell and other family records, 17th-19th Centuries. (1951-53, p. 18.)

UPRICHARD. Uprichard Family (Quaker Records), County Armagh, dated between 1702-1800. (1951-53, p. 287.)

US(S)HER. Us(s)her Family (Quaker Records), County Armagh, dated between 1718-1774; County Down, 1701-1715. Also Us(s)her-Whelan Family Pedigree, (1066)-1800. (1951-53, p. 287.)

VANBERESTEYN. Paulis VanBeresteyn, of Delft, Holland, Pedigree, *ca.* 1548-1800. (1951-53, p. 287.)

VANDER WEL. Vander Wel Family, Middleburg, Holland, Pedigree, *ca.* 1600-1700. (1951-53, p. 287.)

VAN HOMRIGH. Van Homrigh Family Genealogical Notes *ca.* 1600-1800. (1951-53, p. 287.)

VANTRUMPH. Vantrumph Family Genealogical Notes. (1951-53, p. 287.)

VASA. Vasa Family Pedigree, 1521-1718; Pedigree, Sweden, 1451-1800. (1951-53, p. 287.)

VAUGHAN. See Armstrong documents, 1731-1878. (1927, p. 24.)

VEI(T)CH. Vei(t)ch Family Genealogical Notes. (1951-53, p. 287.)

VINCENT. See Armstrong and other family documents, 1666-1859. (1924, p. 10.)

VOWELL. Vowell Family Genealogical Notes, *ca.* 1600-1800. (1951-53, p. 288.)

WADDELL. Waddell Family, Islanderry, County Down and Yorkshire, Pedigree and Notes (Extracts), 1636-1878.

WADDELL. See Chetwode and other family Pedigrees and Notes on, 1222-1878. (1938-45, p. 17.)

WAINWRIGHT. Wainwright Family (Quaker Records), Counties Antrim and Armagh, 1670-1741. (1951-53, p. 289.)

WAKEFIELD. Wakefield Family (Quaker Records), Counties Armagh, 1766-1800; Down, 1745-1800. (1951-53, p. 289.)

WALKER. Walker Family (Quaker Records) of: Cumberland, Eng., 1643; County Armagh, dated between 1650-1786; County Down, 1643-1785; County Monaghan, 1702-1734; County Tyrone, 1727-1786. (1951-53, p. 289.)

WALKER. See Boyd and other family documents, 1660-1811. (1926, p. 9.)

WALLACE. Wallace Family, Ballyhalbert, County Down, Pedigree, 1685-. (1948, p. 116.)

WALLACE. See Andrews and other family documents, 1728-1852. (1925, p. 8.)

WALLACE. See Boyd and other family documents, 1660-1811. (1926, p. 9.)

WALSH. See Arundell and other family documents, 1646-1846. (1926, p. 9.)

WALSH(E). Walsh(e) Family Genealogical Notes, *ca.* 1600-1800. (1951-53, p. 292.)

WARD. Ward Family (Quaker Records), County Antrim, dated between 1677-1686; County Tyrone, 1718-1778. (1951-53, p. 292.)

WARDELL. Wardell Family (Quaker Records), County Antrim, dated between 1714-1787; County Armagh, 1694-1787. (1951-53, p. 293.)

WAR(R)EN. War(r)en Family (Quaker Records), County Armagh, dated between 1732-1796; County Cavan, 1709-1737. (1951-53, p. 293.)

WATERSON. See Andrews and other family documents, 1728-1852. (1925, p. 8.)

WATSON. See Agnew and other family documents, 1718-1830. (1925, p. 8.)

WATSON. See Anderson and other family documents, 1672-1847. (1925, p. 8.)

WATSON. See Andrews and other family documents, 1668-1855. (1925, p. 7.)

WATSON. See Andrews and other family documents, 1728-1852. (1925, p. 8.)

WATSON. See Hays and other family documents, 1697-1819. (1925, p. 7.)

WATT(S). Watt(s) Family (Quaker Records), County Antrim, dated between 1719-1780; County Armagh, 1732-1782. (1951-53, p. 293.)

WAT(T)SON. Wat(t)son Family (Quaker Records). For the following counties and between dates of: Antrim, 1668, 1741-1764; Armagh, 1700-1785; Down, 1703, 1738, 1742, 1780-1793; Kings, 1744-1785. (1951-53, p. 294.)

WAUGH. See Smith-Waugh Family Wills, 1658-1832. (1927, p. 8.)

WEBB. Webb Family (Quaker Records). For the following counties and between dates of: Antrim, also Armagh, 1622-1674; Armagh, 1649-1800; Armagh and Londonderry, 1659-1699; Tyrone, 1742-1783; Dublin, 1694-1794. (1951-53, p. 294.)

WELD. See Boyd and other family documents, 1660-1811. (1926, p. 9.)

WEST. West Family Pedigree. (1951-53, p. 296.)

WETH(E)RAL(L). Weth(e)ral(l), Weatherell, Weth(e)rill, etc., Family (Quaker Records), County Armagh, 1676-1800. (1951-53, pp. 294, 296, 297.)

WHAL(L)(E)Y. Whal(l)(e)y Family Genealogical Notes, *ca.* 1600-1800. (1951-53, p. 297.)

WHE(E)LAN (USSHER). Whe(e)lan (Ussher) Family Pedigree (1066)-1800. (1951-53, p. 297.)

WHIT(E)FIELD, WHITTFIELD. Whit(e)field, Whittfield Family (Quaker Records). For the following counties and between dates of: Armagh, 1702-1735; Cavan, 1793-1800; Down, 1769-1800; Tyrone, 1700-1800. (1951-53, p. 298.)

WHIT(E)SIDE, WHET(T)(E)SIT(T)(E). Whit(e)side, Whet(t)(e)sit(t)(e), etc., Family (Quaker Records). For the following counties and between dates of: Armagh, 1684-1778; Cavan, 1770-1784; Monaghan, 1754-1764; Tyrone, 1628-1796. (1951-53, pp. 298, 299.)

WHITTAKER. Whittaker Family, County Fermanagh, documents, 1796-1900. (1927, p. 7.)

WHITTSITE. See Graves Wills, 1728-1776. (1951-53, p. 17.)

WICLIFF(E). Wicliff(e) Family (Quaker Records), County Armagh, 1670-1720. (1951-53, p. 300.)

WILKIN. See Arundell and other family documents, 1646-1846. (1926, p. 9.)

WILKIN. Wilkin Family, Carrickreagh, County Fermanagh, Pedigree, 1600-1949. (1949-50, p. 5.)

WILKIN(S). Wilkin(s) Family, Carrickreagh, County Fermanagh, Genealogical Notes, 1600-1800. (1951-53, p. 300.)

WILLCOCKS. Willcocks Family (Quaker Records), County Armagh, 1718-1800; County Tyrone, 1721, 1760-1784. (1951-53, p. 300.)

WIL(L)KI(N)SON, WILKESON. Wil(l)ki(n)son, Wilkeson Family (Quaker Records), County Antrim, dated between 1690-1769; County Armagh, 1671-1782. (1951-53, p. 301.)

WILLIAMS. Williams Family (Quaker Records), County Armagh, 1672-1788; County Tyrone, 1721-1784. (1951-53, p. 301.)

WILLIAMSON. Williamson Family (Quaker Records). For the following counties and between dates of: Antrim, 1690-1722; Armagh, 1686-1799; Tyrone, 1734-1738, 1767-1796. (1951-53, pp. 300, 301.)

WIL(L)SON. Wil(l)son Family (Quaker Records). For the following counties and between dates of: Antrim, 1678-1717; Armagh, 1695-1800; Down, 1697-1789; Londonderry, 1717-1772; Tyrone, 1700-1788. (1951-53, pp. 303, 304.)

WIL(L)SON. Wil(l)son Family, Scotland and Ireland Pedigree, 1684-1800. (1951-53, p. 303.)

WIL(L)SON. Wil(l)son Family, Killenure, County Donegal, Genealogical Notes, *ca.* 1610-1655. (1951-53, p. 303.)

WIL(L)SON. Wil(l)son Family, Irish Newspaper extracts, 1707-1800. (1951-53, p. 303.)

WILSON. Wilson and Kirkpatrick Families, Genealogical Table, 1232-1907. (1938-45, p. 19.)

WILSON. Pedigree of the Wilson-Chesney Family, 1641 *ca.* 1918. Also Diary of Capt. Alex. Chesney, 1755-1815. (1951-53, p. 20.)

WILSON. Memoirs of the Chesney and Wilson Family (of County Antrim and to America, 1772), 1684-1783. (1935, p. 19.)

WILSON. See Agnew and other family documents, 1718-1830. (1925, p. 8.)

WILSON. See Anderson and other family documents, 1672-1847. (1925, p. 8.)

WILSON. See Anderson, etc., documents, 1789-1911.

WILSON. See Andrews and other family documents, 1668-1855. (1925, p. 8.)

WILSON. See Evans and other family documents, 1620-1856. (1926, p. 9.)

WINDER. Winder Family Genealogical Notes, *ca.* 1600-1800. (1951-53, p. 305.)

WINTER, WYNTER. Winter, Wynter Family (Quaker Records), County Armagh, dated between 1684-1789. (1951-53, p. 305.)

WISDOM. Wisdom Family in Ireland, 1640-1835. (1946-47, p. 7.)

WODHULL. Wodhull Family Pedigree (extracts), 1410-1702. (1938-45, p. 74.)

WOOD(S). Wood(s) Family (Quaker Records). For the following counties and between dates of: Antrim, 1678-1786; Armagh, 1692-1792; Down, 1717-1771; Tyrone, 1777-1786. (1951-53, p. 306.)

WORKMAN. Workman Family Genealogical Table, 1681-1927. (1928, p. 9.)

WRAY. Short Account of the Wray Family, 1664-1680. (1927, p. 60.)

WRAY. The Wrays of Donegal, Londonderry and Antrim. By Charlotte Violet Trench. Oxford, 1945. (1946-47, p. 9.)

WRAY. See Arundell and other family documents, 1646-1846. (1926, p. 9.)

WRIGHT. Wright Family (Quaker Records), Yorkshire, 1619; County Armagh, 1647-1789. (1951-53, pp. 306, 307.)

WRIXON. Wrixon Family, Blossomfort, County Cork, Pedigree, *ca.* 1918. Also Diary of. (1951-53, p. 307.)

WYL(E)Y, WIL(L)EY. Wyl(e)y, Wil(l)ey Family (Quaker Records). For the following counties and between dates of: Antrim, 1676-1730; Armagh, 1672-1695, 1716-1788; Londonderry, 1696-1708. (1951-53, pp. 300, 307.)

WYNNE. Wynne Family of Sligo, Documents, 1689-1750. (1938-45, pp. 5, 6, 30.)

YARDELL. See Cuningham Pedigree, etc., 1600-1935. (1951-53, p. 19.)

YOUNG. See Anderson and other family genealogical notes and documents, 1671-1858. (1937, p. 8.)

YOUNG. See Armstrong and other family documents, 1666-1859. (1924, p. 10.)

YOUNG. See Armstrong and other family records, 1694-1806. (1924, p. 10.)

YOUNG(E). Young(e) Family Genealogical Notes, 1600-1800. (1951-53, p. 308.)

CHAPTER II

MANUSCRIPTS IN THE PUBLIC RECORD OFFICE OF IRELAND

The following list of family histories, pedigrees and family collections of documents is representative of the records of a genealogical nature, now deposited in the Public Record Office of Ireland, located in the Four Courts, Dublin. Mr. Diarmid Coffey is the Assistant Deputy Keeper of the Records and in charge of the Office.

This indexed list of families and their records is selected from the collections calendared in the *Reports of the Deputy Keeper of the Public Records in Ireland,* namely, the 55th (1928), 56th (1931), 57th (1936) and 58th (1951) *Reports.* They are, in effect, published catalogues of the records.

Mr. Coffey has followed an outline in making his *Reports* to the government, since the fire of 1922. All describe the care, arrangement and indexing of the records. The 55th-57th describe the collections saved from the fire, and the appendices contain detailed indexes of the documents in many collections, by name of the principal, county or more particular residence, nature, year and source of the records.

The 55th-58th *Reports* list in some detail the collections purchased or presented since the fire, as well as the deposits not required by law from other government agencies and the normal increments from various sources.

The purchased and presented collections contain replacements of records destroyed in 1922, and original documents never before deposited. The replacements are certified copies and transcripts, abstracts, lists or notes, made by qualified persons, from all classes of original records, before the fire. These are genealogical materials of great value, being records of wills, grants and bonds (administration), marriage records, census, tax, and court records, parish registers, etc.; also family history, compiled genealogy and pedigrees. The collections represent the life work of many important genealogists, the contributions of other repositories, material from the files of solicitors or legal offices, and the contents of private family archives.

The original documents deposited in this manner are wills never lodged for probate, other testamentary records, deeds, leases, marriage settlements or agreements, affidavits, estate records and other documents of various classes. They have been acquired principally from solicitors, many of whom emptied their vaults of early documents, and from families or individuals who contributed private papers.

All collections of replacements are calendared and described as to class and nature of the records, number of volumes or documents, inclusive dates and area of interest. Items in smaller collections are listed or indexed. The very large collections are self indexed and, with exceptions, the contents could not be included in the indexes of the *Reports,* due to the great number of items. Sir William Betham's collection of 241 volumes of "Genealogical Abstracts" made from the Prerogative Wills, 1535-1800, and other records, is an example of one collection which is only described in the *Reports* and may be consulted in the Search Room of the Public Record Office. Exceptions are the "Gertrude Thrift Collection" of about 3,600 abstracts and transcripts of wills, marriage records, etc., formerly in this Office, and the "J.G.A. Prim Collection" containing many pedigrees, family histories and other items of genealogical nature. The former is indexed in appendices of the 55th and 57th *Reports.* The contents of the latter is described in detail and indexed in the 58th *Report.*

The single items in the collections of original documents, and the smaller manuscript collections, received 1922-1936, are indexed in the appendices of the 55th-57th *Reports.* After 1936, the volume of records received was too great to allow indexing in the 58th *Report* (1951). Card indexes, catalogues, etc., referring to these records are in the Public Search Room.

The following index contains family names, notes regarding the nature of the records and, in parentheses, the number of the *Report* (55th, 56th, 57th or 58th) and the page number on which the family or individual records are described or listed.

As the *Reports* also record the names of families, the history of which has been a subject of study during the period covered by the *Report*, indicating that material relating to such families is in the Office, these names are included in the following index. They are listed with a reference to the *Report* where mentioned, and with an asterisk before the name to indicate the type of reference. These names are included only to indicate that one might be successful in seeking further details during a visit to the Office or by correspondence.

The references in parentheses after the family names in the following index should be mentioned in any written request sent to this Office, asking for details. For further instructions, see VOLUME ONE, PART TWO, CHAPTER V.

Attention is also called to the fact that this family index serves only as a sample of the many thousands of records of a genealogical nature in this Office. It is compiled from 1,255 pages of the 55th-58th *Reports*. If possible, they should be studied for further findings. Full sets of the *Reports*, published 1869-1958, are in the larger genealogical libraries of the United States.

* * * * *

AHMUTY: Deeds affecting lands in Limerick, Longford, etc., 1685-1844, names of Ahmuty, Brady, Dalzell, Lefroy, and Lorton prominent. Also documents of court cases, various names including the above, 1685-1859. (58th, p. 49.)

ALCOCK: Names Alcock, Crofton, Hubbart, Minchin, Seymour and Walcott, prominent in 336 documents, comprising 235 testamentary documents, 1700-1921; miscellaneous documents; deeds, fines, recoveries, custodian grants, etc., for various counties, Tipperary, Limerick, etc. (58th, p. 47.)

ALEXANDER: Alexander family included in the Anderson Bland collection of 601 documents, relating to the following families and estates: Alexander (Co. Antrim); Lord Audley (Co. Cork); Birch (Cos. Dublin and Meath); Burnside (Co. Wicklow); Cameron (Co. Dublin); Campbell (Dublin); Connolly (Co. Donegal); Disney (Dublin and Co. Wexford); Dowdall (Co. Meath); Edgar (Co. Donegal); Ferguson (Co. Tyrone); Findlater (Dublin); Henry (Dublin); Higgenbothem (Dublin); Law (Co. Down); Lecky (Co. Dublin); McIntire (Derry City); Madder (Dublin); Earl of Miltown (Dublin and Co. Kildare); Moorehouse (Dublin); Norris (Co. Tyrone); Ormsby (Cos. Dublin and Roscommon); Pollock (Co. Meath); Riddal (Dublin); Spencer-Cowper (Dublin); Stewart (Co. Tyrone); Tiernan (Dublin); Trotter (Dublin and Co. Meath). (58th, p. 28.)

* ALLEN: Allen family history. (57th, p. 57.)

ALLEY: See Conrahy.

ANNESLEY: See Bolger.

* ARCHER: Archer family history. (55th, p. 14.)

ARCHER: Archer family genealogy. (Prim Coll., no. 95, 58th, p. 67.)

* ARDERY: Ardery family history. (57th, p. 57.)

ARMSTRONG: Armstrong and the following families in 2,268 documents, mainly 18th and 19th centuries; estates, properties and interests. Some records of 1654, 1666, 1677, etc. Families of Armstrong (Cos. Leitrim, Mayo, and Sligo); Armstrong (Mealiffe, Co. Tipperary); Bellingham (Cos. Louth and Monaghan); Bianconi (Ardmayle, Co. Tipperary); Blackwood (Co. Meath); Brabazon (Co. Tipperary); Bradshaw (Cos. Kilkenny and Tipperary); Caldwell (Cos. Meath and Dublin); Carroll (Dublin City and Co. Meath); Clare (Co. Tipperary); Coote (Leix); Cox (Cos. Cork, Kilkenny and Tipperary); Crofton (Dublin); Croker (Co. Limerick); Duckett (Clonmel); Eccles (Dublin and Co. Wicklow); Fennell (Co. Tipperary); French (Cos. Leitrim and Roscommon); Gordon (Cos. Dublin, Louth, Tipperary and

Waterford); Grace (Cos. Tipperary and Waterford); Green (Dublin and Co. Tipperary); Hely-Hutchinson (Cos. Dublin, Meath, Tipperary and Wexford, and Dublin City); Hickson (Westport and Co. Tipperary); Jones (Dublin City and Cos. Meath and Roscommon); Kearney (Dublin); Kemmis (Co. Louth); Larive (Dublin); MacKenzie (Co. Tyrone, Belfast and Armagh); Massey (Co. Dublin); Moore (Cos. Tipperary and Waterford); O'Brien (Dublin); O'Connor (Dublin); Oliver (Cos. Cork, Leitrim and Limerick); O'Neill (Co. Kildare); Osborne (Cos. Leix, Offaly, and Waterford and Dublin City); Palliser (Cos. Clare, Kildare, Limerick, Tipperary and Waterford); Pennefather (Cos. Dublin, Kildare, Offaly, Wicklow, and especially Co. Tipperary); Phaire (Co. Wexford); Poe (Co. Tipperary); Prendergast (Cos. Galway and Tipperary); Purefoy (Co. Tipperary); Quin (Co. Tipperary); Reynell (Co. Westmeath); Robinson (Dublin); Ryan (Co. Tipperary); Saunders (Cos. Cavan and Dublin, also Tipperary and Wicklow); Smyth (Dublin); Staples (Cos. Derry, Mayo, Offaly, Tipperary and Tyrone); Steele (Co. Louth, etc.); Usher (Cos. Cork and Waterford); Woodcock (Co. Limerick). (58th, p. 36.)

* ARMSTRONG: Armstrong family history. 57th, p. 57.)

ARMSTRONG: Archibald Armstrong Will and Grant, Clogher 1770; probate, William Armstrong, Clogher, 1794; Assignment, Armstrong to Armstrong, 1791; lease of Roosky, Armstrong to McDonald, 1802; lease of Derryannin, Co. Fermanagh, Robinson to Collin, 1823, etc. (58th, p. 28.)

ARTHUR: Abstracts of Wills, 1672-1836: Names Arthur, Atkins, Davis, Lisle, Lysaght, Royse, and Smith, with abstracts and court and other documents, relating to the above families and to those of Blood, Bourke, Bridgeman, Brown, Butler, Chinery, Crone, Crosby, England, Fitzgerald, Hewson, Hill, Love, Moland, Morgan, O'Brien, Purefoy, Reddan, Sexton, Shuckburgh, Stritch, Westby and Wolfe, 17th and 18th centuries. Dr. Edward McLysaght collection. (58th, p. 42.)

ATKINS: See Arthur.

ATKINSON: Atkinson, Bellew, Eyre, Silke, deeds and miscellaneous papers relating to property in Galway City and Co., 1740-1894. (58th, p. 41.)

ATTWOOD: See Bolger.

AUCHMUTY: See Bond.

AUDLEY: See Alexander.

BACON: Families of Bacon (Co. Wicklow); Bowen (Co. Leix); Southwell (Co. Leix); Ellis (Dublin); Lowther (Dublin); Meredith (Dublin); Palliser (Dublin); Hamilton (Dublin); Hayes (Cork); Jacob (Co. Tipperary); Latham (Tipperary); Tuckey (Tipperary); Nugent (Westmeath and Longford); Stopford (Wexford); Walcott (Cork and Tipperary); 380 documents, 1578-1875, relating to above families, including leases, marriage settlements, letters patent, rentals, wills, administrations, and miscellaneous papers. (58th, p. 30.)

BAKER: Baker family records. (55th, pp. 14, 34; 57th, p. 330.)

BALFOUR: See Plunkett.

BALL: Ball family: Three deeds, 1557 and 1621 for Dublin and 1595 for part of property of Kilbeggan priory, and some miscellaneous papers, 17th century, relating to the Ball family. (58th, p. 23.)

BANASTRE: Banastre and Langton families. Armorial bearings and seals (printed extract) and, on the back, manuscript genealogical table of the Langton family. (Prim Coll. no. 91. 58th, p. 66.)

BARBOR: See Bond.

* BARKER: Barker family history. (56th, p. 68.)

BARLOW: Barlow and other families: 50 bundles of papers relating to the following estates: Barlow (Co. Meath); Davis (Monkstown, Co. Dublin); Cooper (Co. Kilkenny); Coppinger (Cos. Cork and Tipperary); Despard (Co. Leix); Finn (Co. Kilkenny); Gibb (Dublin); Goslin (Cos. Dublin and Meath); Harden (Dublin and Co. Leitrim); Sparks (Dublin and Co. Leitrim); Hobart-Davis (Dublin and Co. Kildare); Keogh (Co. Clare); Simpson (Cos.

Leitrim, Leix, Roscommon and Waterford); Usher (Cos. Cork and Tipperary); Warburton (Co. Cork); Widenham (Co. Cork); Woodroffe (Cos. Donegal, Dublin and Kilkenny); Wright (Cos. Donegal, Dublin and Kilkenny); also 365 testamentary documents for families connected with above estates, and others, 1660-1919; also 10 bundles of fines, recoveries, abstracts of title, rentals, and other miscellaneous papers regarding court cases, 18th and 19th centuries. 67 deeds previous to 1708. (58th, p. 32.)

BARNARD: Barnard abstracts of Chancery Bills and Equity Exchange Bills and answers (contain genealogy); Barnard family entries from Co. Waterford Subsidy Rolls, copies and abstracts of Prerogative Wills, documents, and other material mainly relating to the Markham family, 1661-1717. (Crosslé Mss., 58th, p. 33.)

* BARNES: Barnes family history. (57th, p. 57.)

BARNEWELL: Barnewell Pedigree (printed), 1891. (58th, p. 11.)

BATEMAN: Bateman Family Papers, 1648-1848, illustrating the history of the descendants of Rowland Bateman,—who settled near Tralee, *ca.* 1654; 474 items: mainly deeds for land, Co. Kerry, 1648-1707. Also 314 documents, 1712-1848. (58th, p. 28.)

BATEMAN: Bateman deeds relating to their property in Cos. Kerry and Limerick, *ca.* 1714-1773, with correspondence, 1726-65. (58th, p. 19.)

BATEMAN: Bateman documents, 1714-1773. See Hamilton.

BATESON: The families of Bateson, McGill, Purdon, Savage, Thompson and others; 77 documents, including deeds, 1682-1892; recoveries, marriage settlements, and miscellaneous documents, relating to lands in Ballymonestragh, Co. Down, Dublin, Co. Cork, etc. Also certificates of decrees of innocence for Nicholas and Mary Gernon, 1663, and copies of Exchequer inquisitions on Gernon family. Mainly 17th century. (58th, p. 30.)

BEATTY: Beatty family records. (55th, p. 10.)

BECK: Extracts of 1821 census for Beck family, Cos. Antrim, Armagh and Down. Also extracts from Freeholders' Registers, 1769-1783 and 1805; Hearthmoney Rolls; Poll Books and Subsidy Rolls for Beck family, Co. Down. (58th, p. 29.)

BELL: Families of Bell, Carpenter, Clarke, deBurgho, Foott and O'Callaghan, etc., 388 documents, 18th to 20th centuries, comprising 280 deeds, 34 testamentary documents, also trusts in Chancery, estate papers, and marriage settlements. (58th, p. 44.)

BELLEW: See Atkinson.

BELLEW: See Carolan.

BELLINGHAM: See Armstrong.

BERESFORD: See Fitzpatrick.

BERMINGHAM: Bermingham Family of Athenry, Co. Galway. Collection of documents in the Lindsay collection. Claim of Edward Bermingham to the Athenry peerage in 1824. (56th, pp. 58, 397.)

* BERRY: Berry family history. (55th, p. 14.)

BIANCONI: See Armstrong.

BIBBY: Bibby family of Co. Kilkenny. Genealogy compiled, 1858. (Prim Coll. no. 94. 58th, p. 67.)

BINGHAM: See Bolger.

BIRCH: See Alexander.

BLACKWOOD: See Armstrong.

BLAKE: Blake Family Records. Calendar printed. (55th, p. 133.)

* BLAKENEY: Blakeney family history. (57th, p. 57.)

BLOOD: See Arthur.

BOLGER: Families of Bolger, Jones, Wade (Co. Dublin); Hendrick (Co. Kildare); Stannard (Co. Kilkenny); Bingham and Vesey (Co. Mayo); also families of Annesley, Attwood, Brisson, Cox, Coyler, Edwards, Harrison, Hatton, Ram, Read, all in Co. Wexford; Snell (Co. Wicklow). (58th, p. 37.)

BOLTON: See Dobbyn.

* BOLTON: Bolton family history. (57th, p. 57.)

BOND: Bond family papers relating to County and Town of Longford, 1688-1863. Chief related names: Auchmuty, Barbor and Montfort. Includes maps of property in Co. Longford, 1764-1855. (58th, p. 29.)

BOURKE: See Arthur.

BOWEN: See Bacon.

* BOXWELL: Boxwell family history. (56th, p. 68.)

BRABAZON: See Armstrong.

BRADSHAW: See Armstrong.

BRADY: Brady family records. (57th, p. 336.)

BRADY: See Ahmuty.

BRICE (BRUCE): Brice or Bruce Family. Counties Antrim and Down, 1655-1873. Deeds, testamentary and some miscellaneous documents relating to this family. (58th, p. 20.)

BRIDGEMAN: See Arthur.

BRISSON: See Bolger.

BRISTOW: See Conrahy.

BRODERICK: See Fitzgerald.

BROUGHTON: Broughton family records. (57th, p. 339.)

BROWN: See Arthur.

BRUCE: See Brice.

BRUCE: See Conrahy.

BUDD: Budd family. See Greene Mss.

BULLOCK: Bullock family, extracts from 1821 census, Cos. Antrim and Armagh. (58th, p. 29.)

BUNBURY: Bunbury family records. (57th, p. 116.)

BURKE: Burke family records. (56th, p. 93; 57th, pp. 117, 340, 428, 429.)

BURNSIDE: See Alexander.

* BURT: Burt family history. (57th, p. 57.)

BUSTEED: Busteed family testamentary documents, 1789-1839. (58th, p. 33.)

BUSTEED: Families of Busteed, Daunt, Dowlin, Hayes, Morgan, and Walton, represented in 434 documents, relating to property in the County and City of Cork, 1667-1920. (58th, p. 43.)

BUTLER: Families of Butler, Keogh, Lawless, Nowlan, and Nugent; names prominent in 428 documents, relating to property in Cos. Meath and Westmeath. Also the Butler claim to the Dunboyne peerage. Includes 222 deeds, 1629-1884. (58th, p. 35.)

BUTLER: Butler Chancery and Exchequer Bills; 12 extracts concerning the Butler family, 1680-1765. (58th, p. 31.)

BUTLER: Butler family records. (56th, pp. 93, 400; 57th, p. 341.)

BUTLER: Butler, see Arthur.

CALBEC: Families of Calbec, Carvill, Connell, Conly, Connolly, Dardis, Fitton, Foss, Fullam, Grehan, Hamill, Kearney, Langan, McDaniell, McDonell, Maffit, Mathews, Seward, Twigg, Vaughn, Wall, Yeo, copies and abstracts of wills, marriage license grants; 1821-1841-1851 census returns; entries in Chapelzoid Parish Register, 1783-1851. Records, 1761-1897. (58th, p. 48.)

CALDWELL: Caldwell, see Armstrong.

CAMERON: Cameron, see Alexander.

CAMPBELL: Campbell, see Alexander.

CANTWELL: Cantwell family notes on. (Prim Coll. no. 103. 58th, p. 67.)

CAREW: Carew Family Papers: Carew family of Castle Boro, Co. Wexford, 18th - early 19th century. Published in Shapland Carew Papers. Dublin, 1946.

CAREW: Carew family, Co. Wexford, documents, memoranda of. (57th, p. 3.)

CAROLAN: Register of births, deaths, and marriages, and miscellaneous documents, concerning the Carolan family of Belpatrick, Co. Louth, post 1730, and extracts of baptisms, and marriages from Collon and Slane Catholic parish registers, and burials in Smarmore, Dunleek, and Grangegeeth cemeteries, with notes on Bellew, Carolan, and Nulty families, 1704-1926. (58th, p. 31.)

CARPENTER: Carpenter, see Bell.

CARROLL: Carroll, see Armstrong.

CARVILL: Carvill, see Calbec.

CHINERY: Chinery, see Arthur.

CHINNERY: Chinnery family records. (57th, p. 344.)

* CHRISTIE: Christie family history. (57th, p. 57.)

* CLARE: Clare family history. (57th, p. 57.)

CLARE: See Armstrong.

CLARKE: Clarke, see Bell.

* CLINTON: Clinton family history. (56th, p. 68.)

COLE: Cole family records. (56th, p. 100; 57th, p. 130.)

COLLES: Colles letters. (Prim Coll. 58th, p. 61.)

COLVILLE: Colville family documents, 1610-1900. 272 items, mainly deeds, relating to property in Dublin, Wexford, and Cos. Antrim, Down, Fermanagh, Kildare, Louth, Meath. Also testamentary documents, etc. (58th, p. 32.)

COMERFORD: Comerford Family in Champagne, France. Notes in French. (Prim Coll. no. 102. 58th, p. 67.)

CONLY: Conly, see Calbec.

CONNELL: See Calbec.

CONNELL: Connell, see O'Connell.

CONNOLLY: Connolly, see Alexander.

CONNOLLY: Connolly, see Calbec.

CONRAHY: Families of Conrahy, Alley, Bristow, Bruce, Delaney, Eyre, Finston, Fivey, Gregory, Lucas, and Stewart, extracts of 21 wills, 1683-1873, and from one deed, 1806. Also Conrahy pedigree chart. (58th, p. 34.)

* COOKE: Cooke family history. (55th, p. 14.)

COOPER: Cooper, see Barlow.

COOTE: Coote, see Armstrong.

COPPINGER: Coppinger, see Barlow.

CORRY: Forty nine notebooks containing genealogical material on the Corry family, Newry, Co. Down. Crosslé Mss. Coll. (58th, p. 33.)

COWLEY (COLLEY): Cowley or Colley family, notes on, 23rd Oct. 1852. (Prim Coll. no. 96. 58th, p. 67.)

COYLER: Coyler, see Bolger.

COX: Cox, see Armstrong.

COX: Cox family records. (57th, pp. 135, 347.)

COX: Cox, see Bolger.

CROFTON: Crofton, see Armstrong.

CROFTON: Families of Crofton, Irwin, Dodwell, Gethin, deeds relating mainly to estates of, in Cos. Sligo and Roscommon, 1615-1828. (58th, p. 22.)

CROFTON: Crofton family of Dublin, and allied families: 6 testamentary documents, 1748-1893; 2 marriage licenses and memorial of marriage articles, 1725-1803. (58th, p. 33.)

CROFTON: Crofton, see Alcock.

CROKER: Croker family: see Greene Mss.

CROKER: Croker, see Armstrong.

CRONE: Crone, see Arthur.

CROOKSHANKS: Crookshanks, see Delap.

CROSBY: Crosby, see Arthur.

DALZELL: Dalzell, see Ahmuty.

DARDIS: Dardis, see Calbec.

DAUNT: Daunt, see Busteed.

DAVIS: Davis, see Arthur.

DAVIS: Davis, see Barlow.

DAVIS: Davis family records (57th, p. 142.)

DAWSON: Dawson family records. (57th, p. 352.)

DE BURGHO: deBurgho, see Bell.

DELANEY: Delaney, see Conrahy.

DELAP: Delap and Crookshanks family records. (57th, pp. 350, 354.)

* DEMPSEY: Dempsey family history. (57th, p. 57.)

DENIS (DENNIS): Denis or Dennis: see Greene Mss.

* DENNEHY: Dennehy family history. (57th, p. 57.)

DENNY: Denny family records. (56th, pp. 109, 238.)

DESPARD: Despard, see Barlow.

* DE VIGNE: De Vigne family history. (55th p. 14.)

DE ZOUCHE: De Zouche family abstracts from testamentary records, and memorials, 1676-1810. (57th, p. 37.)

DICKSON: Dickson family records. (57th, pp. 145, 355.)

DILLON: Dillon, Michael James Robert; claim to Earldom of Roscommon. Papers covering claim: 1792 pedigree (printed), Wills, Marriage records, etc. (57th, pp. 45, 46.)

DISNEY: Disney, see Alexander.

DIXON: Dixon family records. (56th, p. 110; 57th, p. 146.)

DOBBIN: Dobbin family records. (55th, pp. 43, 74; 56th, pp. 110, 238; 57th, pp. 146, 355.)

DOBBYN: Dobbyn, Bolton and West families, 1726-1894. 55 documents, testamentary items, deeds, etc., in Cos. Kilkenny and Waterford, 1715-1717. (58th, p. 33.)

DODWELL: Dodwell family records. (56th, p. 111.)

DODWELL: Dodwell, see Crofton.

DOMVILLE: Sir William Domville, see Montgomery.

* DOWDALL: Dowdall family history. (56th, p. 68.)

DOWDALL: Dowdall, see Alexander.

DOWLIN: see Busteed.

* DROUGHT: Drought family history. (55th, p. 14.)

DROUGHT: Drought family: 167 copies and extracts from wills, leases and marriage settlements of the Drought family, 1698-1905, various counties, especially Offaly (Park and Ballybracken). (58th, p. 34.)

DRURY: Drury family copies of wills and entries referring to Drury family in Chancery and Exchequer Bills, testamentary and matrimonial documents, and parish registers, 17th to 19th centuries. Deeds relating to Drury property near R. Dodder, Co. Dublin, 1751-1862. (58th, p. 34.)

DUCKETT: Duckett, see Armstrong.

DUNNE: Dunne family records. (55th, p. 43; 56th, pp. 113, 114; 57th, pp. 152, 153, 356, 357.)

DURHAM: Transcripts of Durham wills, Armagh diocese, 1763-1793. (58th, p. 34.)

DWYER: Dwyer family documents, 1667-1875. Lands in Cos. Clare, Leix, Limerick, and Tipperary. 267 items including deeds, fines, recoveries, rentals, grants. Stradbally parish, Co. Limerick. (58th, p. 34.)

ECCLES: Eccles, see Armstrong.

* ECKERSLEY: Eckersley family history. (56th, p. 68.)

EDGAR: Edgar, see Alexander.

EDGEWORTH: Edgeworth Papers, late 17th to early 19th centuries regarding property in Co. Longford and town of Kinsale. Also one volume of documents, showing management of family property by Maria Edgeworth.

EDGEWORTH: Edgeworth family documents, 1671-1847; 109 items, mainly deeds, relating to Edgeworth estates in Co. Longford, with a few relating to property in Kinsale, 1693-1695. Includes wills. (58th, p. 31.)

* EDWARDS: Edwards family history. (56th, p. 68.)

EDWARDS: Edwards, see Bolger.

ELLIOT: Elliot (Elliott), see Greene Mss.

ELLIS: Ellis, see Bacon.

ELMES: Elmes family record. (57th, p. 156.)

ENGLAND: England, see Arthur.

EVERARD: Everard, see Plunkett.

EYRE: Eyre family deeds, testamentary documents and miscellaneous papers relating to property in Galway City and County, also property of the White, Hedges and Eyre families in Co. Cork, and property in Limerick City, mainly that of the Pearse family, 1663-1819. Includes "Adventurers Cert." to James Reed and others of the lands of Longford, Castle-fleming, etc., of Queen's Co., 19 October 1666. (58th, p. 24.)

EYRE: Eyre, see Atkinson.

EYRE: Eyre, see Conrahy.

EYRE: Eyre, see Herbert.

FENNELL: Fennell, see Armstrong.

FERGUSON: Ferguson, see Alexander.

FINCH: Finch family records. (57th, p. 360.)

FINDLATER: Findlater, see Alexander.

FINLAY: Finlay family records. (56th, p. 117; 57th, p. 160.)

FINN: Finn, see Barlow.

FINSTON: Finston, see Conrahy.

FINUCANE: Genealogical notes on the Finucane family, containing extracts from Chancery and Exchequer documents. Also 32 testamentary items for Finucane and other families, 1772-1869. (58th, p. 33.)

FINUCANE: Families of Finucane, Co. Clare, and Meredyth, Co. Kilkenny, in 157 deeds and 10 miscellaneous, all dated 1712-1900. (57th, p. 37.)

FITTON: Fitton, see Calbec.

FITZGERALD: Fitzgerald and Broderick families; 129 documents, 1666-1850, relating to property in Co. Cork. (58th, p. 30.)

FITZGERALD: Fitzgerald, see Arthur.

FITZGERALD: See Lombard family history. (57th, p. 57.)

FITZMAURICE: Lord Thomas Fitzmaurice and his Descendants, Co. Kilkenny. (3 pp.) From Lynch's "Feudal Dignities." (Prim Coll. no. 99. 58th, p. 67.)

FITZPATRICK: Papers relating to property of Fitzpatrick and allied families of Beresford, Pearse and Slade, in Cos. Cavan and Galway. 100 items, including 67 deeds, 1703-1840. (58th, p. 29.)

FIVEY: Fivey, see Conrahy.

FLEMING: Fleming family records. (56th, p. 118; 57th, pp. 146, 436.)

FOOTT: Foott, see Bell.

FORBES: Forbes, see Plunkett.

* FORD: Ford family history. (56th, p. 68.)

FOSS: Foss, see Calbec.

* FOX: Fox family history. (55th, p. 14; 57th, p. 57.)

FRAYNE: Frayne Family Pedigree. (Prim Coll. no. 105. 58th, p. 67.)

FRENCH: French family records. (56th, p. 120; 57th, pp. 167, 362.)

FRENCH: French, see Armstrong.

FULLAM: Fullam, see Calbec.

GERNON: Gernon, see Bateson.

GETHIN: Gethin, see Crofton.

GIBB: Gibb, see Barlow.

* GILBERT: Gilbert family history. (57th, p. 57.)

* GLENNY: Glenny family history. (55th, p. 14.)

GODLEY: Godley, see Lane.

GORDON: Gordon, see Armstrong.

* GORMLEY: Gormley family history. (56th, p. 68.)

GOSLIN: Goslin, see Barlow.

GRACE: Grace, see Armstrong.

GRANGER: Granger family records. (57th, p. 176.)

GRAY (GREY): Gray or Grey family records. (56th, p. 124.)

GREEN: Greene or Green, see Armstrong.

* GREEN: Green or Greene family history. (56th, p. 68.)

GREENE: Greene Mss. 5 vols. (copies) from original manuscripts in the National Library, by the Public Record Office. Regarding the Greene family and allied families of Budd, Croker, Denis (Dennis), Elliot (Elliott), Greene (Green), Hunt, Jones, Lewis, Mackesy, Newport, Poulter, Shearman, etc. The manuscripts contain Original Wills, Baptismal, Marriage and Burial Entries, Extracts from Officers' Rolls, Patent Rolls, Abstracts of Wills, Grants and other documents, formerly in the Public Record Office. Families of the parishes of Clonmore, Dunkett, Fiddown, Kilbeacon, and Macully (or Kilculliheen), Diocese of Ossory; Parish of Innislonagh, Diocese of Lismore; St. Finnbarr's Parish, Diocese of Cork; Shanagolden, Diocese of Limerick. (57th, pp. 54, 56.)

* GREER: Greer family history. (57th, p. 57.)

GREGORY: Gregory, see Conrahy.

GREHAN: Grehan, see Calbec.

GREVILLE: Greville family papers concerning the estates of the family in Co. Cavan, early 19th century. (57th, p. 468.)

GREVILLE: Memorandum of the Greville Estate papers. (57th, pp. 3, 522, 523.)

GRUBB: Grubb family testamentary documents, 1669-1885, and miscellaneous papers relating to the Grubb family property in Clonmel, Carrick-on-Suir, and Cos. Tipperary, Waterford and Kilkenny. (58th, p. 20.)

GUINNESS: Guinness family testamentary documents, 1795-1835. (58th, p. 37.)

GUINNESS: Guinness family records. (55th, pp. 14, 76-78; 57th, p. 184.)

HAMILL: Hamill, see Calbec.

HAMILTON: Hamilton, see Bacon.

HAMILTON: Hamilton Deeds, Wills: estate of Sir Hans Hamilton, Co. Down, late 17th and early 18th century. Wills of James, Earl of Clanbrassil (d. 1659); James Hamilton (d. 1693); the Rev. James Hamilton (d. 1721). (58th, p. 22.)

HAMILTON: Hamilton Family Documents, 1547-1776; Bateman family documents, 1714-1773; Nugent family documents, 1637-1848; Ball family documents, 1557-1603; Fitzpatrick family documents, deeds (Barony of Upper Ossory), *ca.* 1587-1656. (57th, pp. 568-69.)

HAMILTON: Hamilton family papers concerning their estates in Cos. Armagh and Down. 17th and 18th centuries. (58th, p. 22.)

* HANDCOCK: Handcock family history. (57th, p. 57.)

HARDIN: Hardin, see Barlow.

HARRISON: Harrison, see Bolger.

HATTON: Hatton, see Bolger.

HAYES: Hayes, see Bacon.

HAYES: Hayes, see Busteed.

HEDGES: Hedges, see Eyre.

HEDGES: Hedges, see Herbert.

HELY-HUTCHINSON: Hely-Hutchinson, see Armstrong.

HENDRICK: Hendrick, see Bolger.

HENRY: Henry, see Alexander.

HERBERT: Herbert family of Cahirnane and Muckross, Co. Kerry: Testamentary documents, deeds, and miscellaneous papers, 1669-1859. Chief related families: Eyre, Hedges, Hussy (Hussey), and White of Bantry. (58th, p. 38.)

HEWSON: Hewson, see Arthur.

HICKSON: Hickson, see Armstrong.

HIGGENBOTHAM: Higgenbotham, see Alexander.

HILL: Hill, see Arthur.

HOBART: Hobart, see Barlow.

HOGAN: Hogan family records. (57th, pp. 196, 197, 442.)

HOLLAND: Holland family records. (56th, p. 130; 57th, pp. 197, 373.)

HOWLIN: Howlin vol. of deeds, correspondence, rent rolls, maps and miscellaneous papers relating to the property of the Howlin family of Ballycronigan, Co. Wexford, 1723-93. (58th, p. 27.)

HUBBART: Hubbart, see Alcock.

HUMPHREY: Testamentary documents, relating to the Humphrey family. Prerogative Wills, Dublin and Leighlin, 1649-1843. (58th, p. 39.)

* HUNT: Hunt family. See Greene Mss.

HUSSEY: Small collection of documents, relating to the Hussey family of Co. Meath, time of Henry VIII. (58th, p. 27.)

HUSSEY: Hussey, see Herbert.

IRWIN: Irwin family records. (56th, p. 133; 57th, p. 374.)

IRWIN: Irwin, see Crofton.

JACOB: Jacob, see Bacon.

* JENNENS: Jennens family history. (57th, p. 57.)

JENNINGS: Ms. vol. (Caulfield Coll.) containing pedigrees, arms, memoranda, entries of births, deaths, marriages, etc., of various Jennings families. (55th, p. 132.)

* JENNINGS: Jennings family history. (55th, p. 14.)

JOHNSON: Johnson family records. (56th, p. 133; 57th, pp. 206, 374.)

JONES: Jones family: see Greene Mss.

JONES: Jones, see Armstrong.

JONES: Jones, see Bolger.

KEARNEY: Kearney, see Armstrong.

KEARNEY: Kearney, see Calbec.

KELLY: Kelly family records. (55th, pp. 51, 80; 56th, p. 135; 57th, pp. 210-212, 444.)

KELLY: Kelly Family: see Walsh Mss. volume.

KEMMIS: Kemmis, see Armstrong.

KENNEDY: Kennedy family records. (56th, p. 136; 57th, p. 212.)

KEOGH: Keogh, see Barlow.

KEOGH: Keogh, see Butler.

KERR. Kerr family records. (55th, p. 51; 56th, p. 137; 57th, p. 213.)

* KING: King family history. (56th, p. 68.)

KING-HARMON: King-Harmon family papers concerning their estates in Cos. Longford, Kildare, Queen's, Westmeath, 1656-1893.

KNARESBOROUGH: Knaresborough family, Co. Kilkenny. (Prim Coll. no. 93; 58th, p. 66.)

* KNIGHT: Knight family history. (56th, p. 68.)

LACY: Lacy family records. (56th, p. 400; 57th, p. 217.)

LANE: Lane, O'Brien and Godley families: 142 documents, 1586-1878, concerning property in many counties, especially in Cork City (Lane property); Dublin City and County (O'Brien and Godley); also Cos. Kildare and Meath. (58th, p. 30.)

LANGAN: Langan, see Calbec.

LANGTON: Langton, see Banastre.

LANGTON: Langton family of Co. Kilkenny: Manuscript genealogical table of Langton family armorial bearings and seals of Banastree and Langton families in printed extract from *Visitation of Lancashire* (Chetham Society). Manuscript draft of portion of proofs on article on Langton family of Kilkenny, etc. (Prim Coll. nos. 91, 92, 97, 98. 58th, p. 66.)

LANGTON: Langton family arms. (Prim Coll. 58th, p. 67.)

LARIVE: Larive family, see Armstrong.

LATHAM: Latham, see Bacon.

* LATIMER: Latimer family history. (56th, p. 68.)

LAW: Law, see Alexander.

LAWLESS: Lawless, see Butler.

LECKY: Lecky, see Alexander.

LEFROY: Lefroy, see Ahmuty.

LEWIS: Lewis family, see Greene Mss.

LEWIS: Lewis family records. (56th, p. 141; 57th, pp. 222, 380.)

* LINTON: Linton family history. (55th, p. 14.)

LISLE: Lisle, see Arthur.

LORTON. Lorton, see Ahmuty.

LOVE: Love, see Arthur.

* LOVEKIN (LUFKIN): Lovekin or Lufkin family history (56th, p. 68.)

LOWTHER: Lowther, see Bacon.

LUCAS: Lucas, see Conrahy.

* LUDLOW: Ludlow family history. (56th, p. 68.)

* LYNCH: Lynch family history. (55th, p. 14; 56th, p. 68; 57th, p. 57.)

LYNCH: Lynch family of Newtown, Co. Mayo: deeds and miscellaneous papers, 1656-1917. (58th, p. 39.)

LYSAGHT: Lysaght, see Arthur.

MACGRATH: Deeds and miscellaneous documents, 1676-1857, relating to the MacGrath family in the Barony of Tulla, Co. Clare, etc. (58th, p. 42.)

MACKENZIE: MacKenzie, see Armstrong.

MADDEN: Madden family records. (57th, pp. 234, 449.)

MADDER: Madder, see Alexander.

MAFFIT: Maffit, see Calbec.

* MAGILL: Magill family history. (56th, p. 68.)

MAKESY: Makesy family: see Greene Mss.

MALONE: Malone family in Cos. Dublin and Westmeath, 1700-1855. Map of Malone estate in Westmeath, 1852. (58th, p. 22.)

MARKHAM: Markham, see Barnard.

MARTIN: Genealogy of the Martin family of Ballynahinch, Co. Galway. (58th, p. 31.)

MARTIN: Martin family records. (Co. Antrim.) (57th, p. 385.)

MARTIN: Rentals relating to the Martin estate, Co. Galway, 1829-57. (58th, p. 39.)

MASSEY: Massey, see Armstrong.

MATHEWS: Mathews family records. (57th, pp. 238, 386, 450.)

MATHEWS: Mathews, see Calbec.

* MCAULEY: McAuley family history. (57th, p. 57.)

MCCLURE: McClure family records. (56th, pp. 146, 147; 57th, p. 382.)

MCDANIELL: McDaniell, see Calbec.

MCDONELL: McDonell, see Calbec.

MCDONNELL: McDonnell, see Barlow.

* MCGARRY: McGarry family history. (56th, p. 68.)

MCGILL: McGill, see Bateson.

MCGURTY: McGurty, papers relating to McGurty and Townsend families, Co. Cork, 1678-1881. (58th, p. 38.)

MCINTIRE: McIntire, see Alexander.

MCKENNA. McKenna family records. (56th, p. 151; 57th, pp. 232, 383.)

MCNAMARA: McNamara family records. (57th, pp. 233, 384.)

MEADE: Wills, copies and abstracts of wills, Meade family, 1595-1831, and population return, 1821, family of Thomas Meade, Merchants Quay, Dublin. (58th, p. 42.)

* MEELL: Meell family history. (57th, p. 57.)

MEREDITH: Meredith, see Bacon.

MEREDYTH: Meredyth, see Finucane.

MILTOWN: Miltown, Earl of: see Alexander.

MINCHIN: Minchin, see Alcock.

MOLAND: Moland, see Arthur.

MOLINEUX: Molineux, see Perry.

MONTFORT: Montfort, see Bond.

MONTGOMERY: Montgomery family (Cos. Cavan and Donegal); Waller family (Cos. Limerick and Cork); Moore family (Co. Louth); Sir William Domville and others (Co. Meath); deeds for these families, late 18th century. Also deeds, 1730-1870, for Dublin City, etc., with some testamentary documents. (58th, p. 23.)

* MOONEY: Mooney family history. (57th, p. 57.)

* MOORE: Moore family history. (55th, p. 14.)

MOORE: Moore, see Armstrong.

MOORE: Moore, see Montgomery.

MOORE: Moore family of Co. Louth, deeds, late 18th century. See Montgomery. (58th, p. 23.)

MOOREHOUSE: Moorehouse, see Alexander.

MORGAN: Morgan family records. (56th, p. 162; 57th, pp. 246, 389.)

MORGAN: Morgan, see Arthur.

MORGAN: See Busteed.

MORRIS: Morris family records. (57th, pp. 247, 389, 453.)

* MORRISON: Morrison family history. (56th, p. 68.)

MORROGH: Morrogh family records. (57th, p. 246.)

MURRAY: Murray family records. (57th, pp. 249, 250, 391, 454.)

NAGHTEN: Naghten Family. See Walsh Mss. volume.

NARROW WATER, CO. DOWN, FAMILIES. (56th, p. 68.)

* NASH: Nash family history. (55th, p. 14.)

* NEEDHAM: Needham family history. (57th, p. 57.)

NEWPORT: Newport family. See Greene Mss.

NORRIS: Norris, see Alexander.

* NORTH: North family history. (56th, p. 68.)

NOWLAN: Nowlan, see Butler.

NUGENT: Nugent family records. (56th, p. 165; 57th, pp. 254, 394, 455.)

NUGENT: Nugent family miscellaneous documents, mainly deeds—and their property in Cos. Westmeath and Galway, and Dublin City, 1637-1848, etc. (58th, p. 21.)

NUGENT: See Bacon.

NUGENT: See Butler.

NULTY: Nulty, see Carolan.

OBINS: Obins family documents: 58 testamentary documents, deeds, fines and recoveries for property in Dublin City and Co., also in counties Armagh, Down, Kerry, Meath and Offaly, 1666-1899. (58th, p. 57.)

O'BRIEN: O'Brien, see Armstrong.

O'BRIEN: O'Brien, see Arthur.

O'BRIEN: O'Brien, see Lane.

O'CALLAGHAN: O'Callaghan, see Bell.

* O'CONNELL. O'Connell family history. (57th, p. 57.)

O'CONNELL: O'Connell family of Darrinane and Co. Clare; lands in Cores, Co. Kerry, 1772-96. (58th, p. 29.)

O'CONNOR: O'Connor, see Armstrong.

* O'FARRELL: O'Farrell family history. (53rd, p. 15.)

* O'FLANAGAN: O'Flanagan family history. (53rd, p. 15.)

O'GRADY: O'Grady family of Kilballyowen, Co. Limerick. (Prim Coll. no. 90. 58th, p. 66.)

* O'HUIGINN: O'Huiginn family history. (56th, p. 68.)

OLIVER: Oliver, see Armstrong.

O'NEILL: O'Neill Wills: Collection in Public Record Office. (53rd.)

O'NEILL: O'Neill, see Armstrong.

ORMSBY: Ormsby, see Alexander.

OSBORNE: Osborne, see Armstrong.

OSBORNE: Osborne family documents, 17th and 18th century, deeds, etc., patents, Prerogative Wills; 31 pre-1708 deeds. Lands: Headfort estate, Co. Meath, also Cos. Limerick and Tipperary. (58th, p. 30.)

O'SHEE: See Shee. Genealogical material for Co. Kilkenny. (Prim Coll. nos. 83, 84, 109, 112. 58th, p. 60.)

* PAINE: Paine family history. (53rd, p. 15.)

PALLISER: Palliser, see Armstrong.

PALLISER: Palliser, see Bacon.

PEARSE: Pearse, see Eyre.

PEARSE: Pearse, see Fitzpatrick.

* PENNEFATHER: Pennefather family history. (57th, p. 57.)

PENNEFATHER: Pennefather, see Armstrong.

PERRY: Perry family and related families of Molineux, Ringwood, Ward and Wilkinson: 13 notebooks and 3 envelopes of loose notes compiled by Dr. W. M. Graham, 18th and 19th centuries. (Perry family of Dublin, violin makers.) (58th, p. 36.)

* PHAIRE: Phaire family history. (56th, p. 68.)

PHAIRE: Phaire, see Armstrong.

* PHAYRE: Phayre family history. (57th, p. 57.)

PLUNKETT: Families of Plunkett, Balfour, Everard, Forbes, Warren, and others in many counties, especially Louth and Meath: Various papers, including deeds, fines, recoveries, leases from Archbishop of Armagh, 1695-1776. Family records, 1658-1827. (58th, p. 29.)

POE: Poe, see Armstrong.

POLLOCK: Pollock, see Alexander.

POULTER: Poulter, see Greene Mss.

PRENDERGAST: Prendergast, see Armstrong.

PURDON: Purdon, see Bateson.

PUREFOY: Purefoy, see Armstrong.

PUREFOY: Purefoy, see Arthur.

PUREFOY COLLES: Purefoy Colles family. (Prim Coll. no. 86 (a) 58th, p. 61.)

QUIN: Quin, see Armstrong.

RAM: Ram, see Bolger.

RAMBAUT. Rambaut family records. (57th, p. 401.)

RAYMOND: Raymond family estate: 14 deeds relating to Ballyloughran, Co. Kerry, 1663-1824. (58th, p. 22.)

READ: Read, see Bolger.

REDDAN: Reddan, see Arthur.

* REDESDALE: Lord Redesdale family history. (55th p. 14.)

REYNELL: Reynell, see Armstrong.

RICE: Rice, see Spring.

* RICHARDSON: Richardson family history. (57th, p. 57.)

RIDDAL: Riddal, see Alexander.

RINGWOOD: Ringwood, see Perry.

ROBERTS: History of the descendants of Mary Sautell (daughter of Major Sautell), and John Roberts of Waterford, including sketches of the families of Roberts, Greham, Makesy, Price, etc. (Caulfield Mss. 55th, p. 132.)

ROBINSON: Robinson family records. (56th, p. 175; 57th, p. 277.)

ROBINSON: Copy of Robinson family tree, Co. Fermanagh and England. (*ca.* 1819.) (58th, p. 46.)

ROBINSON: Robinson, see Armstrong.

ROCHE: Roche family records. (56th, p. 175; 57th, pp. 277, 278, 404, 460.)

ROSSE: Rosse, Countess of. See Alexander.

ROTH: Genealogical material on the Roth family. (Prim Coll. no. 85. 58th, pp. 60, 61.)

* ROWEN: Rowen family history. (57th, p. 57.)

ROYSE: Royse, see Arthur.

* RUTHERFORD: Rutherford family history. (55th, p. 14.)

RUXTON: Charles and Elizabeth Ruxton, fine of 1767 and 22 deeds, mainly Ruxton family of Dublin and Ardee, Co. Louth. (58th, p. 28.)

RYAN: Ryan, see Armstrong.

* SANDES: Sandes family history. (56th, p. 68.)

SANDFORD: Sandford wills and deeds (also for others), Co. Roscommon, 1723-1832. Also list of tenants on Sandford estate, Mullacloe, Co. Westmeath, early 19th century. (58th, p. 34.)

SARSFIELD - VESEY: Sarsfield - Vesey Papers: Concerning property of the Sarsfield and Vesey families of counties Dublin, Wicklow, Kildare and Carlow: Testamentary documents, 1616-; List of Deeds (indexed), 1414-1808; Index to correspondence, 1673-1814; Accounts, Rentals, 1675-. Exchequer Documents, 1407-1696. (56th, p. 342.)

SAUNDERS: Saunders, see Armstrong.

SAVAGE: Savage, see Bateson.

SCOOL: See Scull.

SCOTT: Scott family records. (56th, p. 178; 57th, p. 405.)

SCULL: Notes on the Scool or Scull family, 1500-1638. Paper also of Edmund Sculagh, dated 9 Mar. 1564/5. Grant 11 Feb. 1620/21, to Edmund Skoole of Kilballio-wen. Correspondence relating to the Scull and O'Grady genealogy. Also printed pedigree, and notes, Scull family (1876). (58th, p. 66.)

SEGRAVE: Segrave family records. (56th, pp. 178, 286, 336.)

SEWARD: Seward, see Calbec.

SEXTON: Sexton, see Arthur.

SEYMOUR: Seymour, see Alcock.

* SHANLEY: Shanley family history. (56th, p. 68.)

SHEARMAN: Shearman Family: see Greene Mss.

SHEARMAN: Shearman family pedigree. (Prim Coll. no. 106. 58th, p. 67.)

SHEE: Families of Shee, O'Shee, Rothe, Colles, O'Grady, Scull, Cantwell, Frayne, and Shearman, Co. Kilkenny. Genealogical material: Pedigrees, notes, copies of wills, etc., 1458-1784. (Prim Coll. 58th, pp. 50, 68.)

SHUCKBURGH: Shuckburgh, see Arthur.

SILKE: Silke, see Atkinson.

SIMPSON: Simpson family records. (55th, p. 63; 56th, p. 180; 57th, p. 287.)

SIMPSON: See Barlow.

SINGLETON: Singleton family records. (56th, p. 180; 57th, p. 288.)

SKERRETT: Skerrett family, Galway; two notebooks containing abstracts of deeds and wills. (Crosslé Mss., 58th, p. 33.)

SLADE: Slade, see Fitzpatrick.

SMITH: Smith, see Arthur.

* SMYTH: Smyth family history. (56th, p. 68.)

SMYTH: Smyth, see Armstrong.

SNELL: Snell, see Bolger.

SOUTHWELL: Southwell, see Bacon.

SPARKS: Sparks, see Barlow.

SPENCE: Spence family records. (56th, p. 182; 57th, p. 292.)

SPENCER-COWPER: See Alexander.

SPRING: The Spring and Rice families, in Counties Kerry and Limerick: 290 documents, 1669-1925, relating to these families and their property. Grants, recoveries, leases, rent rolls, will of 1823, etc. (Papers of Monteagle Coll. 58th, p. 43.)

STANNARD: Stannard, see Bolger.

STAPLES: Staples, see Armstrong.

STAWELL: Stawell family of Kilbrittain, Co. Cork, 1667-1891; 40 documents. (58th, p. 30.)

STEELE: Steele, see Armstrong.

STEUART: Steuart testamentary documents, Dublin and Co. Cavan, 1740, 1793, 1808; deeds and fines relating to the lands of Steuart and Young families, Co. Cavan, 1718-1863. (58th, p. 43.)

STEUART: Steuart, see Conrahy.

STEWART: Stewart family records. (56th, p. 183; 57th, pp. 409, 463.)

STEWART: Stewart, see Alexander.

STEWART: Stewart, see Conrahy.

STOPFORD: Stopford, see Bacon.

STRITCH: Stritch, see Arthur.

STYLES: Styles family in counties Roscommon and Donegal,—mid and late 18th century, mainly deeds and rentals. (58th, p. 21.)

TAYLOR: Taylor family records. (55th, p. 64; 56th, pp. 185, 186; 57th, pp. 300, 411.)

THOMPSON: Thompson, see Bateson.

TIERNAN: Tiernan, see Alexander.

TOWNSEND: Townsend, see McGurty.

TRAVERS: Travers family documents, one probate and 29 deeds for Cork City and counties Cavan, Kerry, Offaly, and Tipperary, 1695-1857. (58th, p. 49.)

* TROTTER: Trotter family history. (57th, p. 57.)

TROTTER: Trotter, see Alexander.

TUCKEY: Tuckey, see Bacon.

TWIGG: Twigg, see Calbec.

TWIGG: Twigg, see Winder.

TYRRELL: Tyrrell family records. (57th, pp. 306, 413.)

ULSTER: Collection of Ulster family pedigrees. (57th, p. 57.)

* UPTON: Upton family history. (57th, p. 57.)

USHER: Usher, see Armstrong.

USHER: Usher, see Barlow.

VAUGHAN: Vaughan, see Calbec.

VERDON: Verdon family records. (57th, p. 413.)

* VERNON: Vernon family history. (56th, p. 68.)

VESEY: Vesey, see Bolger.

VESEY: Vesey, see Sarsfield.

VESEY: Vesey family letters, late 17th century or early 18th century. (58th, p. 21.)

* WADDY: Waddy family history. (56th, p. 68.)

WADE: Wade, see Bolger.

WALCOTT: Walcott, see Bacon. See also Alcock.

WALL: Wall, see Armstrong.

WALL: Wall, see Calbec.

* WALLACE: Wallace family history. (55th, p. 14.)

WALLER: Waller family, Co. Meath: 68 documents, 1673-1837, mainly concerning the Waller family, with maps of their estates, 1716-70, and deeds for lands in counties Meath, Galway, Mayo and Monaghan, 1673-1837. (58th, p. 48.)

WALLER: Waller family, Cos. Limerick and Cork, late 18th century. See Montgomery. (58th, p. 23.)

WALSH: Walsh Family Mss. volume, records of the Walsh family, the Kelly, Naghten, and other families, 14th to 19th centuries. Family pedigrees and descents. The Walshes, of Athlone, Carrickmines, Ballygunner, Kilgobbin, Killincarrig, Shanganagh, counties Dublin, Roscommon, Waterford, Wicklow, etc. Contains copies and abstracts of wills, Chancery and Exchequer bills, answers, decrees, depositions, inquisitions, etc. (57th, p. 55.)

* Walsh: Walsh family history. (56th, p. 68.)

WALTON: Walton, see Busteed.

WARBURTON: Warburton, see Barlow.

WARD: Ward, see Perry.

WARREN: Warren, see Plunkett.

WARREN: Warren family records. (56th, p. 191, 57th, pp. 312, 415, 466.)

WATSON: Watson family records. (56th, p. 192; 57th, pp. 313, 314.)

* WEBB: Webb family history. (55th, p. 14.)

WELPLY: Welply family records. (55th, p. 14; 56th, p. 192; 57th, pp. 314, 315, 415.)

WESLEY (WELLESLEY): Wesley or Wellesley: Collection of genealogical material. (58th, p. 27.)

WEST: West, see Dobbyn.

WESTBY: Westby, see Arthur.

WHITE: White probates and deeds relating to the White family, 1721-1827. (58th, p. 27.)

WHITE: White, see Eyre.

WHITE: White family records. (56th p. 193; 57th, pp. 316, 416, 417.)

WHITE: White, see Herbert.

WIDENHAM: Widenham, see Barlow.

* WILDER: Wilder family history. (55th, p. 14.)

WILKINSON: Wilkinson, see Perry.

WILLS: Wills, see Sandford.

* WILSON: Wilson family history. (56th, p. 56; 57th, p. 57.)

WINDER: Winder and Twigg families; papers, 1734-1908, including 11 deeds, for property in Carnmoney, Co. Antrim; Dublin City and Co., and Roscommon. (58th, p. 49.)

WOLFE: Wolfe, see Arthur.

WOLFE: Wolfe family of Forenaghts, Co. Kildare, and its property in counties Dublin, Kildare and Limerick, 18th century papers. (58th, p. 24.)

WOODCOCK: Woodcock, see Armstrong.

WOODROFFE: Woodroffe, see Barlow.

WRIGHT: Wright, see Barlow.

YEO: Yeo, see Calbec.

YOUNG: Young, see Steuart.

---

* Surname has been reported as the subject for study of a family history.

PART THREE

PUBLISHED SOURCES

A BIBLIOGRAPHY
OF REFERENCE MATERIALS
FOR GENEALOGICAL RESEARCH

CHAPTER I

CATALOGUES

IRELAND

ARMAGH:

PUBLIC LIBRARY OF ARMAGH:

Catalogue of Manuscripts in the Public Library of Armagh. Edited by J. Dean. Dundalk, 1928.

BELFAST:

LINEN HALL LIBRARY:

Linen Hall Library, Belfast. General Catalogue. Edited by George Smith. Belfast, 1896.

Linen Hall Library, Belfast. Catalogue of Books in the Irish Section. Belfast, 1917.

PRESBYTERIAN HISTORICAL SOCIETY:

Proceedings of the Presbyterian Historical Society of Ireland, 1938-39. (Lists accessions of manuscripts by the Society.)

PUBLIC RECORD OFFICE OF NORTHERN IRELAND:

Reports of the Deputy Keeper of the Public Records of Northern Ireland, 1924-53.

CORK:

UNIVERSITY COLLEGE LIBRARY:

Catalogue of the Irish Library, University College, Cork. Cork, 1914.

DUBLIN:

GENEALOGICAL OFFICE, DUBLIN CASTLE:

A List of the Manuscripts in the Genealogical Office. (Microfilm.)

IRISH MANUSCRIPTS COMMISSION:

Irish Manuscripts Commission Catalogue of Publications, 1928-50. Dublin Stationery Office, 1950.

NATIONAL LIBRARY OF IRELAND:

National Library of Ireland. Subject Index of Books added, 1894-1903. Dublin, 1911.

National Library of Ireland. Subject Index of Books added, 1904-1915, and those in the General Collection prior to 1894. Dublin, 1926.

Department of Education, National Library of Ireland, Report of the Council of Trustees. 1950-51; 1951-52; 1952-53. 3 vols. Stationery Office, Dublin, 1952-54.

PUBLIC RECORD OFFICE OF IRELAND:

Reports of the Deputy Keeper of the Public Records in Ireland. 58 Reports, 1869-1951. Stationery Office, Dublin.

REGISTRY OF DEEDS:

Report upon the Office of the Registry of Deeds in Ireland. By Richard James Lane. Dublin, 1861.

REPRESENTATIVE CHURCH BODY:

Catalogue of Manuscripts in Possession of the Representative Church Body, 52 St. Stephen's Green, Dublin, collected by the Ecclesiastical Records Committee. Dublin, 1938.

ROYAL DUBLIN SOCIETY:

A Bibliography of the Publications of the Royal Dublin Society, 1731-1951. Dublin, 1951.

ROYAL IRISH ACADEMY:

Catalogue of the Irish Manuscripts in the Royal Irish Academy. By Elizabeth Fitzpatrick and Kathleen Mulchrone, assisted by A. I. Pearson. Dublin, 1948.

Proceedings of the Royal Irish Academy, 1836-.

Transactions of the Royal Irish Academy, 1786-1907.

TRINITY COLLEGE LIBRARY:

Trinity College, Supplemental Catalogue of the Library. 1854.

Catalogue of the Manuscripts in the Library of Trinity College. By T. K. Abbott and E. J. Gwynn. Dublin, 1900.

A Short Guide to some Manuscripts in the Library of Trinity College, Dublin. By Robert H. Murray. Dublin, 1920.

UNIVERSITY COLLEGE, DUBLIN:

Catalogue of the Manuscripts in the Library of University College, Dublin.

LIMERICK:

LIMERICK PUBLIC LIBRARY:

City of Limerick Public Library. Catalogue of the Museum and Reference Library. By R. Herbert. Published in the *Limerick Leader,* 1941. Reprint from the *North Munster Antiquarian Journal,* vol. 2, p. 348.

LOUGH FEA:

LIBRARY OF LOUGH FEA:

Catalogue of the Library at Lough Fea, in Illustration of the History and Antiquities of Ireland. By Sir Evelyn Philip Shirley. London, 1872.

ENGLAND

CAMBRIDGE:

UNIVERSITY LIBRARY, CAMBRIDGE:

A Catalogue of the Bradshaw Collection of Irish Books in the University Library, Cambridge. 3 vols. Cambridge, 1916.

LONDON:

BRITISH MUSEUM:

Catalogue of Manuscripts, Books, Pamphlets and Newspapers relating to the Civil War, the Commonwealth and Restoration, collected by George Thomason, 1640-1661. 2 vols. London, 1908.

Catalogue of Irish Manuscripts in the British Museum.
Vol. I, by Standish Hayes O'Grady. London, 1926.
Vol. II, by Robin Flower. London, 1926.
Vol. III, by Robin Flower. Revised and edited by Dr. Myles Dillon. London, 1953.

LAMBETH PALACE LIBRARY:

Calendar of the Carew Manuscripts Preserved in the Archiepiscopal Library at Lambeth Palace, London, 1515-1624. Edited by J. Brewer and W. Bullen. 6 vols. London, 1867-73.

PUBLIC RECORD OFFICE OF ENGLAND:

A Guide to the Manuscripts Preserved in the Public Record Office of England. By M. S. Giuseppi.

CHAPTER II

GUIDES TO GENEALOGICAL RECORDS

BIOGRAPHICAL SOCIETY OF IRELAND, Publications.

CRISP, F. A., *Ed.* List of Parish Registers and other Genealogical Works. 1909.

CRONE, J. S., *Ed.* Concise Directory of Irish Biography. Dublin, 1928; 2nd edition, 1937.

CURTIS, EDMUND, and R. B. MCDOWELL. Irish Historical Documents, 1172-1922. London, 1943.

DENNY, REV. HENRY L. L. Anglo-Irish Genealogy. Published in *The Kerry Post,* September, 1916.

DENNY, REV. HENRY L. L. A Handbook of County Kerry Family History, Biography, etc. 1923.

DIX, E. R. MC C. A List of Irish Towns and Dates of Earliest Printing in Each. 1903.

GIUSEPPI, M. S. A Guide to the Manuscripts Preserved in the Public Record Office of England. 2 vols. London, 1923-24.

GRIFFITH, MARGARET. A Short Guide to the Public Record Office of Ireland. In *Irish Historical Studies.* Vol. VIII, no. 29, pp. 45-58.

HARRISON, H. G. A Select Bibliography of English Genealogy, with brief lists for Wales, Scotland and Ireland. London, 1937.

HUMPHREYS, ARTHUR L. A Handbook to County Bibliography, being a Bibliography of Bibliographies relating to the Counties and Towns of Great Britain and Ireland. London, 1917.

IRISH COMMITTEE OF HISTORICAL SCIENCES, Bulletin.

IRISH HISTORICAL STUDIES, 1938-. (See continued sections: Bibliography, Writings on Irish History; Reviews; Short Notices; Books and Periodicals Received. Also List of Bibliographical Abbreviations, in Vol. IV, no. 13, pp. 6-33).

IRISH LIBRARY BULLETIN, Dublin. 1940—.

KING, JEREMIAH. County Kerry, Past and Present. A handbook to the local and family history of the county. Dublin, 1931.

LANE, RICHARD JAMES. Report upon the Office for the Registry of Deeds. Dublin, 1861.

LOFTUS, DUDLEY. Collection of Annals, in Marsh's Library, Dublin.

LOMBARD, R. E. FITZGERALD. How to trace Catholic and other Pedigrees in Ireland. In *The Irish Catholic,* April 19, 1913.

MACARTHUR, WILLIAM. Bibliography of Histories of Irish Counties and Towns. In *Notes and Queries,* 1915-16.

MACDONAGH, J. C. T. and EDWARD MACINTYRE. Bibliography of County Donegal. In the *Journal of the County Donegal Historical Society.* Vol. 1, pp. 49-80.

MARSHALL, GEORGE W. The Genealogist's Guide to Printed Pedigrees. 4th edition. 1903.

PENDER, SÉAMUS. A Guide to Irish Genealogical Collections. In *Analecta Hibernica,* No. 7. By the Irish Manuscripts Commission.

PENDER, SÉAMUS. Studies in Waterford History. (A series published in the *Journal of the Cork Historical and Archaeological Society.*) Vols. lii-lviii.

QUINN, D. B. Irish Records, 1920-1933: A Survey. In *Bulletin, Institute of Historical Research.* Vol. 11.

REYNOLDS, HENRY FITZGERALD. A List of Articles published in *Notes and Queries,* Dec. 1917-1941. In *Irish Genealogist.* Vol. 1.

RUSHEN, PERCY C. The Genealogist's Legal Dictionary. (Pocket Library.) 1909.

SIMMS, SAMUEL. A Select Bibliography of the United Irishmen, 1791-1798. In *Irish Historical Studies.* Vol. 1, no. 2, pp. 158-180.

WALSH, ROISIN. The Dublin Libraries. (In Lord Mayor's *Handbook.* Dublin Municipal Annual. 1942, pp. 42-45.)

WOOD, HERBERT. Guide to the Records deposited in the Public Record Office in Ireland. Dublin, 1919.

CHAPTER III

GEOGRAPHICAL SOURCES

1. ATLASES AND MAPS

BACON, G. W. & Co., London. Motoring and Cycling Road Maps of Ireland.

BADDESLEY, M. J. B. Thorough Guide Series. Ireland. Part I. London, 1897.

BARTHOLOMEW, J. Pocket Atlas of Ireland. Index and Statistical Notes. London, 1887.

BARTHOLOMEW & SON. Revised Quarter-Inch Maps, Ireland. Scale, ¼ inch to 1 mile. 5 sheets. 34 x 23 inches. London, 1957.

BEAUFORT, REV. DANIEL AUGUSTUS. Map of Ireland, Civil and Ecclesiastical. W. Faden, 3rd edition. London, 1813. (Shows Provinces, Counties, Dioceses.)

EACHARD, LAURENCE. An Exact Description of Ireland ——. London, 1691. A Topographical Dictionary containing 37 maps.

ESSO ROAD MAP NO. 8, IRELAND. This current, very detailed map, prepared and printed by Edward Stanford, Ltd., for the Esso Petroleum Co., Ltd., price one sixpence, may be obtained through the Esso Petroleum Co., U. S. A., Size 22″ x 26″, both sides of one sheet. Besides the principal and other roads throughout Ireland, with mileages, it shows the boundary line between Northern Ireland and the Republic of Ireland, all county boundaries, height of land above sea level, and all cathedrals, abbeys, and castles are named and located. Also 1,900 cities, towns and villages are named, located on the map, and listed in an index with locating key. Each city, town or village on the map has its symbol showing population: (1) over 10,000; (2) 5,000-10,000; (3) 2,500-5,000; (4) 1,000-2,500; (5) 500-1,000; under 500.

GREEN, E. R. R. A Catalogue of Estate Maps, etc. Downshire Office, Hillsborough, Co. Down. In *Ulster Journal of Archaeology*. Vol. XII, pp. 1-25.

JANSSON, JOHANN. Hibernia Regnum vulgo Ireland. Amsterdam, 1659. Five sheets, 23 x 20 inches. One general map and one of each of the four provinces.

JOYCE, P. W. Atlas and Geography of Ireland. London, *ca.* 1870.

LEWIS, SAMUEL. Lewis's Atlas, comprising the counties of Ireland, and a General Map of the Kingdom. London, 1837.

MOLL, HERMAN. A Set of Twenty New and Correct Maps of Ireland, with the Great Roads and Principal Cross-Roads, showing the Computed Miles from Town to Town. London, 1728.

MUIRHEAD, L. RUSSELL. The Blue Guides. Ireland, with a complete Atlas of Ireland, ——. Rand McNally, Chicago, New York, etc. 1932, 1949, etc.

ORDNANCE SURVEY MAPS OF IRELAND. Scale ¼ inch to 1 mile. 1: 253440. Dublin, 1835-1836; revised 1898-1899. 16 sheets. 18 x 12 inches.

ORDNANCE SURVEY MAPS OF IRELAND. Scale ½ inch to 1 mile. 1: 126720. Dublin, 1835-1836; revised 1956. 25 sheets. 27 x 18 inches.

ORDNANCE SURVEY MAPS OF IRELAND. Scale 1 inch to 1 mile. 1: 63360. Dublin and Belfast, 1835-1836; revised 1936-1956. 163 sheets. 24 x 20 inches.

ORDNANCE SURVEY MAPS OF IRELAND. Scale 6 inches to 1 mile. 1: 10560. Dublin, 1835-1842; revised. 2,000 sheets approx. 36 x 24 inches.

ORDNANCE SURVEY MAPS OF IRELAND. Scale 25 inches to 1 mile. 1: 2500. Dublin, 1835-1842; revised. 21,000 sheets approx. 36 x 25 inches.

PETTY, WILLIAM. Hiberniae Delineatio quoad hactenus licuit Perfectissima Studio Guilielmi Petty Eqtis. Aurati. London, 1685. The first printed atlas of Ireland.

PETTY, WILLIAM. A Geographical Description of ye Kingdom of Ireland. With 38 maps. London, 1685. Another edition, 1720.

PETTY, WILLIAM. The Down Survey, 1655-1658. Dublin, 1908. 221 sheets. 28 x 20 inches, unbound. All baronies mapped except those in Galway, Mayo and Roscommon—these had been done by the Strafford Survey of 1637. Each map shows a barony, the parishes within the barony, the names of the parishes, towns (sometimes shown as inserts to a larger scale), villages, townlands, castles, churches, some manor houses, etc.

PHILIPS' HANDY ATLAS OF THE COUNTIES OF IRELAND. Constructed by John Bartholomew. Revised by P. W. Joyce. London, 1881, 1885. With Index. Very detailed.

PROBATE MAP OF IRELAND. Principal Probate and District Registries of the Court of Probate, established in 1857. Printed by Forster & Co. In the *3rd Report of the Deputy Keeper of the Public Records in Ireland.* (Shows the area of each district.)

REVENUE MAP. A Map of Ireland showing the counties and dioceses, constructed for and included in *The Report of Her Majesty's Commissioners on the Revenue and Condition of the Established Church (Ireland), 1868, and Appendix.*

SCALE, BERNARD. An Hibernian Atlas; or General Description of Ireland ——. London, 1809. With 37 maps.

TAYLOR, JOHN and ANDREW SKINNER. Maps of the Roads of Ireland, surveyed in 1777 and corrected down to 1783. Second edition, 1883. 289 maps.

WARD, LOCK & CO'S Illustrated Guide Books. London, 1913.

2. PLACE-NAMES, TOPOGRAPHICAL DICTIONARIES

GOBLET, Y. M., *Ed.* A Topographical Index of Parishes and Townlands of Ireland in Sir William Petty's Manuscript Barony Maps (*ca.* 1655-59). Dublin, 1932.

HARRIS, WALTER, *Ed.* Hibernica; or some ancient pieces relating to Ireland: Containing a Survey of the Six Escheated Counties of Ulster, —— 1 December 1618-28 March 1619, by Capt. Nicholas Pynnar. Dublin, 1747.

HOGAN, S. J. Description of Ireland, 1598. Dublin, 1878.

JOYCE, P. W. Origin and History of Irish Place-Names. 3 vols. 1869, 1875, 1913 (Reprint) *ca.* 1953.

LEWIS, SAMUEL. Topographical Dictionary of Ireland —. 2 vols. London, 1837, 1839.

MACGIVNEY, REV. JOSEPH. Place-Names of the County Longford. 1908.

MASON, WILLIAM SHAW. A Statistical Account or Parochial Survey of Ireland. 3 vols. 1814.

PARLIAMENTARY GAZETTEER OF IRELAND. 3 vols. Dublin, London, etc., 1844-46.

POWER, PATRICK. Place-Names of Decies. 1907.

PRICE, LIAM. Place-Names of County Wicklow. 6 booklets. Dublin Institute for Advanced Studies. Dublin, 1958.

THOM, ALEXANDER, *Ed.* The General Alphabetical Index to the Townlands and Towns, Parishes and Baronies of Ireland. Published with the Census of Ireland. Dublin, 1861. Other editions published with the Census of Ireland, 1904, 1913.

TOPOGRAPHICAL INDEX. Government of Northern Ireland publication with the Census of Population of Northern Ireland: 1926. An Alphabetical Index to the Townlands and Towns, Parishes and Baronies (with their various districts, divisions, etc.). Belfast, 1926. Reprint, 1947.

YOUNG, ARTHUR. A Tour in Ireland (1776-1779), edited with Introduction and Notes by Arthur Wollaston Hutton. 2 vols. London, 1892.

CHAPTER IV

ARMS, HERALDRY, AND NOMENCLATURE

1. ARMS AND HERALDRY

ARMS: Some lesser Known Family Arms. In *The Genealogical Quarterly*, London. Vol. XIII. (Many Irish Family Arms included.)

ARMS, COATS OF: Coats of Arms from the Irish Funeral Entries (or Certificates) which were copied from an original manuscript volume now in the British Museum (Add. MS. 4820), but formerly one of a series of eighteen manuscript volumes of Funeral Entries, late 16th century to 18th century in the Office of Arms, Dublin Castle. The above copies were published in the *Journal of the Association for the Preservation of the Memorials of the Dead*, Vols. VII and VIII, and later reprinted in one volume.

ARMSTRONG, E. C. R. Irish Seal-Matrices and Seals. Dublin, 1913.

BIGGER, FRANCIS, and HERBERT HUGHES. Armorial Sculptured Tomb Stones. In the *Ulster Journal of Archaeology*. Second series, Vols. VI, VII, VIII, IX (1900-1903).

BURKE, JOHN. A Genealogical and Heraldic History of the Landed Gentry or Commoners of Great Britain and Ireland. 4 vols. London, 1837-1838.

BURKE, JOHN and JOHN BERNARD BURKE. Genealogical and Heraldic History of the Extinct and Dormant Baronetcies of England, Ireland and Scotland. 1844.

BURKE, JOHN, and JOHN BERNARD BURKE. A Genealogical and Heraldic Dictionary of the Landed Gentry of Great Britain and Ireland. 3 vols. London, 1849.

BURKE, JOHN and JOHN BERNARD BURKE. Encyclopedia of Heraldry, or General Armory of England, Scotland and Ireland. 3rd edition with a Supplement. 1851.

BURKE, J. B. Examples of Irish Bookplates.

BURKE, SIR BERNARD. A Visitation of the Seats and Arms of the Noblemen and Gentlemen of Great Britain and Ireland. London, 1855.

BURKE, SIR BERNARD. Landed Gentry of Great Britain and Ireland. 2 vols. London, 1871.

BURKE, SIR BERNARD. General Armory of England, Scotland and Ireland. London, 1878.

BURKE, SIR BERNARD. Genealogical and Heraldic History of the Peerages of England, Ireland and Scotland; Extinct, Dormant and in Abeyance. London, 1883.

BURKE, SIR BERNARD. A Genealogical and Heraldic Dictionary of the Landed Gentry of Ireland. London, 1899.

BURKE, SIR BERNARD. A Genealogical and Heraldic History of the Landed Gentry of Ireland. Revised and edited by A. C. Fox-Davies. London, 1912. Supplement, 1937.

BURKE. Burke's Genealogical and Heraldic History of the Landed Gentry of Ireland. Edited by L. G. Pine. Fourth edition. London, 1958.

COKAYNE, G. E. State of the Peerage of Ireland, 1801-1889. With list of Knights of St. Patrick, 1783-1888. Edited, 1889.

COKAYNE, G. E. The Complete Peerage of England, Scotland, Ireland ——. New edition. London, 1910.

COKAYNE, G. E. The Complete Peerage of England, Scotland, Ireland, Great Britain and the United Kingdom, extant, extinct or dormant. New Edition, revised and much enlarged by Hon. Vicary Gibbs and others. Vols. 1-2, pt. 1, and 13 (all published), 13 vols.

CROSSLY, AARON. The Peerage of Ireland, —— with a Historical and Genealogical Account ——. Dublin, 1725.

ENCYCLOPAEDIA OF IRELAND. Irish Heraldry, Topography and Modern History. Part I contains the coats of arms of over seven hundred Irish family names printed in their proper colors and a comprehensive delineation of the thirty-two counties, with a colored map of each. Part II contains the History of Ireland—with special articles and history of the Irish exiles in Australia. Dublin & New York, 1904.

FAIRBAIRN'S BOOK OF CRESTS of the Families of Great Britain and Ireland. Fourth edition, revised and enlarged. 2 vols. London, 1905.

FOSTER, J. Stemmata Britannica: A Genealogical Account of the Untitled Nobility and Gentry of Great Britain and Ireland. London, 1877.

HOWARD, J. J. and FREDERICK A. CRISP. Visitation of Ireland. 6 vols. 1897-1918. Pedigrees of 160 families with coats of arms, portraits, etc.

KIMBER, EDWARD. The Peerage of Ireland. 1788.

LASCELLES, ROWLEY, *Ed.* Liber Munerum Publicorum Hiberniae. London, 1824-1830. Second edition, 2 vols. London, 1852. Includes copies of Patents of Creation of Peers, Peerage Lists, etc.

LODGE, JOHN. The Peerage of Ireland: or a Genealogical History of the Present Nobility of that Kingdom. With engravings of their paternal coats of arms. Revised, enlarged and continued to the present time, by Mervyn Archdall. 7 vols. Dublin, 1789.

MACLYSAGHT, EDWARD. Irish Families, Their Names, Arms and Origins. Dublin, 1957. With illustrations (in color) of 243 armorial bearings, by Myra Maguire, Heraldic Artist to the Genealogical Office, Dublin Castle, Dublin.

MORRIS, JOHN PAYNE. A bound volume containing the emblazoned arms of the Lords Lieutenants of Ireland, etc., *ca.* 1830.

NICHOLS, FRANCIS. The Irish Compendium. 1735.

O'HART, JOHN. Irish Pedigrees: or the Origin and Stem of the Irish Nation. 5th edition, 1887-1892, 2 vols. Dublin, New York.

PHILLIMORE, W. P., *Ed.* Law and Practice of Grants of Arms and Registration of Pedigrees in England, Scotland and Ireland. London, 1905.

PHILLIPS, T. Knights of Ireland, temp. Elizabeth.

ROBSON, T. The British Herald; or cabinet of armorial bearings of the nobility and gentry of Great Britain and Ireland. Sunderland, 1830.

ROONEY, JOHN. A Genealogical History of Irish Families, with their Crests and Armorial Bearings. New York, 1896.

SALMON. A Short View of the Families of the Present Nobility; their Marriages, Issue, Descents and immediate Ancestors; their Arms, etc. London, 1759.

SKEY, WILLIAM. The Heraldic Calendar: a list of the Nobility and Gentry whose Arms are registered and Pedigrees recorded in the Heralds Office in Ireland. Dublin, 1846.

STEPHENSON, JEAN. Heraldry for the American Genealogist. Issued by the National Genealogical Society (reprint). Washington, D. C., 1959.

WAGNER, ANTHONY RICHARD. Heralds and Heraldry in the Middle Ages. Oxford, 1939.

WAGNER, ANTHONY RICHARD. Irish Coats in Continental Rolls of Arms. In the *Journal of the Royal Society of Antiquaries of Ireland.* Vol. XXII.

WAGNER, ANTHONY RICHARD. The Records and Collections of the College of Arms. London, 1952. Includes records from the Office of Arms, Dublin Castle, Dublin.

WEENER, JOHN. Ancient Funeral Monuments of Ireland.

2. NOMENCLATURE

BEARDSLEY, C. W. Dictionary of English and Welsh Surnames, with Special American Instances. London, 1901.

CENSUS OF IRELAND: The Publication of the Census of Ireland, 1761-1872. 2 vols. By the Registrar General. Contains: The Surnames in Ireland and where located principally. Also derivation of Irish surnames.

HARRISON, HENRY. Surnames of the United Kingdom. London, 1912.

MACGIOLLA-DOMHNAIGH, PADRAIG. Some Anglicised Surnames in Ireland. Dublin, 1923.

MACLYSAGHT, EDWARD. Irish Families, their Names, Arms and Origin. Dublin, 1957. Section on Nomenclature.

MATHESON, ROBERT E. Varieties and Synonymes of Surnames and Christian Names in Ireland: For the guidance of Registration Officers and the Public in Searching the Indexes of Births, Deaths, and Marriages. Dublin, 1901.

MATHESON, ROBERT E. Special Report on Surnames in Ireland. Dublin, 1909.

MUSGRAVE, SIR WILLIAM. General Nomenclature and Obituary prior to 1800. 6 vols. Harleian Society, London, 1899-1901.

WOULFE, REV. PATRICK. Sloinnte Gaedheal is Gall. Irish Names and Surnames. Dublin, 1923.

CHAPTER V

ANCIENT GENEALOGY

ANNÁLA RÍOGHACHTA ÉIREANN. Annals of the Kingdom of Ireland, by the Four Masters (Michael, Conary, Cucogry O'Clery, and Ferfessa O'Mulconry) from the earliest period to 1616. With Translation and Notes by John O'Donovan. 7 vols. Dublin, 1851.

ANNALES HIBERNIAE. Jacobi Grace, Kilkenniensis, Annales Hiberniae, A. D. 1074-1504. Edited with Translation and Notes, by Rev. Richard Butler. Dublin, 1842.

ANNALS OF CLONMACNOISE. Being Annals of Ireland from the Earliest Period to A. D. 1408. Translated into English, A. D. 1627, by Connell Mageoghagan—. Edited by Rev. Denis Murphy. Dublin, 1896.

ANNALS OF CONNACHT, A. D. 1224-1544. Edited with Introduction, Translation, Notes and Indexes, by A. Martin Freeman. Dublin, 1944.

ANNALS OF INISFALLEN, A. D. 433-1320. Edited with Introduction, Translation, Notes and Indexes, by Seán MacAirt. Dublin, 1951.

ANNALS OF IRELAND, 1171-1616. Translated from the Original of the Four Masters, by Owen Connellan with Annotations by Philip MacDermott and the Translator. Dublin, 1846.

ANNALS OF IRELAND, to 1600. By Friar John Clyn—and Thady Dowling—together with the Annals of Ross. Edited from manuscripts in the Library of Trinity College, Dublin, with Introductory Remarks by Richard Butler. Dublin, 1849.

ANNALS OF IRELAND, A. D. 571-913. Three Fragments, copied from Ancient Sources by Dubhaltach MacFirbisigh; edited with Translation and Notes by John O'Donovan. Dublin, 1860.

ANNALS OF THE KINGDOM OF IRELAND, by the Four Masters, from the Earliest Period to the Year 1616. Edited with Translation and Copious Notes by John O'Donovan. 7 vols. Dublin, 1854.

ANNALS OF LOCH CÉ. A Chronicle—from A. D. 1014 to A. D. 1590. Edited with Translation by William M. Hennessy. 2 vols. Dublin, 1939.

ANNALS, MISCELLANEOUS IRISH. Edited with Introduction, Translation and Indexes, by Séamus ó h-Innse. Dublin, 1947.

ANNALS OF TIGERNACH. Edited with Translation by Whitley Stokes. Paris, 1895-1897.

ANNALS OF ULSTER. Otherwise Annala Senait, Annals of Senat; a Chronicle—from A. D. 431 to A. D. 1540. Edited with Translation, Notes and Index, by William M. Hennessy and B. MacCarthy. 4 vols. Dublin, 1887-1901.

BOOK OF FENAGH. Edited by William M. Hennessy and D. H. Kelly, 1875. Reproduction by the Irish Manuscripts Commission, Dublin, 1939.

BOOK OF LECAN, THE. With Foreword by Eoin MacNéill and Indexes by Kathleen Mulchrone. Contains 15th Century Pedigrees. A collotype facsimile by the Irish Manuscripts Commission. Dublin, 1937.

BOOK OF UÍ MAINE. With Introduction and Indexes by R.A.S. Macalister. From a 14th century manuscript known as the *Book of the O'Kellys.* A collotype facsimile by the Irish Manuscripts Commission. Dublin, 1942.

CAREW MANUSCRIPTS, CALENDAR OF, 1515-1624. Edited by J. S. Brewer and W. Bullen. London, 1867-1873.

COMPOSSICION BOOKE OF CONOUGHT, THE, 1585. Transcribed and edited by A. Martin Freeman. Irish Manuscripts Commission, Dublin, 1936.

HORE, H. J. The Social State of the Southern and Eastern Counties of Ireland in the Sixteenth Century; being the Presentments of Gentlemen, Commonalty and Citizens of Carlow, Cork, Kilkenny, Tipperary, Waterford, and Wexford, made in the Reigns of Henry VIII and Elizabeth. (From the Public Record Office, London.) Dublin, 1870.

IRISH MANUSCRIPTS COMMISSION: Analecta Hibernica, No. 3 (1931); No. 7 (1935.) (See VOL. II, PART ONE, CHAPTER VII.)

KEATING, GEOFFREY. A General History of Ireland—Illustrated with above One Hundred and Sixty Coats of Arms of the Ancient Irish, with Particular Genealogies of Many Noble Families. 3rd edition, with Appendix. London, 1738.

MACLYSAGHT, EDWARD. Irish Families, Their Names, Arms, and Origins. Dublin, 1957.

O'DÁLAIGH, AENGUS. The Tribes of Ireland, together with an Historical Account of the Family of O'Daly. Edited by John O'Donovan. Dublin, 1852.

ORMOND DEEDS, CALENDAR OF: 1172-1603. Edited by E. Curtis. 6 vols. Irish Manuscripts Commission, Dublin, 1932-1943.

CHAPTER VI

CHURCH RECORDS

1. CONGREGATIONAL

ARCHIBALD, JAMES E. A Century of Congregationalism: The Story of Donegal Street Church, Belfast, 1801-1901. Belfast, 1901.

2. CHURCH OF IRELAND

CHURCH REGISTERS:

CAULFIELD, RICHARD. The Parish Registers of Holy Trinity, Cork, 1643-1668. 1877.

JOURNAL OF THE ASSOCIATION FOR THE PRESERVATION OF THE MEMORIALS OF THE DEAD, IRELAND. Vol. X, nos. 5 and 6 (1919, 1920). Extracts from the Burials in some County Wexford Parish Registers: Parish of Kilpatrick, Burials, 1834-1864; Parish of Rathmacknee, Burials, 1813-1866; Parish of Templescobin, Burials, 1835-1864.

JOURNAL OF THE IRISH MEMORIALS ASSOCIATION. Formerly the Association for the Preservation of the Memorials of the Dead in Ireland, and now incorporating the Dublin Parish Register Society. Vol. XI, nos. 1-6 (1921-1925); DUBLIN PARISH REGISTERS:

No. 1. St. Michan's Parish Register ---- Marriages, 1700-1800.
No. 2. St. Mary's Donnybrook Register -- Marriages, 1712-1800.
No. 3. St. John's Register --- Marriages, 1700-1798.
No. 4. St. Nicholas Within Register -- Marriages, 1671-1800.
No. 5. St. Michael's Register ---------- Marriages, 1656-1800.
No. 6. Finglass Register ------ Burials, 1664-1729.
No. 6. St. Nicholas Within Register ------ Burials, 1671-1823.

JOURNAL OF THE IRISH MEMORIALS ASSOCIATION, etc. Vol. XII, nos. 1-6 (1926-1932); Vol. XIII, no. 1; PARISH REGISTERS AND VISITATION RETURNS:

Vol. XII, No. 1. St. Audoen's, Dublin, Register — Burials, 1672-1692.

Aney, Co. Limerick, Register, ——— Baptism, 1760-1802; Marriage, 1761-1803; Burial, 1759-1802.

No. 2. St. Mary's Crumlin, Co. Dublin, Index to the deaths in the old register of the parish, A-K, 1740-1830; L-Y, 1740-1830.

No. 3. A List of Burials at Crumlin, Diocese of Dublin, which were recorded in the Visitation Returns, 1785-1810. Also a List of Baptisms and Marriages, 1740-1830.

No. 4. The Parish Church of Belfast, Marriage Register, 4 vols. 1745-1799.

No. 6. St. Andrew's Church, Dublin, Register — Marriages 1801-1819.

St. Nicholas Within, Dublin, Register — Burials, 1825-1863.

Vol. XIII, No. 1. St. Paul's, Dublin, ——— Burials, 1702-1718.

PARISH REGISTER SOCIETY OF DUBLIN. 12 vols. Dublin, 1906-1915.

VOL. I. The Registers of St. John the Evangelist, Dublin. Baptism, Marriage and Burial, 1619-1699. Edited by James Mills. Dublin, 1906.

VOL. II. The Registers of Baptisms, Marriages, and Burials in the Collegiate and Cathedral Church of St. Patrick, Dublin, 1677-1800. Transcribed by C. H. P. Price. Edited by J. H. Bernard. Dublin, 1907.

Vol. III. The Registers of the Church of St. Michan, Dublin. Baptism, Marriage and Burial, 1636 to 1685. Edited by Henry F. Berry. Dublin, 1907.

VOL. IV. The Registers of the Rev. Samuel Winter, D. D., Provost of Trinity College, Dublin, 1650 to 1660, and of the Liberties of Cashel (Co. Tipperary), 1654-1657. London, 1907.

VOL. V. The Registers of St. Catherine, Dublin, 1636-1715. Being: Extracts from the Registers of the Parish of St. Catherine and St. James, Dublin, 1636-1687. Register of St. Catherine's Parish. Baptism, Marriage, and Burial, 1679-1715. Edited by Herbert Wood. London, 1908.

VOL. VI. The Register of the Union of Monkstown, Co. Dublin, 1679-1786, and Parochial Returns of the Union of Monkstown, 1783-1800. Edited by Henry Seymour Guinness. London, 1908.

Vol. VII. The Registers of the Church of St. Michan, Dublin. Part 2. Baptism, Marriage and Burial, 1686-1700. With Index (for Vols. III and VII), 1636-1700. Edited by Henry F. Berry. Dublin, 1909.

VOL. VIII. The Register of Derry Cathedral (St. Columb's), Parish of Templemore, Londonderry. Baptism, Marriage and Burial, 1642-1703. With Preface by the Rev. Richard Hayes. London, 1910.

Vol. IX. The Register of the Parish of St. Peter and St. Kevin, Dublin. Baptism, Marriage and Burial, 1669-1761. With Preface by James Mills. London, 1911.

VOL. X. The Register of the Parish of St. Nicholas Without, Dublin. Baptism, Marriage and Burial, 1694-1739. With Preface by James Mills. Exeter, 1912.

VOL. XI. Marriage Entries from the Registers of the Parishes of St. Andrew, St. Anne, St. Audoen, and St. Bride, Dublin. 1632-1800: St. Andrew, 1672-1800; St. Anne, 1719-1800; St. Audoen, 1672-1800; St. Bride, 1632-1800. Edited by D. A. Chart. London, 1913.

VOL. XII. Marriage Entries in the Registers of the Parishes of: St. Marie, Dublin, 1697-1800; St. Luke, Dublin, 1716-1800; St. Catherine, Dublin, 1715-1800; St. Werburgh, Dublin, 1704-1800. Edited by A. E. Langman. London, 1915.

CLERGY OF THE CHURCH OF IRELAND; BIOGRAPHICAL SUCCESSION LISTS OF:

Ardfert and Aghadoe Clergy and Parishes. By the Rev. James B. Leslie. 1940.

Armagh Clergy and Parishes. By the Rev. James B. Leslie. 1911.

Belfast; A History of the Church of Ireland in St. Mary Magdalene Parish. By W. S. Leathem. Belfast, 1939.

Clogher Clergy and Parishes. By the Rev. James B. Leslie. 1929.

Cork, Cloyne, and Ross; Clerical and Parochial Records of. By William M. Brady. 3 vols. 1864.

Cork, Cloyne, and Ross; Church and Parish Records of the United Diocese of. By the Rev. J. H. Cole. Cork, 1903. (A sequel to the above.)

Derry Clergy and Parishes. By the Rev. James B. Leslie. 1937.

Down; Biographical Succession Lists of the Clergy of the Diocese of. By the Rev. James B. Leslie and Very Rev. H. B. Swanzy. 1936.

Dromore; Succession Lists of the Diocese of. By the Rev. James B. Leslie and the Very Rev. Henry B. Swanzy. 1933.

Dublin; Succession of Clergy in the Parishes of St. Bride, St. Michael Le Pole, and St. Stephen. By W. G. Carroll. 1884.

Dublin; The Fasti of St. Patrick's. By H. J. Lawlor, D. D. 1930.

Ferns Clergy and Parishes. By the Rev. James B. Leslie. 1936.

Newry; Vicars of. By the Very Rev. H. B. Swanzy. 1927.

Ossory Clergy and Parishes. By the Rev. James B. Leslie. 1933.

Raphoe Clergy and Parishes. By the Rev. James B. Leslie. 1940.

MARRIAGE LICENCE BONDS, CHURCH OF IRELAND:

Cloyne, Ireland, Index to the Marriage Licence Bonds of the Diocese of, 1630-1800. Edited by T. G. H. Green. Cork, 1899-1900.

Cork and Ross, Ireland, Index to the Marriage Licence Bonds of the Diocese of, for the Years 1623-1750. Edited by Herbert Gillman. Cork, 1896-1897.

Dublin, Index to the Marriage Licence Bonds of the Diocese of, *ca.* 1650-1853. Printed in the Appendices to the *Reports of the Deputy Keeper of the Public Records in Ireland.* Dublin, 1895, 1899.

Ferns Marriage Licences, 1662-1806. In the *Journal of the County Kildare Archaeological Society.* Vols. 9 and 10.

Kildare Marriage Licence Bonds, Index to, 1662-1806. Edited by Major G. O'Grady. In the *Journal of the County Kildare Archaeological Society.* Vols. 11 and 12.

3. HUGUENOT

AGNEW, D. C. Protestant Exiles from France in the Reign of Louis XIV; or the Huguenot refugees and their descendants in Great Britain and Ireland. 2nd edition with Index volume. London, 1871-1874.

CARRE, ALBERT. L'influence des Huguenots Francais en Irelande aux XVII et XVIII Siecles, 1937.

GIMLETTE, THOMAS. The History of the Huguenot Settlers in Ireland, and other Literary Remains. 1888.

HUGUENOT SOCIETY OF LONDON, PUBLICATIONS OF:

VOL. VII. Registers of the French Conformed Churches of St. Patrick and St. Mary, Dublin. Edited by J. J. Digges La Touche. Dublin, 1893. St. Patrick's, Baptisms, 1668-1687; Marriages, 1680-1716; Deaths, 1680-1716. St. Mary's Baptisms, 1705-1716; Marriages, 1705-1715; Deaths, 1705-1715. United Churches, Baptisms, 1716-1818; Marriages, 1716-1788; Deaths, 1716-1830.

VOL. XIV. Registers of the French Non-Conformist Churches of Lucy Lane and Peter Street, Dublin. Edited by T. P. Le Fanu. Aberdeen, 1901. Baptisms, 1701-1731; Marriages, 1702-1728; Burials, 1702-1731, and 1771-1831.

VOL. XIX. French Church of Portarlington: Registers of. 1694-1816. London, 1908.

HUGUENOT SOCIETY OF LONDON, PROCEEDINGS OF: The French Churches in Dublin. Vol. VIII, pp. 87-139.

LAWLOR, HUGH JACKSON. The Fasti of St. Patrick's, Dublin. Dundalk, 1930. (Appendix contains records, 1666-1816: Ministers of the French Church; Biographical and Genealogical Notices.)

LEE, GRACE LAWLESS. The Huguenot Settlements in Ireland. London, 1936.

LEFANU, T. P. Huguenot Veterans in Dublin. In the *Journal of the Royal Society of Antiquaries of Ireland.* Vol. 72, pp. 64-70.

MCCALL, R. A. The Huguenots in Ulster. 1915.

O'HART, JOHN. Irish Pedigrees. Vol. II. Dublin, 1892. (Names of Huguenot Refugees who settled in Great Britain and Ireland before the reign of, and during the reign of Louis XIV, of France; their French origins and descendants named in some notes, pp. 463-497.)

O'MULLANE, BRIGID. The Huguenots in Dublin. In *Dublin Historical Record.* Vol. VIII.

SMILES, SAMUEL. The Huguenots: Their Settlements, Churches and Industries in England and Ireland. 1889.

ULSTER JOURNAL OF ARCHAEOLOGY. First Series, vols. 1-4. 1853-1856. Huguenot Settlement Records (with family notes).

4. METHODIST

CROOK, WILLIAM. Ireland and the Centenary of American Methodism. London, 1866.

CROOKSHANK, C. H. History of Methodism in Ireland. 3 vols. Belfast, 1885-1858.

HAIRE, ROBERT. Wesley's One-and-Twenty Visits to Ireland. London: Epworth Press.

HARTE, REV. FREDERICK E. The Road I Have Traveled: Experiences of an Irish Methodist Minister. Belfast, n. d.

5. PRESBYTERIAN

ADAIR, PATRICK. A True Narrative of the Rise and Progress of the Presbyterian Government in Northern Ireland . . . 1622-1670 (copied from the original Adair MS., 1850). Belfast, 1866.

ANNUAL PRESBYTERIAN REGISTER. 21 vols. 1759-1783.

BECKETT, J. C. Protestant Dissent in Ireland. 1948.

BELFAST RECORDS:

Historic Memorials of the First Presbyterian Church, Belfast. 1887. (Contains: Roll of Ministers, 1642-1887; Baptismal Register, 1757-1790; Funeral Register, 1712-1736; Earliest List of Members, 1760; Earliest Complete List of Constituents, 1775; List of Subscribers and Constituents for 1781, 1790, 1812, 1831, 1877. List of Treasurers, Sextons, etc., 1712-1886.)

Fitzroy Avenue Presbyterian Church, Past and Present. By R. E. Alexander.

May Street Presbyterian Church: A History of the Congregation, 1829-1929. By John Williamson. 1929.

Reformed Presbyterian Congregation, Belfast, 1832-1932.

Rosemary Street Presbyterian Church, Belfast. Belfast, 1923. (Contains: Church records of Baptisms, 1722-1760, 1761-1812; Marriages, 1741-1761, 1762-1811.)

Townsend Street Presbyterian Church, Belfast: A Memorial Sketch. By the Rev. William Johnston. 1880.

BURT, CO. DONEGAL, RECORDS:

Burt Presbyterian Church Register Book. Edited by the Rev. James B. Woodburn. Baptisms, 1676/7-1683, 1683-1687/8; Marriages, 1690-1715/16; Elders listed.

CARSON, JAMES. The Cahans Exodus. In *The Irish Presbyterian* (May-July, 1914).

CASTLEREAGH, CO. DOWN: Castlereagh Presbyterian Church, 1650-1950. By James Little. 1950.

COLERAINE: A Century of Congregational History of Terrace Row Presbyterian Church, Coleraine. By R. B. Wylie. 1925.

CULLYBACKEY, CO. ANTRIM: A Short History of the Reformed Presbyterian Congregation, Cullybackey. By William Shaw. 1912.

CUMBER, CO. LONDONDERRY: Cumber Presbyterian Church and Parish. By the Rev. John Rutherford. Londonderry, 1939. (Mostly a collection of biographical notes on the various Presbyterian ministers who served in the Lower and Upper Cumber from the 17th century to the present day.)

DRUMBO, CO. DOWN: The History of Drumbo Presbyterian Church, with Notes on the District. 1937.

DUBLIN: Registers of the Presbyterian Congregations of Bull Alley and Plunkett Street, Dublin. Vol. I, 1672-1765; Vol. II, 1790-1835.

ENNISKILLEN: Enniskillen, Parish and Town. By W. H. Dundas. 1913. (Contains biographies of Presbyterian pastors of Enniskillen.)

FASTI OF THE IRISH PRESBYTERIAN CHURCH. Compiled by the Rev. James McConnell and revised by the Rev. S. G. McConnell. Edited by the Rev. F. J. Paul and the Rev. Dr. David Stewart. Belfast, 1935. (A dictionary of brief biographical records of Presbyterian ministers, 1613-1840, including some ministers who were sent to America.)

FERGUSON, REV. SAMUEL. Some Items of Historic Interest about Waterside. Londonderry, 1902. (Includes Tables of Householders in Glendermott Parish, 1663, 1740.)

HAMILTON, THOMAS. History of the Irish Presbyterian Church. Edinburgh, 1886.

IRISH PRESBYTERIANS. Brief Biographies. 1915.

IRWIN, CHARLES H. A History of Presbyterians in Dublin and the South and West of Ireland. 1890.

KILLEN, REV. W. D. History of Congregations of the Presbyterian Church in Ireland, and Biographical Notices of Eminent Presbyterian Ministers and Laymen. Belfast, 1886. A continuation of Reid's *History of the Presbyterian Church in Ireland,* London, 1853.

KILLINCHY: Killinchy Presbyterian Church; a History of its Origin. By the Rev. David Stewart.

KIRKPATRICK, REV. T. Millisle and Ballycopeland Presbyterian Church. 1934.

LATIMER, W. T. History of the Irish Presbyterians. Belfast, 1893, 1902.

LECKY, A. G. The Laggan and its Presbyterianism. 1905.

LECKY, A. G. In the Days of the Laggan Presbytery. 1908.

MCCREEVY, ALEXANDER. The Presbyterian Ministers of Killeleagh.

NEWRY: Newry Presbyterian Congregation (First). Its History and Relationships. 1904.

PEARSON, A. F. S. Puritan and Presbyterian Settlements in Ireland, 1560-1660. 2 vols.

PRESBYTERIAN HISTORICAL SOCIETY OF IRELAND ANNUAL RECORDS. Belfast, 1908-1916, 1918.

RANDALSTOWN: History of Randalstown Presbyterian Congregation: Covering Three Centuries. "By a member of the Society".

REID, JAMES SEATON. History of the Presbyterian Church in Ireland. 3 vols. London, 1853. (Contains much biography.)

STEPHENSON, S. M. The Parish and Congregation of Grey-Abbey. Belfast, 1828. (Grey-Abbey, Co. Down.)

STEWART, ANDREW. A Short Account of the Church of Christ as it was amongst the Irish: Appendix to Adair's *True Narrative*. Belfast, 1866.

STEWART, DAVID. History of the Presbyterian Settlements in Ireland, 1641-1760. (Larmor Trust Lectures, vol. 3.)

STEWART, REV. DAVID. The History and Principles of the Presbyterian Church in Ireland. Belfast, 1908.

STEWART, REV. DAVID. The Seceders in Ireland. Belfast, 1950.

ULSTER, RECORDS OF THE GENERAL SYNOD OF ULSTER. 1691-1820. 3 vols. Belfast, 1890-1898. (Records of the ministers, elders, etc.)

WITHEROW, THOMAS. Historical and Literary Memorials of Presbyterianism in Ireland, 1623-1731. Belfast, 1879. (Biographies of fifty Presbyterian ministers with some genealogical records.)

WOODBURN, REV. JAMES B. The Ulster Scot, His History and Religion. London, 1914.

6. QUAKER

FULLER, A. and T. HOLMES. A Compendious View of Some Extraordinary Sufferings of the People Called Quakers ... in the Kingdom of Ireland, from 1655 to the end of the Reign of George, the First. 1731.

GOUGH, JOHN. History of the People Called Quakers. 4 vols. Dublin, 1789.

GRUBB, ISABEL. Quakers in Ireland, 1654-1900. London, 1927.

MYERS, ALBERT COOK. Immigration of the Irish Quakers into Pennsylvania, 1682-1750; with their early history (records) in Ireland. 1902.

PENN, WILLIAM. Brief Account of the People Called Quakers. Reprinted for R. Jackson. Dublin.

QUAKERS: Narrative Events that have lately taken place in Ireland among the Society called Quakers. 1804.

QUAKER RECORDS: Quaker Records, Dublin; Abstracts of Wills. Edited by P. Beryl Eustace and Olive Goodbody. Dublin, 1957.

R., J. M. Six Generations of Friends in Ireland, 1655-1890. 1893.

RUTTY, JOHN. A History of the Rise and Progress of the People called Quakers in Ireland, from the Year 1653 to 1700 . . . by Thomas Wright of Cork. Now revised and enlarged. To which is added a Continuation of the same History to the Year of Our Lord, 1751. Dublin, 1751, 1811.

7. ROMAN CATHOLIC

ARCHIVIUM HIBERNICUM. Published by the Catholic Record Society of Ireland. Dublin, 1912-1913.

CATHOLIC DIRECTORY AND ALMANAC, 1837.

D'ALTON, JOHN. King James's Irish Army List, 1689. 2 vols. Second edition, enlarged. Dublin, 1860. (Memoirs, origins and brief genealogical notices of the Septs and Families of some 500 officers commissioned on King James II Army List; their army achievements, and some of their descendants.)

FASTI ECCLESIAE HIBERNICAE: The Succession of the Prelates and Members of the Catholic Bodies in Ireland. Edited by Henry Cotton. 4 vols. Dublin, 1855.

HISTORIES: See the histories of the counties and towns which are located in the provinces of Leinster, Munster and Connaught. These are, for the most part, especially rich in Catholic genealogical and personal records. See County and Town Histories in PART ONE (p. 77).

KELLY'S DIRECTORY: Roman Catholic Parishes and Parish Priests. 1936. (Complete list to 1936.)

O'CONNELL, MRS. MORGAN JOHN. The Last Colonel of the Irish Brigade, Count O'Connell and Old Irish Life at Home and Abroad, 1745-1833. 2 vols. London, 1892. (Pedigrees of many Irish families.)

PRYNNE'S RECORDS, 1665. 3 vols.

CHAPTER VII

DEATH RECORDS

FUNERAL CERTIFICATES: Irish Funeral Entries (or Certificates) which were copied from an original manuscript volume now in the British Museum (Add. MS. 4820), but formerly one of a series of eighteen manuscript volumes of Funeral Entries, late 16th century to 18th century, now in the Genealogical Office, Dublin Castle, Dublin. The above copies were published in the *Journal of the Association for the Preservation of the Memorials of the Dead,* Vols. VII and VIII, and later printed as one volume.

INQUISITIONS POST MORTEM: Inquisitionum in Officio Rotulorum Cancellariae Hiberniae Asservatarum, Repertorium, 1603-1649 (Leinster and Ulster). 1826-1829.

TOMBSTONE RECORDS:

BIGGER, FRANCIS JOSEPH, and HERBERT HUGHES. Armorial Sculptured Stones of the County Antrim. In the *Ulster Journal of Archaeology.* Second series, Vols. VI through IX. (Over 250 sketches of Arms with inscriptions.) Also includes tombstone records of the Old Abbey Church of Bangor, County Down.

CASSIDY, WILLIAM, JR. Lambeg Churchyard, Lisburn, County Antrim: Inscriptions on Old Tombstones, 1626-1837.

CLARE, REV. WALLACE. Monumental Inscriptions in the Cathedral Burial-Ground at Glendalough, County Wicklow. In *The Irish Genealogist.* Vol. II, pp. 88-93.

DAVIES, O. Drakestown Graveyard, County Meath. In the *Journal of the Royal Society of Antiquaries of Ireland.* Vol. 71.

DUNDAS, W. H. Tombstone Inscriptions, Enniskillen. Published in *Enniskillen, Parish and Town.* 1913.

LESLIE, REV. JAMES B. Tombstone Inscriptions and Memorials of the Dead. Published in *The History of Kilsaran Union of Parishes, County Louth. Appendix IV*, pp. 282-319.

LONGFIELD, ADA K. Some Eighteenth Century Irish Tombstones. In the *Journal of the Royal Society of Antiquaries of Ireland.* Vols. 73-76.

MACALISTER, R. A. S. The Memorial Slabs of Clonmacnoise, King's County. Dublin, 1909.

MASTERSON, VERY REV. M. J. CANON. Inscriptions on Tombstones and Monuments. In the *Journal of Ardagh and Clonmacnoise Antiquarian Society,* No. 6.

MCDONAGH, MICHAEL. Irish Graves in England. *Evening Telegraph,* Dublin. Reprint, No. 6. 1888.

MEMORIALS OF THE DEAD: The Journals of the Irish Memorial Association; formerly the Association for the Preservation of the Memorials of the Dead in Ireland, and in 1937, incorporating the Dublin Parish Register Society. Edited by Thomas Ulick Sadleir. Vols. I-XIII, no. 2. 1892-1937. Contains many thousands of tombstone inscriptions throughout Ireland.

O'PHELAN, JOHN. Epitaphs on the Tombs in the Cathedral Church of St. Canice, Kilkenny. Dublin, 1813.

QUINN, REV. WILLIAM. Athlone Grave Stones. In the *Journal of Ardagh and Clonmacnoise Antiquarian Society,* No. 8.

VICARS, SIR ARTHUR. Index to the Births, Marriages and Deaths, in *Anthologia Hibernica,* 1793-1794. Published as an *Appendix* in *Irish Marriages.* By Henry Farrar. 2 vols. London, 1897. (Vol. II.)

CHAPTER VIII

DIRECTORIES AND SCHOOL REGISTERS

1. DIRECTORIES

BASSETT, G. H. Published directories for a number of Irish counties in the second half of the nineteenth century.

BELFAST PAROCHIAL GUIDE. 1901 and 1904.

BRADSHAW: Bradshaw's Belfast Directory. 2 vols. Belfast, 1819. (Includes a secondary list, arranged by trades.)

CLARE, REV. WALLACE. A Brief Directory of the City of Cork, 1758. Extracted from the *Cork Evening Post* advertisements. Also, A Brief Directory of the City of Cork, 1769-1770. Extracted from the *Hibernian Chronicle*. Published in *The Irish Genealogist,* Vol. I, nos. 8-9, 1941.

CONNOR, JOHN. Directory of Cork. *ca.* 1820-1830.

DENNAN, JOSEPH. The First Hundred Years of the Dublin Directory. A historical account, in the *Biographical Society of Ireland Publications*. Vol. I, no. 7.

ERCK, J. C. The Irish Ecclesiastical Register for the Year 1818.

FERRAR, JOHN. The Limerick Directory, 1769.

GUINNESS, H. S. Dublin Directories, 1751-1760. A report on Dublin Directories. Published in the *Irish Book Lover,* Vol. XIV, pp. 84-6.

HALY, JAMES. Directory of Cork, 1795.

HORE, H. J. The Social State of the Southern and Eastern Counties of Ireland in the Sixteenth Century; being the presentments of gentlemen, commonalty, and citizens of Carlow, Cork, Kilkenny, Tipperary, Waterford, and Wexford, made in the reigns of Henry VIII and Elizabeth. (From the Public Record Office, London.) Edited by Hore and Graves. Dublin, 1870.

IRISH CHURCH DIRECTORY, THE. Published since 1862.

KELLY'S DIRECTORY: Roman Catholic Parishes and Parish Priests. 1936-.

KILKENNY: The New Commercial Directory. Kilkenny, 1839. (Includes Waterford, Kilkenny, Clonmel, Carrick-on-Suir, New Ross and Carlow.)

KING'S COUNTY DIRECTORY, THE. Includes a short history. Parsonstown, 1890.

LEET, AMBROSE. A Directory to the Market Towns, Villages, Gentlemen's Seats and Other Noted Places in Ireland. 1814.

LENNOX, WILLIAM. New Commercial Directory. 1840. (Covers most of the mid-Ulster towns.)

LUCAS, RICHARD. Lucas' Directory of Cork (and south-east towns, Youghal to Kinsale). 1787; 1821.

LUCAS, RICHARD. General Directory of Ireland (27 towns of the south half of Ireland, excepting those in his 1787 Directory). 1788.

MACCABE. Directory of Drogheda. 1830.

MACLOSKIE, CHARLES. Handbook or Directory for the County of Fermanagh. 1848.

MARTIN. Martin's Belfast Directory. 1835, 1841.

PARLIAMENTARY GAZETTEER OF IRELAND. 10 vols. Dublin, 1844-1846.

PETTIGREW AND OULTON. Dublin Directory (names arranged by streets and houses). 1834.

PIGOT. Pigot's Commercial Directory of Ireland, Scotland, etc. 1820.

PIGOT. The City of Dublin and Hibernian Provincial Directory. Pigot and Co. 1824.

SLATER, I. (Late Pigot and Co.) The National Commercial Directory of Ireland, 1846, and at later intervals. Includes all cities, and market and post towns of Ireland, with alphabetical directories of the larger cities. Lists, for each location, of the nobility, gentry, and lists by trades and professions.

SMYTH, JOSEPH. Belfast Directory. 1807, 1820.

STEWART, JOHN WATSON. The Gentleman's and Citizen's Almanack. 1816, 1823, 1826, 1827. (Included in the Treble Almanac with the English Court Registry and Wilson's Dublin Directory, with a new correct plan of Dublin.)

THOM: Thom's Irish Almanac and Official Directory. Dublin (each of four years) 1842-1847.

THOM: Thom's Directory. 1848-1864.

WATSON, JOHN. Gentleman's and Citizen's Almanack, Dublin. 67 vols. 1736-1844.

WILSON. Wilson's Directory of Dublin, 1751 (earliest). Issued every year (except 1754-1759) until 1837.

2. SCHOOLS, REGISTERS OF; HISTORIES OF, ETC.

ARMAGH: Armagh Royal School, 1667-1931. Edited by Major L. M. Ferrar. Belfast, 1933.

BELFAST: The Book of the Royal Belfast Academical Institution. 1810-1910. Belfast, 1913. Includes names of students, 1814-1912, with residence and names of parents or guardians.

BRENAN, REV. MARTIN. The Schools of Kildare and Leighlin, 1775-1835. Dublin, 1935. Includes Roman Catholic and Protestant schools. Records of Head Masters.

CORCORAN, REV. T. Clongowes School Register, 1814-1932. Dublin, n. d.

DUBLIN: Alumni Dublinensus, 1593-1860. Edited by the late George Dames Burtchaell and T. U. Sadleir. Dublin, 1924, 1935. A Register of the Students, Graduates, Professors and Provosts of Trinity College in the University of Dublin. Presents in dictionary form, by date of entry, the name of each student, his school classification, date of entry, age at entry, parentage, place of birth, place of previous schooling, name of tutor, etc.

DUBLIN: Registers of King's Inns, Dublin. (Use as a guide to the Inn's of Court Registers, London, which contain more information on the students, including Irish law students required to study in London.)

DUNDAS, W. H. Enniskillen, Parish and Town. 1913. Contains the records of Portora Royal School, Enniskillen: History and biography of the Head Masters, 1618-1904; list of pupils from 1641-1722, including name and age of pupil, father's name, and place of birth.

GLASGOW, UNIVERSITY OF, SCOTLAND: Matriculation Albums of the University of Glasgow, 1728-1858. Edited by W. Innes Addison. Glasgow, 1913. Includes records of many students from Ireland.

KILKENNY: Register of Kilkenny College, 1684-1800. Edited by Thomas U. Sadleir. In the *Journal of the Royal Society of Antiquaries of Ireland*. Vol. 54. 1924. (Also a Supplement to the above, edited by W. E. J. Dobbs, published in vol. 76.)

LONDON: Inns of Court (London) Admission Registers: Gray's Inn, 1521-1889, edited by Joseph Foster, 1889; Inner Temple, 1547-1660, edited 1877; Lincoln's Inn, 1420-1893, 2 vols., 1896.

LONDONDERRY: Foyle College, Londonderry, Register of: 1814-1834; 1847-1853. Published in *Our School Times*. 1926-29.

O'CONNELL, PHILIP. The Schools and Scholars of Breiffne. Dublin, 1942. (Breiffne covers much of the diocese of Kilmore and includes the present Co. Cavan with the northwest half of Co. Leitrim and small sections of counties Meath, Fermanagh and Sligo. Notes on teachers of many schools and some emigrations to America.)

RATHMINES, CO. DUBLIN: Rathmines School Roll, from the beginning of the school in 1858 till its close in 1899. Dublin, 1932. Records of 2,190 students; birth date or age, entrance date, residence, parentage and some notes on career and death dates.

CHAPTER IX

GOVERNMENT RECORDS

CENSUS, EMIGRATION, NATURALIZATION, TAX, VITAL RECORDS

CENSUS: See County, Town, Diocesan, and Parish Histories, PART ONE (p. 76). Many contain extracts from census returns. Historical magazines of county or regional interest often contain such lists. Examples are:

CONLON, M. V. The Census of the Parish of St. Mary Shandon, Cork (*ca.* 1830). In the *Journal of the Cork Historical and Archaeological Society.* Vol. 49, pp. 10-18.

LESLIE, REV. JAMES B. History of Kilsaran Union of Parishes in the County of Louth. Dundalk, 1908. (Extracts and lists from 1821, etc, census returns.)

MacIVOR, REV. DERMOT. Townland Survey of County Louth. In the *Journal of the County Louth Archaeological Society.* Vol. 12.

MARTIN, SAMUEL. Historical Gleanings from County Derry. Dublin, 1955. (Contains lists of inhabitants; Aghanloo and Tamlaght Finlagan Parishes, Co. Derry, 1831; also some 1821 census lists for baronies of County Fermanagh.)

O'DONNCHADHA, TADHG. Extracts from an Old Census (Parish of Dunbullogue (Carrignavar) County Cork). In the *Journal of the Cork Historical and Archaeological Society.* Vol. 51, pp. 69-77.

PENDER, SÉAMUS. Inhabitants of Waterford City in 1663 (by trades and profession). In the *Journal of the Cork Historical and Archaeological Society.* Vol. 51, pp. 108-125.

CENSUS RETURNS:

KING, VERY REV. DEAN R. G. S. A Particular of the "Howses and Famyles" in Londonderry, 15 May 1628. Reprint from the *Sentinel,* Londonderry, 1936.

PENDER, SEAMUS, *Ed.* A Census of Ireland, *ca.* 1659. Irish Manuscripts Commission, Dublin, 1939.

PRIOR, THOMAS. List of the Absentees of Ireland, and an Estimate of the Yearly Value of their Estates and Incomes spent abroad. Dublin, 1767.

EMIGRATION:

BLAKE, JOHN W. Transportation from Ireland to America, 1653. Published in *Irish Historical Studies,* vol. 3, no. 11 (1943), pp. 267-281.

DRUMGOOLAND VESTRY BOOK: 1892. Notes of Ulster Emigration to America, 1789-1828. (Other unpublished vestry books contain notes on emigrants.)

HANDLIN, OSCAR. Irish Emigration to Boston.

MacDONAGH, OLIVE. The Irish Catholic Clergy and Emigration during the Great Famine. Published in *Irish Historical Studies,* vol. 5, no. 20 (Sept. 1947), pp. 287-302.

MARTIN, SAMUEL. Historical Gleanings from County Derry. Dublin, 1955. (Contains lists of emigrants, 1833-1834, from the County Londonderry parishes of Aghanloo, Aghadowey, Balteagh, Bovevagh, Coleraine (town), Drumachose Parish and Limavady, Dunboe, Magilligan, Tamlaght Finlagan.)

NEWSPAPERS: Lists of local emigrants printed in local newspapers throughout Ireland. Examples are:

Belfast News Letter: Sailing notices in: Issues of 10 September 1754, 8 October 1754, 27 May 1755, 21 October 1755, 26 September 1755; all cover the sailings of Arthur Dobbs' colonists to North Carolina.

Nation: Issue of 8 December 1850, has March 1850 Record of Sailings of Catholics from Ireland via Liverpool.

NEW ENGLAND HISTORICAL AND GENEALOGICAL REGISTER, vols. 60, 61, 62, 66. Ireland Passenger Lists, 1803.

REPORT OF THE DEPUTY KEEPER OF THE PUBLIC RECORDS OF NORTHERN IRELAND, 1929: Appendix B indexes the name, residence and year of sailing of emigrants from counties Antrim, Armagh, Down, Fermanagh, Londonderry and Tyrone, 1804-1806.

STEWART, REV. DAVID. Fasti of the American Presbyterian Church . . . Ministers (136 of Irish Origin . . . in America). Presbyterian Historical Society. 1943.

NATURALIZATION: (See also: Inquisitions, and Patent Rolls.)

SHAW, W. A. *Ed.* Letters of Denization and Acts of Naturalization for Aliens in England and Ireland, 1603-1700. Published by the Huguenot Society, vol. 18. London, 1911.

STEWART, REV. DAVID, *Ed.* The Scots in Ulster; their Denization and Naturalization, 1605-1634. Parts One and Two. Presbyterian Historical Society, Belfast, 1952. Part One: Scots Undertakers, Grants of Naturalization, 1610-1614. Part Two: Early Scots Settlers in: Co. Antrim, 1607-1633; Co. Armagh, 1610-1619; Co. Cavan, 1610-1629; Co. Donegal, 1610-1629.

STEWART, REV. DAVID, *Ed.* The Scots in Ulster, their Denization and Naturalization. Presbyterian Historical Society, Belfast, 1954. Contains: Early Scots Settlers in Co. Down, 1606-1629; Co. Fermanagh, 1610-1629; Co. Londonderry, 1616-1625; Co. Monaghan, 1615-1630.

STEWART, REV. DAVID, *Ed.* The Scots in Ulster, the Years Between 1636 and 1642. Presbyterian Historical Society, Belfast, 1955.

TAX RECORDS: HEARTHMONEY ROLLS: (Householder's tax on each hearth.)

ANTRIM (COUNTY):

Parish of Carnmoney, Hearthmoney Roll of 1669. Published in *Three Centuries in South East Antrim.* By Rev. H. J. St. J. Clarke.

Parish of Lisburn, Hearthmoney Rolls. Edited by Rev. J. Smyth. In the *Journal of the Down and Connor Historical Society.* Vol. 7, pp. 85-92.

ARMAGH (COUNTY):

County Armagh Hearthmoney Rolls, 1664. Edited by Rev. L. P. Murray. In *Archivium Hibernicum,* vol. 8, pp. 121-202. 1936.

Hearthmoney Rolls, Parish of Creggan, 1664. Published in *History of the Parish of Creggan (in Barony of Upper Fews).* By the Rev. Lawrence P. Murray. Dundalk, 1940.

LONDONDERRY (COUNTY): OR (COUNTY DERRY):

Hearthmoney Rolls, Parish of Aghanloo, 1663. In *Historical Gleanings from County Derry.* By Samuel Martin. Dublin, 1955.

DONEGAL (COUNTY):

Hearthmoney Rolls of County Donegal, 1665. Edited by R. J. Dickson. In the *Journal of the County Donegal Historical Society.* Vol. 1, nos. 2, 3 (1949).

DUBLIN (COUNTY):

Hearthmoney Rolls, of County Dublin, 1664. In the *Journal of the County Kildare Archaeological Society.* Vols. 10, 11 (1927-30).

FERMANAGH (COUNTY):

Hearthmoney Rolls for Enniskillen, County Fermanagh, 1665 and 1666. Published in *Enniskillen, Parish and Town.* By W. H. Dundas. 1913.

LOUTH (COUNTY):

Hearthmoney Rolls for the Parishes of Kilsaran, Gernonstown, Stabannan, Manfieldstown and Dromiskin, 1664, 1666-7. Published in the *History of Kilsaran Union of Parishes in the County of Louth.* By the Rev. James B. Leslie. Dundalk, 1908.

MONAGHAN (COUNTY):

Hearthmoney Roll of County Monaghan, 1663, 1665. Published in *The History of Monaghan for Two*

Hundred Years: 1660-1860. By Denis Carolan Rushe. Dundalk, 1921. Pp. 291-338.

TIPPERARY (COUNTY):

Tipperary's Families: Being the Hearthmoney Records for 1665-6-7. Edited by Thomas Laffan. Dublin, 1911. (Published earlier in the *Journal of the Cork Historical and Archaeological Society.* Vols. 5 and 6.)

WICKLOW (COUNTY):

Hearthmoney Rolls for County Wicklow. In the *Journal of the Royal Society of Antiquaries of Ireland.* Vol. 61.

VITAL RECORDS:

Births Registered in Ireland: General Index. Births registered in Ireland in 1864-1866. Fol. H.M.S.O. Thom: Dublin, 1873-1876.

Baptisms, Marriages and Deaths, recorded in the *Hibernian Chronicle,* 1769-1795; Index volumes (in the National Library, Dublin, and in the Public Record Office of Northern Ireland, Belfast).

FARRAR, HENRY, *Ed.* Irish Marriages: Being an Index to the Marriages in *Walker's Hibernian Magazine,* 1771-1812. With an Appendix of the Births, Marriages and Deaths in the *Anthologia Hibernica,* 1793 and 1794, from the Notes of Sir Arthur Vicars. 2 vols. London, 1897.

Newspapers: Lists of Vital Records in the local news.

CHAPTER X

LAND RECORDS

1. EARLY COLLECTIONS

BROOKS, ERIC ST. JOHN, *Ed.* Register of the Hospital of St. John, the Baptist, without the New Gate, Dublin, *ca.* 1190-1473. Irish Manuscripts Commission, Dublin, 1936.

BROOKS, ERIC ST. JOHN, *Ed.* Knight's Fees in Counties Wexford, Carlow, and Kilkenny. I. M. C., Dublin, 1950. (13th and 14th century records showing feudal descents.)

CALENDAR OF CHRIST CHURCH DEEDS, DUBLIN, *ca.* 1174-1684. Printed in the *Twentieth Report of the Deputy Keeper of the Public Records in Ireland,* 1888. Pp. 36-122.

CLARKE, M. V., *Ed.* The Register of Tristernagh (Abbey, Co. Westmeath). Irish Manuscripts Commission, Dublin, 1941. Mid-fourteenth century records relating to property and the early settlement of Co. Meath by the Anglo-Normans.

CURTIS, EDMUND, *Ed.* Calendar of Ormond Deeds, 1172-1603. 6 vols. Irish Manuscripts Commission, Dublin, 1932-1943. (The most important extant collection of mediaeval documents in Ireland.)

LONGFIELD, A. K., *Ed.* The Shapland Carew Papers. Irish Manuscripts Commission, Dublin, 1946. Records of the Carew and other families in Wexford and Waterford counties, 1740-1822.

MACLYSAGHT, EDWARD, *Ed.* The Kenmare Manuscripts. Irish Manuscripts Commission, Dublin, 1942. Kenmare, Earls of; family estate records, rentals, etc., counties Kerry, Limerick and Cork, mostly 18th century.

MACLYSAGHT, EDWARD, *Ed.* Calendar of Orrery Papers. Irish Manuscripts Commission, Dublin, 1941. Rent Rolls, wills, marriage settlements, leases, etc., 1620-1689.

McNeill, Charles, Rev. A. Gwynn, and S. J. and A. J. Otway-Ruthven, *Editors.* Dowdall and Peppard Deeds. 2 vols. Irish Manuscripts Commission, Dublin.

Smyly, J. S., *Ed.* Old Deeds in the Library of Trinity College. A series, running in *Hermathena,* vols. 69-74.

White, Newport B., *Ed.* The Red Book of Ormond. Irish Manuscripts Commission, Dublin, 1932.

White, Newport B., *Ed.* Irish Monastic and Episcopal Deeds, . . . (13th-16th cent.). Includes documents regarding marriage, legitimacy, inheritance. Irish Manuscripts Commission, Dublin, 1936.

2. FORFEITURES: LAND CONFISCATION AND REDISTRIBUTION

Book of Postings and Sale of the Forfeited and Other Estates and Interests in Ireland: pre-23 June 1703. (In National Library of Ireland, Dublin.)

Butler, W. F. Cromwellian Confiscation in Muskerry. In the *Journal of the Cork Historical and Archaeological Society,* Series II, vols. 21-23, 26.

Chichester House Claims: A list of Claims as they are entered with the Trustees at Chichester House, Dublin, on or before 10 August 1700, with manuscript rulings (regarding forfeited estates by Catholics after the Battle of the Boyne). Dublin, 1701.

Frost, James. The History and Topography of the County of Clare. Dublin, 1893. Contains: (1) Connaught Certificates, Act of Settlement, 1653 (pp. 390-399); (2) County Clare Forfeitures and Distributions (of land), 1659, showing the owner in 1641, the name of person to whom land was disposed of in 1659 and names of townlands involved (pp. 399-526); (3) Abstracts of the Petitions before the Court of Claims for return of forfeited land (1689), sold . . . 1700 (pp. 570-603).

Rentals, Incumbered Estates Court: Published in *Landed Estates Court and Land Judges.*

Report of the Commissioners Appointed by Parliament to enquire into the Irish Forfeitures . . . London, reprinted Dublin, 1700.

Report of the Deputy Keeper of the Public Records in Ireland (5th, 1873). Contains: Recoveries (of forfeited estates) Suffered in the Palatine of Tipperary. (Appendix, pp. 69-81.)

Report of the Deputy Keeper of the Public Records in Ireland (19th, 1887). Contains: Abstracts of the Court of Claims for the Tryall of Innocents (who forfeited estates), 1662, 1663.

SIMMS, J. G. The Williamite Confiscation in Ireland, 1690-1703. London, 1956.

Second Report of the Trustees Appointed by Parliament for the Sale of the Forfeited Estates in Ireland. London, 1701.

Williamite Confiscations in Ireland: 131 Petitions, Claims, Counter-Claims, etc., from individuals, groups of individuals, and corporations, *ca.* 1702-1703. Privately printed for distribution among the members of Parliament and others of influence by those Irish whose estates were about to be confiscated . . .

Note: Many county and town histories contain records of forfeitures, land confiscation and redistribution. See list in PART ONE (p. 77).

3. PLANTATION RECORDS

The Carew Manuscripts, 1603-1624. Published by the British Government, a series of Reports made by the Commissioners appointed by the King, to visit landlords in Ulster . . .

DUNLOP, ROBERT. Ireland Under the Commonwealth. 2 vols. Manchester, 1913.

HILL, REV. GEORGE. An Historical Account of the Macdonnells of Antrim. Belfast, 1873.

HILL, REV. GEORGE. The Montgomery Manuscripts, 1603-1706. Compiled from Family Papers by William Montgomery and edited by the Rev. George Hill. Belfast, 1869.

HILL, REV. GEORGE. An Historical Account of the Plantation of Ulster . . . 1608-1620. Belfast, 1877.

HILL, REV. GEORGE. Plantation Papers or the Great Ulster Plantation in the Year 1610. Belfast, 1889.

LOWRY, T. K., *Ed.* The Hamilton Manuscripts: Containing Some Account of the Territories of the Upper Clandeboye, Great Ardes, and Dufferin, in the County of Down, by Sir James Hamilton (pre-1703). Belfast, 1868.

MOODY, T. W. The Londonderry Plantation, 1609-1641: The City of London and the Plantation in Ulster. Belfast, 1939.

PHILLIPS, SIR THOMAS. Londonderry and the London Companies, 1609-1629: Being a survey and other documents submitted to King Charles I, by Sir Thomas Phillips. Belfast, 1928.

PRENDERGAST, JOHN P. The Cromwellian Settlement in Ireland. 2nd edition, 1875.

"Records of Ireland, Fifteenth Annual Report, 1825". (1) Abstracts of Grants under the Acts of Settlement and Explanation, 1666-1684. (2) Index to the Inrolements for Adventurers, Soldiers, etc., 1666.

4. SURVEYS

FREEMAN, A. MARTIN, *Ed.* The Compossicion Booke of Conought. With Index, compiled by G. A. Hayes-MacCoy. 2 vols. Dublin, 1936-1942.

GRIFFITH, RICHARD. General Valuation of Ireland. 1844-1860. A survey of property in Ireland and occupants by Poor Law Unions. These are, however, identified in each title by the county or counties in which the Union falls, such as: "Union of Oughterard and Ballinrobe in the Counties of Galway and Mayo"; "Union of Carrickmacross, County Monaghan"; "Union of Athlone, County Westmeath". Printed as a Government project.

O'FLANAGHAN, REV. MICHAEL. Ordnance Survey Letters Containing Information relative to the Antiquities of the Counties, collected during the progress of the Ordnance Survey of 1835-1840. Reproduced under the direction of Rev. Michael O'Flanaghan. Bray, 1927, 1928. 35 vols.

O'SULLIVAN, WILLIAM. The Strafford Inquisition of County Mayo. Irish Manuscripts Commission, Dublin, 1958.

PYNNAR, NICHOLAS. Survey of Ulster: Counties of Armagh, Tyrone, Donegal, Cavan and Fermanagh, together with the Works and Plantation by the City of London in the City of Londonderry. December 1, 1618-March 28, 1619. Published by Walter Harris in *Hibernica: or Some Ancient Pieces*. Dublin, 1770.

SIMINGTON, ROBERT, *Ed.* Books of Survey and Distribution. 2 vols. Dublin, Irish Manuscripts Commission, 1949. Vol. I, County Roscommon. Vol. II, County Mayo.

SIMINGTON, ROBERT, *Ed.* The Civil Survey, A. D. 1654-1656. 9 vols. Irish Manuscripts Commission, Dublin, 1931-1953. Vol. I, Tipperary, East and South. Vol. II, Tipperary, West and North. Vol. III, Donegal, Derry, and Tyrone. Vol. IV, Limerick. Vol. V, Meath. Vol. VI, Waterford, Muskerry Barony, and Kilkenny City. Vol. VII, Dublin County. Vol. VIII, Kildare. Vol. IX, Wexford.

Statistical and Agricultural Surveys of the following Irish counties:

Antrim. By Rev. John Dubourdieu. 1812.

Armagh. By Sir Charles Coote. 1804.

Cavan. By Sir Charles Coote. 1802.

Clare. By Hely Dutton. 1808.

Cork. By Horatio Townsend. 2 vols. 1815.

Donegal. By James McParlan. 1802.

Down. By Rev. John Dubourdieu. 1802.

Dublin. By Joseph Archer. 1801.

Dublin (Observations on). By Hely Dutton. 1802.

Galway. By Hely Dutton. 1824.

Kildare. By Thomas James Rawson. 1807.

Kilkenny. By William Tighe. 1802.

King's County. By Sir Charles Coote. 1801.

Leitrim. By James McParlan. 1802.

Londonderry. By Rev. George V. Sampson. 1802.

Meath. By Robert Thompson. 1802.

Monaghan. By Sir Charles Coote. 1801.
Queen's County. By Sir Charles Coote. 1801.
Roscommon. By Isaac Weld. 1832.
Sligo. By James McParlan. 1802.
Tyrone. By John McEvoy. 1802.
Wexford. By Robert Fraser. 1807.
Wicklow. By Robert Fraser. 1801.

THOM, ALEXANDER. Return of Owners of Land of One Acre and Upwards in the Several Counties, Counties of Cities, and Counties of Towns in Ireland. Dublin, 1876.

YOUNG, ARTHUR. Arthur Young's Tour in Ireland (1776-1779), edited with Introduction and Notes, by Arthur Wollaston. 2 vols. London, 1892.

CHAPTER XI

MILITARY AND NAVAL RECORDS

BALLYMENA: Old Ballymena, a History of Ballymena during the 1798 Rebellion. In the *Ballymena Observer*, 1857, under the title, "Walks about Ballymena."

BIGGER, FRANCIS JOSEPH. The Northern Leaders of '98. Dublin, 1906.

BLAKE, BUTLER T. King Henry VIII's Irish Army List. Published in *The Irish Genealogist*, vol. 1, pp. 3-13, 36-38.

BORLASE, EDMUND. History of the Execrable Irish Rebellion; traced from many preceding Acts to the Grand Eruption, the 23rd of October, 1641, and pursued to the Act of Settlement, 1662. London, 1680. Reprint: Dublin, 1743.

BOULGER, DEMETRIUS CHARLES. The Battle of the Boyne, 1688-1691. London, 1911.

D'ALTON, JOHN. Illustrations Historical and Genealogical of King James's Irish Army List, 1689. 2 vols. Dublin. (2nd edition.) 1860.

DUNDAS, W. H., *Ed.* Muster Roll of 1631 and other Military Records to 1700, published in *Enniskillen, Parish and Town.* 1913. Pp. 146-156.

DWYER, REV. PHILIP, *Ed.* The Siege of Derry in 1689, as set forth in the Literary Remains of Col. The Rev. George Walker. 1893.

FERRAR, M. L. Officers of the Green Howards, 1688-1921. Belfast, 1931.

GROVES, TENISON. List of Officers of the Kildare Militia, 1794-1817. In the *Journal of the County Kildare Archaeological Society.* Vol. 12, no. 4 (1939).

HAYES-MCCOY, G. A. Scots Mercenary Forces in Ireland, 1565-1603. Dublin, 1937.

HAYES, RICHARD. Irish Swordsmen of France. Dublin, 1934.

IRISH SWORD, THE. A Military Journal, 1951.

JOURDAIN, LT. COL. H. F. and E. FRASER. The Connaught Rangers. 3 vols. London, 1924-1928.

KING, ARCHIBALD. The Irish Rebellion . . . Dublin, 1713.

LATIMER, W. T., *Ed.* The Actions of the Enniskillen Men, 1688-1689. Belfast, Dublin, 1896.

LUDLOW, LIEUT. GEN. EDMUND. The Memoirs of Edmund Ludlow, Lieutenant General in the Army of the Commonwealth of England, 1625-1672. Edited with Appendixes of letters illustrative documents, by C. H. Firth. 2 vols. Oxford, 1894. (A previous edition (2nd) of 3 vols., London, 1721, is entitled, *Memoirs of Edmund Ludlow, Esq., Lieutenant General of the Horse, Commander in Chief of the Forces in Ireland.*)

MARTIN, SAMUEL, *Ed.* The Muster Roll of Newtown Limavady, County Londonderry, 1666. Published in *Historical Gleanings of County Derry.* Dublin, 1955.

MCANALLY, SIR HENRY. The Irish Militia, 1793-1816. Dublin, 1949.

MCSKIMIN, SAMUEL. Annals of Ulster, 1790-1798. 1906.

Militia Officers for the Counties of Ireland. A rare printed work. One volume in the Armagh Library.

MILLIGAN, CECIL DAVIS. History of the Siege of Londonderry, 1689. Belfast, 1951.

MUNSTER MILITARY JOURNAL, THE. A Monthly Magazine. New series vol. 1, no. 1, January 1888.

O'BYRNE, W. R. *Ed.* Naval Biographical Dictionary. Edited, 1849 and 1859-1862.

O'CALLAGHAN, J. C. History of the Irish Brigades in the Service of France. Dublin, 1854.

O'CONNOR, ARTHUR. A List of the Officers of the several Regiments and Battalions of Militia, and of the several Regiments of Fencible Cavalry and Infantry upon the Establishment of Ireland, with the dates of their respective commissions and an alphabetical index, 1 September 1789. Dublin, 1797-1801.

O'CONOR, MATTHEW. The Irish Brigades; or Memoirs of the Most Eminent Irish Military Commanders . . . in the Elizabethan and Williamite Wars . . . Dublin, 1855.

O'HART, JOHN. Irish and Anglo-Irish Landed Gentry when Cromwell Came to Ireland. Dublin, 1884. Contains: (1) A List of Commissioned Officers (and their arrears) who served under Charles I in the wars in Ireland, before 5 June 1649 (no ranks or residence given); (2) Soldiers of the Commonwealth in Ireland (name and county given). These lists taken from *The Records of Ireland,* 1816-1825.

PATERSON, T. G. F. The County Armagh Volunteers of 1778-1793. In the *Ulster Journal of Archaeology,* 1941.

PHILLIPS, SIR THOMAS. Londonderry and the London Companies, 1609-1629. Belfast, 1928. Contains Muster Rolls of Londonderry and Coleraine, 1622.

PRENDERGAST, JOHN P. The Cromwellian Settlement of Ireland. Dublin, 1875.

WHITE, MAJOR JAMES GROVE. Record of the Doneraile Rangers with a List of the Volunteer Corps in the County of Cork. 1778-1783. In the *Journal of the Cork Historical and Archaeological Society,* January, 1893.

WITHEROW, THOMAS. The Boyne and Aghrim; or the Story of some famous Battlefields outside Ulster. 1879.

WITHEROW, THOMAS. Derry and Enniskillen in the Year 1689. 1885.

YOUNG, WILLIAM R. The Fighters of Derry. London, 1933. (Biographical and genealogical notes on those who were present at the Siege of Derry, 1689.)

Note: See also, under LAND RECORDS: *Plantation Records,* the works of the Rev. George Hill, and the Hamilton Manuscripts, which contain early Muster Rolls.

CHAPTER XII

NEWSPAPERS AND PERIODICALS

The following provides sources of information concerning the past publication of Irish newspapers and periodicals; the cities and towns wherein they were published, dates of publication, existing issues, present location and details of extant numbers in many collections.

Irish newspapers supply many birth, marriage and death notices for the cities and towns represented. They offer a wealth of miscellaneous news items regarding individuals and families. Emigration notices were also published. Many newspapers and periodicals ran a series of genealogical articles and biographical sketches.

A chapter in VOLUME I is devoted to newspapers and periodicals, listing the 17th, 18th and early 19th century publications, by city and town, with notations as to the dates and location of extant issues in many collections.

BIBLIOGRAPHY OF SOURCES:

BRADSHAW COLLECTION: A Catalogue of the Bradshaw Collection of Irish Books in the University Library, Cambridge (England). 3 vols. Cambridge, 1916.

BRITISH MUSEUM: Catalogue of Printed Books. Supplement: Newspapers published in Great Britain and Ireland, 1801-1900. IV. Irish Newspapers. London, 1905.

CAULFIELD, RICHARD. Antiquarian and Historical Notes: Early Cork Newspapers. In the *Journal of the Cork Historical and Archaeological Society*. Vol. XI, pp. 93-95.

CRONE, JOHN S. Ulster Bibliography (Londonderry). In the *Ulster Journal of Archaeology*. Second series, Vol. X, pt. 4; Vol. XI, pts. 1, 3, 4; Vol. XII, pt. 3; Vol. XIV, pt. 3; Vol. XV, pts. 2 and 3.

DENNY, REV. H. L. L. A Handbook of County Kerry Family History, Biography, Etc. (Newspapers with much family history, genealogy, etc., p. 11.)

DIX, E. R. McC. Bibliography, Ulster: A series, by county; includes Ulster newspapers. In the *Ulster Journal of Archaeology.* Vols. VII, VIII, IX, XIII, XIV, XV.

DIX, E. R. McC. The Earliest Cork Newspapers. In the *Journal of the Cork Historical and Archaeological Society.* Vol. I, A., pp. 83-4. Cork Newspapers Printed at Cork in the 18th Century. Vol. IX. (Second series), p. 267.

DIX, E. R. McC. Irish Bibliography. Tables Relating to some Dublin Newspapers: a list of Dublin newspapers of the 18th century (with dates of extant issues and locations of the various collections in Dublin). Dublin, 1910.

LINEN HALL LIBRARY, BELFAST: Belfast Library and Society for Promoting Knowledge (Linen Hall Library). Catalogue of the Books in the Irish Section. Belfast, 1917. (See also, catalogues of other libraries, listed under CATALOGUES, p. 199.)

MADDEN, R. R. History of Irish Periodical Literature. 2 vols. 1867.

NEWSPAPER PRESS DIRECTORY: The Newspaper Press Directory. (Contains full particulars of every newspaper, magazine, review, and periodical published in the United Kingdom and the British Isles. Annual.) London, 1846.

O'KELLEY, F. Survey of Newspapers Printed in Ireland Before 1801. In the *Bulletin of the Irish Committee of Historical Sciences,* No. 7. Dublin.

SLATER, I. National Commercial Directory of Ireland. London, 1846. (Under each city and town, a listing of newspapers presently being published, the days on which they appear, and the names of the publishers.)

STEPHEN, REV. J. and S. J. BROWN. The Dublin Newspaper Press: a bird's-eye view, 1659-1916. Published in *Studies,* Vol. XXV, pp. 109-122.

CHAPTER XIII

RECORDS OF PUBLIC OFFICES, FREEHOLDERS AND GUILDS

The biographical dictionaries and publications of collected pedigrees, listed in PART ONE, CHAPTER III, provide information about those who held the more important public offices. Many of the excellent county and town histories contain the rolls of those who have, from the seventeenth century or earlier, represented their county in the Irish Parliament, and also lists of past mayors, burgesses, sheriffs, etc. Footnotes regarding many of these men add biographical and genealogical details. Some additional sources are herein presented.

The Guild Records and Rolls of Freemen now extant are largely unpublished. Several of the records and rolls have been transcribed, however, for genealogical purposes. Some of these have been printed and the sources are noted below.

BALL, F. ELRINGTON. The Judges in Ireland, 1221-1921. 2 vols. London, 1926.

BELMORE, THE EARL OF. Parliamentary Memoirs of Fermanagh County and Borough, from 1613 to 1835. Dublin, 1885.

BERRY, H. F. The Goldsmith's Company of Dublin. In the *Journal of the Cork Historical and Archaeological Society.* Vol. 8 (1902), pp. 29-50. Contains a list of Master Wardens (compiled from the *Journals,* etc.), 1636-1800. Also a list of Apprentices, 1653-1752, which provides the name of the father, mother, or guardian of each apprentice, place of residence and name of the master to whom bound.

BURTCHAELL, GEORGE DAMES. Genealogical Memoirs of the Members of Parliament for the County and City of Kilkenny. Dublin, 1888.

CONLON, M. V. The Honorary Freemen of Cork, 1690-1946. In the *Journal of the Cork Historical and Archaeological Society.* Vol. 52, pp. 74-86.

DUNDAS, W. H. Enniskillen, Parish and Town. Dundalk, 1913. Contains a list of the Freemen, 1747-1768.

FAHY, E. M. The Cork Goldsmith's Company. In the *Journal of the Cork Historical and Archaeological Society*. Vol. 58, pp. 33-38.

GILBERT, JOHN T. History of the Viceroys of Ireland; with Notices of the Castle of Dublin and its Chief Occupants in Former Times. Dublin, 1865.

GIVEN, MAXWELL. High Sheriffs of County Antrim, 1603-1854. In the *Ulster Journal of Archaeology*. Vol. XI, pt. 2, pp. 78-83.

GRAY, EDWARD STEWART. Notes on the High Sheriffs of County Donegal. In *The Irish Genealogist*. Vol. II, pp. 165-177.

GUILD RECORDS: Lesser Known Documents in the City Muniment Room of Dublin. In the *Dublin Historical Record*. Vol. II, no. 3, pp. 119-20.

GUILDS, DUBLIN: Dublin Guilds. In the *Journal of the Royal Society of Antiquaries of Ireland*. Vols. 26, 30, 31, 33, 35, 36, 48, 49, 52, 60. See Volume Indexes.

LIBER MUNERUM PUBLICORUM HIBERNIAE ab an. 1152 usque ad 1827; or, The Establishment of Ireland from the Nineteenth of King Stephen to the Seventh of George IV. 2 vols. London, 1852. Consists of appointments by patent to offices under the Crown in Ireland over a period of 675 years. It was compiled by Rowley Lascelles from transcripts made by John Lodge of the now destroyed Patent Rolls. An index is being compiled for publication by the Irish Manuscripts Commission.

LIMERICK: The Freemen of Limerick, List of (with explanatory Introduction): In the *North Munster Antiquarian Society Journal*. Vol. IV, Appendix I, pp. 103-130.

MARYBOROUGH (Queen's Co.): A Handlist of the Voters of Maryborough Corporation, 1760. This is taken from a notebook which forms part of the Drogheda Manuscript, in the National Library of Ireland. This manuscript contains a rough alphabetical list of the freemen and burgesses of the borough, 1 March 1738/9-29 September 1754; additions and corrections to 1759; an amended list to 1760. List printed in the *Irish History Review*. Vol. IX, no. 33 (March, 1954), pp. 67-85.

PENDER, SÉAMUS. Studies in Waterford History, V. Lists of Freemen, Council Members, Masters and Wardens of Guilds of the Waterford Corporation, 1656-1665; also Bonds of Apprentices from 1664 to 1677, and a list of the Guild Officers and Freemen for 1664-1677. Information taken from the old Council-Books of the Corporation of Waterford. In the *Journal of the Cork Historical and Archaeological Society*. Vol. 53, no. 177, pp. 39-59.

PENDER, SÉAMUS. Studies in Waterford History, IX, X. The Guilds of Waterford, 1650-1700. In the *Journal of the Cork Historical and Archaeological Society*. Vol. 58, pp. 14-19; 67-76. (A list of the Waterford Freeholders is also published in the *Journal of the Waterford and South East of Ireland Archaeological Society*.)

QUEEN'S COUNTY: Queen's County Freemen, 1758-1775, a List of. In the *Journal of the County Kildare Archaeological Society*. See Indexes.

RABBITTE, REV. J., S. J. Historical Account of the Wardens of Galway. In the *Journal of the Galway Archaeological and Historical Society*. Vol. XVII.

SADLEIR, T. U. Kildare Members of Parliament, 1559—. In the *Journal of the County Kildare Archaeological Society*. Vols. 1911-1924.

SLATER, I. National Commercial Directory of Ireland. London, 1846. (See also other Almanacs and Directories listed on pp. 229-231.)

SMYTH, C. J. Chronicle of the Law Officers of Ireland. London, 1839.

STEWART, JOHN WATSON. A List of the Justices of the Peace in the Several Counties of Ireland in 1797-1798. Taken from *The Gentleman's and Citizen's Almanack*, compiled by John Watson Stewart for the year of our Lord, 1797 and

1798. Dublin, n. d. A list for the counties of Antrim, Cavan and Fermanagh is published in the *Ulster Journal of Archaeology,* 2nd series, Vol. VII (1901), pp. 138-141.

TENISON, CHARLES MCCARTHY. Cork Members of Parliament, 1559-1800. In the *Journal of the Cork Historical and Archaeological Society.* 2nd series, Vols. I and II.

TENISON, CHARLES MCCARTHY. Old Dublin Bankers. *ibid.* Vol. II.A., and Vol. I, 2nd series.

TENISON, CHARLES MCCARTHY. Private Bankers of Cork and the South of Ireland. *ibid.* Vol. I.A., and II.A.

TIPPERARY: Tipperary County Freeholders of 1776: a printed list in the Royal Irish Academy, Dublin.

VIGORS, COL. P. D. Alphabetical List of the Free Burgesses of New Ross, County Wexford, from 1658 to 30 September 1839. (Contains genealogical notes on many.) In the *Journal of the Royal Society of Antiquaries of Ireland.* Vol. XXI, pp. 298-309.

WEBB, J. J. The Guilds of Dublin. Dublin, 1929.

WESTROPP, M. S. D. The Goldsmiths of Cork. In the *Journal of the Cork Historical and Archaeological Society.* Vol. 12, pp. 37-43.

WOODS, CECIL C. The Goldsmiths of Cork, 1601-1850. Gives names, earliest record of, latest notice of, with many death notations. 82 names, with notes on each. In the *Journal of the Royal Society of Antiquaries of Ireland.* Vol. 25, pp. 218-223.

YOUGHAL, COUNCIL BOOK OF THE CORPORATION OF: From 1610 to 1659, from 1666 to 1687, 1690-1800. Edited by Richard Caulfield. Contains Guild and Freemen's records of admission and concellation (see index).

YOUNG, R. M. The Town Book of the Corporation of Belfast, 1613-1816. Belfast, 1892. Contains Roll of Freemen, 1635-1796. (Pp. 246-300; 336-338.)

CHAPTER XIV

STATE PAPERS AND COURT RECORDS

A bibliography of printed calendars of State Papers, published abstracts or extracts from documents, lists of transcripts of destroyed documents, name indexes to existing documents, etc., all of which contain genealogical information.

CAREW MANUSCRIPTS, CALENDAR OF: Calendar of the Carew Manuscripts at Lambeth Palace (London), 1515-1624. With the Book of Howth, the Conquest of Ireland, and Miscellany (including pedigrees). Edited by J. S. Brewer and W. Bullen. 5 vols. 1867-1873.

CAVEL, RICHARD, and J. WATTS. A List of Such of the Names of the Nobility, Gentry, and Commonalty of England and Ireland, Assembled in Dublin, 7th May 1689, before the Late King James, Attainted of High Treason. London, 1690.

CHANCERY INQUISITIONS: Inquisitionum in officio Rotulorum Cancellariae Hiberniae Asservatarum repertorium, 1603-1649. Vol. I. Leinster. 1826. Vol. II. Ulster. 1829. Published by the Record Commission.

FORFEITURE: The Report of the Commissioners appointed by Parliament to enquire into the Irish Forfeiture. London, 1700.

GILBERT, JOHN T. and LADY GILBERT, *Editors*. Calendar of Ancient Records of Dublin. 13 vols. Dublin, 1889-1907.

GRIFFITH, MARGARET. The Irish Record Commission, 1810-1830. In *Irish Historical Studies*. Vol. VII, no. 25 (March, 1950), pp. 17-38.

GRIFFITH, MARGARET. A Short Guide to the Public Record Office of Ireland. In *Irish Historical Studies*. Vol. VIII, no. 29 (March, 1952), pp. 45-58.

HATCHELL, GEORGE. Abstract of the Deeds enrolled in Chancery pursuant to the Act 4 and 5, William IV. 1840.

LISMORE PAPERS: The Lismore Papers (1st series); Autobiographical Notes, Remembrances and Diaries of Sir Richard Boyle, First and "Great" Earl of Cork. Edited by the Rev. Alex. B. Grosart. 5 vols. 1886. The Lismore Papers (2nd series); Selections from the Private and Public (or State) Correspondence of Sir Richard Boyle, First and "Great" Earl of Cork. Edited by the Rev. Alex. B. Grosart. 5 vols. 1887-1888.

MILLS, JAMES and MARGARET C. GRIFFITH, *Editors.* Calendar of the Justiciary Rolls or proceedings in the Court of the Justiciar of Ireland, 1295-1314. 3 vols. Dublin, 1905-1956.

PARLIAMENTARY GAZETEER OF IRELAND. 10 vols. Dublin, 1844-46.

PATENT ROLLS:

COLLINGRIDGE, J. H., *Ed.* Calendar of the Patent Rolls of Elizabeth, 1558-60. Vol. I. London, 1941.

ERCK, JOHN CAILLARD, *Ed.* Patent Rolls, 1603-1606/7. A Repertory of the enrollments of the Patent Rolls of Chancery in Ireland, commencing with the Reign of King James I. Dublin, 1846.

LIBER MUNERUM PUBLICORUM HIBERNIAE ab an. 1152 usque ad 1827; or, The Establishment of Ireland from the Nineteenth of King Stephen to the Seventh of George IV. 2 vols. London, 1852. The Liber Munerum consists of appointments by patent to offices under the Crown in Ireland over a period of 675 years. It was compiled, with some additions, by Rowley Lascelles from transcripts made by John Lodge of the now destroyed patent rolls. An index is being compiled by the Irish Manuscripts Commission. (An Index to *Liber Munerum Publicorum Hibernae* was printed in the Ninth *Report of the Deputy Keeper of the Public Records in Ireland,* pp. 21-58.)

MORRIN, JAMES, *Ed.* Calendar of the Patent and Close Rolls of Chancery in Ireland, of the Reigns of Henry VIII, Edward VI, Mary and Elizabeth, to 1575. Vol. I. Dublin, 1861.

MORRIN, JAMES, *Ed.* Calendar of the Patent and Close Rolls of Chancery in Ireland, of the Reign of Elizabeth, 1575-1603. Vol. II. Dublin, 1862.

MORRIN, JAMES, *Ed.* Calendar of the Patent and Close Rolls of Chancery in Ireland, of the Reign of Charles I, 1625-1633. Dublin, 1863.

RECORD COMMISSION: Calendar of Patent Rolls of James I, 1603-1625. The first volume, Calendar of the Patent Rolls of James I: from 1 to 16 James I, printed by the Record Commission (no date). The second volume, Calendar of the Patent Rolls of James I: from 16-22 James I, printed by Alexander Thom. 1867-1868. An Index to persons mentioned in entries relating to Counties Antrim, Armagh, Down, Fermanagh, Londonderry and Tyrone, contained in the printed but unindexed volumes of Irish Patent Rolls of James I, with a key to the dates of the instruments 24 March 1603-1625, has been printed in the *Report of the Deputy Keeper of the Public Records of Northern Ireland,* 1938-1945, pp. 76-127.

ROLUTORUM PATENTIUM ET CLAUSARUM CANCELLARIAE HIBERNIAE CALENDARIUM. Published by the Record Commission, 1828. Contains enrollments of patents of Henry II, John, Henry III and Edward I, and Patent Rolls, 31 Edward I to 21 Henry VII.

WOOD, D. C., *Ed.* Calendar of the Patent Rolls, Philip and Mary, 1557-1558. London, 1941.

PUBLIC RECORD OFFICE OF IRELAND, PUBLICATIONS: *Reports of the Deputy Keeper of the Public Records in Ireland.* Calendars and repertories of records: See 53rd-58th *Reports.*

CHANCERY PLEADINGS: A Cause List of Chancery Pleadings of the Palatine Court, County Tipperary, from 1662 to 1669. (*Report* No. 6 (1874), Appendix V, pp. 47-72.)

CHANCERY ROLLS: Rolls of the Chancery of the Regalities and Liberties of the County Palatine of Tipperary, containing Fee-farm Grants from the Duke of Ormond. 12 Rolls, 1636-1707 (125 documents calendared). (*Report* No. 6, pp. 73-88.)

COURT OF CLAIMS: Abstract of the Decrees of the Court of Claims for the Tryall of Innocents. Beginning 13 January 1662/3, ending 21 August 1662. Table of the Pedigrees of the Claimant, how he descends from the proprietor who was in possession of the family land in 1641; county of estate; number of acres. (19th *Report,* pp. 42-87.)

COURT OF RECORD: Records of the Court of Record of the County Palatine of Tipperary: Fines Levied in the Palatine of Tipperary, 1664-1715 (5th *Report* (1873), Appendix III, pp. 41-68). Recoveries Suffered in the Palatine of Tipperary. (*ibid.,* pp. 68-81).

COURT RECORDS: Transcripts of destroyed records, calendars and repertories of:

1. Ferguson collection of transcripts of old exchequer records. (55th *Report,* pp. 122-123.)

2. Lodge collection of transcripts mainly from patent rolls. (55th *Report,* pp. 116-122.)

3. Record Commissioners Transcripts, Calendars, Repertories. (55th *Report,* pp. 111-116.)

COURT RECORDS:

1. Chancery documents presented, official and certified copies, etc., list of (indexed by name or place, etc.). (56th *Report,* Appendix III, pp. 203-300.)

2. Equity and Revenue Exchequer documents presented, certified copies, etc., list of (indexed by name of person or place, etc.). (*ibid.,* Appendix III, pp. 309-341.) Also indexed list continued, together with Common Pleas documents (57th *Report,* Appendix II, pp. 421-467).

DEEDS: Church of Ireland. Calendar of Christ Church Deeds. Abstracts of 467 deeds, *ca.* 1174-1684. (20th *Report,* pp. 36-122.)

FIANTS: Printed Calendars; being brief abstracts of "Fiants" or Warrants to the Court of Chancery under the Privy Seal and signature of the sovereign or the chief governor of Ireland, directing letters patent be passed: Enrolled Fiants or warrants, pardons, leases, grants of English liberty, presentations, grants of office, grants of pensions, liveries, pardons, licences of alienation, grants in fee, appointments, etc. Printed in the *Reports*, as follows:

Fiants, Henry VIII (1521/2-1546/7, and some without date), No. 1 - No. 548 and index. (7th *Report*, Appendix X, pp. 33-110.)

Fiants, Edward VI (1546/7-1553), No. 1—No. 1257 and index. (8th *Report*, Appendix IX, pp. 27-230.)

Fiants, Philip and Mary (1553 - 1558), No. 1 - No. 276, and index. (9th *Report*, Appendix IV, pp. 59-104.)

Fiants, Elizabeth (1558 - 1570), No. 1-No. 1614. (11th *Report*, Appendix III, pp. 31-242.)

Fiants, Elizabeth (1570 - 1576), No. 1615 - No. 2935. (12th *Report*, Appendix V, pp. 17-194.)

Fiants, Elizabeth (1576 - 1583), No. 2936 - No. 4253. (13th *Report*, Appendix IV, pp. 16-220.)

Fiants, Elizabeth (1583 - 1586), No. 4254 - No. 4935. (15th *Report*, Appendix I, pp. 15-174.)

Fiants, Elizabeth (1586 - 1595/6), No. 4936 - No. 5973. (16th *Report*, Appendix II, pp. 17-278.)

Fiants, Elizabeth (1595/6 - 1601), No. 5974 - No. 6564. (17th *Report*, Appendix IV, pp. 29-276.)

Fiants, Elizabeth (1601 - 1603), No. 6565 - No. 6792. (18th *Report*, Appendix VI, pp. 27-146.)

Fiants, Henry VIII, seven additional Fiants. (*ibid.*, pp. 147-148.)

Fiants, Edward VI, eight additional Fiants. (*ibid.*, pp. 149-150.)

Fiants, Philip and Mary, four additional Fiants. (*ibid.*, p. 150.)

Index to Calendar of Fiants of Elizabeth. (21st *Report*, Appendix III, pp. 29-254; 22nd *Report*, Appendix VI, pp. 255-862.)

STATE PAPERS:

Calendar of Documents relating to Ireland, 1171-1307. Edited by H. S. Sweetman and G. F. Handcock. 5 vols. 1875-1886.

Calendar of State Papers (Ireland), 1509-1573; 1588-1603, 1606-1670. With Addenda, 1625-1660 and Adventures for Land, 1642-1659. Edited by C. H. Hamilton and others. 20 vols. 1860-1910.

Journals of the House of Commons of Ireland, 1613-1800. With Appendix and Index to the first eleven volumes. 41 vols. Dublin, 1763-1800.

Journal of the House of Lords, 1634-1752. 3 vols. Dublin, 1782-1784.

CHAPTER XV

WILLS

Copies or abstracts of wills may be found in a number of county, town, and regional histories. Many are also printed in historical and archaeological society journals and in periodicals such as *Notes and Queries, The Irish Genealogist, Brown's Cases,* and in the *Journals of the Association for the Preservation of the Memorials of the Dead,* etc. Other sources are as follows:

CANTERBURY: Calendar of Irish Wills, 1634-1652, from the Prerogative Court of Canterbury (England); Wills now at Somerset House, London. Edited by John Ainsworth. In the *Journal of the Royal Society of Antiquaries of Ireland.* Vol. 78, pt. 2, pp. 24-37.

CARY, GEORGE SYDNEY, *Ed.* Index to the Wills of the Diocese of Kildare, in the Public Record Office of Ireland. Dublin, 1905. (Reprint from the *Journal of the County Kildare Archaeological Society.* Vol. IV, no. 6.)

CARY, GEORGE SYDNEY. Index to the Intestate Administrations of the Diocese of Kildare. Dublin, 1907. (Reprint from the *Journal of the County Kildare Archaeological Society.* Vol. V, no. 3.)

CATHOLIC EPISCOPAL: Catholic Episcopal Wills. Printed in *Archivum Hibernicum,* vols. 1-4.

CHARITABLE BEQUESTS: Details of Charitable Bequests, contained in the Wills registered in the Prerogative and Consistorial Offices of Dublin, were published in the *Dublin Gazette,* from *ca.* 1825. Names of the testator and executors, dates of the will and probate are furnished.

CLARE, REV. WALLACE, *Ed.* Irish Genealogical Guides: A Calendar of Wills in various collections that have escaped destruction. 1930.

GENEALOGICAL OFFICE: Will Abstracts in the Genealogical Office, Dublin Castle, Dublin: Index to the Wills. Prepared by Miss P. Beryl Eustace. Published in *Analecta Hibernica,* No. 17, pp. 147-348. (Publications of the Irish Manuscripts Commission, Dublin, 1949.)

PHILLIMORE INDEXES TO IRISH WILLS:

VOL. I. Indexes to Irish Wills in the Dioceses of Ossory, Leighlin, Ferns, Kildare. Edited by W. P. W. Phillimore. London, 1909. (Ossory, 1536-1800; Leighlin, 1652-1800; Ferns, 1601-1800; Kildare, 1661-1800.)

Vol. II. Indexes to the Irish Wills in the Dioceses of Cork and Ross, Cloyne. Edited by W. P. W. Phillimore. London, 1910. (Cork and Ross, 1548-1800; Cloyne, 1621-1800.)

VOL. III. Indexes to Irish Wills in the Dioceses of Cashel and Emly, Waterford and Lismore, Killaloe and Kilfenora, Limerick, Ardfert and Aghadoe. Edited by Gertrude Thrift. London, 1913. (Cashel and Emly, 1618-1800; Waterford and Lismore, 1645-1800; Killaloe and Kilfenora, 1653-1800; Limerick, 1615-1800; Ardfert and Aghadoe, 1690-1800.)

VOL. IV. Indexes to Irish Wills in the Dioceses of Dromore, Newry, and Mourne. Edited by Gertrude Thrift. London, 1918. (Dromore, 1678-1858; Newry and Mourne, 1727-1858.)

VOL. V. Indexes to Irish Wills in the Dioceses of Derry and Raphoe. Edited by Gertrude Thrift. London, 1920. (Derry, 1612-1858; Raphoe, 1684-1858.)

PREROGATIVE WILLS:

Index to the Prerogative Wills of Ireland. 1536-1810. Edited by Sir Arthur Vicars, Ulster King of Arms. Dublin, 1897.

PUBLIC RECORD OFFICE OF IRELAND, DUBLIN:

Index to the Act or Grant Books and to the Original Wills of the Diocese of Dublin, to the year 1800. (Appendix to the 26th *Report of the Deputy Keeper of the Public Records in Ireland.* Dublin, 1895.)

Index to the Act or Grant Books and to the Original Wills of the Diocese of Dublin, 1800-1858. (Appendix to the 30th *Report*. Dublin, 1899.)

Calendars of collections of wills (original, copies, abstracts), acquired 1922-1951; indexes of wills surviving 1922, and documents acquired, 1922-1936. Printed in 55th-58th *Reports of the Deputy Keeper of the Public Records in Ireland*.

PUBLIC RECORD OFFICE OF NORTHERN IRELAND, BELFAST:

Wills: Original unproved wills, plain and official copies of wills, transcripts, abstracts, etc., presented since 1924, included in the general index to the records, printed in the *Reports of the Deputy Keeper of the Public Records in Northern Ireland*. 20 vols. 1924-1953.

QUAKER WILLS:

Quaker Records, Dublin, Abstracts of Wills. Edited by P. Beryl Eustace and Olive C. Goodbody. Published by the Irish Manuscripts Commission, Dublin, 1957.

REGISTRY OF DEEDS, DUBLIN:

Registry of Deeds, Dublin, Abstracts of Wills. Edited by P. Beryl Eustace. Vol. I, 1708-1745. Vol. II, 1746-1785. Published by the Irish Manuscripts Commission, Dublin, 1956.

PART FOUR

MICROFILMS

COLLECTIONS OF MICROFILMS FOR REFERENCE, WITH A KEY TO LOCATION OF RECORDS

MICROFILMS

The following provides a list of microfilms of some of the more important Irish manuscripts, lists and indexes, which are a rich source of material for genealogists.

In 1941, Dr. Richard J. Hayes, Director of the National Library of Ireland, Dublin, initiated a policy of microfilming every important manuscript collection relating to Ireland and its people, dated from ancient to modern times. Irish scholars had long been searching the public and private repositories of records and family archives throughout Ireland, Great Britain, Europe and America for documents of this nature. Further discovery of records, selection and microfilming of collections by the National Library has resulted in many thousands of manuscripts of a genealogical, historical, or literary nature being recorded on film. This has now made a wealth of genealogical source materials available to the public.

The *Reports of the Council of Trustees, National Library of Ireland,* 1950-51, 1951-52, 1952-53 (3 vols.), contain lists of the microfilms of manuscript collections made by the National Library which are in public repositories. These lists of microfilms have been arranged under the name of the city or town in which the library or repository owning the records is situated. The same plan will be followed in this bibliography with respect to all microfilms listed below.

As it is impossible to transcribe here the full list of microfilms of genealogical interest, it is suggested that reference be made to the *Reports.* They may be purchased for four shillings each, at the Government Publications Sale Office, G. P. O. Arcade, Dublin; also at the Hodges Figgis Book Shop, and at other book shops in Dublin.

The *Reports* do not contain lists of the microfilms which have been made of many privately owned collections of manuscripts. These have been calendared by the National Library with typed, annotated lists or indexes to the contents of each film. The indexes of more extensive private collections have also been microfilmed.

Many of the privately owned manuscripts, thus recorded on film, yield a wealth of genealogical material, consisting of pedigrees, diaries, letters, family legal or personal documents, wills, marriage records, and estate records including leases, lists of tenants, and their affairs. Privately owned collections of records of past government officials, such as the Annesley Collection, have great genealogical value. It contains the most complete set of records extant, regarding Forfeited Estates, 1690-1770. Also the "Books of Survey and Distribution" for each county of Ireland except Meath, have been microfilmed as a part of the Annesley Collection. *Analecta Hibernica,* Nos. 16 and 20, published by the Irish Manuscripts Commission, give a full description and history of the Annesley Collection.

Since 1950, the National Library has been microfilming many hundreds of Roman Catholic Parish Registers. Under the direction of Dr. Hayes, these registers have been sent to the Library, about fifty at a time, for recording on film, until all parish records of one diocese were completed. So far, the records of sixteen dioceses in the Republic of Ireland have been filmed.

Dr. Hayes has also pursued a policy of microfilming rare published records which are growing too old and valuable for longer use by the public. Directories, of great value for locating people, such as Lucas' Directory of the City of Cork, 1787, and the same for the South East of Ireland, 1788; also Pigot's Directory of 1820, and others, have been filmed. Rare early newspapers such as *The Freeman's Journal,* Dublin, are being indexed for subjects and for personal items, notices of birth, marriage, death, emigration, etc. The index cards are being microfilmed.

Dr. Hayes has recognized the need for adequate indexing of the Irish historical journals and periodicals. Only the *Journal of the Royal Society of Antiquaries,* the *Cork Historical and Archaeological Society Journal,* and the *Ulster Journal of Archaeology* have maintained excellent indexes. Card indexes for the other publications are being prepared and microfilmed.

The National Library has also filmed the records of the Society of Friends, Dublin. Copies of the four films are in Friends Historical Library, Swarthmore, Pennsylvania.

The records of the Society of Friends, Lisburn, Northern Ireland, have been recorded on four films by the Queen's University, Belfast. Copies of these films are also in Friends Historical Library, Swarthmore, Pennsylvania.

A program of microfilming the important manuscript collections in the Public Record Office of Ireland, Dublin, has been pursued in the past few years. The following announcement was made in the 58th *Report of the Deputy Keeper of the Public Records in Ireland* (1958), p. 9: "Microfilm copies have been made of a large number of records. These are being stored in a separate building." As no list or index to these films is printed, reference must be made to this repository for further information.

The Genealogical Society of the Church of Jesus Christ of Latter-Day Saints (Mormon), Salt Lake City, Utah, has made a great contribution to Irish genealogy by an extensive microfilming program in Ireland. When their representatives came to Ireland in the hope of obtaining permission to microfilm extensive genealogical collections, indexes, and source materials, Dr. Richard J. Hayes sponsored their cause. In return, the National Library was rewarded with copies of all films made by the Mormon representatives in Ireland. These include about 127 films of the entire collection of manuscripts in the Genealogical Office, Dublin Castle, Dublin. As the records of this office which are included in the manuscript collections are not open to the public, it is now possible for anyone to see them on microfilm in the National Library of Ireland, or in the Genealogical Society Library, Salt Lake City, Utah. One especially valuable collection in the Genealogical Office, Dublin, comprises the 39 volumes of Pedigree Charts, made from the Prerogative Wills of Ireland, 1536-1800, by Sir William Betham, Ulster King of Arms, from his genealogical abstracts of the wills which he first compiled in his collection of notebooks, now deposited in the Public

Record Office of Ireland, Dublin. Dr. Hayes, in 1955, sent copies of the microfilms of the above Betham collection of Pedigree Charts to the Library of Congress, Washington, D. C. The published *Index to the Prerogative Wills of Ireland, 1536-1810,* by Sir Arthur Vicars, 1897, is the guide to every will represented in Betham's Pedigree Charts, 1536-1800. Another important guide to the microfilms of the manuscript collections in the Genealogical Office, Dublin, is the "Index of Will Abstracts in the Genealogical Office, Dublin", published in *Analecta Hibernica,* No. 17 (1949), by the Irish Manuscripts Commission. About 7,500 abstracts are indexed by name of the testator, with residence, year of probate or date of will, and the notation as to the name of the manuscript collection in which it is deposited.

The representatives from Salt Lake City also microfilmed the two extensive indexes in the Registry of Deeds, Dublin, between the dates when the records began, 1708 to 1904. The Names Index is recorded on 122 films, and the Land Index on 283 films. Copies of the films are in the National Library of Ireland as well as in the Genealogical Society Library, Salt Lake City, Utah. An index to the contents of the films has been printed for the National Library. This is a necessary guide in the use of the films. It has been included in this publication, VOL. I, PART TWO, CHAPTER I, under "Registry of Deeds", following the explanation of the records, indexes, and methods of ordering copies of deeds, leases, marriage settlements, etc.

A guide for the following bibliography is provided below, with key numbers for all repositories of the microfilms. The key numbers in parentheses, before listed items, will indicate where the microfilms are located.

REPOSITORIES OF MICROFILMS

(1) Armagh, Northern Ireland (County Museum).

(2) Belfast, Northern Ireland (Public Record Office of Northern Ireland).

(3) Belfast, Northern Ireland (The Queen's University Library).

(4) Donegal, Ireland (Donegal County Library).

(5) Dublin, Ireland (Genealogical Office, Dublin Castle).

(6) Dublin, Ireland (National Library of Ireland).

(7) Dublin, Ireland (Ordnance Survey Office).

(8) Dublin, Ireland (Public Record Office of Ireland).

(9) Dublin, Ireland (Registry of Deeds).

(10) Dublin, Ireland (Royal Irish Academy).

(11) Dublin, Ireland (Royal Society of Antiquaries Library).

(12) Dublin, Ireland (Society of Friends (Quaker) Library).

(13) Dublin, Ireland (Trinity College Library).

(14) Edinburgh, Scotland (H. M. Register House).

(15) Galway, Ireland (University College Library).

(16) Lisburn, Northern Ireland (Friends Meeting House).

(17) London, England (British Museum).

(18) London, England (Public Record Office).

(19) Oxford, England (Bodleian Library).

(20) Salt Lake City, Utah, U. S. A. (Genealogical Society).

(21) Swarthmore, Pennsylvania, U. S. A. (Friends Historical Library).

(22) Washington, D. C., U. S. A. (Library of Congress).

(23) Washington, D. C., U. S. A. (The National Archives).

MICROFILMS

List arranged by cities and repositories where original records are located. Microfilm items arranged in order of the number of the negative film.

ARMAGH (COUNTY MUSEUM)

Key	Ms. No.	Contents	Film neg.	Film pos.
(1) (6)		Life of L. Gillespie, M.D. 1836.	11	205
(1) (6)		Autobiography of Col. W. Blacker. Vol. I-VII. 19th cent.	11,12	205-6
(1) (6)		Brownlow Estate Survey, 1667; Rental, 1635.	12	206
(1) (6)		Freeholders book of Co. Armagh, 18th c.	12	206
(1) (6)		Muster Roll of Ulster, 1630 (copy).	12	206
(1) (6)		Hearthmoney Roll, Orrier Barony, Co. Armagh, 1664 (copy).	13	207
(1) (6)		Griffith's Valuation of Co. Armagh, 1839. 28 vols.	419	99
(1) (6)		Survey of R. Johnston's estate, Co. Down, Co. Armagh, Co. Monaghan, 1731.	809	1,014
(1) (6)		Armagh Militia records, 1793-1908.	809	1,014

BELFAST (PUBLIC RECORD OFFICE OF NORTHERN IRELAND)

Key	Ms. No.	Contents	Film neg.	Film pos.
(2) (6)		The Drennan Letters.	291-297	349-355
(2) (6)		McCartney letter books.	297-305	355-363
(2) (6)		Bellew Papers.	305	363

Key	Ms. No.	Contents	Film neg.	Film pos.
		DONEGAL (THE COUNTY LIBRARY)		
(4) (6)		Donegal Grand Jurors: Books of Presentments, 1768-1783; 1815-1856.	753	975
(4) (6)		Register of Freeholders, Co. Donegal, 1767-1768.	753	975
		DUBLIN (GENEALOGICAL OFFICE, DUBLIN CASTLE)		
(6) (20)		Annotated list of manuscripts.	One film	
(6) (20)		Entire Mss. collection of 701 vols. and 23 legal size boxes of original documents and transcripts.	127 films	
(6) (20) (22)		Betham collection of Pedigree Charts made from all Prerogative Wills, Admns., 1536-1800, included in above (39 vols.).		
		DUBLIN (NATIONAL LIBRARY OF IRELAND)		
(6)	2-23, 27, 29-36, 38, 43, 59	Annesley Collection (original at Castlewellan, Co. Down) concerning Forfeited Estates, etc., 1690-1770. Miscel. rec. of earlier dates.	26-34	259-267
(6)		Annesley Collection *(ibid.)*, vols. for all Counties but Meath, "Survey and Distribution".	35-42	267-275

Key	Ms. No.	Contents	Film neg.	Film pos.
(6)		All Catholic Parish Registers (originals in local custody) in the dioceses of Achrony, Ardagh and Clonmacnoise, Cashel and Emly, Clonfert, Ferns, Galway, Kerry, Kildare and Leighlin, Killala, Killaloe, Limerick, Meath, Raphoe, Tuam, Waterford and Lismore.		
(6)		List of Roman Catholic Parish Registers with inclusive dates of records, now microfilmed.		
(6)		Freeman's Journal, index (on microcards), 1763-80, 1783-86 (some nos.).		
(6)		Indexes of Historical, etc., Journals, on microcards.		
(6)		Rare books, directories, etc. Lucas' Directories, of Cork City, 1787; South-east Ireland, 1788. Pigot's Directory, 1820.		
(6)		Tithe Applotment Books of Irish parishes, 1824-1840, with names of property owners and occupiers.		
		DUBLIN (ORDNANCE SURVEY OFFICE)		
(6) (7)		J. O'Donovan Name Books, Co. Carlow	583	935

Key	Ms. No.	Contents	Film neg.	Film pos.
		J. O'Donovan Name Books, Co. Cavan	477,478	793,794
		J. O'Donovan Name Books, Co. Clare	811-813	1,016-18
		J. O'Donovan Name Books, Co. Cork	938-44	1,032-38
		J. O'Donovan Name Books, Co. Donegal	378-80	593-95
		J. O'Donovan Name Books, Co. Roscommon	553-54	924-25
		DUBLIN (PUBLIC RECORD OFFICE)		
(6) (8)		Hearthmoney Roll, Co. Antrim, 1666 (copy).	13	207
		Hearthmoney Roll, Fews Barony, Co. Armagh, 1664 (copy).	13	207
		Hearthmoney Roll, Orrier Barony, Co. Armagh, 1664 (copy).	13	207
		Co. Armagh Poll Book, 1753 (copy).	13	207
(6) (8)		Diocese of Elphin Census Book, 1749.	542	923
		DUBLIN (REGISTRY OF DEEDS)		
(6) (9) (20)		Names Index to Deeds, Leases, etc. 1708-1904.	2001-2122	2001-2122
(6) (9) (20)		Land Index, by townlands, city street. 1708-1904.	2123-2406	2123-2406
		DUBLIN (ROYAL IRISH ACADEMY)		
(6) (10)	12 R 9-14	Charlemont Correspondence, 1707-87.	96	288
(6) (10)	12 R 15-20	Charlemont Correspondence, 1790-99.	97	289
(6) (10)	12 R 21	Charlemont Correspondence.	97,98	289,290

Key	Ms. No.	Contents	Film neg.	Film pos.
(6) (10)	12 R 23-25	Charlemont Correspondence, 1782-1803.	98	290
(6) (10)	12 R 22	Castlereagh Letters, 1791.	98	290
		DUBLIN (ROYAL SOCIETY OF ANTIQUARIES)		
(6) (11)		Corporation Book of Bannow, 1744.	607	938
(6) (11)		Corporation Book of Callan, 1739.	607	938
(6) (11)		Corporation Book of Gowran, 1736.	607	938
(6) (11)		Corporation Book of Thomastown, 1752.	607	938
		DUBLIN (SOCIETY OF FRIENDS)		
(6) (12) (20) (21)		Records of births, marriages, deaths, Carlow, Cork, to 1859.	820	1,021
(6) (12) (20) (21)		Records of births, marriages, Dublin, to 1859.	820	1,021
(6) (12) (20) (21)		Records of deaths, Dublin, to 1736.	820	1,021
(6) (12) (20) (21)		Records of deaths, Dublin, 1736-1859.	820	1,022

Key	Ms. No.	Contents	Film neg.	Film pos.
(6) (12) (20) (21)		Records of births, marriages, deaths, to 1859, for Edenderry, Grange, Lisburn, Limerick, Lurgan, Moate.	821	1,022
(6) (12) (20) (21)		Records of births, marriages, deaths, to 1859, for Mountmellick, Richhill.	822	1,023
(6) (12) (20) (21)		Records of births, marriages, deaths, to 1859, for Co. Tipperary, Waterford, Co. Wexford, Wicklow, Youghal.	823	1,024
(6) (12) (20) (21)		Records of birth, throughout Ireland, 1859-1887.	823	1,024
(6) (12) (20) (21)		Records of marriages throughout Ireland, 1859-1887, 1893-1947.	823	1,024
(6) (12) (20) (21)		Records of deaths throughout Ireland, 1859-1949.	823	1,024
		DUBLIN (TRINITY COLLEGE LIBRARY)		
(6) (13)	1,339 (H. 2.18)	Book of Leinster.	24	257
(6) (13)	1,212 (E. 3.2)	Pedigrees of Irish Families, 17th c.	706	948

Key	Ms. No.	Contents	Film neg.	Film pos.
(6) (13)	1,213 (F. 3.23)	Pedigrees of Irish Families, *ca.* 1700.	706	948
(6) (13)	1,214 (F. 3.25)	Pedigrees of English Families, *ca.* 1700.	706	948
(6) (13)	1,215 (F. 3.26)	Pedigrees of Lancashire and Yorkshire Families, *ca.* 1700.	706	948
(6) (13)	1,216 (F. 3.27)	Pedigrees of Irish Families, *ca.* 1700.	706	948
		EDINBURGH (H. M. REGISTER HOUSE)		
(6) (14)	N 2/3	Papers relating to the Plantation of Ulster.	808	1,013
		GALWAY (UNIVERSITY COLLEGE LIBRARY)		
(6) (15)		Galway Corporation Minute Books, 1485-1815.	349,350	399,400
		LISBURN (SOCIETY OF FRIENDS)		
(3) (16) (21)		Grange Monthly Meeting (1 vol.) records of birth, marriage, and burial, 1658-1800. Areas in Cos. Antrim, Tyrone, Londonderry.		
(3) (16) (21)		Lisburn Monthly Meeting (1 vol.) records of Lisburn and dist., birth, marriage and burial, certificates of removal, some family records, and testimonies, 1650-1859.		

Key	Ms. No.	Contents	Film neg.	Film pos.
(3) (16) (21)		Lurgan Monthly Meeting (4 vols.) records of Lurgan and dist., birth, marriage and burial. Records by families. Some English origins. 1650-1789. List of members to 1883.		
(3) (16) (21)		Ulster Province Meeting (earliest book at Friends Society, Dublin, 10/11/1674, to Aug. 1693). Ulster Province Minutes (1 vol.), includes marriage certificates, testimonials, certificates of removal, and some family notes, 1694-1717; 1717-1750.		
(3) (16) (21)		Ulster Quarterly Meeting (1 vol.). Contains marriage certificates, 1731-1812; marriage register, 1812-1848; minutes of meetings, testimonials, certificates of removal, etc.		
(3) (16) (21)		Ulster Family Records (1 vol.), contains marriage certificates, baptismal and burial registers, 1658-1815.		
		LONDON (BRITISH MUSEUM)		
(6) (17)	Sloane Ms. No. 33	Troops sent to Ireland, *ca.* 1596. (Extracts)	666	1
(6) (17)	Sloane Ms. No. 856	Warrants relating to Army and other appointments in Ireland, *ca.* 1661-2. (Extracts)	666	1

Key	Ms. No.	Contents	Film neg.	Film pos.
(6) (17)	Sloane Ms. No. 1,301	Pedigrees, Essex, Clare, LeGros, Cogan, 17th cent. (Extracts)	84	2
(6) (17)	Sloane Ms. No. 3,328	List of men of the Armie, Dublin, *ca.* 1655. (Extract)	94	3
(6) (17)	Sloane Ms. Nos. 4,038-9	Letters of P. Lloyd and Rev. J. MacBride, 1700-1703; 1707-13. (Extracts)	95	4
(6) (17)	Sloane Ms. No. 4,056	Letters of J. Copping and R. MacBride, 1739-1740. (Extracts)	95	4
(6) (17)	Sloane Ms. No. 4,057	Letters of J. Copping and R. MacBride, 1741-1742. (Extracts)	95	4
(6) (17)	Sloane Ms. No. 4,227	Memoirs of the life of Roger Boyle, Earl of Orrery, by Rev. T. Maurice.	386	5
(6) (17)	Add. 4,760	Warrants, licences, etc., granted by Essex, 1672-1677.	388,389	7,8
(6) (17)	Add. 4,766	Warrants of the Lord Lieutenant, 1676-1678.	391	10
(6) (17)	Add. 4,770	Muster Roll of the Province of Ulster.	392	11
(6) (17)	Add. 4,772	Crown-rents, Waterford, Cork, Tipperary, etc., 1625. List of persons indicted for treason, 1641-1642.	392	11
(6) (17)	Add. 4,773-6	Crown-rents, Ireland, 1667-1669.	392-394	11-13
(6) (17)	Add. 4,448	Grants, fiants, pardons by Essex, 1672-1677.	394	13

Key	Ms. No.	Contents	Film neg.	Film pos.
(6) (17)	Add. 4,815	Grants of Arms in Ireland. Collection for an Irish Peerage.	531	17
(6) (17)	Add. 4,820	Funeral Certificates, Irish Nobility and Gentry, 1634-1729.	533	19
(6) (17)	Add. 4,821	Miscel. Coll. for Irish History and Irish Family History.	265	434
(6) (17)	Add. 4,974	Arms of Irish Nobility and Gentry, by S. Walker, 17th cent.	533	19
(6) (17)	Add. 5,482	Knights made in Ireland by Essex, 1599. (Extract)	533	19
(6) (17)	Add. 5,524	Arms of Visct. Wentworth and of Sir O. St. John. (Extracts)	533	10
(6) (17)	Add. 5,751	Papers . . . presentation of plate to certain nobles in Ireland, 1550. (Extracts)	533	19
(6) (17)	Add. 6,113	Creations of Irish Earls, 16th cent. (Extracts)	535	21
(6) (17)	Add. 6,297	Fees of Irish Nobility to Officers of Arms. n. d. (Extract)	543	22
(6) (17)	Add. 6,313	Peerage of England, Ireland, 1787. (Extract)	543	22
(6) (17)	Add. 8,163	List of conservators of peace, Dublin, 1803.	543,544	22,23

Key	Ms. No.	Contents	Film neg.	Film pos.
(6) (17)	Add. 8,666-8,790	Grants of land in Cork to the Roche family.	851,852	574-5
(6) (17)	Add. 9,714	Papers relating to Kinsale and the Southwell family, 1637-1778.	573	24
(6) (17)	Add. 9,718	Papers of H. de Ruvigny, Earl of Galway, 1692-1701.	580	25
(6) (17)	Add. 9,762	Irish Army lists and other papers of Secr. Blathwait, 1686-1705.	585	26
(6) (17)	Add. 9,763	List of King James's Army in Ireland, 1689.	585	26
(6) (17)	Add. 9,805	Index of names to pedigrees in the Harleian Mss.	585	26
(6) (17)	Add. 11,722	Names, ages, occupations of the inhabitants of Carrick-on-Suir, 1799.	619	28
(6) (17)	Add. 13,956	Survey of forfeited estates in Galway, 1701.	643	30
(6) (17)	Add. 14,318	Arms of Irish families, A to D, 18th c.	645	31
(6) (17)	Add. 14,405	Trustees (for forfeited estates) survey, 1701, for counties Leitrim, Mayo, Sligo.	645	31
(6) (17)	Add. 14,406	Survey of forfeited lands, Co. Donegal.	645	31
(6) (17)	Add. 14,410	Knights of St. Patrick, 1783. (Extracts)	645	31
(6) (17)	Add. 14,422	Irish and English Catholics, 1666, and 1789.	645	31
(6) (17)	Add. 14,838-9	Pedigrees of Irish Peers.	645,656	31,32

Key	Ms. No.	Contents	Film neg.	Film pos.
(6) (17)	Add. 15,973	Forfeitures, County Dublin, 1703.	779	505
(6) (17)	Add. 17,508	Forfeited estates, Co. Cork, survey, (1691?).	779	505
(6) (17)	Add. 17,774	Report, Trustees for Forfeited Estates, Ireland, 1703.	780	506
(6) (17)	Add. 18,022	Public Revenues, Ireland, 1615-1714. Return of houses and people in Dublin, 1695.	780	506
(6) (17)	Add. 18,718	Forfeited estates, Co. Dublin, 1702-3.	780	506
(6) (17)	Add. 18,735	Muster Book of Undertakers, etc., Leinster, Ulster, 1618.	780	506
(6) (17)	Add. 19,264	Grants of land in Decies Barony, Co. Waterford, 1655.	852	575
(6) (17)	Add. 19,829	Minutes, Courts of Assembly, —— Burgesses of Banagher, 1693-1749.	782	508
(6) (17)	Add. 19,837-42	Ireland: Court of Chancery Entry book of recognizances (4 vols.), 1570-1634.	783-784	509,510
(6) (17)	Add. 19,851-54	Ireland: Court of Exchequer: Notes of cases (4 vols.) . . . 1732-40.	785,786	511,512
(6) (17)	Add. 19,859	Limerick City: Acts and orders of the General Assembly and Common Council, 1672-80. Copied by Betham, 1818.	786	512

Key	Ms. No.	Contents	Film neg.	Film pos.
(6) (17)	Add. 19,865	Papers relating to the Sexton family of Limerick, and other docts. relating to Limerick, 19th cent. copies.	787	513
(6) (17)	Add. 19,868	Papers relating to the Roche family of Co. Cork, 1543-1740.	787	513
(6) (17)	Add. 19,997	Register of elections of burgesses of Newtown, Co. Down.	788	514
(6) (17)	Add. 20,715	Paper relating to the Roche family of Co. Cork, and Crosbie of King's Co., 16th to 19th cent.	794	520
(6) (17)	Add. 21,126	List of church dignitaries, judges, etc., 1660-1727.	794	520
(6) (17)	Add. 21,130	Pedigrees, Burkes of Clanrickarde, 18th cent.	795	521
(6) (17)	Add. 21,131	Co. Down estate of the Southwell family, 18th cent.	795	521
(6) (17)	Add. 21,372	Arms of Irish Families, 18th cent.	4	523
(6) (17)	Add. 22,230	History of the Wentworth family. (Extract)	436	528
(6) (17)	Add. 22,267	Family memoranda of the Earl of Cork, 1631. (Extracts)	436	528
(6) (17)	Add. 23,684-5	Genealogical collections of Sir William Betham, vols. 1 and 2.	437	529
(6) (17)	Add. 23,686-7	Ditto. Vols. 3 and 4.	528	530

Key	Ms. No.	Contents	Film neg.	Film pos.
(6) (17)	Add. 26,688	Pedigrees, inquisitions, visitations, etc., coll. by Sir William Betham, Vol 1.	528	530
(6) (17)	Add. 23,689	Ditto. Vol. 2.	528,529	530-531
(6) (17)	Add. 23,690	Pedigree and peerage cases collected by Betham.	529	531
(6) (17)	Add. 23,691	McMorogh Kavanagh family history, by Betham.	529	531
(6) (17)	Add. 23,692	Barony of Kinsale papers by Betham.	529	531
(6) (17)	Add. 23,693	Lodge's Irish Pedigrees, notes by Betham. Vol. 1.	529,530	531,532
(6) (17)	Add. 23,694-7	Ditto. Vols. 2-5.	530	532
(6) (17)	Add. 23,698	Ditto. Vol. 6.	530,586	532,533
(6) (17)	Add. 23,699-702	Ditto. Vols. 7-10.	586	533
(6) (17)	Add. 23,703	Lodge's Peerage of Ireland, with additions by the author.	586,587	533,534
(6) (17)	Add. 23,704-5	Ditto. Vols. 2-3.	587	534
(6) (17)	Add. 23,706	Ditto. Vol. 4.	587,588	534,535
(6) (17)	Add. 23,707-8	Ditto. Vol. 5-6.	588	535
(6) (17)	Add. 23,709	Notes relating to Irish Nobility, by Lodge.	588	535
(6) (17)	Add. 23,710	Collections for a baronage of Ireland, with additions by Betham.	588,589	535,536
(6) (17)	Add. 23,711	Entry book fees on patents, creations, pardons, 1752-83.	589	536

Key	Ms. No.	Contents	Film neg.	Film pos.
(6) (17)	Add. 24,331	Pedigree of the Earl of Desmond, by Sir William Betham, 1834.	592	539
(6) (17)	Add. 24,451	Monteagle and Darcy families. Pedigrees by Sir William Betham, 15th and 16th cent.	592,593	539,540
(6) (17)	Add. 24,481	Charters of families of Devereux, Bouchier, Roche, 1820-36.	593	540
(6) (17)	Add. 26,676	Arms of Irish nobility, 17th cent.	624	546
(6) (17)	Add. 26,685	Arms of Irish families, 16th cent.	624	546
(6) (17)	Add. 26,704	Arms of the nobility of Ireland, 1634. By J. Chaloner.	624	546
(6) (17)	Add. 28,937-49	Miscellaneous papers relating to Ireland and the Duke of Ormond. Vols. 1-10, 1583-1743. Vols. 11-13, n. d.	628-704	550-556
(6) (17)	Add. 30,515	Notes on the De Burgho, Bourke family, 19th cent.	861	743
(6) (17)	Add. 30,988	Account of the Carew family, 1589. Also, Grant of Arms to Visct. Dungannon, 1662.	861	743
(6) (17)	Add. 30,999	Arms and desc. of McCarthy, serving in the French army, 1715. (Extract)	861	743
(6) (17)	Add. 31,248	Papers relating to Irish Catholics, 1692-1709.	861	743
(6) (17)	Add. 31,883	Bonds on marriage licences, diocese of Killaloe, 1680-1762.	863	745

Key	Ms. No.	Contents	Film neg.	Film pos.
(6) (17)	Add. 32,627	Life of A. Chesney of Ballymena, Co. Antrim, 1772-1821.	873	755
(6) (17)	Add. 34,766	List of Knights, etc., by Sir William Betham, 19th cent.	889	771
(6) (17)	Add. 35,928	Pension list of Ireland, 1801.	917,918	992,993
(6) (17) (23)	Add. 35,932	List of Passengers sailing from Ireland to America, 1803-1806.	918	993
(6) (17)	Add. 37,067	Index to Wills preserved in Barbados, 1776-1800. By E. Fitzpatrick.	922	997
(6) (17)	Add. 37,514	Genealogical collection for the Emerson family in Ireland.	930	1,005
(6) (17)	Add. 47,209-16	Conveyances by the Committee for Claims of lands in King's Co., 1654-90.	924	999
(6) (17)	Add. 47,217-22	Ditto, for lands in Co. Limerick, 1653-90.	924	999
(6) (17)	Add. 47,223	Ditto, for lands in Co. Meath, 1666.	924	999
(6) (17)	Add. 47,224-29	Ditto, for lands in Queen's Co., 1654-66.	924	999
(6) (17)	Add. 47,230-37	Ditto, for lands in Co. Waterford, 1654-66.	924	999
(6) (17)	Add. 47,238	Ditto, for lands in Co. Westmeath, 1666.	924	999
(6) (17)	Egerton 1,075	Earl of Pembroke's pedigree. (Extract)	774	69
(6) (17)	Egerton 1,628-30	Edward Southwell's diary, 1659-99. Memoranda, 1691-93. Property at Kinsale, 1750-54.	782	508
(6) (17)	Egerton 1,765	Copies of Charters, registers of Dublin trade guilds, 1296-1824, made by Monck Mason.	854	577

Key	Ms. No.	Contents	Film neg.	Film pos.
(6) (17)	Egerton 1,976	Letters of members of the Sheridan family, 1799-1820.	99	585
(6) (17)	Egerton 2,168	Papers relating to the family of Penn, 17th and 18th cent.	289	587
(6) (17)	Egerton 2,642	Family history of M'Carty More, Burke, Lacy; late 16th cent.	876	758
		LONDON (PUBLIC RECORD OFFICE)		
(6) (18)	C.O. 384/16	Irish applicants for emigration to North America, 1827.	90	285
(6) (18)	E. 101	Irish Exchequer Rolls, nos. 234-239; 540, 547.	490-492	796-798
		OXFORD (BODLEIAN LIBRARY)		
(6) (19)	Carte 1(10,447)	History of the Butler family. Correspondence of Thomas, Earl of Ormonde, 1577-1612. Correspondence of James, 1st Duke of Ormonde, 1633-1641, etc.	155	601
(6) (19)	Carte 2(10,488)-4-0(10,486).	Correspondence of 1st Duke of Ormonde, 1641-1651. Docts. relating to the history and estates of the Butler family, etc. (See annotated indexes for the entire Carte Mss. collection, in the National Library.)	156-180; 371-377; 426-431	602-640

PART FIVE

A BIBLIOGRAPHY FOR PRELIMINARY RESEARCH IN THE UNITED STATES

FOR THE PURPOSE OF OBTAINING BASIC INFORMATION REGARDING THE IMMIGRANT ANCESTOR

A BIBLIOGRAPHY FOR PRELIMINARY RESEARCH IN THE UNITED STATES

EXPLANATION OF THE SELECTED RECORDS

An important message is here being repeated. The following bibliography has been prepared in response to urgent requests from the directors and their assistants in some of the principal repositories of genealogical records in Ireland. Their requests have been made to this compiler during every personal interview in the past ten years, when the plan for this two-volume guide was being discussed. They wish Americans to know that their attitude toward all who make genealogical inquiries is one of friendly inclination to cooperate. They are disappointed, however, over their inability to help the large number of Americans, whose letters asking for genealogical help fail to supply basic information regarding the emigrant ancestor. They call these "vague inquiries", and believe each case to be an indication that little, if any, serious research has been attempted with the use of American source materials in an effort to discover all records concerning the immigrant ancestor and his immediate family. They regretfully reply that they can be of no help without further information.

Thus, not enough can be said to stress the advantage of learning everything possible about the Irish or Scotch-Irish immigrant ancestor through a preliminary search of American records, before proceeding with the Irish work. Among the genealogical and historical sources of the states wherein the Irish or Scotch-Irish made original settlements before the last century, much basic information has been discovered regarding various first generation settlers in America.

Records to be sought and some often found, are those of the parentage, brothers, sisters, or other relatives, of the immigrant in Ireland or America; the Irish locality of his birth, or home (at least the county) from which he emigrated; his certain or approximate age upon departure; the exact or probable time and place of settlement in America, as well as records of marriage, children, death, or burial.

The given names of the immigrant's father, brothers, sisters, and of any children in order of their birth, particularly any unusual given name, might help to identify him with a certain Irish family. The record of the time of marriage will indicate whether he was a householder in Ireland and, if so, had some leased or owned property to dispose of before emigration. Information about his wife's family and its origin, if Irish, could guide the search for his residence in Ireland. Knowledge of the place of origin of his Irish-American neighbors, if they came at or about the same time, would offer a clue to his own Irish locality for, before 1800, these emigrants were prone to move in groups. Each item discovered can help to narrow the choice of Irish records later to be searched.

Therefore, the following selected bibliography of published works is offered as an aid to preliminary research in the genealogical libraries of the United States. It lists the guides, and many published records which will lead to, or offer information concerning the first generation Irish and Scotch-Irish in America, from the seventeenth century through the early years of the nineteenth century. It therefore covers only the states in which original settlements of the first or second generation in America were made during this period. Fortunately, many of the listed sources will also serve for a study of later arrivals who settled in these early states.

The parentage, Irish origin, and other records of those who came during the great immigration from Ireland, beginning in the 1830s and increasing tremendously through the 1850s, are more easily traced, regardless of where they settled throughout the country. The available records include family papers, Bible records, newspaper obituaries, biographies in local histories, tombstone records which in some cases give the place of birth, as well as the public sources of genealogical records in all states.

It is impossible to include here a list of the hundreds of county, town, and regional histories of the early states. Guides to such works for all states are listed, and good collections are available in various American genealogical libraries. Local histories throughout the country, mostly written after 1850, are a rich source of information regarding the origins of first settlers and the ancestry of later residents who played some part in the community. These sources should in all cases be located and examined for the short biographies, etc., even if it is necessary to page through without the aid of an index. While local biographies are, for the most part, classed as secondary evidence, those for the late colonial or following settlers have usually been compiled from records supplied by elderly descendants in the second or third generation, or by the later immigrant himself. Their traditions are often exaggerated or confused, but a statement of the name of a specific county or locality of birth or residence in the old country often can be relied upon as evidence of origin, except in some cases when the place name is that of a port of embarkation. Such place names should be suspect, if given as tradition. A less well-known name of a place of origin may be forgotten in favor of a well-known port city from which the emigrant sailed.

Many local histories and church publications include copies of tombstone inscriptions. In numerous cases the place of birth or origin is named. Scharf's *History of Western Maryland* lists many such records of Irish settlers. Another source, *Some Early Georgia Epitaphs,* offers nearly one-hundred named places of Irish birth or origin. Likewise, there are published *Abstracts of Wills of Chatham County, Georgia,* which furnish notable examples of many cases wherein the Irish place of origin of the testator, or residence of a close relative, is named. These abstracts of wills illustrate the importance of locating the published or unpublished wills of all immigrants.

A thorough search of pertinent American genealogical source materials for the records of any immigrant will largely contribute to future success in Irish research. The results will help to direct the choice of records to be examined in Ireland and, on the whole, time and expense will eventually be saved.

GENEALOGICAL GUIDES TO AMERICAN RECORDS

AMERICAN ASSOCIATION FOR STATE AND LOCAL HISTORY. Historical Societies in the United States and Canada. Directory of, 1959.

AMERICAN BIOGRAPHY, DICTIONARY OF. 22 vols. New York, 1928-1944.

AMERICAN GENEALOGICAL BIOGRAPHICAL INDEX. 1952—. (32 vols., published to 1960.)

AMERICAN SOCIETY OF GENEALOGISTS. Genealogical Research: Methods and Sources. Washington, D. C., 1960.

BAILEY, ROSALIE FELLOWS. Guide to Genealogical and Biographical Sources for New York City (Manhattan), 1783-1898.

BENNETT, ARCHIBALD F. Advanced Genealogical Research. Bookcraft, Inc., Salt Lake City, Utah, 1959.

BENNETT, ARCHIBALD F. A Guide for Genealogical Research. Salt Lake City, Utah, 1951.

BOWEN, RICHARD LE BARON. Massachusetts Records. A Handbook for Genealogists, Historians, Lawyers, and Other Researchers. Rehoboth, Mass. 1957.

BRIGHAM, CLARENCE S. History and Bibliography of American Newspapers, 1690-1820. 2 vols. Worcester, 1947. (Newspaper collections in American libraries listed.)

BROWN, KARL. American Library Directory. 20th edition. New York, 1954. (Lists of all U. S. libraries, with special collections.)

COLKET, MEREDITH B., JR. Genealogical Bibliography. (Washington, D. C., 1955. Published for the American University School of Social Sciences and Public Affairs.)

COLKET, MEREDITH B., JR., and E. H. PRESTON. Local History and Genealogical Reference Section, Library of Congress. Published in *The American Genealogist.* Vol. 17, October, 1940.

CRITTENDEN, CHRISTOPHER, and DORIS GODARD, *Editors.* Historical Societies in the U. S. A. and Canada, A Handbook of. 1936, 1944.

CURRY, CORA C. Records of the Roman Catholic Church in the U. S. A., as a Source for Authentic Genealogical Historical Material. Published by the National Genealogical Society, as *Special Publication No. 5.* 1935.

DAUGHTERS OF THE AMERICAN REVOLUTION, NATIONAL SOCIETY OF. Catalogue of Genealogical and Historical Works. Washington, D. C., 1940.

DAUGHTERS OF THE AMERICAN REVOLUTION, NATIONAL SOCIETY OF. Is that Lineage Right? By the Genealogical Advisory Committee to the Registrar General; Dr. Jean Stephenson, National Chairman. Washington, D. C., 1958.

DOANE, REV. GILBERT HARRY. Searching for Your Ancestors. Minneapolis, 1948. 2nd ed. 1960.

DORMAN, JOHN FREDERICK. Some Sources for Kentucky Genealogical Research. In the *National Genealogical Society Quarterly,* Washington, D. C. March, 1954.

DRAUGHTON, WALLACE R. North Carolina Genealogical Reference; A Research Guide. 1956.

DURRIE, DANIEL S. Bibliographia Genealogica Americana. An Alphabetical Index to American Genealogies and Pedigrees Contained in State, County, and Town Histories, Printed Genealogies, etc. Albany, 1868.

EASTERBY, J. H. Guide to the Study and Reading of South Carolina History; A General Classified Bibliography. 1953.

EVERTON, GEORGE B. and GUNNAR RASMUSON. Handy Book for Genealogists. The Everton Publishers. Logan, Utah, 1953.

FLAGG, CHARLES ALLCOTT. An Index to Pioneers from Massachusetts to the West. 1915.

FOTHERGILL, GERALD. A List of Emigrant Ministers to America, 1690-1811. 1904.

GOODSPEED'S BOOK SHOP. (Catalogues.) Genealogy and Local History. Boston.

GREGORY, WINIFRED, *Ed.* American Newspapers (U. S. and Canada), 1821-1936. New York, 1937.

HISTORY: A General Classified Bibliography. 1953.

JACOBUS, DONALD LINES. Genealogy as a Pastime and Profession. New Haven, 1930.

JACOBUS, DONALD LINES. Index to Genealogical Periodicals. Vol. I, New Haven, 1932; Vol. II, 1948; Vol. III (including "My Own Index"), 1953.

JOHNSON, J. PERCY H., *Ed.* Directory of Newspapers and Periodicals. (Annual publication for U. S. A., Canada, etc.) N. W. Ayer & Sons.

KIRKHAM, E. KAY. The ABC's of American Genealogical Research. Salt Lake City, 1954.

KIRKHAM, E. KAY. Research in American Genealogy. Salt Lake City, 1956.

LANCOUR, ADLORE H. Passenger Lists of Ships Coming to North America, 1607-1825; A Bibliography. In the *New York Public Library Bulletin.* Vol. 41, no. 5. 1937.

LONG ISLAND HISTORICAL SOCIETY, Brooklyn, N. Y. Catalogue of American Genealogies in the Library of. Brooklyn, 1935.

MORIARITY, JOHN H. Directory Information Material (printed), for New York City Residents, 1626-1786. A Bibliographic Study. In the *New York Public Library Bulletin.* Vol. XLVI, pp. 807-64.

MORTON, C. B. Bibliography of the State of Maine. New York, 1852.

MUNSELL'S. Munsell's Genealogical Index. South Norwalk, Conn. 1933.

MUNSELL'S, JOEL SONS (Publishers). Index to American Genealogist, being a Catalogue of Family Histories. A Bibliography . . ., from 1771 to 1900. 5th edition. Albany, 1900.

MUNSELL'S, JOEL SONS (Publishers). Index to American Genealogies and to Genealogical Material Contained in all Works such as Town Histories, County Histories, Local Histories . . . 5th edition. Albany, 1900.

NEWSPAPERS: Irish American Papers, A Check List of. In *The Recorder, American-Irish Historical Society,* New York. Vol. 4, no. 5. January, 1931.

PARKER, DONALD DEAN. Local History, How to Gather It, Write It, and Publish It. (Revised and Edited by Bertha E. Josephson.) 1944.

PASSANO, E. P. An Index to the Source Records of Maryland, Genealogical, Biographical, Historical. 1940.

PENNSYLVANIA HISTORICAL AND MUSEUM COMMISSION. Bibliography of Pennsylvania History. 1957.

PETERSON, C. STEWART. Bibliography of County Histories of the 3,111 Counties in the 48 States. Baltimore, 1946.

PRESBYTERIAN HISTORICAL SOCIETY LIBRARY, PHILADELPHIA, PA. Catalogue of Church Records.

REED, EVAN L. Ways and Means of Identifying Ancestors. Chicago, 1947.

RIDER, FREMONT, *Ed.* The American Genealogical Index. 48 vols. Middletown, Conn., 1942-1952.

RIDER, FREMONT, *Ed.* The American Genealogical Biographical Index —. 32 vols. (Published A-D, and continuing.) 1952-1960. Middletown, Conn.

ROMAN CATHOLIC: The Official Catholic Directory, 1822-1943. New York, 1943.

ROMAN CATHOLIC RECORDS: Records of the Library of the Catholic University of America, Washington, D. C. (Records of many thousands of Catholics.)

RUBINCAM, MILTON. The Lure and Value of Genealogy. In *The Pennsylvania Genealogical Magazine.* Vol. 17, pp. 33-44. June, 1949.

SEVERSMITH, HERBERT F. Long Island Genealogical Source Material. National Genealogical Society *Special Publication No. 9.* Washington, D. C., 1948-49.

STETSON, OSCAR FRANK. The Art of Ancestor Hunting. New York, 1946.

STEVENSON, NOEL C. The Genealogical Reader. Salt Lake City, Utah, 1958.

STEVENSON, NOEL C. Search and Research. Whittier, Cal. 1959.

STEWART, ROBERT ARMISTEAD. Index to Printed Virginia Genealogies. 1930.

SWEM, EARL GREGG. Virginia Historical Index. 2 vols. 1934, 1936.

UNITED STATES, DEPARTMENT OF THE INTERIOR: Official Register of the United States. (Contains names of the officials in all departments of government service from 1843, giving address, place of birth, etc.) Washington, D. C. (Various publications.)

UNITED STATES LIBRARY OF CONGRESS: American and English Genealogies in the Library of Congress. 2nd edition. Washington, D. C., 1919.

UNITED STATES LIBRARY OF CONGRESS: Check List of the American 18th Century Newspapers in the Library of Congress. Government Printing Office, 1936.

UNITED STATES LIBRARY OF CONGRESS: Check List of Foreign Newspapers in the Library of Congress. Government Printing Office, Washington, D. C., 1929.

WALDENMAIER, INEZ, *Ed.* The Genealogical News Letter. Vol. I, No. 1 (1955); Vol. VI, No. 3 (1960). (Mimeographed.) Contains an important, cumulative bibliography of newly published genealogical source materials, genealogy, etc.

WRIGHT, CARROLL D. Report on the Custody and Condition of the Public Records of Parishes, Towns, and Counties (of Massachusetts). Boston, 1889.

WRITINGS ON AMERICAN HISTORY. 40 vols. 1902-1952, et seq. Washington, D. C. (1904-5; 1941-7, omitted.)

YENAWINE, WAYNE STEWART. A Check List of Source Material for the Counties of Georgia. In *The Georgia Historical Quarterly*, September, 1948.

GENERAL REFERENCE AND SOURCE MATERIALS

AMERICAN CATHOLIC HISTORICAL SOCIETY OF PHILADELPHIA, Records of the.

AMERICAN GENEALOGIST, THE. Edited by Donald Lines Jacobus. New Haven, 1923—. (First published as *The New Haven Genealogical Magazine.*)

AMERICAN-IRISH HISTORICAL SOCIETY, JOURNAL OF. Boston —New York, 1898-1941. 32 vols.

RECORDER, THE. Bulletin of the American-Irish Historical Society. Vols. 1 to 23. New York, 1901-1960.

ANDREWS, CHARLES M. The Colonial Period of American History. 4 vols. 1934-1938.

BAGENAL, PHILIP H. Irish in America. London, 1882.

BANCROFT. History of the U. S. A. 7 vols. London, 1857.

BANKS, CHARLES EDWARD. The Planters of the Commonwealth; A Study of the Emigration in Colonial Times. 1930. Passenger lists, 1620-1640. (Use with care.)

BENNETT, WILLIAM H. Some Pre-Civil War Militiamen. In the *Journal of the American-Irish Historical Society.* Vol. XXI, New York, 1922.

BESSE, JOSEPH. A Collection of the Sufferings of the People Called Quakers, 1654-1690. 2 vols.

BOLTON, CHARLES KNOWLES. Scotch-Irish Pioneers in Ulster and America.

BREED, WILLIAM P. Presbyterians and the Revolution. Philadelphia, 1876.

BRIGGS, CHARLES AUGUSTUS. American Presbyterianism; Its Origin and Early History. Edinburgh, New York, 1885.

CAMPBELL, JOHN H. History of the Friendly Sons of St. Patrick, and the Hibernian Society for the Relief of Emigrants from Ireland. March 17, 1771-March 17, 1892. Philadelphia, 1892. (Contains nearly 2,000 biographies of members of the Society, past and present, with records of wills, marriages, tombstone inscriptions, etc. Also information gathered in Philadelphia from Irish and Americans of Irish lineage.)

CARTER, CLARENCE E. The Territorial Papers of the United States. 4 vols. 1934-.

CASSON, HERBERT N. The Irish in America. In the *Journal of the American-Irish Historical Society.* Vol. VI. Boston, 1906.

COBB, IRVIN S. The Lost Tribes of the Irish in the South. In the *Journal of the American-Irish Historical Society.* Vol. XVI, Concord, N. H., and New York, 1917.

CONDON, EDWARD O'MEAGER. Irish Immigration to the United States Since 1790. In the *Journal of the American-Irish Historical Society.* Vol. IV, Boston, 1904.

CONDON, EDWARD O'MEAGHER. The Irish Race in America. Glasgow and London, 189?

COYLE, JOHN G., M.D. The Scot, the Ulster Scot and the Irish. In the *Journal of the American-Irish Historical Society.* Vol. XII, 1912-13.

CRAIGHEAD, REV. J. G. Scotch and Irish Seeds in American Soil. The early history of the Scotch and Irish Churches and their relations to the Presbyterian Church of America. Philadelphia, 1878.

CRIMMINS, JOHN D. American-Irish Historical Miscellany: Relating to New York City and vicinity, as well as the seaboard colonies, together with much interesting material relative to other parts of the country. Also biographical sketches of some 500 Irish-Americans of note. New York, 1905.

DESMOND, HUMPHREY J. The Colonial Irish. In the *Journal of the American-Irish Historical Society.* Vol. XXI, New York, 1922.

DOMINICK, JAMES. Bishops of the United States, of Irish Birth or Descent. Published by the *American-Irish Historical Society.* New York, 1936.

EARLY IRISH EMIGRANTS TO AMERICA, 1803-1806. In *The Recorder, American-Irish Historical Society.* Vol. III, no. 5, New York, June, 1926.

EMMET, THOMAS ADDIS, M. D. Irish Emigration During the Seventeenth and Eighteenth Centuries. In the *Journal of the American-Irish Historical Society.* Vol. II, Boston, 1899.

FORD, HENRY JONES. The Scotch-Irish in America. Princeton, N. J., 1915.

FREEMAN, DOUGLAS SOUTHALL. George Washington. 3 vols. 1948.

GILLETT, E. H. History of the Presbyterian Church in the United States. 2 vols. Philadelphia, 1864.

GLASGOW, MAUDE. The Scotch-Irish in North Ireland and in the American Colonies. New York, 1936.

GREEN, SAMUEL SWETT. Scotch-Irish in America. Worcester, 1895.

GRIFFIN, MARTIN I. J. Irish Builders of the White House. In the *Journal of the American-Irish Historical Society.* Vol. VII, Boston, 1907.

HACKETT, J. D. The Pedigree Irish. In the *Journal of the American-Irish Historical Society.* Vol. X, 1910-11.

HALTIGAN, JAMES. Irish in the American Revolution and Their Early Influence in the Colonies. Washington, 1908.

HANNA, CHARLES A. The Scotch-Irish, or, the Scot in North Britain, North Ireland, and North America. 2 vols. New York, 1902.

HANNA, CHARLES A. The Wilderness Trail. 2 vols. London, New York, 1911.

HARLLEE, WILLIAM CURRY. Kinfolks. 3 vols. 1934-1937. (Various families. See Vol. I: Chapter on county and state records, 10 southern states.)

HASBROUCK, J. E. Some Irish Revolutionary Soldiers. In *The Recorder, American-Irish Historical Society.* Vol. III, no. 2, May, 1925.

HENNESSY, MICHAEL EDMUND. Men of Irish Blood Who Have Attained Distinction in American Journalism. In the *Journal of the American-Irish Historical Society.* Vol. III, Boston, 1900.

HILL, WILLIAM. American Presbyterianism. Washington, 1839.

HINSHAW, WILLIAM WADE. Encyclopedia of American Quaker Genealogy. 6 vols., 1936-1950. (North Carolina, Philadelphia Yearly Meeting, New York and Long Island, Ohio (2 vols.), Virginia.)

HODGE, CHARLES. History of the Presbyterian Church in the United States. 2 vols. Philadelphia, 1851.

HURLEY, DORAN. Medal of Honor Men of Irish Birth or Irish Ancestry in the United States Army and Navy. In the *Journal of the American-Irish Historical Society.* Vol. XXXII, 1941.

IRISH IN AMERICA BEFORE 1700, THE. In *The Recorder, American-Irish Historical Society.* Vol. V, no. 4, New York, 1932.

LAWRENCE, RUTH, *Ed.* Colonial Families of America. 15 vols. 1928.

LEECH, ARTHUR BLENNERHASSETT. Irish Riflemen in America. London, New York, 1875.

LINCHAN, JOHN C. and THOMAS HAMILTON MURRAY. Irish Schoolmasters in the American Colonies, 1640-1775; . . . and after the . . . Revolution. Published by the *American-Irish Historical Society.* Washington, D. C., 1898.

LINEHAN, JOHN C. The Irish Scotch and the Scotch Irish. Published by the *American-Irish Historical Society.* New York, 1902.

MACLEAN, JOHN PATTERSON. An Historical Account . . . Settlements of Scotch Highlanders in America Prior to . . . 1783. 1900. (Includes Scotch-Irish.)

MAGUIRE, JOHN F. Irish in America. London, 1868.

MARSHALL, W. F. Ulster Sails West. Belfast, 1943-44.

MCGEE, THOMAS D'ARCY. A History of the Irish Settlers In North America, from the Earliest Period to the Census of 1850. Boston, 1851, 1852, 1855.

MOLONEY, MAURICE T. Irish Pioneers of the West and Their Descendants. In the *Journal of the American-Irish Historical Society.* Vol. VIII, 1909.

MURPHY, M. J. Ulster Settlers in America. Published in the *Ulster Journal of Archaeology.* Belfast, 1895-96.

MURRAY, THOMAS HAMILTON. Echoes From Out The Past; Historical Notes relating to Irish Pioneers in America. Published by the *American-Irish Historical Society,* New York, 1905.

MURRAY, THOMAS HAMILTON. Some Voices from Ye Old Time. In the *Journal of the American-Irish Historical Society.* Vol. IV, Boston, 1904.

MURRAY, THOMAS HAMILTON. Walsh's Irish Regiment of Marine Artillery. In the *Journal of the American-Irish Historical Society,* Boston, 1907.

MURTAGH, DEARMIUD. Irish in the 17th U. S. Cavalry. Published in *Irish Sword.* Vol. I, Dublin, 1953.

NATIONAL GENEALOGICAL SOCIETY QUARTERLY. Washington, D. C., 1912-.

NETTELS, C. P. The Roots of American Civilization, a History of American Colonial Life. 1939.

NEW CENTURY CYCLOPEDIA OF NAMES. New York, 1954.

New York: Arrival of Ships from Ireland in 1811. In *The Recorder, American-Irish Historical Society.* Vol. III, no. 1, New York, March, 1925.

New York: List of Passengers from the Ships *Radius, Clark,* from Cork, 1811. In *The Recorder, American-Irish Historical Society.* Vol. II, no. 6. New York, March, 1924.

O'BRIEN, MICHAEL J. A Glance at Some Pioneer Irish in the South. In the *Journal of the American-Irish Historical Society.* Vol. VII, Boston, 1907.

O'BRIEN, MICHAEL J. Births, Marriages and Burials and Other Records of the Irish in America in and About the Eighteenth Century. In the *Journal of the American-Irish Historical Society.* Vol. XII, 1912-13.

O'BRIEN, MICHAEL J. Early Irish Settlers in the Champlain Valley. In the *Journal of the American-Irish Historical Society.* Vol. XXVI, New York, 1927.

O'BRIEN, MICHAEL J. George Washington's Associations With the Irish. New York, 1937.

O'BRIEN, MICHAEL J. Historical Papers. (A collection reprinted from the *Journal of the American-Irish Historical Society.* Vol. XXV.) 1926.

O'BRIEN, MICHAEL J. Immigration, Land, Probate Records of the Irish in America in and About the Eighteenth Century. In the *Journal of the American-Irish Historical Society.* Vol. XIII, 1913-14. Continued, Vol. XIV, 1914-15.

O'BRIEN, MICHAEL J. Irish Immigrants from English Ports in the Eighteenth Century. In the *Journal of the American-Irish Historical Society.* Vol. XVIII, New York, 1919.

O'BRIEN, MICHAEL J. The Irish in the American Colonies. In the *Journal of the American-Irish Historical Society.* Vol. XXVI, New York, 1927.

O'BRIEN, MICHAEL J. Irish Pioneers and Schoolmasters. In the *Journal of the American-Irish Historical Society.* Vol. XVIII, New York, 1919.

O'BRIEN, MICHAEL J. Irish Schoolmasters in the American Colonies. In the *American-Irish Historical Society* "Historical Papers," New York, 1926.

O'BRIEN, MICHAEL J. Items Culled from the National Gazette and Literary Register. In the *Journal of the American-Irish Historical Society.* Vol. XXVII, New York, 1928.

O'BRIEN, MICHAEL J. The Scotch-Irish in the War of the Revolution. In the *Journal of the American-Irish Historical Society.* Vol. XXVIII, New York, 1930.

O'BRIEN, MICHAEL J. Some Examples of the Scotch-Irish in America. In the *Journal of the American-Irish Historical Society.* Vol. XIV, 1914-15.

O'DOWD, M. Irish Settlements of the Atlantic and Pacific Railroad Lands. St. Louis, 1875.

O'DWYER, GEORGE. Irish Immigrations to America, 1861-1865. In the *Journal of the American-Irish Historical Society.* Vol. XXX, 1932.

O'FARRELL, CHARLES. Irish Family Names Anglicized and Altered. In the *Journal of the American-Irish Historical Society.* Vol. XXII, New York, 1923.

O'HANLON, VERY REV. JOHN, CANON. Irish American History of the United States. Dublin, 1903.

O'HART, JOHN. Irish Pedigrees; or The Origin and Stem of the Irish Nation. 2 vols. 5th edition, Dublin, New York, 1892.

O'HART, JOHN. The Irish and Anglo-Irish Landed Gentry When Cromwell Came to Ireland, or a Supplement to Irish Pedigrees. Dublin, 1884.

PASSENGER LISTS: Irish Passenger Lists; Ireland to the U. S. A., 1803-1806. In the *New England Historical and Genealogical Register*. Vols. 60, 61, 62, and 66.

PERKINS, JAMES H. Annals of the West. Cincinnati, 1846.

PERRY, A. L. Scotch-Irish in New England. Boston, 1890.

PETERS, MADISON D. Irish Builders of the American Nation. In the *Journal of the American-Irish Historical Society*. Vol. X, 1910-11.

PETERSON, C. S. The American Pioneer in Forty-eight States. 1945.

PRESBYTERIAN CHURCH: Records of the Presbyterian Church in America from 1706 to 1788. Philadelphia, 1841.

PURCELL, RICHARD J. Irish Colonists in the British West Indies. In the *Journal of The American-Irish Historical Society*. Vol. XXXI, pp. 47-54.

REID, WHITELAW. The Scot in America and the Ulster Scot. 1912.

REILLY, DESMOND. Irish Refugees in American Chemistry. In *The Recorder, American-Irish Historical Society*. Vol. 14, New York, 1952.

ROCHE, JAMES JEFFRY. Irish Ability in the United States. In the *Journal of the American-Irish Historical Society*. Vol. VII, Boston, 1907.

ROSS, PETER. The Scot in America. New York, 1896.

SCHRIER, ARNOLD. Ireland and The American Emigration, 1850-1900. Minneapolis, Minn., 1958.

SCOTCH-IRISH IN AMERICA: Proceedings of the Scotch-Irish Congress. 10 vols. Cinncincinnati, Nashville, 1889-1901.

SHEPPARD, J. HAVERGAL. Irish Preachers and Educators in the Early History of the Presbyterian Church in America. In the *Journal of the American-Irish Historical Society*. Vol. XXIV, New York, 1925.

SHEPPARD, REV. J. HAVERGAL. The Irish in Protestant Denominations in America. In the *Journal of the American-Irish Historical Society.* Vol. IX, 1910.

SPRAGUE, WILLIAM B. Annals of the American Pulpit. (Vols. 3, 4, and 9, *Biographies of Presbyterian Mininsters.)* New York, 1860.

SWEENEY, WILLIAM M. A Ship from Newry, 1786. In *The Recorder, American-Irish Historical Society.* Vol. VII, no. 3, New York, April, 1935.

"THE SONS OF CAVAN" (Co. Ireland). In *The Recorder, American-Irish Historical Society.* Vol. IV, no. 3, January, 1930.

WALSH, DR. JAMES J. Irish Physicians and Surgeons. In *The Recorder, American-Irish Historical Society.* Vol. VI, no. 3, New York, June, 1933.

WEBSTER, RICHARD. History of the Presbyterian Church in America. Philadelphia, 1857.

WEIS, THE REV. FREDERICK LEWIS. The Colonial Clergy of Maryland, Delaware and Georgia. Lancaster, Mass., 1950.

WEIS, THE REV. FREDERICK LEWIS. The Colonial Clergy of Virginia, North Carolina and South Carolina. Boston, 1955.

"WHAT CONGRESS OWES TO IRELAND". In *The Recorder, American-Irish Historical Society.* Vol. IX, no. 3, New York, June, 1938.

WINDSOR, JUSTIN. Westward Movement. Boston, 1897.

WITTKE, CARL. The Irish in America. Baton Rouge, 1956.

WOODBURN, REV. JAMES BARKLEY. The Ulster Scot, His History and Religion. London, 1914.

WOODBURN, REV. JAMES BARKLEY. Emigration to America, Its Causes and Its Extent. In *The Ulster Scot,* pp. 212-229.

WRIGHT, LOUIS B. The Atlantic Frontier, 1607-1763. 1947.

IRISH AND SCOTCH-IRISH SOURCE MATERIALS OF EARLY STATES

ALABAMA

ALABAMA: State Department of Archives and History, Montgomery, Alabama. (Contains an important genealogical and biographical collection for southern states.)

ALABAMA GENEALOGICAL REGISTER. 1959-.

ALABAMA: Historical and Biographical History of Northern Alabama. 1888.

ALABAMA HISTORICAL QUARTERLY. Vols. 1-22, 1960.

ALABAMA WILLS, INDEX TO, 1808-1870. Compiled by the Alabama Society, D. A. R., 1955.

BRANT AND FULLER PUBLISHING CO. Memorial Record of Alabama. 2 vols. (Personal memoirs of early settlers.)

BREWER, WILLIS. Alabama—Her History—Public Men, etc. 1872.

HAMILTON, PETER J. Colonial Mobile. 1910.

JONES, KATHLEEN. Alabama Records.

MELL, A. R. W. Revolutionary Soldiers Buried in Alabama. 1904.

OWEN, THOMAS M. History of Alabama and the Directory of Alabama Biography. 1921.

OWEN, THOMAS M. Revolutionary Soldiers in Alabama. 1911. (Some biographical data.)

RILEY, REV. B. F. History of the Baptists of Alabama. Birmingham, 1895.

SAUNDERS, JAMES EDMONDS. Early Settlers of Alabama. 1899. Reprint, 1959. (Contains genealogical connections of over 1,000 early settlers.)

SMITH AND DELAND. Northern Alabama, Historical and Biographical. 1888.

WEST, ANSON. A History of Methodism in Alabama. Nashville, 1893.

CALIFORNIA

BANCROFT, HUBERT H. History of California, The. (Includes a "Pioneer Register.")

BANCROFT LIBRARY, BERKELEY, CAL.: See Record Collection of Pioneers. Contains history and origins.

CENTENNIAL ROSTER—CALIFORNIA PIONEERS, THE SOCIETY OF. 1948. (Lists members since 1850 for descendants of, or pioneers arrived before 1850, giving date of arrival in California, etc. Many Irish.)

CONNOLLY, JAMES. The Historical Place of Irishmen in California. In the *Journal of the American-Irish Historical Society*. Vol. III, Boston, 1900.

CROWLEY, REV. GEORGE T. S. J. The Irish in California. Published in Ireland, in *Studies,* Vol. XXV, pp. 451-62. 1936.

O'CONNOR, R. C. The Irish in California. In the *Journal of the American-Irish Historical Society.* Vol. XV, Concord, N. H., and New York, 1916.

QUIGLEY, DR. The Irish Race in California and on the Pacific Coast. San Francisco, 1878.

CONNECTICUT

AMERICAN GENEALOGIST, THE. (Formerly The New Haven Genealogical Magazine.) 1922 —. Donald Lines Jacobus, Editor.

BAILEY, FREDERICK WILLIAM. Early Connecticut Marriages as Found in Ancient Church Records, Prior to 1800. 7 vols. 1896-1906.

BOWEN, CLARENCE WINTHROP. The History of Woodstock (Windham Co.), Connecticut. 8 vols. 1926-43.

CONNECTICUT: Connecticut Historical Society, Hartford, "Collections". 1860-.

CONNECTICUT: Irish Settlers in Connecticut. In the *Journal of the American-Irish Historical Society.* Vol. XXIV, New York, 1925.

CONNECTICUT: The Public Records of the Colony of Connecticut, 1636-1776. 15 vols. Hartford, 1850-1890.

CONNECTICUT: The Public Records of the State of Connecticut. 3 vols. Hartford, 1894-1922, et seq.

CONNECTICUT MAGAZINE, THE. 12 vols. Hartford, 1895-1908.

CUTTER, WILLIAM RICHARD. Genealogical and Family History of the State of Connecticut. 4 vols. New York, 1911. (Use with care.)

ENCYCLOPEDIA of Connecticut Biography, Genealogical—Memorial. 4 vols. Boston and New York. 1917. (Use with care.)

HALL, EDWARD A. The Irish Pioneers of the Connecticut Valley. In the *Journal of the American-Irish Historical Society.* Vol. IV, Boston, 1904.

MANWARING, CHARLES WILLIAM. A Digest of the Early Connecticut Probate Records. 3 vols. Hartford, 1904-06.

MORRISON. History of Windham Conn. (Some copied Parish Records of Londonderry (Ireland) appear in the Supplement.)

O'BRIEN, MICHAEL J. The Connecticut Irish in the Revolution. In the *Journal of the American-Irish Historical Society.* Vol. XXII, New York, 1923.

O'BRIEN, MICHAEL J. Irish Pioneers in Hartford County, Connecticut. In the *Journal of the American-Irish Historical Society.* Vol. XXVII, New York, 1928.

O'BRIEN, MICHAEL J. Irish Pioneers of New London. In the *Journal of the American-Irish Historical Society.* New York, 1927.

DELAWARE

DELAWARE: A Calendar of Delaware Wills, New Castle County. 1682-1800. (National Society, Colonial Dames of America in Delaware.)

DELAWARE: Historical Society of Delaware, Papers of 1879—.

DELAWARE: Maryland and Delaware Genealogist. 1959—. Raymond Clark, Washington, D. C., Editor.

DELAWARE PUBLIC ARCHIVES COMMISSION: Delaware Archives. Vol. I, 1911—.

FERRIS, BENJAMIN. A History of the Original Settlements on the Delaware, From Its Discovery—to—William Penn. Wilmington, 1846.

MURRAY, THOMAS HAMILTON. The Irish Chapter in the History of Brown University. In the *Journal of the American-Irish Historical Society.* Vol. II, Boston, 1899.

O'BRIEN, MICHAEL J. Irish Pioneers in Delaware. In the *Journal of the American-Irish Historical Society.* Vol. XVIII, New York, 1919.

PURCELL, RICHARD J. Irish Settlers in Early Delaware. In the *Pennsylvania Magazine of History and Biography.* Vol. XVI.

SCHARF, J. THOMAS. The History of Delaware, 1609-1888. 2 vols. Philadelphia, 1888.

GEORGIA

BOWEN, ELIZA A. Wilkes County, The Story of. Marietta, 1950.

COULTER, ELLIS MERTON. A List of the Early Settlers of Georgia. Athens, 1949.

CRIMMINS, JOHN D. One Hundreth Anniversary of the Founding of the Hibernian Society of Savannah, Georgia. In the *Journal of the American-Irish Historical Society.* Vol. XI, 1911-12.

CHANDLER, ALLEN D. Revolutionary Records of the State of Georgia. 3 vols. Atlanta, 1908.

DAVIDSON, GRACE. Records of Richmond County, Formerly St. Paul's Parish. Athens, 1929.

FLANIGAN, JAMES C. Marriages of Hancock County, 1806-1943. Hapeville, 1943.

GEORGIA: Catalogue of the Georgia Society, D. A. R. (N. S. D. A. R. Library.)

GEORGIA: Colonial Records of the State of Georgia. 18 vols. Atlanta, 1904-08.

GEORGIA: The Georgia Historical Quarterly. 1917-.

GEORGIA: The Georgia Historical Society, Collections of. Savannah, 1840-.

GEORGIA: Historical Collections of the Georgia Chapters, D. A. R. 4 vols. 1929-32.

GEORGIA: The Irish in Atlanta, Georgia (List Appended). In the *Journal of the American-Irish Historical Society.* Vol. XXX, 1932.

GEORGIA: The Irish in Georgia. In *The Recorder, American-Irish Historical Society.* Vol. VI, no. 3, New York, 1933.

GILMER, GEORGE. Sketches of Some of the First Settlers of Upper Georgia. Americus, 1926.

HOUSTON, MARTHA L. Marriages of Hancock County, 1806-1850. Washington, 1947.

JONES, CHARLES C., JR. The History of Georgia. 2 vols. Boston, 1883.

LA FAR, MABLE FREEMAN and CAROLINE PRICE WILSON. Chatham County, Georgia, Abstracts of Wills of, 1773-1817. (National Genealogical Society, Washington, D. C., 1936.)

LUNCEFORD, ALVIN MELL. Early Records of Taliaferro County, Georgia. Crawfordsville, Georgia, 1956.

MCCALL, HUGH. History of Georgia. 2 vols. Savannah, 1812.

MELDRIM, MRS. PETER W. Some Early Epitaphs in Georgia. (Compiled by the Georgia Society of the Colonial Dames of America.) Durham, N. C., 1924.

SMITH, MRS. HERSCHEL W. Marriage Records of Green County, 1787-1875, and Oglethorpe County, 1795-1852. Atlanta, 1949.

STEVENS, WILLIAM B. History of Georgia. 2 vols. New York, 1847. Philadelphia, 1859.

KENTUCKY

ALLEN, WILLIAM B. History of Kentucky. Louisville, 1882.

ARDERY, MRS. W. B. Kentucky Records. (Contains Early Wills and Marriages, Old Bible Records and Tombstone Inscriptions. Records from 17 Counties.) Volume I, 1926. Reprint, 1958. Volume II contains Court Records of many Counties. 1932.

ARMSTRONG AND CO., J. M., *Publishers*. Biographical Encyclopedia of the Dead and Living Men of the Nineteenth Century. 1878.

BUTLER, MANN. History of Kentucky. Frankfort, 1824.

COLLINS, RICHARD H. History of Kentucky. 2 vols. Covington, 1882.

DAVIDSON, ROBERT. History of the Presbyterian Church in the State of Kentucky. New York, 1847.

DRAKE, DANIEL. Pioneer Life in Kentucky. Cincinnati, 1873.

ELY, WILLIAM. Big Sandy Valley. A History of the People and Country from the Earliest Settlement to the Present Time. 1887.

FILSON CLUB PUBLICATIONS. Louisville, 1884-.

FITZPATRICK, EDWARD. Early Irish Settlers in Kentucky. In the *Journal of the American-Irish Historical Society*. Vol. II, Boston, 1899.

FOWLER, I. E. Kentucky Pioneers and Their Descendants. 1850.

GREEN, THOMAS H. Historic Families of Kentucky. Cincinnati, 1889.

KENTUCKY HISTORICAL SOCIETY: Register of.

LINEHAN, JOHN C. Irish Pioneers and Builders of Kentucky. In the *Journal of the American-Irish Historical Society*. Vol. III, Boston, 1900.

MCADAMS, MRS. HARRY K. Pioneer and Court Records. Abstracts of Wills, Deeds, and Marriages from Court Houses and Records of Old Bibles, Churches, etc. Records from fourteen counties. 1929.

McCLUNG, JOHN A. Sketches of Western Adventure, 1755-1794. Dayton, 1854.

PERRIN, W. H., J. C. BATTLE and G. C. KNIFFIN. A History of Kentucky. Louisville, 1886.

SCOTT, H. M. Scott's Papers: Kentucky Court and Other Records. 1953.

TINSLEY, H. B. North Creek, History of, with Genealogical and Biographical Section. 1953.

WILSON, SAMUEL M. Catalogue of Revolutionary Soldiers and Sailors of the Commonwealth of Virginia,— Warrants granted to, by Virginia. 1953.

LOUISIANA

ARTHUR, STANLEY C. Old Families of Louisiana. Genealogy. 1931.

FORTIER, ALCEE. A History of Louisiana. 4 vols. 1904.

GAYARRE, CHARLES. History of Louisiana. 4 vols. New Orleans, 1903.

LOUISIANA HISTORICAL QUARTERLY. New Orleans, 1917-.

PERRIN, WILLIAM. Southwest Louisiana, Biographical and Historical. 1891.

SEABOLD, HERMAN B. Old Plantation Louisiana: Life, Homes, Family trees. 1941.

MAINE

GREENLEAF, JONATHAN. Ecclesiastical History of Maine. Portsmouth, 1821.

HOUGH, FRANKLIN B. Pemaquid, Papers Relating to. Albany, 1856.

LITTLE, GEORGE THOMAS. Genealogical and Family History of the State of Maine. 4 vols. 1909. (Use with care.)

MAINE: Collections of the Maine Historical Society. Portland, 1831-.

MAINE: The Maine Genealogist and Biographer. (Quarterly.) 3 vols. 1875-1878.

MAINE: The Maine Historical and Genealogical Recorder. 9 vols. 1884-1898.

MAINE: Province and Court Records of Maine. 4 vols. Portland, 1928, 1931, 1947, 1958.

NOYES, SYBIL, CHARLES THORNTON LIBBY, and WALTER GOODWIN DAVIS. Genealogical Dictionary of Maine and New Hampshire. Portland, 1928-1939.

O'BRIEN, MICHAEL J. The Early Irish in Maine. In the the *Journal of the American-Irish Historical Society.* Vol. X, 1910-11.

O'BRIEN, MICHAEL J. The Lost Town of Cork, Maine. In the *Journal of the American-Irish Historical Society.* Vol. XII, 1912-13.

O'DWYER, GEORGE F. Irish Pioneers of Maine. In the *Journal of the American-Irish Historical Society.* Vol. XIX, XX, 1920-1921. (Also see, "Other Pioneers".)

PATTERSON, WILLIAM D., *Ed.* Probate Reports of Lincoln County, Maine. Portland, 1895.

POPE, CHARLES HENRY. The Pioneers of Maine, and New Hampshire, 1623-1660. 1908.

RIDLON, G. T. Saco Valley Settlements and Families. Historical, Biographical and Genealogical. Portland, 1895.

SARGENT, WILLIAM MITCHELL. Maine Wills, 1640-1760. Portland, 1887.

SIBLEY, JOHN L. History of Union. Boston, 1851.

SPRAGUE. Sprague's Journal of Maine History. 14 vols. 1913-1926.

STAHL, JOSEPH. History of Old Broad Bay and Waldoboro. *ca.* 1956.

WHITNEY, S. H. Kennebec Valley: Early History of the Valley. 1887.

WILLIAMSON, W. D. History of the State of Maine. 2 vols. Hallowell, 1832.

WILLIS, WILLIAM. History of Portland from 1632 to 1864. Portland, 1865.

WILLIS, WILLIAM. Journals of the Rev. Thomas Smith and Rev. Samuel Deane, Pastors of the First Church of Portland. Portland, 1849.

MARYLAND

BALTIMORE: The Irish in Baltimore. In *The Recorder, American-Irish Historical Society.* Vol. IX, no. 2, New York, 1936.

BROMWELL, HENRIETTA ELIZABETH. Old Maryland Families: A Collection of Charts Compiled from Public Records, Wills, Family Bibles, Tombstone Inscriptions, and Other Original Sources. 1916.

CARROLL: The Life of Charles Carroll of Carrollton, 1737-1832, with His Correspondence and Public Papers. 2 vols. New York, 1898.

COTTON, JANE BALDWIN. Maryland Calendar of Wills, 1635-1743. 8 vols. 1901-1928.

FORD, H. P. Manoken Presbyterian Church, History of. 1910.

IRISH: Irish Pioneers in Maryland. In the *Journal of the American-Irish Historical Society.* Vol. XIV, 1914-15.

JOHNSTON, GEORGE. History of Cecil County and the Early Settlements Around the Head of Chesapeake Bay and on the Delaware River, with Sketches of Some of the Old Families of Cecil County. Elkton, 1881.

MAGRUDER, JAMES MOSBY. Index of Maryland Calendar of Wills, 1634-1777, at Land Office, Annapolis, Md. 3 vols. *ca.* 1933.

MAGRUDER, JAMES MOSBY. Magruder's Maryland Colonial Abstracts: Wills, Accounts and Inventories, 1772-1777. 5 vols. *ca.* 1934.

MARYLAND: Archives of Maryland. 30 vols. 1883-1910.

MARYLAND: Collections of the Maryland Historical Society. Baltimore, 1867-.

MARYLAND: Maryland and Delaware Genealogist. Edited by Raymond Clark. Washington, D. C., 1959-.

MARYLAND: The Maryland Genealogical Bulletin. January, 1930-.

MARYLAND: The Maryland Historical Magazine. 1906-. (A Card Index to Personal Names is in the Maryland Historical Society.)

O'BRIEN, MICHAEL J. The Irish in Maryland, 1778. In the *Journal of the American-Irish Historical Society*. Vol. XXIV, New York, 1925.

RICHARDSON, MRS. HESTER (DORSEY). Sidelights on Maryland History, with Sketches of Early Maryland Families. 2 vols. 1913.

RIDGELY, HELEN WEST. A Calendar of Memorial Inscriptions Collected in the State of Maryland. 1906.

SCHARF, J. THOMAS. Baltimore, The Chronicles of. Baltimore, 1874.

SCHARF, J. THOMAS. History of Baltimore City and County, from the Earliest Period to the Present Day, Including Biographical Sketches, —. Philadelphia, 1881.

SCHARF, J. THOMAS. History of Maryland. 3 vols. Baltimore, 1879.

SCHARF, J. THOMAS. History of Western Maryland. 2 vols. Philadelphia, 1882.

SCULLY, D. J. Irish Influence in the Life of Baltimore. In the *Journal of the American-Irish Historical Society*. Vol. VII, Boston, 1907.

TORRENCE, CLAYTON. Old Somerset on the Eastern Shore of Maryland. 1935.

WEIS, THE REV. FREDERICK LEWIS. The Colonial Clergy of Maryland, Delaware and Georgia. Lancaster, Mass. 1950.

MASSACHUSETTS

ACKLAND, THOMAS. The Kelts of Colonial Boston. In the *Journal of the American-Irish Historical Society*. Vol. VII, Boston, 1907.

AMERICAN ANTIQUARIAN SOCIETY, WORCESTER. Index to Obituary Notices in the "Boston Transcript," 1875-1930. 5 vols. (Typed.) Worcester, 1938-40.

BOSTON: Boston Society Publications. Vols. I-XII, and 2nd series, Vols. I-IV. Boston, 1886-1924.

BOSTON: Report of the Commissioners of Boston. Edited by W. H. Whitmore and W. S. Appleton. 39 vols. 1876-1909.

BOSTON PUBLIC LIBRARY. Genealogical Index of over 50,000 names which have appeared in the Genealogical Section of the "Boston Transcript". Index is located at 1118 Tremont Street, Boston.

BOSTON PUBLIC LIBRARY. Index of All Names which have appeared in the Genealogical Section of the "Boston Transcript".

CAMBRIDGE: Looking Back at Old Cambridge, Massachusetts. In the *Journal of the American-Irish Historical Society*. Vol. VII, Boston, 1907.

CHAMBERLAIN, SAMUEL. The Berkshires: Berkshire, Massachusetts. New York, 1956.

COLONIAL SOCIETY OF MASSACHUSETTS: Publications, 1892-. Index to Vols. I-XXV, 1932.

CRANE, ELLERY BICKNELL. Historic Homes and Institutions and Genealogical and Personal Memoirs of Worcester County, Massachusetts. 4 vols. 1907.

CULLEN, J. B. Irish in Boston: The Story of the Irish in Boston, together with Biographical Sketches of Representative Men and Noted Women. Boston, 1889.

CUTTER, WILLIAM RICHARD. Genealogical and Personal Memoirs Relating to Families of Boston and Eastern Massachusetts. 4 vols. 1910. (Use with care.)

CUTTER, WILLIAM RICHARD. Historic Homes and Places and Genealogical and Personal Memoirs Relating to Families of Middlesex County, Massachusetts. 4 vols. 1908. (Use with care.)

DONOVAN, GEORGE FRANCIS. The Pre-Revolutionary Irish in Massachusetts. Menasha, Wisconsin, 1931.

ESSEX ANTIQUARIAN, THE. 13 vols. 1897-1909.

ESSEX INSTITUTE: Historical Collections, 1859-.

HANDLIN, OSCAR. The Irish in Boston: Boston's Immigrants, 1790-1865. Cambridge; London; Oxford, 1941.

HOLLAND, JOSIAH G. History of Western Massachusetts. 2 vols. Springfield, 1855.

HUDSON, CHARLES. History of the Town of Lexington, Middlesex County, Massachusetts, from its First Settlement to 1868. 2 vols. Vol. II, *Genealogies,* Boston, New York, 1913.

HUNNEWELL, JAMES F. Charlestown: A Century of Town Life. A History of Charlestown, 1775-1887. Boston, 1888.

HURD, CHARLES EDWIN. Genealogy and History of Representative Citizens of the Commonwealth of Massachusetts. 1902.

LANGTRY, ALBERT P., *Ed.* Metropolitan Boston. 5 vols. New York, 1929.

LEE, THOMAS Z. The Charitable Irish Society of Boston. In the *Journal of the American-Irish Historical Society.* Vol. XXIV, New York, 1925.

LINEHAN, JOHN C. Irish Pioneers in Boston and Vicinity. In the *Journal of the American-Irish Historical Society.* Vol. VI, Boston, 1906.

LINEHAN, MARY LESSEY. The Irish Settlers of Pelham, Mass. In the *Journal of the American-Irish Historical Society.* Vol. III, Boston, 1900.

LYNCH, JOHN E. Early Irish Settlers in Worcester, Massachusetts. In *The Recorder, American-Irish Historical Society.* Vol. X, 1939.

MASSACHUSETTS HISTORICAL SOCIETY: Collections, 1792-; Proceedings, 1859-.

MASSACHUSETTS MAGAZINE. 11 vols. (in 10), 1908-1918.

MULLANEY, K. F. Catholic Pittsfield and Berkshire (Mass.). 1897.

O'BRIEN, MICHAEL J. Irish Names from Boston Probate Records. In the *Journal of the American-Irish Historical Society.* Vol. XV, Concord, N. H., and New York, 1916.

O'BRIEN, MICHAEL J. The Pioneer Irish of Essex County, Massachusetts. In the *Journal of the American-Irish Historical Society.* Vol. XXVI, New York, 1927.

O'BRIEN, MICHAEL J. Pioneer Irishmen of Northampton, Massachusetts. In the *Journal of the American-Irish Historical Society.* Vol. XVII, New York, 1918.

O'BRIEN, MICHAEL J. Some Traces of the Irish Settlers in the Colony of Massachusetts Bay. In the *Journal of the American-Irish Historical Society*. Vol. XVIII, New York, 1919.

O'DWYER, GEORGE F. Early Irish Names on the Ipswich Vital Records. In the *Journal of the American-Irish Historical Society*. Vol. XVI, Concord, N. H., and New York, 1917.

O'DWYER, GEORGE F. Historical Gleanings from Massachusetts Records. In the *Journal of the American-Irish Historical Society*. Vol. XVIII, New York, 1919.

O'DWYER, GEORGE. Memorials of the Dead. (Old Calvary Cemetery, Springfield, Massachusetts, and Old Cabotsville Cemetery, Chicopee, 1840-1850.) In the *Journal of the American-Irish Historical Society*. Vol. XXIX, 1930-31.

O'DWYER, GEORGE. Some Massachusetts Wills, 1753. In the *Journal of the American-Irish Historical Society*. Vol. XXIX, 1930-31.

O'MALLEY, CHARLES J. American Irish Progress in Boston. In the *Journal of the American-Irish Historical Society*. Vol. XXIV, New York, 1925.

SMITH, J. E. A. Pittsfield, History of, 1734-1876. 2 vols., 1869-76.

WALL, C. A. Worcester, Reminiscences of, from the Earliest Period. Historical and Genealogical. 1877.

WALL, C. A. North Worcester: Its First Settlers and Old Farms. 1890.

WORCESTER: Early Irish Settlers at Worcester, Massachusetts. In the *Journal of the American-Irish Historical Society*. Vol. XVIII, New York, 1919.

WORCESTER: Early Irish Settlers in Worcester. In *The Recorder, American-Irish Historical Society*. Vol. 10, no. 1, New York, 1939.

WRIGHT, H. B. and E. D. HARVEY. Oakham Settlement and Story of. 2 vols., 1947.

WYMAN, THOMAS BELLOWS. Charlestown, Middlesex County, the Genealogies and Estates of, 1629-1818. 2 vols. Boston, 1879.

MICHIGAN

BURTON HISTORICAL COLLECTION, DETROIT. (Includes biographies giving origins of settlers.)

DETROIT SOCIETY FOR GENEALOGICAL RESEARCH: Magazine of.

MICHIGAN PIONEER AND HISTORICAL SOCIETY: Collections of the. Lansing, 1874-1915.

MINNESOTA

MINNESOTA: The Irish Colonies in Minnesota. In *The Recorder, American-Irish Historical Society.* Vol. VII, no. 2, New York, 1934.

MINNESOTA HISTORICAL SOCIETY, ST. PAUL. (See biographical file of early residents of the State, giving origins of settlers.)

NEW ENGLAND

BLAIKIE, ALEXANDER. Presbyterianism in New England. Boston, 1882.

BOLTON, ETHEL STANWOOD. Immigrants to New England, 1700-1775. Salem, 1931.

CUSHING, THE MOST REV. RICHARD J., ARCHBISHOP. The Irish in New England in the Seventeenth Century. (Subject of an Address.) In *The Recorder, American-Irish Historical Society.* Vol. XIV, 1952.

CUTTER, WILLIAM RICHARD. New England Families, Genealogical and Memorial. 4 vols. New York, 1913, 1914, 1915. (Use with care.)

NEW ENGLAND HISTORICAL AND GENEALOGICAL REGISTER (Quarterly), Boston, 1847—. Index of Persons, vols. 1-50. 3 vols. Boston, 1905-07. Index of Persons, vols. 51-100. Boston, 1959.

NEW ENGLAND: New Ireland in New England. In *The Recorder, American-Irish Historical Society.* Vol. X, no. 1, New York, 1939.

O'BRIEN, MICHAEL J. An Authoritative Account of the Earliest Irish Pioneers in New England. In the *Journal of the American-Irish Historical Society.* Vol. XVIII, New York, 1919.

O'BRIEN, MICHAEL J. Irish Marriages in New England. In the *Journal of the American-Irish Historical Society.* Vol. XVII, New York, 1918.

O'BRIEN, MICHAEL J. Pioneer Irish in New England. New York, 1937.

NEW HAMPSHIRE

BELNAP, JEREMY. History of New Hampshire. 3 vols. Dover, 1812.

BRENNAN, JAMES F. The Irish Pioneers and Founders of Peterborough, New Hampshire. In the *Journal of the American-Irish Historical Society.* Vol. II, Boston, 1899.

BRENNAN, JAMES F. The Irish Settlers of Southern New Hampshire. In the *Journal of the American-Irish Historical Society.* Vol. IX, 1910.

COCHRANE, R. W. History of Antrim, New Hampshire.

DUBLIN: The History of Dublin, New Hampshire, Containing . . . A Register of Families. Boston, 1855.

GOSS, WINIFRED LANE. Colonial Gravestone Inscriptions in the State of New Hampshire. Dover, N. H., 1942.

HAZEN, HENRY A. Congregational and Presbyterian Ministry and Churches of New Hampshire.

LAWRENCE, ROBERT F. New Hampshire Churches, Congregational and Presbyterian. Claremont, 1856.

LINEHAN, JOHN C. Early New Hampshire Irish. In the *Journal of the American-Irish Historical Society.* Vol. III, Boston, 1900.

NEW HAMPSHIRE: Antiquarian Society Collections. (4 numbers), 1 vol. 1874-1879.

NEW HAMPSHIRE GENEALOGICAL RECORD. 7 vols. 1903-1910.

NEW HAMPSHIRE HISTORICAL SOCIETY: Collections, 1824—. Proceedings, 1874—.

NEW HAMPSHIRE: Probate Records of the Province of New Hampshire—1635—1771. *New Hampshire State Papers Series,* vols. 31-39. Concord, N. H., 1907-41.

NEW HAMPSHIRE: Probate Records of the Province of New Hampshire. 1907—.

NEW HAMPSHIRE: Provincial, State and Town Papers, 1867—.

NEW HAMPSHIRE: New Hampshire Provincial Papers, 1623-1792. 10 vols.

NEW HAMPSHIRE: New Hampshire State Papers, 1679-1771. 15 vols. Nashua and Concord, various dates.

NEW HAMPSHIRE: New Hampshire Town Papers, 1680-1800. 3 vols.

NOYES, SYBIL, CHARLES THORNTON LIBBY and WALTER GOODWIN DAVIS. Genealogical Dictionary of Maine and New Hampshire. Portland, 1928-1939.

O'BRIEN, MICHAEL J. Irish Pioneers in New Hampshire. In the *Journal of the American-Irish Historical Society.* Vol. XXV, New York, 1926.

O'BRIEN, MICHAEL J. Some Irish Names Culled from the Official Records of New Hampshire. In the *Journal of the American-Irish Historical Society.* Vol. XVIII, New York, 1919.

PARKER, EDWARD L. History of Londonderry, New Hampshire. Boston, 1851.

SMITH, ETTA M. Peterborough, History of. 2 vols. Book One—Narrative. By George A. Morison. Book Two—Genealogies. By Etta M. Smith. Ringe, 1954.

STEARNS, EZRA SCOLLAY. Genealogical and Family History of the State of New Hampshire. 4 vols. 1908. (Use with care.)

NEW JERSEY

BARBER, JOHN WARNER and HENRY HOWE. Historical Collections of the State of New Jersey; Containing a General Collection of the Most Interesting Facts, Traditions, Biographical Sketches, Anecdotes, etc. New York, 1884.

COOLEY, ELI F. Trenton. Genealogy of Early Settlers in Trenton and Ewing, "Old Hunterdon County", New Jersey. 1883.

GENEALOGICAL MAGAZINE OF NEW JERSEY. Newark, 1925—.

GORDON, THOMAS F. History of New Jersey. Trenton, 1834.

HATFIELD, E. F. History of Elizabeth (N. J.). New York, 1868.

LEE, FRANCIS BAZLEY. Genealogical and Memorial History of the State of New Jersey. 4 vols. 1910. (Use with care.)

LITTELL, JOHN. Passaic Valley Genealogies. Feltville, 1851.

MAHONEY, W. H. The Irish Element in Newark, New Jersey. In the *Journal of the American-Irish Historical Society*. Vol. XXI, New York, 1922.

MAHONEY, WILLIAM H. Irish Settlers in Union County, New Jersey. In the *Journal of the American-Irish Historical Society*. Vol. XXVIII, New York, 1930.

MAHONEY, WILLIAM H. The Melting Pot; Irish Footsteps in New Jersey. In the *Journal of the American-Irish Historical Society*. Vol. XXV, New York, 1926.

MORRIS COUNTY: Early History of Presbyterianism in Morris County. (*American Presbyterian Review*, vol. 17, April, 1868.)

MORRISTOWN: "The Record", First Presbyterian Church, Vol. I, no. 1, to Vol. V, no. 36 (complete); "The Combined Registers," 1742-1885; A History of the Church. 1880-1885.

NELSON, WILLIAM. Church Records in New Jersey (a bibliography). 1904.

NELSON, WILLIAM. Church Records of New Jersey. In the *Journal of the Presbyterian Historical Society*, Philadelphia. Vol. II, pp. 173-188; 251-266.

NEWARK: Records of the Town of Newark, From its Settlement in 1666, to its Incorporation as a City in 1836. Newark, 1864.

NEW JERSEY ARCHIVES. 19 vols. Newark and Trenton, 1880—.

NEW JERSEY: New Jersey Bibliography for Early Irish Settlers. In *The Recorder, American-Irish Historical Society.* Vol. XIII, no. 1, pp. 27-30. New York, 1951.

NEW JERSEY: Collections and Proceedings of the New Jersey Historical Society. New York and Newark, 1846—. (A magazine of history, biography, and notes on families, 1st-3rd series, and new series.)

NEW JERSEY: The Story of New Jersey. 5 vols. New York, 1945.

O'BRIEN, MICHAEL J. The Irish in the New Jersey Probate Records. In the *Journal of the American-Irish Historical Society.* Vol. XXVII, New York, 1928.

O'BRIEN, MICHAEL J. Some Early Irish Settlers and Schoolmasters in New Jersey. In the *Journal of the American Irish Historical Society.* Vol. XI, 1911-12.

PURCELL, PROF. RICHARD J. Irish Settlers in Early New Jersey. In *The Recorder, American-Irish Historical Society.* Vol. XIII, no. 1, New York, 1951.

SHERMAN, ANDREW M. Washington and His Army in Morris County. In the *Journal of the American-Irish Historical Society.* Vol. X, 1910-11.

SHOURD, THOMAS. Fenwick's Colony, History and Genealogy of. 1876.

SMITH, SAMUEL. History of the Colony of Nova Caesaria, or New Jersey. Burlington, 1765; reprint, Trenton, 1877.

STEARNS, J. F. Newark: Historical Discourses Relating to the First Presbyterian Church. 1853.

STILLWELL, JOHN EDWIN. Historical and Genealogical Miscellany: Data Relating to the Settlement and Settlers of New York and New Jersey. 5 vols. New York, 1903-1932.

WHITEHEAD, WILLIAM A. Contributions to the Early History of Perth Amboy and Adjoining Country. New York, 1856.

WHITEHEAD, WILLIAM A. East Jersey Under the Proprietary Governments. Newark, 1846.

NEW YORK

ALBANY: Collections of the History of Albany, from Its Discovery to the Present Time, with . . . Biographical Sketches, etc. 4 vols. 1865-1871.

ALBANY: Early Records of the City and County of Albany and the Colony of Rensselaerwyck. 4 vols. 1869, 1916-1919.

ALEXANDER, S. D. History of the Presbytery of New Jersey. New York, 1887.

ANJOU, GUSTAVE. Ulster County Probate Records. 2 vols. 1906.

BANNAN, THERESA. Pioneer Irish of Onondaga County, New York, 1776-1847. New York, 1911.

BARBER, JOHN W., and HENRY HOWE. Historical Collections of New York. New York, 1844.

BERGEN, TUNIS G. Genealogies of the State of New York. Long Island Edition, 3 vols., 1915.

BERGEN, TUNIS G. Hudson—Mohawk Genealogical and Family Memoirs. 4 vols., 1911.

COYLE, JOHN G. Irish Militiamen in New York Province. In the *Journal of the American-Irish Historical Society*. Vol. XV, Concord, N. H., and New York, 1916.

CRIMMINS, JOHN D. St. Patrick's Day: Its Celebration in New York— 1737-1845. New York, 1902. (Contains 550 short biographies.)

CUNNINGHAM, RT. HON. S. The Early Irish in Old Albany, New York. Belfast, 1903.

CUTTER, WILLIAM R. Genealogy and Family History of Northern New York. 3 vols. New York, 1910. (Use with care.)

CUTTER, WILLIAM R. Genealogy and Family History of Central New York. 3 vols. New York, 1912. (Use with care.)

CUTTER, WILLIAM R. Genealogy and Family History of Western New York. 3 vols. New York, 1912. (Use with care.)

DANAHER, FRANKLIN M. Early Irish in Old Albany New York. (Paper read before the American-Irish Historical Society, 1903.)

DONOVAN, HERBERT D. A. Fenian Memories in Northern New York. In the *Journal of the American-Irish Historical Society.* Vol. XXIII, 1930.

DUNLAP, WILLIAM: History of New Netherlands and New York. 2 vols. New York, 1839-1840.

FERNOW, BERTHOLD. Calendar of Wills on File and Recorded at Albany—1626-1836. New York, 1896.

FOLEY, JANET WETHY. Early Settlers of New York State; Their Ancestors and Descendants. 6 vols. Akron, New York, 1934-40. (Index to many thousands of names, with births, marriages, deaths, residences.)

FOLEY, JANET WETHY. Early Settlers of Western New York State, Their Ancestors and Descendants. 8 vols. Akron, New York, 1934-42.

FREELAND, DANIEL N. Chronicles of Monroe in the Olden Time. New York, 1898.

FRENCH, J. H. Historical and Statistical Gazetteer. Syracuse, 1860.

HACKETT, J. DOMINICK. Passenger Lists Published in "The Shamrock or Irish Chronicle" (Newspaper of N. Y. C.), 1811. In the *Journal of the American-Irish Historical Society.* Vol. XXVIII, New York, 1930.

HALSEY, FRANCIS WHITNEY. The Old New York Frontier. New York, 1901.

HARLOW, HENRY A. Presbytery of Hudson, History of the. New York, 1888.

HASKETT, D. C. Checklist of Newspapers and Official Gazettes in the New York Public Library. 1915.

HASTINGS, HUGH. Irish Stars in the Archives of the New York Province. In the *Journal of the American-Irish Historical Society.* Vol. IX, 1910.

HUGHES, THOMAS P. *Ed.* Genealogies of Columbia County, New York. Published in *American Ancestry*. Vol. 2, Albany, 1887.

IRISH: Some Irish Arrivals in New York, Philadelphia and Baltimore, in 1811. In *The Recorder, American-Irish Historical Society*. Vol. III, no. 6.

LAMB, MARTHA J. New York City, History of. 2 vols. New York, 1877-80.

LONG ISLAND HISTORICAL SOCIETY: Catalogue of American Genealogies in the Library. 1935.

LOSSING, BENSON J. The Empire State. Hartford, 1888.

MCGUIRE, EDWARD J. Gleanings of New York Irish Records. In the *Journal of the American-Irish Historical Society*. Vol. XVI, Concord, N. H., and New York, 1917.

MCMANUS, TERENCE. A Few Outstanding Figures of Irish Ancestry at the Bench and Bar of New York. In the *Journal of the American-Irish Historical Society*. Vol. XXIII, New York, 1924.

MEEHAN, THOMAS F. A Bit of New York History. In the *Journal of the American-Irish Historical Society*. Vol. VII, Boston, 1907.

MUNSELL, JOEL. The Annals of Albany. 10 vols. Albany, 1850-59.

MUNSELL, JOEL. Collections on the History of Albany. 4 vols. Albany, 1865-71.

NEW YORK: Calendar of New York Historical Manuscripts. 2 vols. Albany, 1868.

NEW YORK: Collections and Proceedings of the New York Historical Society. New York, 1811—.

NEW YORK: Documents Relating to the Colonial History of New York, 1663-1778. 15 vols. Albany, 1853-1887.

NEW YORK: Irish Property Owners of Old New York. In the *Journal of the American-Irish Historical Society*. Vol. XV, Concord, N. H., and New York, 1916.

NEW YORK: Names of Persons for Whom Marriage Licenses were Issued by the Secretary of the Province of New York, prior to 1784. 1860, with Supplement, 1898.

NEW YORK: New York Historical Society Collections; Abstracts of Wills on File in . . . The City of New York . . . 1665-1801. 17 vols. 1893-1913.

NEW YORK: New York in the Revolution. Albany, 1887.

NEW YORK: New York State Historian: Ecclesiastical Records, State of New York. 7 vols. 1901-1916.

NEW YORK: Survey of the Manuscript Collections in the New York Historical Society. 1941.

NEW YORK: Some Irish Arrivals in New York in 1810-1811. In *The Recorder, American-Irish Historical Society.* Vol. II, no. 2, New York, 1923.

NEW YORK GENEALOGICAL AND BIOGRAPHICAL RECORD (Quarterly). January, 1870—. Subject Index (Vols. I—XXXVIII), 1907; Surname Index (Vols. I-XX), 1950.

NIAGARA FRONTIER MISCELLANY. Published by the Buffalo Historical Society. Buffalo, 1947.

O'BRIEN, MICHAEL J. In Old New York. The Irish deceased, in Trinity and St. Paul's Church-yards. (*American-Irish Historical Society.* New York, 1928.)

O'BRIEN, MICHAEL J. The Irish and the Dutch in Albany, New York. Colonial Records. In the *Journal of the the American-Irish Historical Society.* Vol. XXVI, New York, 1927.

O'BRIEN, MICHAEL J. The Irish and the Dutch Records of Ulster County, New York. In the *Journal of the American-Irish Historical Society.* Vol. XXVI, New York, 1927.

O'BRIEN, MICHAEL J. The Irish Burghers of New Amsterdam and Freemen of New York. In the *Journal of the American-Irish Historical Society.* Vol. XVII, New York, 1918.

O'BRIEN, MICHAEL J. Irish Colonists in New York. *New York State Historical Association,* New York, 1906.

O'BRIEN, MICHAEL J. The Irish in Old New York. In *The Recorder, American-Irish Historical Society.* Vol. III, no. 6, 1926.

O'BRIEN, MICHAEL J. The Irish in the Dutch Records of the City of New York. In the *Journal of the American-Irish Historical Society.* Vol. XXVII, New York, 1928.

O'BRIEN, MICHAEL J. Irish Settlers in Orange County New York. In the *Journal of the American-Irish Historical Society.* Vol. XXVII, New York, 1928.

O'BRIEN, MICHAEL J. Irish Settlers in Queen's County, City of New York. In the *Journal of the American-Irish Historical Society.* Vol. XXVII, New York, 1928.

O'BRIEN, MICHAEL J. Some Pre-Revolutionary Ferrymen of Staten Island. In the *Journal of the American-Irish Historical Society.* Vol. XV, Concord, N. H., and New York, 1916.

O'BRIEN, MICHAEL J. Irish Schoolmasters in the City of New York. In the *Journal of the American-Irish Historical Society.* Vol. XXVII, New York, 1928.

O'CALLAGHAN, E. B., *Ed.* Documentary History of New York. 4 vols. Albany, 1849-1851.

PEARSON, JONATHAN. Contributions for the Genealogies of the First Settlers of the Ancient County of Albany, from 1600-1800. Albany, 1872.

PEARSON, JONATHAN. Contributions for Genealogy of Descendants of First Settlers of Patent and City of Schenectady, 1662-1800.

PELLETREAU, W. S., *Ed.* Westchester County, Early Wills of, from 1664-1784, with Genealogical and Historical Notes. New York, 1898.

PRESBYTERIAN SYNOD: Records of the Presbyterian Synod of New York and Philadelphia. Philadelphia, 1841.

PURCELL, PROF. RICHARD J. Irish Residents in Albany, 1783-1865. In *The Recorder, American-Irish Historical Society.* Vol. XII, no. 1, New York, 1950.

REYNOLDS, CUYLER. Genealogy and Family History of Southern New York and Hudson River Valley. 3 vols, 1914. (Use with care.)

ST. NICHOLAS SOCIETY OF THE CITY OF NEW YORK. Genealogical Record. Vols. I-IV, 1905-1934. (Hereditary

Society: Members descended from New York residents, there prior to 1785. Records of each member since 1935, with ancestry.)

SAWYER, JOHN. History of Cherry Valley, from 1740 to 1898. Cherry Valley, 1898.

SCHOONMAKER, MARIUS. The History of Kingston, Ulster County, New York, from its Early Settlement to the Year 1820. New York, 1888.

SEVERSMITH, HERBERT F. Long Island Genealogical Source Material. National Genealogical Society, *Special Publication No. 9*. Washington, D. C., 1948-49.

SHAMROCK OR HIBERNIAN CHRONICLE, THE. A file of, 1810-1817, in the American-Irish Historical Society Library, New York City. In *The Recorder*, Vol. II, no. 1, 1923.

SIMMS, JEPHTHA R. Frontiersmen of New York. 2 vols. Albany, 1882-3.

SMITH, WILLIAM. History of the Province of New York. New York, 1814.

SOCIETY OF THE FRIENDLY SONS OF ST. PATRICK. Roll of Members (membership list from 1784). New York, 1909.

SPENCER, ALFRED. Spencer's Roster of Native Sons. 1941.

STILLWELL, JOHN EDWIN. Historical and Genealogical Miscellany: Data Relating to the Settlement and Settlers of New York and New Jersey. 5 vols. 1903-32.

STOKES: Iconography. Vol. II. (Contains a list of the N. Y. C. newspapers, 1725-1811.)

SWINNERTON, H. U. Historical Account of the Presbyterian Church of Cherry Valley. Cherry Valley, 1876.

TURNER, ORSAMUS. History of the Pioneer Settlements of Phelps and Gorham's Purchase, and Morris' Reserve. 1852.

TURNER, ORSAMUS. Pioneer History of the Holland Purchase of Western New York. 1850.

ULSTER HISTORICAL SOCIETY. Publications of the Ulster Historial Society. Kingston, 1862—.

NORTH CAROLINA

CLARKE, DESMOND. Arthur Dobbs, Esquire (Gov. of North Carolina), 1689-1765. London, 1958.

CORBITT, DAVID L. The Formation of the North Carolina Counties. 1950.

GRIMES, J. B. Abstracts of North Carolina Wills—to 1760. 1910.

HANNON, W. B. Irish Builders in North Carolina. In the *Journal of the American-Irish Historical Society*. Vol. X, 1910-11.

HATHAWAY, J. R. B., *Ed.* The North Carolina Historical and Genealogical Register. 3 vols. 1900-1903.

NORTH CAROLINA: Colonial and State Records of North Carolina. 30 vols. 1886-1907.

NORTH CAROLINA HISTORICAL COMMISSION: The Historical Records of North Carolina. 3 vols. 1938-39.

NORTH CAROLINA HISTORICAL REVIEW. Raleigh, 1924.

THE NORTH CAROLINIAN. 1955 —. (A Quarterly Journal of Genealogy and History.)

OLDS, FRED A. Abstract of North Carolina Wills from About 1760 to about 1800. 1925.

OWEN, MARY B. Old Salem. 1846.

RAY, WORTH S. The Lost Tribes of North Carolina. 3 Parts, Baltimore, 1956. Part I: Index and Digest to Hathaway's North Carolina Historical and Genealogical Register, With Notes and Annotations. Part II: Colonial Granville and Its People; also records of Caswell, Chatham and Franklin Counties. Part III: Mecklenburg Signers and Their Neighbors. (3 vols.)

SEMMES, LT. RAPHAEL. Extracts from the County Records of Guilford County, North Carolina. In *The Recorder, American-Irish Historical Society*. Vol. III, New York, 1925.

OHIO

FORD, KATE B. History of Cincinnati, with Illustrations and Biographical Sketches. 1881.

HANNA, CHARLES A. Historical Collections of Harrison County. With Lists of the First Land-Owners, Early Marriages (to 1841), Will Records (to 1861), Burial Records of the Early Settlements and Numerous Genealogies.

HANNA, CHARLES A. Ohio Valley Genealogies. Relating Chiefly to Families in Harrison, Belmont and Jefferson Counties, Ohio, and Washington, Westmoreland and Fayette Counties, Pennsylvania. 1900. (These counties have had large settlements of the Scotch-Irish.)

HOWE, HENRY. Historical Collections of Ohio. 2 vols. Cincinnati, 1875.

OHIO: Irish Among the Ohio Troops in the War of 1812. In *The Recorder, American-Irish Historical Society.* 1925.

OHIO ARCHAEOLOGICAL AND HISTORICAL QUARTERLY. Vol 1, 1888.

OLD NORTHWEST GENEALOGICAL QUARTERLY. 15 vols. Columbus, 1898-1912.

PENNSYLVANIA

ARMOUR, WILLIAM C. Scotch-Irish Bibliography of Pennsylvania. (Proceedings Scotch-Irish Society of America, Vol. VIII. Nashville, 1897.)

ARMOUR, WILLIAM C. Lives of the Governors of Pennsylvania. Philadelphia, 1872.

CAMPBELL, JOHN H. History of the Friendly Sons of St. Patrick. Philadelphia, 1892.

CHAMBERS, GEORGE. A Tribute to the Principles, Virtues, Habits, and Public Usefulness of the Scotch and Irish Early Settlers of Pennsylvania. Chambersburg, 1856.

CLYDE, REV. JOHN C. "Irish Settlement"; Genealogies, Necrology and Reminiscenses of the now Northampton County, Pennsylvania. 1879.

COLONIAL RECORDS OF PENNSYLVANIA. 16 vols., 1851-1853. (Continued as *Pennsylvania Archives.*)

COYLE, DR. JOHN G. American-Irish Governors of Pennsylvania. In the *Journal of the American-Irish Historical Society*. Vol. XIV, 1914-15.

CRAIG, NEVILLE B. History of Pittsburgh. Pittsburgh, 1851.

CRAIG, NEVILLE B. The Olden Time. 2 vols. Pittsburgh, 1846, 1848. (A magazine. Reprint, Cincinnati, 1876.)

CRAIGHEAD, JAMES G. Scotch and Irish Seeds in American Soil. Philadelphia, 1878.

DAY, SHERMAN. Historical Collections of Pennsylvania. Philadelphia, 1843.

DE HASS, WILLS. History of the Early Settlement and Indian Wars of Western Virginia. Wheeling, 1851. (Includes Pennsylvania records.)

DODDRIDGE, JOSEPH. Notes on the Settlement and Indian Wars of the Western Parts of Virginia and Pennsylvania, from 1763 to 1783. Wellsburg, W. Va., 1824; (reprint) Albany, 1876.

DUNAWAY, WAYLAND. The Scotch-Irish of Colonial Pennsylvania. 1944.

EGLE, WILLIAM H. History of Pennsylvania. 1876, 1883.

EGLE, WILLIAM H. Historical Register (magazine). 2 vols. Harrisburg, 1883-84.

EGLE, WILLIAM H., *Ed.* "Notes and Queries" (reprint from the Harrisburg "Daily Telegraph", 1878-1901). 12 vols. Harrisburg, 1894-1901.

EGLE, WILLIAM H. Pennsylvania Genealogies. Harrisburg, 1886 and 1896. (Scotch-Irish and German families.)

EGLE, WILLIAM H. Matrons of the Revolution. Harrisburg, 1899.

ELLIS, FRANKLIN. History of Juniata and Susquehanna Valleys. 2 vols. Philadelphia, 1886.

ENGLAND, C. E. *Ed.* The Molly Maguires of Pennsylvania, or Ireland in America; A True Narrative, Told by Ernest W. Lucy, U. S. A. London, 1883 (?).

FISHER, SYDNEY GEORGE. The Making of Pennsylvania. Philadelphia, 1896.

FISHER, SYDNEY GEORGE. Pennsylvania: Colony and Commonwealth. Philadelphia, 1897.

FISKE, JOHN. Dutch and Quaker Colonies. 2 vols. Boston, 1899.

FRIENDLY SONS OF ST. PATRICK. Samuel Hood and Others. Philadelphia, 1844.

FULTON, ELEANORE JANE. An Index to the Will Books and Intestate Records of Lancaster County, Pennsylvania, 1729-1850. 1936.

FUTHEY, J. SMITH, and GILBERT COPE. History of Chester County, Pennsylvania. Philadelphia, 1881.

GARLAND, ROBERT. The Scotch-Irish in Western Pennsylvania. 1923.

HACKETT, JAMES DOMINICK. Philadelphia Irish. (Irish Burials in St. Mary's Churchyard.) In the *Journal of the American-Irish Historical Society*. Vol. XXX, 1932.

HISTORICAL JOURNAL, THE: A Quarterly Record of Local History and Genealogy, Devoted Principally to Northern Pennsylvania. 2 vols. 1888-1894.

HISTORICAL RECORD OF WYOMING VALLEY, THE. 14 vols. 1887-1908.

JONES, U. J. Early Settlement of the Juniata Valley. Harrisburg, 1889.

JORDAN, JOHN WOOLF. Colonial and Revolutionary Families of Pennsylvania. 3 vols. New York, Chicago, 1911.

JORDAN, JOHN WOOLF. Encyclopedia of Pennsylvania Biography. 5 vols. New York, 1914-1915. (A sixth volume published, New York, 1919.)

JORDAN, JOHN WOOLF. Genealogy and Personal History of the Allegheny Valley. 3 vols. 1913.

JORDAN, JOHN WOOLF. Genealogy and Personal History of Northern Pennsylvania. 3 vols. 1913.

JORDAN, JOHN WOOLF. Genealogy and Personal History of Western Pennsylvania. 3 vols. 1915.

JORDAN, JOHN WOOLF. Historic Homes and Institutions and Genealogical Memoirs of the Lehigh Valley. 2 vols. 1905. (Use all Jordan publications with care.)

JOURNALS: Journal of the Rev. Charles Beatty, London, 1768; Journal of the Rev. Philip V. Fithian, 1775. Harrisburg, 1883-1884.

KEITH, CHARLES PENROSE. Chronicles of Pennsylvania from the English Revolution to the Peace of Aix-la-Chapelle, 1688-1748. 2 vols. 1917.

KITTOCHTINNY HISTORICAL SOCIETY: Papers of. 1900 —.

KULP, GEORGE B. Families of the Wyoming Valley. 3 vols. Wilkes-Barre, 1886-90.

LANCASTER COUNTY HISTORICAL SOCIETY: Historical Papers and Addresses. 1897 —.

LINN, JOHN BLAIR. Annals of Buffalo Valley. Harrisburg, 1877.

LOUDON, ARCHIBALD. Narratives of the Outrages Committed by the Indians. 2 vols. Carlisle, 1808, 1811. Reprint, Harrisburg, 1888.

MARTIN, JOHN H. Chester and Its Vicinity. Philadelphia, 1877.

MEGINNESS, JOHN F. Otzinachson; or a History of the West Branch Valley of the Susquehanna. 1856. Philadelphia, 1867. Williamsport, 1889.

MEGINNESS, JOHN F. Biographical Annals of the West Branch Valley. Williamsport, 1889.

MEGINNESS, JOHN F., *Ed.* Historical Journal (magazine). 2 vols. Williamsport, 1888, 1894.

MYERS, ALBERT COOK. The Immigration of the Irish Quakers Into Pennsylvania, 1682-1750. Philadelphia, 1902.

MYERS, ALBERT COOK. Quaker Arrivals at Philadelphia, 1682-1750; Being a List of Certificates of Removal Received at Philadelphia Monthly Meeting of Friends. Reprint, 1957.

O'BRIEN, MICHAEL J. The Cumberland County Pennsylvania Militia in the Revolution. In the *Journal of the American-Irish Historical Society.* Vol. XXI, New York, 1922.

O'BRIEN, MICHAEL J. The First Regiment of the Pennsylvania Line. In the *Journal of the American-Irish Historical Society.* Vol. XXI, New York, 1922.

O'BRIEN, MICHAEL J. Irish Pioneers in Berks County, Pennsylvania. In the *Journal of the American-Irish Historical Society*. Vol. XXVII, New York, 1928.

O'BRIEN, MICHAEL J. Irish Settlers in Pennsylvania. In the *Journal of the American-Irish Historical Society*. Vol. VI, Boston, 1906.

PARKE, JOHN E. Recollections of Seventy Years. Boston, 1886.

PATTERSON, A. W. History of the Back Woods. Pittsburgh, 1843.

PENNSYLVANIA ARCHIVES: 1st to 7th Series. 90 volumes. 1852-1914.

PENNSYLVANIA: Colonial Records. 16 vols. Harrisburg, 1838-56.

PENNSYLVANIA HISTORICAL SOCIETY: Collections; Cope Manuscripts, etc.

PENNSYLVANIA GENEALOGICAL MAGAZINE. 1895 —. (Before 1948, *Publications of the Genealogical Society of Pennsylvania.*)

PENNSYLVANIA HISTORICAL AND MUSEUM COMMISSION: Guide to the Published Archives of Pennsylvania, Covering the 138 Volumes of Colonial Records and Pennsylvania Archives. 1949.

PENNSYLVANIA MAGAZINE OF HISTORY AND BIOGRAPHY. Philadelphia, 1877 —. Indexes, vols. 1-75 (1877-1951). 1954.

PENNSYLVANIA: Memoirs of the Historical Society of Pennsylvania. Philadelphia, 1826 —.

READER, F. S. Some Pioneers of Washington County, Pennsylvania. 1902.

RUPP, I. DANIEL. Early History of Western Pennsylvania. Harrisburg, 1846.

SCHARF, J. THOMAS, and THOMPSON WESCOTT. History of Philadelphia County. 3 vols. 1884.

SMITH, JOSEPH. History of Jefferson College. Pittsburgh, 1857.

SMITH, WILLIAM H., *Ed.* St. Clair Papers. 2 vols. Cincinnati, 1882.

VAN VOORHIS, JOHN S. The Old and New Monongahela. Pittsburgh, 1893.

WATSON, JOHN F. Annals of Philadelphia. 2 vols. 1870.

WESTERN PENNSYLVANIA HISTORICAL MAGAZINE. 1918 —.

WYOMING HISTORICAL AND GENEALOGICAL SOCIETY: Proceedings and Collections. 1858.

PENNSYLVANIA PRESBYTERIAN RECORDS

In Library, Presbyterian Historical Society, Philadelphia.

CARLISLE: Carlisle Presbytery, Centennial Memorial of. 2 vols. Harrisburg, 1889.

CLYDE, JOHN C. History of Allen Township Presbyterian Church. Philadelphia, 1876.

DONALDSON, ALEXANDER. History of Blairsville Presbytery. Pittsburgh, 1874.

EATON, S. J. M. History of Erie Presbytery. New York, 1868.

EATON, S. J. M. Lakeside: A Memorial of the Planting of the Church in Northwestern Pennsylvania. Pittsburgh, 1880.

EVANS, SAMUEL. History of Donegal Church. Columbia, 1880.

FUTHEY, J. SMITH. Upper Octorara Presbyterian Church. Philadelphia, 1870.

GIBSON, WILLIAM J. History of Huntingdon Presbytery. Bellefonte, 1874.

GIBSON, WILLIAM J. Historic Memorial of Huntingdon Presbytery, 1795-1895. Philadelphia, 1895.

KLETT, GUY S. Presbyterians in Colonial Pennsylvania. Philadelphia, 1937.

MCALARNEY, MATHIAS W. History of the Sesqui-Centennial of Paxtang Church. Harrisburg, 1890.

MURPHY, THOMAS. Presbytery of the Log College. Philadelphia, 1889.

NEVIN, ALFRED. Churches of the (Cumberland) Valley. Philadelphia, 1852.

NEVIN, ALFRED. Men of Mark of the Cumberland Valley, 1776-1876. Philadelphia, 1876.

NEVIN, ALFRED. Presbyterian Encyclopedia.

NEVIN, ALFRED. History of Philadelphia Presbytery. Philadelphia, 1888.

OSMOND, J. History of Luzerne Presbytery. Wilkes-Barre, 1897.

PHILADELPHIA: Records of Philadelphia Presbytery and of the Synods of New York and Philadelphia, 1706-1788. Philadelphia, 1841.

PITTSBURGH: Centennial Volume of the First Presbyterian Church of Pittsburgh. 1884.

REDSTONE: Diary of David McClure, 1772-1773. New York, 1899.

REDSTONE: Minutes of the Presbytery of, 1781-1831. Cincinnati, 1878.

REDSTONE: Presbytery of Redstone, History of. Washington, 1899.

REDSTONE: Redstone Centennial Celebration of the Presbytery of. Uniontown, 1882.

SCHENCK, HARRIS R. Falling Spring Presbyterian Church. Chambersburg, 1894.

SCOULLER, JAMES B. History of Big Spring Presbytery. Harrisburg, 1879.

SCOULLER, JAMES B. United Presbyterian Church, Manual of the. Pittsburgh, 1888.

SMITH, JOSEPH. Old Redstone (Presbytery), or Historical Sketches of Western Presbyterianism. Philadelphia, 1854.

SPRAGUE. Annals of the American Pulpit.

SWOPE, GILBERT E. History of Big Spring Presbyterian Church. Newville, 1898.

SWOPE, BELLE M. History of Middle Spring Presbyterian Church. Newville, 1900.

TURNER, D. K. History of Neshaminy Presbyterian Church. Philadelphia, 1876.

WASHINGTON: History of Washington (Pa.) Presbytery. Philadelphia, 1889.

WESTERN PENNSYLVANIA: Centenary Memorial of the Planting and Growth of Presbyterianism in Western Pennsylvania and Adjacent Parts. Pittsburgh, 1876.

WHITE, WILLIAM P. The Presbyterian Church in Philadelphia. 1895.

WILSON. Presbyterian Historical Almanac and Annual Remembrancer, 1858-1868.

WING, CONWAY P. History of the First Presbyterian Church of Carlisle. 1877.

WYLIE, S. S. and A. NEVIN POMEROY. Rocky Spring Presbyterian Church. Chambersburg, 1895.

RHODE ISLAND

ARNOLD, JAMES NEWELL. Vital Records of Rhode Island, 1636-1850. 21 vols. 1891-1911.

LEE, THOMAS Z. The Irish in Rhode Island. In the *Journal of the American-Irish Historical Society.* Vol. XV, New York, 1916.

MCCANNA, FRANCIS I. Study of History and Jurisdiction of Rhode Island Courts. In the *Journal of the American-Irish Historical Society.* Vol. XXII, New York, 1923.

MURRAY, REV. THOMAS HAMILTON. Irish Rhode Islanders in the American Revolution. Providence, 1903.

MURRAY, THOMAS HAMILTON. The Irish Vanguard of Rhode Island. In the *Journal of the American-Irish Historical Society.* Vol. IV, Boston, 1904.

MURRAY, THOMAS HAMILTON. Mss. A Rhode Island Thousand: Being a List of Ten-hundred Men and Women of Irish Birth and Lineage, who Contributed to the Upbuilding of the Colony and State. 2 vols. 1908.

MURRAY, THOMAS HAMILTON. Sketch of an Early Irish Settlement in Rhode Island. In the *Journal of the American-Irish Historical Society.* Vol. II, Boston, 1899.

NARRAGANSETT: The Narragansett Historical Register. 9 vols. 1882-91.

O'BRIEN, MICHAEL J. Obituary Notices in the Providence, Rhode Island Newspapers. In the *Journal of the American-Irish Historical Society*. Vol. XXV, New York, 1926.

RHODE ISLAND: Representative Men and Old Families of Rhode Island. 3 vols. 1908. (Use with care.)

RHODE ISLAND (COLONY) GENERAL ASSEMBLY: Records of the Colony (and the State) of Rhode Island and Providence Plantations, 1636-1792. 10 vols. 1856-65.

RHODE ISLAND HISTORICAL MAGAZINE, THE. 7 vols. 1880-1887. (First four volumes: *The Newport Historical Magazine.*)

RHODE ISLAND HISTORICAL SOCIETY: Collections, 1827 —; Proceedings, 34 vols.; Publications, 8 vols., 1893-1900.

SOUTH CAROLINA

CARROLL, B. R. Historical Collections. 2 vols. New York, 1836.

CHARLESTON FREE LIBRARY: Index to Wills of Charleston County, South Carolina, 1671-1868. 1950.

COSGROVE, JOHN I. The Hibernian Society of Charleston, South Carolina. In the *Journal of the American-Irish Historical Society*. Vol. XXV, New York, 1926.

DRAYTON, J. Memoirs of the American Revolution in South Carolina. Charleston, 1821.

HEWAT, ALEXANDER. History of South Carolina. London, 1779.

HOWE, GEORGE. Presbyterian Church in South Carolina, History of. 2 vols. Columbia, 1870, 1883.

LOGAN, JOHN H. History of the Upper Country. Charleston, 1859.

MCCRADY, E. South Carolina Under Royal Government. New York, 1899.

MILLS, R. Statistics of South Carolina. Charleston, 1826.

O'BRIEN, MICHAEL J. Irish in South Carolina. In the *Journal of the American-Irish Historical Society.* Vol. XXV, New York, 1926.

O'BRIEN, MICHAEL J. "Limerick Plantation" . . . Berkeley County, South Carolina. In the *Journal of the American-Irish Historical Society.* Vol. XXV, New York, 1926.

O'BRIEN, MICHAEL J. Marriage Notices Published in the South Carolina Gazette. In the *Journal of the American-Irish Historical Society.* Vol. XXV, New York, 1926.

O'NEALL, JOHN B. Bench and Bar of South Carolina. 2 vols. Charleston, 1859.

O'NEALL, JOHN B. and J. A. CHAPMAN. Annals of Newberry. Charleston, 1892.

RAMSAY, DAVID. History of South Carolina. 2 vols. Charleston, 1809.

REVILL, JANIE. A Compilation of the Original Lists of Protestant Immigrants to South Carolina, 1763-1773. Columbia, 1939.

SALLEY, ALEXANDER SAMUEL. Death Notices in the "South Carolina Gazette," 1732-1775. 1917.

SALLEY, ALEXANDER SAMUEL. Marriage Notices in the "South Carolina and American General Gazette," from May 30, 1766 to February 28, 1781; and in its Successor, "Royal Gazette", 1781-1782. 1914.

SALLEY, ALEXANDER SAMUEL. Marriage Notices in the "South Carolina Gazette," and "County Journal", 1765-1775; and in the "Charleston Gazette", 1778-1780. 1904.

SALLEY, ALEXANDER SAMUEL. Marriage Notices in the "South Carolina Gazette" and Its Successors, 1732-1801. 1902.

SALLEY, ALEXANDER SAMUEL. Warrants for Lands in South Carolina, 1672-1711. 3 vols.

SOUTH CAROLINA: Collections of the Historical Society of South Carolina. Charleston, 1857 —.

SOUTH CAROLINA HISTORICAL COMMISSION: Collections, 1857 —; Proceedings, 1931 —.

SOUTH CAROLINA HISTORICAL AND GENEALOGICAL MAGAZINE, THE (Quarterly). Charleston, 1900 —.

WALSH, PATRICK. The Irish in South Carolina, Georgia, Alabama, Louisiana, and Tennessee. In the *Journal of the American-Irish Historical Society*. Vol. III, Boston, 1900.

TENNESSEE

ACKLEN, JEANETTE T. Tennessee Records; Bible Records and Marriage Bonds. 1933. Tombstone Inscriptions and Manuscripts, Historical and Biographical. 2 vols.

EAST TENNESSEE HISTORICAL SOCIETY PUBLICATIONS. Nos. I-XXXI.

HAYWOOD, JOHN. History of Tennessee. Knoxville, 1823. Reprint, Nashville, 1891.

LEDFORD, ALLEN JAMES. Methodism in Tennessee, 1783-1866. 1941.

PHELAN, JAMES. History of Tennessee. Boston, 1888.

PUTNAM, A. W. History of Middle Tennessee. Nashville, 1859.

RAMSEY, J. G. M. Annals of Tennessee. Philadelphia, 1860.

TENNESSEE: History of Tennessee, with Sketches of Montgomery, Robertson, Humphreys, Stewart, Dickson, Cheatham, and Houston Counties. Nashville, 1886.

WEST TENNESSEE: Old Times in West Tennessee. Memphis, 1873.

TEXAS

IRISH IN TEXAS, THE. In *The Recorder, American-Irish Historical Society*. Vol. IV, no. 5, 1931.

LINEHAN, JOHN C. Irish Pioneers in Texas. In the *Journal of the American-Irish Historical Society*. Vol. II, Boston, 1899.

RICE, BERNADINE. Irish in Texas. In the *Journal of the American-Irish Historical Society*. Vol. XXX, 1932.

VERMONT

CARLETON, HIRAM. Genealogy and Family History of the State of Vermont. 2 vols. 1903. (Use with care.)

DE GOESBRIAND, LOUIS. Catholic Memoirs of Vermont and New Hampshire. 1886.

DODGE, PRENTISS CUTLER. Encyclopedia of Vermont Biography. 1912.

GILMAN, MARCUS DAVIS. The Bibliography of Vermont. 1897.

HALL, B. H. History of Eastern Vermont. New York, 1858.

HEMENWAY, ABBY MARIA. The Vermont Historical Gazetteer. 5 vols. 1868-1891. Index, 1923.

O'BRIEN, MICHAEL J. Stray Historical Items from the Green Mountain State. In the *Journal of the American-Irish Historical Society.* Vol. XVIII, New York, 1919.

THOMPSON, ZADOCK. History of Vermont. Burlington, 1842.

ULLERY, JACOB G. Men of Vermont: An Illustrated Biographical History. 1894.

VERMONT HISTORICAL SOCIETY: "Collections". 2 vols. 1870-1871. "Proceedings", 1860 —.

VIRGINIA

ACKERLY, MARY D. and LULA E. J. PARKER. Our Kin. The Genealogies of Some of the Early Families Who Made History in the Founding and Development of Bedford County. 1930.

BELL, LANDON COVINGTON. Cumberland Parish, Lunenberg County, Virginia, 1746-1816. Richmond, 1930.

BOOGHER, WILLIAM FLETCHER. Gleanings of Virginia History. An Historical and Genealogical Collection, Largely from Original Sources. 1903.

BROCK, ROBERT ALONZO. Virginia and The Virginians. 2 vols. 1888.

BROCKMAN, WILLIAM E. Orange County, Virginia Families. 2 vols. 1956.

CAMPBELL, JOHN W. History of Virginia, to 1781. Petersburg, 1813.

CHALKLEY, LYMAN. Chronicles of the Scotch-Irish Settlement in Virginia: Extracted from the Original Court Records of Augusta County, 1745-1800. 3 vols. 1912.

CLEMENS, WILLIAM MONTGOMERY. Virginia Wills Before 1799. 1924.

COCKE, W. R., III. Hanover County Chancery Wills and Notes. A Compendium of Genealogical, Biographical and Historical Material Contained in Cases of the Chancery Suits. 1940.

COOKE, JOHN ESTEN. History of Virginia. Boston, 1883.

CROZIER, WILLIAM ARMSTRONG. Early Virginia Marriages. 1907.

CROZIER, WILLIAM ARMSTRONG. A Key to Southern Pedigrees. 1911.

CROZIER, WILLIAM ARMSTRONG. Virginia Colonial Militia, 1651-1776. 1905.

CROZIER, WILLIAM ARMSTRONG. Westmoreland County. 1913. (Has Abstracts of the County Wills, 1655-1794.)

CROZIER, WILLIAM ARMSTRONG. Williamsburg Wills. 1906.

EARLY, R. H. Campbell (Co.). Chronicles and Family Sketches, Embracing a History of Campbell County, Virginia, 1782-1926. 1927.

FISKE, JOHN. Old Virginia and Her Neighbors. 2 vols. Boston, 1897.

FLEET, BEVERLY. Virginia Colonial Abstracts. 34 vols. 1937 —.

FOOTE, WILLIAM H. Sketches of Virginia. (Includes Presbyterian Churches and Ministers.) Philadelphia (First Series), 1850; Philadelphia (Second Series), 1855.

FOTHERGILL, MRS. AUGUSTA BRIDGLAND (MIDDLETON). Wills of Westmoreland County, 1655-1794.

GREER, J. C. Early Virginia Immigrants, 1623-1666. 1912.

HALE, JOHN P. Trans-Allegheny Pioneers. Cincinnati, 1886.

HAYDEN, HORACE EDWIN. Virginia Genealogies. A Genealogy of the Glassell Family of Scotland and Virginia; also of the Families of Ball, Brown, Bryan, Conway, Daniel, Ewell, Holladay, Lewis, Littlepage, Moncure, Peyton, Robinson, Scott, Taylor, Wallace, and others of Virginia and Maryland, 1891. Reprinted, 1931. (Several Scotch-Irish Families here.)

HOWE, HENRY. Historical Collections of Virginia. Charleston, S. C., 1845.

JEFFERSON, THOMAS. Notes on Virginia. Philadelphia, 1788.

JOHNSON, DAVID EMMONS. A History of Middle New River Settlements and Contiguous Territory. 1906.

JOHNSON, THOMAS CARY. Virginia Presbyterianism and Religious Liberty.

KEGLEY, FREDERICK BITTLE. Kegley's Virginia Frontier; the Beginnings of the Southwest: The Roanoke of Colonial Days, 1740-1783. Roanoke, 1938.

KERCHEVAL, SAMUEL. History of the Valley. Winchester, 1833.

LAWLESS, JOSEPH T. Some Irish Settlers in Virginia. In the *Journal of the American-Irish Historical Society.* Vol. II, Boston, 1899.

LINEHAN, JOHN C. Early Irish Settlers in Virginia. In the *Journal of the American-Irish Historical Society.* Vol. IV, Boston, 1904.

MACJONES, W., *Ed.* Goochland: The Douglas Register, being a Detailed Record of Births, Marriages and Deaths, together with Other Interesting Notes, as kept by the Rev. William Douglas, from 1750 to 1797. An Index to Goochland Wills, etc. 1928.

MCWHORTER, LUCULLUS VIRGIL. The Border Settlers of Northwestern Virginia, from 1768 to 1795. 1915.

MEADE, WILLIAM. Old Churches, Ministers, and Families of Virginia. 2 vols. Philadelphia, 1897. (See Wise's Digested Index.) Richmond, 1910.

NUCKOLLS, B. F. Grayson County, Pioneer Settlers of. 1914. (Much genealogical data.)

O'BRIEN, MICHAEL J. Extracts from Virginia Church Records. In the *Journal of the American-Irish Historical Society.* Vol. XVIII, New York, 1919.

O'BRIEN, MICHAEL J. George Washington's Virginia Regiment. In the *Journal of the American-Irish Historical Society.* Vol. XXV, New York, 1926.

O'BRIEN, MICHAEL J. Land Grants to Irish Settlers of Virginia. In the *Journal of the American-Irish Historical Society.* Vol. XXIV, New York, 1925.

O'BRIEN, MICHAEL J. Pioneer Irish Families in Virginia. In the *Journal of the American-Irish Historical Society.* Vol. XXV, New York, 1926.

O'BRIEN, MICHAEL J. Some First Families of Virginia. In the *Journal of the American-Irish Historical Society.* Vol. XXVI, New York, 1927.

O'BRIEN, MICHAEL J. Virginia Irish in the Revolution. In the *Journal of the American-Irish Historical Society.* Vol. XXVII, New York, 1928.

THE RESEARCHER: A Magazine of History and Genealogical Exchange. 2 vols. 1926-1928.

STEWART, ROBERT ARMISTEAD. Index to Printed Virginia Genealogies. (Including Key and Bibliography.) Richmond, 1930.

SUMMERS, LEWIS PRESTON. Annals of Southwest Virginia, 1769-1800. Abingdon, Va., 1929.

SWEENY, WILLIAM J. Some Pioneer Irishmen of Virginia and North Carolina. In *The Recorder, American-Irish Historical Society.* Vol. 2, no. 6, New York, 1924.

SWEENEY, WILLIAM M. Some Virginia Records. In the *Journal of the American-Irish Historical Society.* Vol. XXVIII, New York, 1930.

SWEENEY, WILLIAM M. Virginia County Records. In the *Journal of the American-Irish Historical Society.* Vol. XXX, 1932.

SWEM, EARL GREGG. Virginia Historical Index. 2 vols. Roanoke, 1934.

TORRENCE, CLAYTON. Virginia Wills and Administrations, 1632-1800; An Index of Wills Recorded in Local Courts of Virginia, 1632-1800. Richmond, 1931.

TYLER'S QUARTERLY HISTORICAL AND GENEALOGICAL MAGAZINE. Richmond, July, 1919 —.

VAN DEVANTER, JOSEPH. Loudoun Valley Legends: True Stories from the Lives and Times of the People of Loudoun County, Virginia. Purcellville, Va., 1955.

VAN METER, BENJAMIN FRANKLIN. Genealogies and Sketches of Some Old Families Who Have Taken Prominent Part in the Developement of Virginia and Kentucky, Especially. 1901.

VIRGINIA CALENDAR OF STATE PAPERS. 11 vols. Richmond, 1875 —.

VIRGINIA COUNTY RECORDS. 11 vols. New York, 1905-1913.

VIRGINIA GENEALOGIST, THE. Edited by John Frederick Dorman, Washington, D. C. 1957 —.

VIRGINIA HISTORICAL SOCIETY: "Collections." 11 vols. Richmond, 1874 —.

VIRGINIA MAGAZINE OF HISTORY AND BIOGRAPHY. Richmond, 1893 —.

WALDENMAIER, INEZ. A Finding List of Virginia Marriage Records before 1853. (See *Genealogical News Letter*, edited by Inez Waldenmaier, Washington, D. C. 1955 —.)

WAYLAND, J. W. Virginia Valley Records. Genealogical and Historical Materials of Rockingham County and Related Regions. 1930.

WEIS, THE REV. FREDERICK LEWIS. The Colonial Clergy of Virginia, North Carolina and South Carolina. Boston, 1955.

WILLIAM AND MARY QUARTERLY. Williamsburg, 1892 —. (Formerly *William and Mary College Quarterly Historical Magazine.* 3 series.)

WINGFIELD, MARSHALL. Franklin County Marriage Bonds, 1786-1858. 1939.

WEST VIRGINIA

DE HASS, WILLS. Indian Wars of West Virginia. Wheeling, 1851.

DODDRIDGE, JOSEPH. Notes on the Settlement and Indian Wars of the Western Parts of Virginia and Pennsylvania, 1763-1783. Wellsburg, 1824. Reprint, Albany, 1876.

NEWTON, J. H., G. G. NICHOLS, A. G. SPRANKLE, and J. A. CALDWELL. Panhandle of West Virginia, History of The. Wheeling, 1879.

WITHERS, ALEXANDER SCOTT. Chronicles of Border Warfare. Clarksburg, 1831. Reprint, Cincinnati, 1895.

WISCONSIN

DESMOND, HUMPHREY J. Early Irish Settlers in Milwaukee. In the *Journal of the American-Irish Historical Society*. Vol. XXIX, 1930-31.

SCANLON, CHARLES M. History of the Irish in Wisconsin. In the *Journal of the American-Irish Historical Society*. Vol. XIII, 1913-14.

WISCONSIN MAGAZINE OF HISTORY. Madison, 1917 —.

WISCONSIN STATE HISTORICAL SOCIETY: "Collections". (See also the great "Draper Manuscript collection of original documents, letters, etc., of Kentucky and Tennessee.")

INDEX

This is a subject index. The names of authors, editors, titles of books, magazine articles, manuscripts, microfilms, and the surnames of family collections of records and documents, are arranged under the various subject headings so as not to require a listing in this index.